Advanced Mathematical Methods in Intelligent Multimedia: Security and Applications

Advanced Mathematical Methods in Intelligent Multimedia: Security and Applications

Editors

Ximeng Liu
Yinbin Miao
Zuobin Ying

MDPI • Basel • Beijing • Wuhan • Barcelona • Belgrade • Manchester • Tokyo • Cluj • Tianjin

Editors
Ximeng Liu
Fuzhou University
Fuzhou, China

Yinbin Miao
Xidian University
Xi'an, China

Zuobin Ying
Nanyang Technological University
Singapore

Editorial Office
MDPI
St. Alban-Anlage 66
4052 Basel, Switzerland

This is a reprint of articles from the Special Issue published online in the open access journal *Mathematics* (ISSN 2227-7390) (available at: https://www.mdpi.com/journal/mathematics/special_issues/Advanced_Mathematical_Methods_in_Intelligent_Multimedia_Security_and_Applications).

For citation purposes, cite each article independently as indicated on the article page online and as indicated below:

LastName, A.A.; LastName, B.B.; LastName, C.C. Article Title. *Journal Name* **Year**, *Volume Number*, Page Range.

ISBN 978-3-0365-8330-3 (Hbk)
ISBN 978-3-0365-8331-0 (PDF)

© 2023 by the authors. Articles in this book are Open Access and distributed under the Creative Commons Attribution (CC BY) license, which allows users to download, copy and build upon published articles, as long as the author and publisher are properly credited, which ensures maximum dissemination and a wider impact of our publications.

The book as a whole is distributed by MDPI under the terms and conditions of the Creative Commons license CC BY-NC-ND.

Contents

Preface to "Advanced Mathematical Methods in Intelligent Multimedia: Security and Applications" vii

Hengxiao Chi, Ji-Hwei Horng and Chin-Chen Chang
Reversible Data Hiding Based on Pixel-Value-Ordering and Prediction-Error Triplet Expansion
Reprinted from: *Mathematics* **2021**, *9*, 1703, doi:10.3390/math9141703 1

Yongjin Hu, Xiyan Li and Jun Ma
A Novel LSB Matching Algorithm Based on Information Pre-Processing
Reprinted from: *Mathematics* **2022**, *10*, 8, doi:10.3390/math10010008 21

Jianguang Lu, Juan Tang, Bin Xing and Xianghong Tang
Stochastic Approximate Algorithms for Uncertain Constrained K-Means Problem
Reprinted from: *Mathematics* **2022**, *10*, 144, doi:10.3390/math10010144 37

Ji-Hwei Horng, Si-Sheng Chen and Chin-Chen Chang
A (k, n)-Threshold Secret Image Sharing Scheme Based on a Non-Full Rank Linear Model
Reprinted from: *Mathematics* **2022**, *10*, 524, doi:10.3390/math10030524 51

Shenling Wang, Yifang Zhang and Yu Guo
A Blockchain-Empowered Arbitrable Multimedia Data Auditing Scheme in IoT Cloud Computing
Reprinted from: *Mathematics* **2022**, *10*, 1005, doi:10.3390/math10061005 71

Yinfeng Chen, Yu Guo, Yaofei Wang and Rongfang Bie
Toward Prevention of Parasite Chain Attack in IOTA Blockchain Networks by Using Evolutionary Game Model
Reprinted from: *Mathematics* **2022**, *10*, 1108, doi:10.3390/math10071108 89

Limengnan Zhou, Chongfu Zhang, Asad Malik and Hanzhou Wu
Efficient Reversible Data Hiding Based on Connected Component Construction and Prediction Error Adjustment
Reprinted from: *Mathematics* **2022**, *10*, 2804, doi:10.3390/math10152804 109

Xin Li, Baodong Qin, Yiyuan Luo and Dong Zheng
A Differential Privacy Budget Allocation Algorithm Based on Out-of-Bag Estimation in Random Forest
Reprinted from: *Mathematics* **2022**, *10*, 4338, doi:10.3390/math10224338 125

Zuobin Ying, Wusong Lan, Chen Deng, Lu Liu and Ximeng Liu
DVIT—A Decentralized Virtual Items Trading Forum with Reputation System [†]
Reprinted from: *Mathematics* **2023**, *11*, 429, doi:10.3390/math11020429 141

Fangwei Wang, Zerou Ma, Xiaohan Zhang, Qingru Li and Changguang Wang
DDSG-GAN: Generative Adversarial Network with Dual Discriminators and Single Generator for Black-Box Attacks
Reprinted from: *Mathematics* **2023**, *11*, 1016, doi:10.3390/math11041016 165

Xin Zhang, Hua Zhang, Kaixuan Li and Qiaoyan Wen
Privacy-Preserving Public Route Planning Based on Passenger Capacity
Reprinted from: *Mathematics* **2023**, *11*, 1546, doi:10.3390/math11061546 183

Cunqun Fan, Peiheng Jia, Manyun Lin, Lan Wei, Peng Guo, Xiangang Zhao and Ximeng Liu
Cloud-Assisted Private Set Intersection via Multi-Key Fully Homomorphic Encryption
Reprinted from: *Mathematics* **2023**, *11*, 1784, doi:10.3390/math11081784 201

Mungwarakarama Irénée, Yichuan Wang, Xinhong Hei, Xin Song, Jean Claude Turiho and Enan Muhire Nyesheja
XTS: A Hybrid Framework to Detect DNS-Over-HTTPS Tunnels Based on XGBoost and Cooperative Game Theory
Reprinted from: *Mathematics* **2023**, *11*, 2372, doi:10.3390/math11102372 . . . . **221**

Preface to "Advanced Mathematical Methods in Intelligent Multimedia: Security and Applications"

The area of intelligent multimedia involves the real-time computer processing and understanding of perceptual input from speech, textual and visual sources. It contrasts with the traditional display of text, voice, sound and video/graphics, possibly with touch and virtual reality linked in. The benefits of intelligent multimedia include improved productivity and efficiency, better flexibility and agility and increased profitability. It also contains many applications that can improve automation, machine-to-machine communication, manufacturing oversight and decision making. However, despite the advantage of intelligent multimedia, it also brings many security and privacy issues such as information confidentiality, data security and secure communication. Most of these security and privacy issues can be solved with mathematical cryptology methods. However, heavyweight cryptosystems still cannot be applied to various types of multimedia, which restricts their applications in intelligent multimedia applications.

The present book contains the 13 articles accepted and published in the Special Issue "Advanced Mathematical Methods in Intelligent Multimedia: Security and Applications" of the MDPI journal "Mathematics". The 13 articles, which appear in the present book in the order in which they were published in Volumes 11(10), 11(8), 11(6), 11(4), 11(2), 10(22), 10(15), 10(7), 10(6), 10(3), 10(1), 9(14) of the journal, cover a wide range of topics connected to the area of intelligent multimedia, security systems and privacy methods.

It is hoped that the book will be interesting and useful for those working in the area of security systems and privacy methods, as well as for those with the proper mathematical background who are willing to become familiar with recent advances in security mathematics and privacy-preserving systems.

As the Guest Editor of the Special Issue I am grateful to the authors of the papers for their quality contributions, to the reviewers for their valuable comments towards the improvement of the submitted works and to the administrative staff of the MDPI publications for their support in completing this project. Special thanks are due to the Managing Editor of the Special Issue, Ms. Jeannie Liu, for her excellent collaboration and valuable assistance.

Ximeng Liu, Yinbin Miao, and Zuobin Ying
Editors

Article

Reversible Data Hiding Based on Pixel-Value-Ordering and Prediction-Error Triplet Expansion

Heng-Xiao Chi [1], Ji-Hwei Horng [2,*] and Chin-Chen Chang [1,*]

1. Department of Information Engineering and Computer Science, Feng Chia University, Taichung 40724, Taiwan; hx9704@gmail.com
2. Department of Electronic Engineering, National Quemoy University, Kinmen 89250, Taiwan
* Correspondence: horng@email.nqu.edu.tw (J.-H.H.); ccc@o365.fcu.edu.tw (C.-C.C.)

Abstract: Pixel value ordering and prediction error expansion (PVO+PEE) is a very successful reversible data hiding (RDH) scheme. A series of studies were proposed to improve the performance of the PVO-based scheme. However, the embedding capacity of those schemes is quite limited. We propose a two-step prediction-error-triplet expansion RDH scheme based on PVO. A three-dimensional state transition map for the prediction-error triplet is also proposed to guide the embedding of the two-step scheme. By properly designing the state transitions, the proposed scheme can embed secret data or expand without embedding by modifying just a single entry of the triplet. The experimental results show that the proposed scheme significantly enlarges the embedding capacity of the PVO-based scheme and further reduces the distortion due to embedding.

Keywords: reversible data hiding; pixel-value-ordering; prediction-error triplet expansion; prediction-error histogram

Citation: Chi, H.-X.; Horng, J.-H.; Chang, C.-C. Reversible Data Hiding Based on Pixel-Value-Ordering and Prediction-Error Triplet Expansion. *Mathematics* **2021**, *9*, 1703. https://doi.org/10.3390/math9141703

Academic Editors: Ximeng Liu, Yinbin Miao and Zuobin Ying

Received: 22 June 2021
Accepted: 19 July 2021
Published: 20 July 2021

Publisher's Note: MDPI stays neutral with regard to jurisdictional claims in published maps and institutional affiliations.

Copyright: © 2021 by the authors. Licensee MDPI, Basel, Switzerland. This article is an open access article distributed under the terms and conditions of the Creative Commons Attribution (CC BY) license (https://creativecommons.org/licenses/by/4.0/).

1. Introduction

With the rapid development of computer and communication technologies, the privacy and security of data transmission have become more and more important. In order to make data transmission more secure, researchers developed various encryption algorithms to convert data into unrecognizable ciphertext. To make unrecognizable ciphertext appear less conspicuous, researchers developed various data hiding algorithms to embed the secret data into digital media, such as images, for transmission. Since a modified digital medium with confidential information is very similar to the original one, it will not draw the eavesdroppers' attention.

Data hiding methods are mainly divided into two types: reversible and irreversible. Reversible data hiding (RDH) [1–6] can extract secret data and restore the original digital objects without distortion. Irreversible data hiding (IRDH) [7,8] can only extract secret data and cannot restore the original digital objects losslessly.

So far, researchers have developed many efficient and easy-to-implement image reversible data hiding (RDH) technologies, such as differential expansion (DE) [9–11], histogram shift (HS) [12–14], prediction error expansion (PEE) [15–17], and so on. The DE method embeds secret data by extending the pixel difference. In HS technology, the image intensity histogram must be generated first and then modified for data embedding. Data embedding based on the PEE algorithm needs to generate the prediction error histogram (PEH) first, then modify it according to specific rules.

Due to the inherent characteristics of PEE-based technology, the embedding performance is related to the generated PEH, and the degree of image distortion is related to the modification rules. Therefore, work improving on PEE has focused on the design of a more concentrated PEH, such as rhombus predictor [18] and interpolation prediction [19], etc., while other works were dedicated to designing rules for minimum distortion. In addition, there is also a method called pairwise PEE, which uses the joint distribution between two prediction errors to generate a two-dimensional (2D) PEH and embeds secret data into the cover image, the digital image used to carry secret information, by modifying the generated 2D PEH [20].

The pixel value ordering (PVO) algorithm proposed by Li et al. [21] flexibly divides the cover image into scalable non-overlapping blocks to obtain a more desirable prediction error histogram. Then, the algorithm modifies the maximum and minimum values in each block to embed the data. The maximum value (minimum value) in each block is either increased (decreased) by one or unchanged so that the order of pixel values does not change after the data is embedded, thus ensuring reversibility. The improved PVO (IPVO) algorithm proposed by Peng et al. [22] takes the spatial relationship between pixels into consideration to improve the prediction method and PEH modification rules. In order to make better use of the spatial relationship between pixels, flexible spatial location-based PVO (FSL-PVO) was proposed by He et al. [23]. In [24], Ou et al. proposed a pairwise PEE to expand the embedding capability of PVO. In addition, researchers also developed various improved algorithms for PVO [25–28]. An example approach is to simultaneously embed data at the first k maximum values (minimum values) of a pixel block, such as PVO-k [26], k-pass PVO [27], and improved k-pass PVO [28].

PVO-based RDH schemes have the advantage of very low image distortion. That means this series of data hiding schemes can produce a stego-image, the digital image embedded with secret information, with a high peak-signal-to-noise ratio (PSNR) value. However, their embedding capacity is quite limited. As we outline in the next section, the existing PVO-based RDH schemes are all based on the two-dimensional state transition of prediction errors. In order to improve the embedding capacity, the new scheme proposed in this paper extends the state space of the prediction errors into three dimensions. More specifically, a prediction-error-triplet expansion RDH scheme based on PVO is proposed. Through an ingenious design of a three-dimensional state transition map for prediction-error triplets, the embedding of secret data or expansion for vacating rooms can be performed by modifying just a single entry of the triplet. The new scheme can improve the embedding capacity of the traditional PVO-based schemes while preserving the visual quality of the stego images.

The rest of this paper is organized as follows. The second section briefly introduces various typical PVO-based RDH schemes. The third section introduces the proposed scheme in detail. The experimental results and comparisons with related works are provided in Section 4. Finally, this paper is summarized in Section 5.

2. Related Works

In this section, PVO [21], IPVO [22], and Pairwise-PVO [24] are briefly introduced, and the embedding maps of typical PVO-based schemes are summarized. This series of RDH schemes are all based on the same problem formulation.

The PVO-based RDH schemes need to divide the cover image into non-overlapping equal-sized pixel blocks first. Each pixel block contains n pixel values $(x_1, x_2, \ldots, x_n)$. Then, the n pixel values are sorted into the sequence $x_{\sigma(1)} \leq x_{\sigma(2)} \leq \ldots \leq x_{\sigma(n)}$, where $(\sigma(1), \sigma(2), \ldots, \sigma(n))$ represents the original location as a function of the current order. That is, the function $\sigma : \{1, 2, \ldots, n\} \to \{1, 2, \ldots, n\}$ is the unique one-to-one and onto mapping. In the case of equal value, pixels are ordered by

$$\sigma(i) < \sigma(j), \text{ if } x_{\sigma(i)} = x_{\sigma(j)} \text{ and } i < j. \tag{1}$$

Finally, the pixels of maximum values (minimum values) are exploited to calculate prediction errors and embed secret data.

2.1. PVO

The original PVO data hiding scheme [21] uses the second largest value $x_{\sigma(n-1)}$ (second smallest value $x_{\sigma(2)}$) to predict the maximum value $x_{\sigma(n)}$ (minimum value $x_{\sigma(1)}$), the prediction errors PE_{max} and PE_{min} can be calculated by

$$\begin{cases} PE_{max} = x_{\sigma(n)} - x_{\sigma(n-1)} \\ PE_{min} = x_{\sigma(1)} - x_{\sigma(2)} \end{cases}. \quad (2)$$

According to the histogram distributions of PE_{max} and PE_{min}, the peak bins are exploited to embed secret data. The embedding rules for PE_{max} and PE_{min} are given by

$$PE'_{max} = \begin{cases} PE_{max}, & \text{if } PE_{max} = 0 \\ PE_{max} + b, & \text{if } PE_{max} = 1 \\ PE_{max} + 1, & \text{if } PE_{max} > 1 \end{cases}; \quad (3)$$

$$PE'_{min} = \begin{cases} PE_{min}, & \text{if } PE_{min} = 0 \\ PE_{min} - b, & \text{if } PE_{min} = -1 \\ PE_{min} - 1, & \text{if } PE_{min} < -1 \end{cases}, \quad (4)$$

where $b \in \{0, 1\}$ is the binary secret bit to be embedded. Then, the maximum pixel value $x_{\sigma(n)}$ is modified to

$$x'_{\sigma(n)} = x_{\sigma(n-1)} + PE'_{max} = \begin{cases} x_{\sigma(n)}, & \text{if } PE_{max} = 0 \\ x_{\sigma(n)} + b, & \text{if } PE_{max} = 1 \\ x_{\sigma(n)} + 1, & \text{if } PE_{max} > 1 \end{cases}, \quad (5)$$

while the minimum pixel value $x_{\sigma(1)}$ is modified to

$$x'_{\sigma(1)} = x_{\sigma(2)} + PE'_{min} = \begin{cases} x_{\sigma(1)}, & \text{if } PE_{max} = 0 \\ x_{\sigma(1)} - b, & \text{if } PE_{max} = -1 \\ x_{\sigma(1)} - 1, & \text{if } PE_{max} < -1 \end{cases}. \quad (6)$$

The rest pixels in the block remain unchanged. To make the embedding rules easier to understand, the prediction errors can be translated into a location-based representation, as introduced in [25] by

$$\begin{cases} e^1_{max} = x_u - x_{\sigma(n-2)} \\ e^2_{max} = x_v - x_{\sigma(n-2)} \end{cases}, \quad (7)$$

where

$$\begin{cases} u = min(\sigma(n), \sigma(n-1)) \\ v = max(\sigma(n), \sigma(n-1)) \end{cases}. \quad (8)$$

Based on the location-based prediction error pair (e^1_{max}, e^2_{max}), the embedding rules of the PVO scheme can be illustrated by the state transition map, as given in Figure 1a. For each pixel block, its corresponding prediction error pair can be mapped to a 'state' on the map. The solid purple lines indicate the state transition rules for embedding the embeddable states, while the pink dashed lines indicate the expansions of non-embeddable states. The states without any guiding line are non-embeddable states with no expansion required. During the secret data embedding phase, the maximum value (minimum value) is either increasing (decreasing) or unchanged. The order of the pixel values is preserved, which is crucial for reversibility. In the secret data extraction phase, the prediction errors PE'_{max} and PE'_{min} can be calculated in the same way. Then, the secret data extraction and the pixel value restoration processes can be designed according to their corresponding embedding rules.

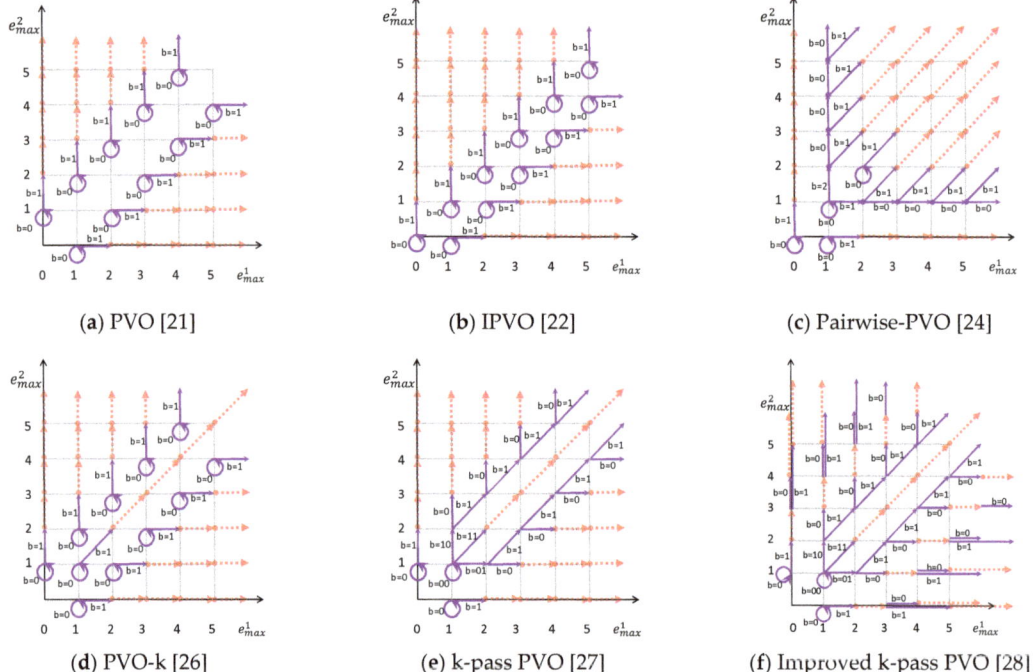

Figure 1. The state transition map for PVO-based RDH schemes. (**a**) PVO [21]; (**b**) IPVO [22]; (**c**) Pairwise-PVO [24]; (**d**) PVO-k [26]; (**e**) k-pass PVO [27]; (**f**) Improved k-pass PVO [28].

2.2. IPVO

In the PVO scheme, bin 1 of the PE_{max} histogram and bin -1 of the PE_{min} histogram are exploited to embed the secret data. Bin 0 is kept unchanged. That is, the states on the main diagonal line of the state transition map (Figure 1a) are left unexploited. The IPVO scheme [22] defines a new prediction error calculation method, which takes the position information into account. The prediction error PE_{max} is defined by

$$PE_{max} = x_u - x_v, \qquad (9)$$

where u and v are defined the same as Equation (8). The embedding rules for IPVO are given by

$$PE'_{max} = \begin{cases} PE_{max} - 1, & \text{if } PE_{max} < 0 \\ PE_{max} - b, & \text{if } PE_{max} = 0 \\ PE_{max} + b, & \text{if } PE_{max} = 1 \\ PE_{max} + 1, & \text{if } PE_{max} > 1 \end{cases}. \qquad (10)$$

The corresponding pixel value modification rules are given by

$$x'_{\sigma(n)} = \begin{cases} x_{\sigma(n)} + 1, & \text{if } PE_{max} < 0 \\ x_{\sigma(n)} + b, & \text{if } PE_{max} = 0 \\ x_{\sigma(n)} + b, & \text{if } PE_{max} = 1 \\ x_{\sigma(n)} + 1, & \text{if } PE_{max} > 1 \end{cases}. \qquad (11)$$

Again, the modification of prediction errors and pixel values can be translated into a state transition map, as shown in Figure 1b. Prediction error states that satisfy $e^2_{max} = e^1_{max}$ are exploited instead of $e^2_{max} = e^1_{max} + 1$. According to the experiments, the IPVO scheme outperforms the original PVO scheme in embedding capacity. That is, the accumulated value of the histogram bins exploited by IPVO is greater than that of PVO for the conventional test images.

2.3. Pairwise-PVO

To improve the embedding capacity, the pairwise-PVO scheme [24] allows two maximum-valued pixels to be increased by one at the same time. The prediction error pair (e_{max}^1, e_{max}^2) is defined the same way as in Equations (7) and (8). The corresponding state transition map of the pairwise-PVO is given in Figure 1c. The diagonal guiding lines indicate the simultaneous increase of two maximum-valued pixels for embedding or expansion. There are more embeddable states near the origin. Additionally, the state of $(e_{max}^1, e_{max}^2) = (1,1)$ is exploited to embed a ternary digit.

Although the embedding capacity is effectively increased, the simultaneous increase of pixel values severely degrades the visual quality of the stego images. A complexity measure is applied to classify the image blocks into different categories. Only low complexity blocks are embedded with the pairwise-PVO scheme. Median complexity blocks are embedded with the IPVO scheme, while high complexity blocks are left unembedded.

2.4. Other Typical PVO-Based Schemes

To further improve the embedding capacity, studies [26–28] were conducted to embed secret data by modifying the k maximum-valued pixels. The corresponding state transition maps for PVO-k [26], k-pass PVO [27], and improved k-pass PVO [28] schemes are given in Figure 1d–f.

Although their motivation is to modify k maximum-valued pixels, the concluded feasible value of k is still 2. Further extension of the k value leads to an unbearable degradation of image quality. The only difference between PVO-k and the original PVO, referring to Figure 1a,d, is the usage of $(e_{max}^1, e_{max}^2) = (1,1)$ with the required additional expansions. In k-pass PVO, the state $(e_{max}^1, e_{max}^2) = (1,1)$ is exploited to embed two bits at a time, as shown in Figure 1e. The improved k-pass PVO further exploits the states of $|e_{max}^1 - e_{max}^2| = 3$ to embed secret data, as shown in Figure 1f. As a result, the pixel value may be increased by two.

The image quality degradation caused by modifying two pixel-values at a time is still not solved. The improved PVO-based data hiding schemes [26–28] are all hybrid methods. Only smooth blocks are processed with the newly proposed schemes. The remaining complex blocks are embedded with IPVO or left unembedded.

3. Proposed Scheme

As discussed in the previous section, the embeddable states are concentrated in the smooth blocks of a cover image. To enlarge the embedding capacity, the improved PVO versions vacate more states for embedding by expanding the surrounding states outward. In most cases, this results in the simultaneous modification of two pixel-values and thus degrades the image quality.

In this section, a new PVO reversible data hiding scheme based on a prediction-error triplet is proposed. By extending the state space from two dimensions to three dimensions (3D), the space for vacating embeddable states can be effectively expanded. By modifying, at most, one of the three maximum-valued pixels in a block, the proposed scheme can embed secret data with the least sacrifice in image quality.

The flowcharts of the proposed data embedding and extraction processes are given in Figure 2. In the following subsections, the framework and pre-process are introduced first. Then, the new proposed 3D state transition map is presented. The complete data embedding process of two example blocks is given in the third subsection, and then their corresponding data extraction and pixel value recovery are demonstrated. Finally, an additional complex block exclusion process is provided to skip non-embeddable blocks.

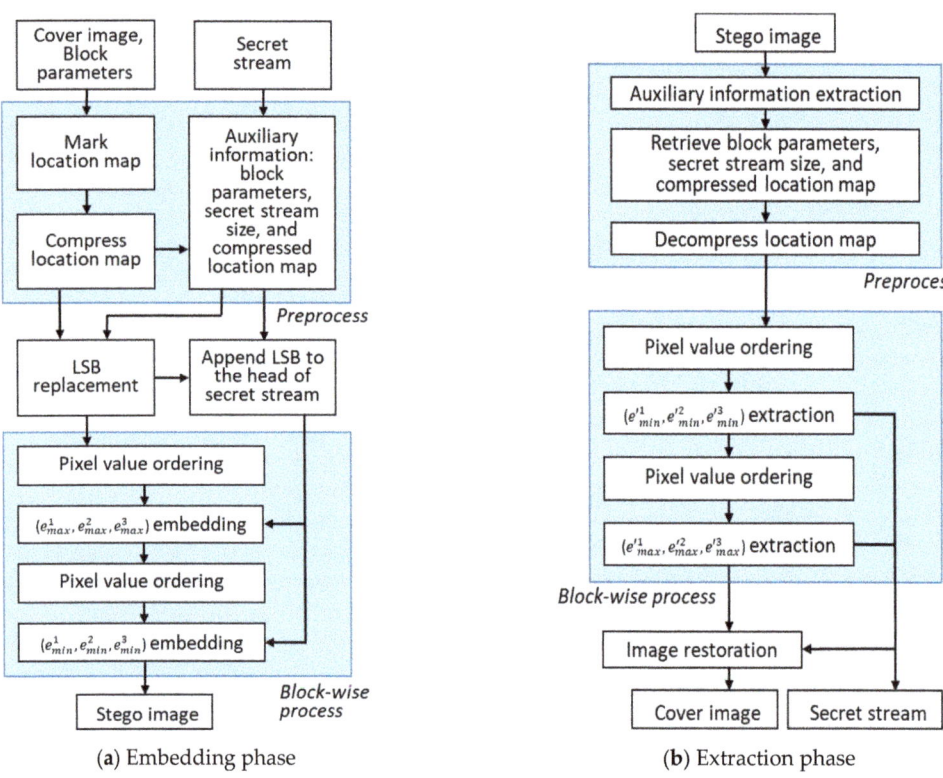

Figure 2. Flowcharts of the proposed scheme. (**a**) Embedding phase; (**b**) Extraction phase.

3.1. Framework and Preprocess

As shown in Figure 2, the data embedding phase consists of a pre-process and a block-wise process. The cover image, the secret data stream, and the block size and complexity threshold parameters are provided as the input information. The framework of block processing is introduced first. Then, the required pre-process to ensure perfect recovery of both the cover image and secret data is presented.

Like all the PVO-based schemes, the RDH scheme proposed in this paper first divides the cover image into non-overlapping and equally sized blocks. Then, the pixels in each block is rearranged into a sequence of n pixels $(x_1, x_2, \ldots, x_n)$ in the raster scan order. The secret data embedding process includes two steps: the maximum-prediction-error expansion (max-PEE) and the minimum-prediction-error expansion (mini-PEE). In the first step, the n pixel values are sorted to obtain the sequence $x_{\sigma(1)} \leq x_{\sigma(2)} \leq \cdots \leq x_{\sigma(n)}$, where $\sigma(i)$ represents the original location index of the i-th term after sorting. When repeated pixel value occurs, the spatial order of pixels with the same value is preserved as given in Equation (1). The 4-th pixel $x_{\sigma(n-3)}$ is used to predict the three maximum-valued pixels $\left(x_{\sigma(n)}, x_{\sigma(n-1)}, x_{\sigma(n-2)}\right)$ and three prediction errors are obtained. The specific operation is as follows: first sort the spatial indices $(\sigma(n), \sigma(n-1), \sigma(n-2))$ to obtain $a_1 < a_2 < a_3$. That is, the three pixels $\left(x_{\sigma(n)}, x_{\sigma(n-1)}, x_{\sigma(n-2)}\right)$ are resorted in their original raster-scanned order into $(x_{a_1}, x_{a_2}, x_{a_3})$. Then, calculate the prediction errors $\left(e_{max}^1, e_{max}^2, e_{max}^3\right)$ by

$$\begin{cases} e_{max}^1 = x_{a_1} - x_{\sigma(n-3)} \\ e_{max}^2 = x_{a_2} - x_{\sigma(n-3)} \\ e_{max}^3 = x_{a_3} - x_{\sigma(n-3)} \end{cases}. \tag{12}$$

The prediction error triplet $(e_{max}^1, e_{max}^2, e_{max}^3)$ is a process in a similar manner as the PVO-based schemes introduced in the related works to embed secret data except for the state transition map is expanded to 3D space. The proposed 3D state-space transition map is provided in the next subsection. Suppose the prediction error triplet $(e_{max}^1, e_{max}^2, e_{max}^3)$ is modified into $(e_{max}'^1, e_{max}'^2, e_{max}'^3)$ after data embedding or expansion, the three maximum-valued pixels $(x_{a_1}, x_{a_2}, x_{a_3})$ are modified accordingly by

$$x'_{a_i} = x_{\sigma(n-3)} + e'^i_{max}, \ (i=1,2,3). \tag{13}$$

In our design, the modification of the maximum-valued pixels is always incremented or unchanged, while the remaining pixels are kept unchanged. The maximum-valued group can be preserved. Further, the three pixels are resorted in their spatial order. This order cannot be altered even if their order in value is changed during the embedding process. Therefore, the embedding scheme's reversibility can be ensured.

In the second step, the modified pixel sequence obtained in the previous step $(x'_1, x'_2, \ldots, x'_n)$ is sorted again to obtain $x'_{\sigma(1)} \leq x'_{\sigma(2)} \leq \ldots \leq x'_{\sigma(n)}$. The indices $(\sigma'(1), \sigma'(2), \sigma'(3))$ are then resorted according to their spatial order to obtain $c_1 < c_2 < c_3$. The prediction errors of the three minimum-valued pixels $(e_{min}^1, e_{min}^2, e_{min}^3)$ are calculated by Equation (14). The second round of data embedding is executed by modifying $(e_{min}^1, e_{min}^2, e_{min}^3)$ according to the same 3D state transition map into $(e_{min}'^1, e_{min}'^2, e_{min}'^3)$. The corresponding modification of pixel values is given by Equation (15). Again, the three minimum-valued pixels are decremented or unchanged to ensure reversibility. The remaining pixels are kept unchanged, and the final stego pixel sequence $(x''_1, x''_2, \ldots, x''_n)$ of the block can be obtained.

$$\begin{cases} e_{min}^1 = x'_{\sigma'(4)} - x'_{c_1} \\ e_{min}^2 = x'_{\sigma'(4)} - x'_{c_2} \\ e_{min}^3 = x'_{\sigma'(4)} - x'_{c_3} \end{cases}. \tag{14}$$

$$x''_{c_i} = x'_{\sigma'(4)} - e'^i_{min}, \ (i=1,2,3). \tag{15}$$

The pre-process is illustrated in Figure 2a. There are some auxiliary messages, including the length and width of a block (4 bits), the threshold of block complexity (8 bits), and the secret data size (16 bits). To avoid overflow and underflow, a block that contains any 0-valued or 255-valued pixel is classified as a non-embeddable block and is marked by 1 in the location map. Then, the compressed location map and the other auxiliary messages are hidden in the LSB of the pixels in the first two rows of the cover image, and these two rows are skipped in the embedding process. The original LSB bits of these two lines are appended to the front of the secret stream and embedded into the cover image. At the receiving end, these auxiliary messages are retrieved first to help extract the secret data and restore the cover image.

3.2. 3D State Transition Map

To design a proper 3D state transition map for a prediction-error triplet $(e_{max}^1, e_{max}^2, e_{max}^3)$, the 3D histogram of the triplet is investigated first. Figure 3 shows the 3D histogram of prediction-error triplet for cover image 'Lena' slice-wise. As shown in the figure, the maximum value appears at $(1,1,1)$, which is a common phenomenon for ordinary cover images. A 3D view of the histogram is given in Figure 4, where a cross-sectional view at the maximum value is also plotted. The values of the prediction error triplets of an entire cover image are highly concentrated near the state $(1,1,1)$, and the population gradually decreases outward.

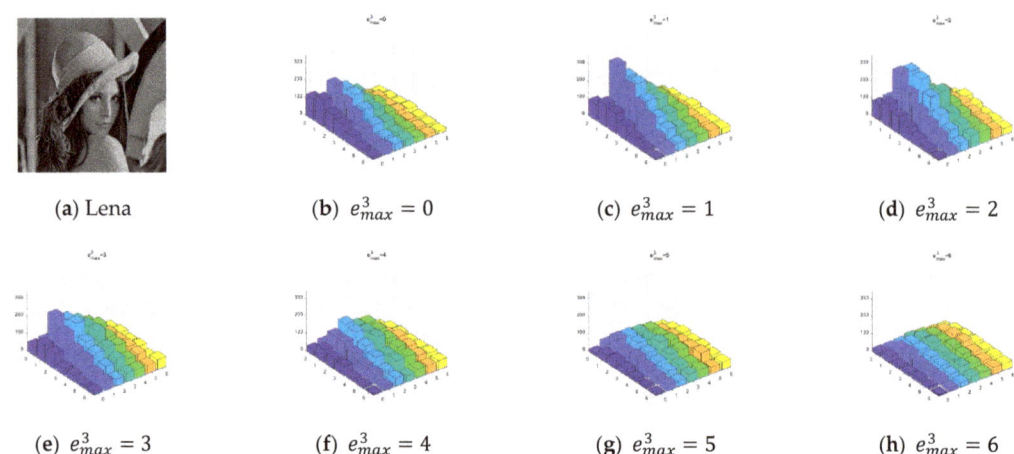

Figure 3. Slice representation of 3D prediction error histogram. (**a**) Lena; (**b**) $e^3_{max} = 0$; (**c**) $e^3_{max} = 1$; (**d**) $e^3_{max} = 2$; (**e**) $e^3_{max} = 3$; (**f**) $e^3_{max} = 4$; (**g**) $e^3_{max} = 5$; (**h**) $e^3_{max} = 6$.

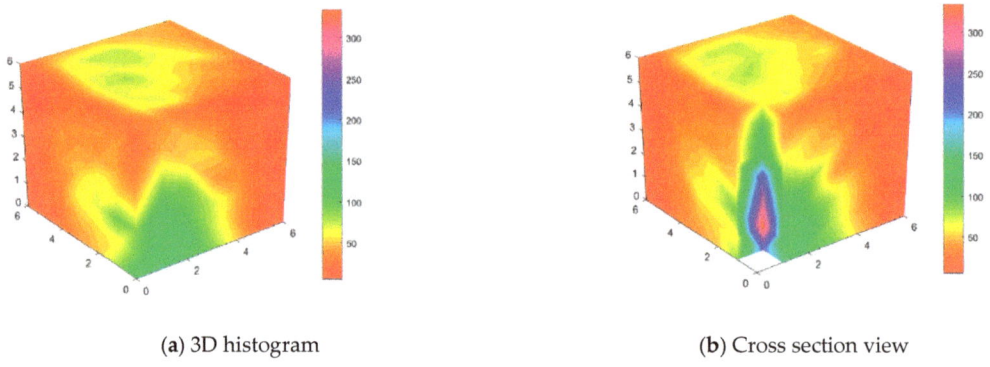

Figure 4. 3D prediction error histogram with a view at the maximum value. (**a**) 3D histogram; (**b**) Cross section view.

A rule of thumb for transition map design is to select the maximum bins in the histogram as the embedding targets while reducing the required expansion of non-embeddable bins. The 3D prediction-error space is divided into layered structures according to the equation

$$L_p = \left\{ \left(e^1_{max}, e^2_{max}, e^3_{max}\right) \middle| \min\left(e^1_{max}, e^2_{max}, e^3_{max}\right) = p. \right\}, \quad (16)$$

where L_p is the set of all states included in the p-th layer. The layered structure is illustrated in Figure 5. In fact, the 0-th layer is the boundary surface of an octant in the 3D space. More specifically, the p-th layer contains all of the states on three quarter plane

$$\begin{cases} e^1_{max} = p, e^2_{max} \geq p, e^3_{max} \geq p \\ e^2_{max} = p, e^1_{max} \geq p, e^3_{max} \geq p \\ e^3_{max} = p, e^1_{max} \geq p, e^2_{max} \geq p \end{cases}. \quad (17)$$

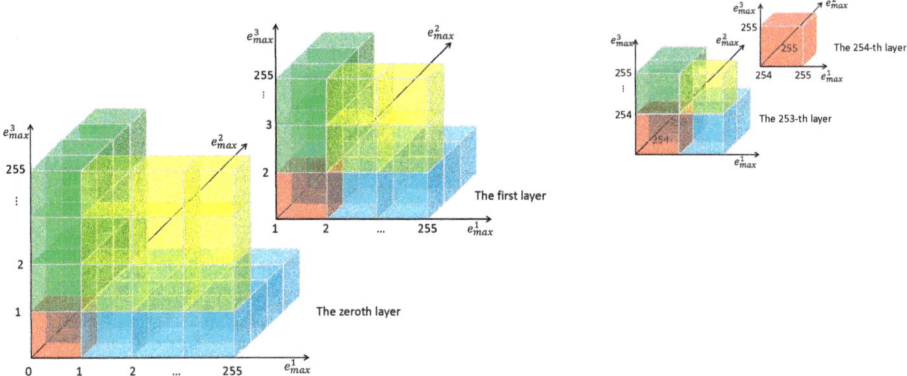

Figure 5. Layered structure of the 3D transition map.

Since the maximum value of the 3D prediction-error histogram appears at $(1, 1, 1)$, which is located on the 1-st layer, the 3D state transition map for the 0-th layer and the remaining layers are designed differently, as shown in Figures 6 and 7, respectively. In each figure, the state transition maps for the three quarter-planes are given in (a–c), while their projection versions are given in (d–f) for convenience. The major difference between the 0-th layer and the remaining layers is that the state $(0, 0, 0)$ is left unembedded, while the states (p, p, p), $p \neq 0$ are embedded with two bits each. Thus, the highest bin of $(1, 1, 1)$ is efficiently exploited. On each quarter plane, the embeddable states are aligned on two diagonal lines, and the secret data is embedded by expanding the states along the horizontal and the vertical axes. This design can reduce the embedding distortion to a minimum since only a single value of the prediction-error triplet is modified. Based on the 3D state transition map, the proposed PVO scheme can efficiently embed the secret data with the least sacrifice of image quality. The corresponding rules for data embedding or pixel value expansion of the proposed scheme are summarized as follows.

For the 0-th layer (L_0):

1. $e_{max}^3 = 0$:

$$\left(e_{max}^{\prime 1}, e_{max}^{\prime 2}, e_{max}^{\prime 3}\right) = \begin{cases} \left(e_{max}^1, e_{max}^2, e_{max}^3\right), & e_{max}^1 = e_{max}^2 = 0 \\ \left(e_{max}^1 + 1, e_{max}^2, e_{max}^3\right), & e_{max}^1 - 1 > e_{max}^2 \\ \left(e_{max}^1 + b, e_{max}^2, e_{max}^3\right), & e_{max}^1 - 1 = e_{max}^2 \\ \left(e_{max}^1, e_{max}^2 + b, e_{max}^3\right), & e_{max}^1 = e_{max}^2 \neq 0 \\ \left(e_{max}^1, e_{max}^2 + 1, e_{max}^3\right), & 0 \neq e_{max}^1 < e_{max}^2 \end{cases}. \quad (18)$$

2. $e_{max}^2 = 0$:

$$\left(e_{max}^{\prime 1}, e_{max}^{\prime 2}, e_{max}^{\prime 3}\right) = \begin{cases} \left(e_{max}^1, e_{max}^2, e_{max}^3 + 1\right), & e_{max}^1 < e_{max}^3 - 1 \\ \left(e_{max}^1, e_{max}^2, e_{max}^3 + b\right), & e_{max}^1 = e_{max}^3 - 1 \\ \left(e_{max}^1 + b, e_{max}^2, e_{max}^3\right), & e_{max}^1 = e_{max}^3 \neq 0 \\ \left(e_{max}^1 + 1, e_{max}^2, e_{max}^3\right), & e_{max}^1 > e_{max}^3 \neq 0 \end{cases}. \quad (19)$$

3. $e_{max}^1 = 0$:

$$\left(e_{max}^{\prime 1}, e_{max}^{\prime 2}, e_{max}^{\prime 3}\right) = \begin{cases} \left(e_{max}^1, e_{max}^2, e_{max}^3 + 1\right), & e_{max}^2 < e_{max}^3 - 1 \\ \left(e_{max}^1, e_{max}^2, e_{max}^3 + b\right), & e_{max}^2 = e_{max}^3 - 1 \\ \left(e_{max}^1, e_{max}^2 + b, e_{max}^3\right), & e_{max}^2 = e_{max}^3 \neq 0 \\ \left(e_{max}^1, e_{max}^2 + 1, e_{max}^3\right), & e_{max}^2 > e_{max}^3 \neq 0 \end{cases}. \quad (20)$$

For the p-th (except for 0) layer ($L_{p\neq 0}$):

1. $e_{max}^1 = e_{max}^2 = e_{max}^3 = p$:

$$\left(e_{max}^{\prime 1}, e_{max}^{\prime 2}, e_{max}^{\prime 3}\right) = \begin{cases} (e_{max}^1, e_{max}^2, e_{max}^3), & b_1 b_0 = 00 \\ (e_{max}^1 + 1, e_{max}^2, e_{max}^3), & b_1 b_0 = 01 \\ (e_{max}^1, e_{max}^2 + 1, e_{max}^3), & b_1 b_0 = 10 \\ (e_{max}^1, e_{max}^2, e_{max}^3 + 1), & b_1 b_0 = 11 \end{cases}. \quad (21)$$

2. $e_{max}^3 = p$:

$$\left(e_{max}^{\prime 1}, e_{max}^{\prime 2}, e_{max}^{\prime 3}\right) = \begin{cases} (e_{max}^1 + 1, e_{max}^2, e_{max}^3), & e_{max}^1 - 1 > e_{max}^2 \\ (e_{max}^1 + 1, e_{max}^2, e_{max}^3), & e_{max}^1 - 1 = e_{max}^2 = p \\ (e_{max}^1 + b, e_{max}^2, e_{max}^3), & e_{max}^1 - 1 = e_{max}^2 \neq p \\ (e_{max}^1, e_{max}^2 + b, e_{max}^3), & e_{max}^1 = e_{max}^2 \neq p \\ (e_{max}^1, e_{max}^2 + 1, e_{max}^3), & p \neq e_{max}^1 < e_{max}^2 \end{cases}. \quad (22)$$

3. $e_{max}^2 = p$:

$$\left(e_{max}^{\prime 1}, e_{max}^{\prime 2}, e_{max}^{\prime 3}\right) = \begin{cases} (e_{max}^1, e_{max}^2, e_{max}^3 + 1), & e_{max}^1 < e_{max}^3 - 1 \\ (e_{max}^1, e_{max}^2, e_{max}^3 + 1), & e_{max}^1 = e_{max}^3 - 1 = p \\ (e_{max}^1, e_{max}^2, e_{max}^3 + b), & e_{max}^1 = e_{max}^3 - 1 \neq p \\ (e_{max}^1 + b, e_{max}^2, e_{max}^3), & e_{max}^1 = e_{max}^3 \neq p \\ (e_{max}^1 + 1, e_{max}^2, e_{max}^3), & e_{max}^1 > e_{max}^3 \neq p \end{cases}. \quad (23)$$

4. $e_{max}^1 = p$:

$$\left(e_{max}^{\prime 1}, e_{max}^{\prime 2}, e_{max}^{\prime 3}\right) = \begin{cases} (e_{max}^1, e_{max}^2, e_{max}^3 + 1), & e_{max}^2 < e_{max}^3 - 1 \\ (e_{max}^1, e_{max}^2, e_{max}^3 + 1), & e_{max}^2 = e_{max}^3 - 1 = p \\ (e_{max}^1, e_{max}^2, e_{max}^3 + b), & e_{max}^2 = e_{max}^3 - 1 \neq p \\ (e_{max}^1, e_{max}^2 + b, e_{max}^3), & e_{max}^2 = e_{max}^3 \neq p \\ (e_{max}^1, e_{max}^2 + 1, e_{max}^3), & e_{max}^2 > e_{max}^3 \neq p \end{cases}. \quad (24)$$

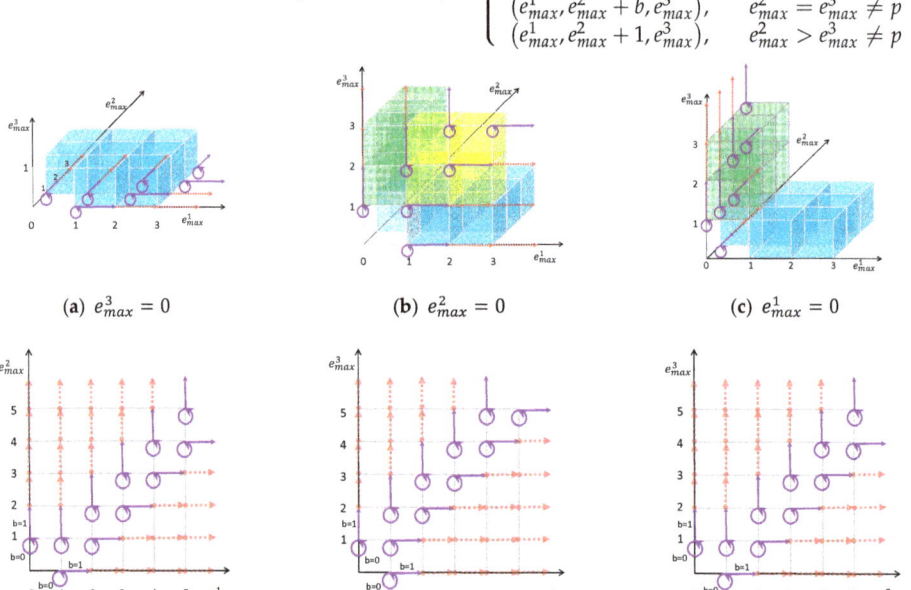

Figure 6. (**a**–**c**) 3D state transition map for the 0-th layer $L_{p=0}$; (**d**–**f**) the projection versions.

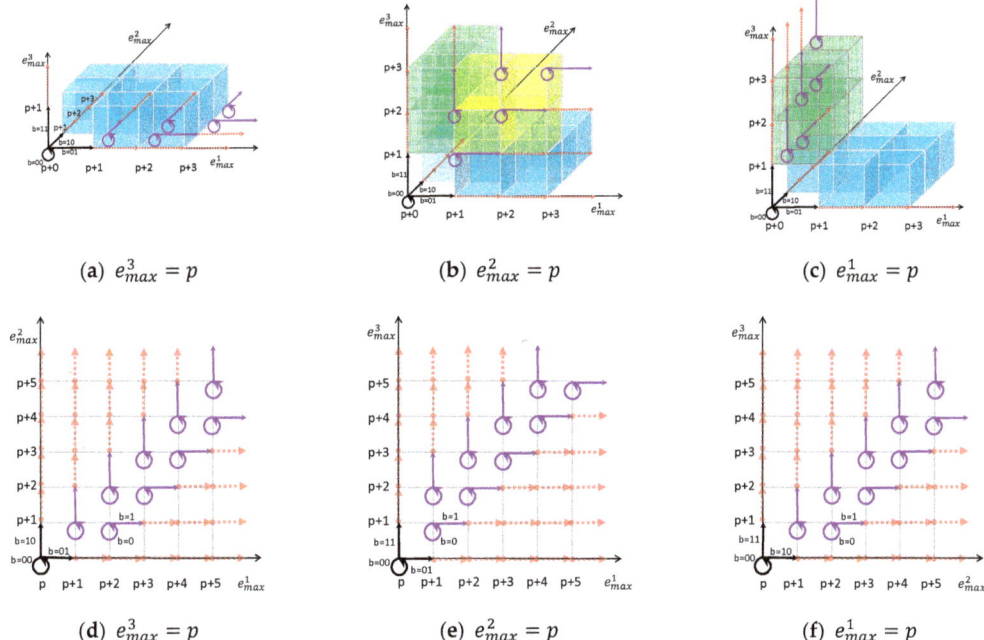

Figure 7. (**a**–**c**) 3D state transition map for the p-th layer $L_{p\neq 0}$; (**d**–**f**) the projection versions.

3.3. Examples of Secret Data Embedding

In this subsection, two example image blocks sized 2×2 are provided to demonstrate the data embedding process of the proposed scheme. The first example is shown in Figure 8a. The first step is to execute the max-PEE. The sorted sequence is $(192, 192, 192, 193)$, the maximum-valued pixels in their spatial order are $(x_2, x_3, x_4) = (192, 192, 193)$, and the minimum-valued pixel is $x_1 = 192$. The prediction error triplet can be calculated by $(e^1_{max}, e^2_{max}, e^3_{max}) = (x_2 - x_1, x_3 - x_1, x_4 - x_1) = (0, 0, 1)$ and its corresponding layer $p = \min(e^1_{max}, e^2_{max}, e^3_{max}) = e^2_{max} = 0$. According to the state transition map of the 0-th layer (see Figure 6e or Equation (19)), suppose the data to be embedded is $b = 1$, the triplet $(e^1_{max}, e^2_{max}, e^3_{max})$ is modified from $(0, 0, 1)$ to $(0, 0, 2)$. Consequently, (x_2, x_3, x_4) is modified from $(192, 192, 193)$ to $(x'_2, x'_3, x'_4) = (192, 192, 194)$. Then, the second step of the mini-PEE has proceeded. The sorted pixel sequence is $(192, 192, 192, 194)$ and the minimum-valued pixels in their spatial order is (x'_1, x'_2, x'_3). The prediction error triplet is given by $(e^1_{min}, e^2_{min}, e^3_{min}) = (x'_4 - x'_1, x'_4 - x'_2, x'_4 - x'_3) = (2, 2, 2)$ and its corresponding layer is $p = \min(e^1_{min}, e^2_{min}, e^3_{min}) = e^2_{min} = 2$. According to the state transition map of the 2-nd layer (see Figure 7e or Equation (23)), suppose the two bits of data to be embedded are $b_1 b_0 = 01$, $(e^1_{min}, e^2_{min}, e^3_{min})$ is modified from $(2, 2, 2)$ to $(3, 2, 2)$. Consequently, (x'_1, x'_2, x'_3) is modified from $(192, 192, 192)$ to $(x''_1, x''_2, x''_3) = (191, 192, 192)$. The second example block is given in Figure 8b. In the first embedding step, the maximum-valued pixels in their spatial order is $(x_1, x_2, x_4) = (194, 195, 193)$. The prediction error triplet is therefore $(e^1_{max}, e^2_{max}, e^3_{max}) = (x_1 - x_3, x_2 - x_3, x_4 - x_3) = (2, 3, 1)$. According to the state transition map of the 1-st layer (see Figure 7d or Equation (22)), the state is not embeddable and $(e^1_{max}, e^2_{max}, e^3_{max})$ is expanded from $(2, 3, 1)$ to $(2, 4, 1)$. Consequently, (x_1, x_2, x_4) is modified from $(194, 195, 193)$ to $(x'_1, x'_2, x'_4) = (194, 196, 193)$. In the second embedding step, the minimum-valued pixels in spatial order is $(x'_1, x'_3, x'_4) = (194, 192, 193)$. The triplet is $(e^1_{min}, e^2_{min}, e^3_{min}) = (x'_2 - x'_1, x'_2 - x'_3, x'_2 - x'_4) = (2, 4, 3)$. According to the state transition map of the 2-th layer (see Figure 7f or Equation (24)), suppose the data to be embedded is $b = 1$, $\left(e_{min}^1, e_{min}^2, e_{min}^3\right)$ is modified from $(2,4,3)$ to $(2,5,3)$. Consequently, $\left(x_1', x_3', x_4'\right)$ changes from $(194, 192, 193)$ to $\left(x_1'', x_3'', x_4''\right) = (194, 191, 193)$.

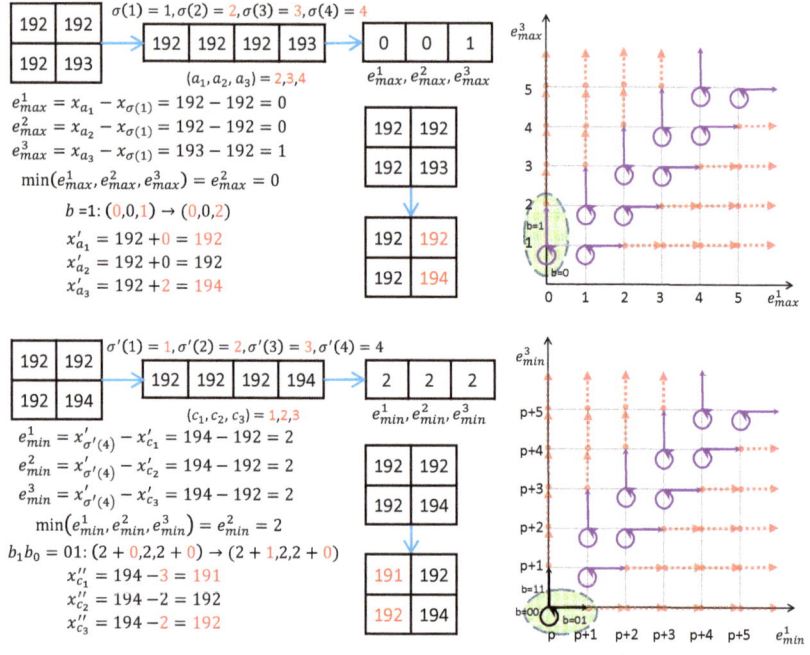

(a) Embedding Example 1.

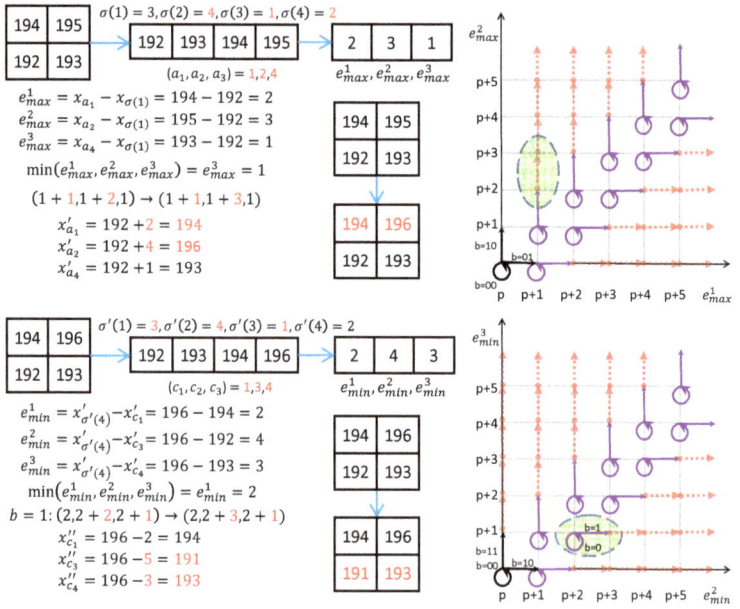

(b) Embedding Example 2.

Figure 8. Two examples of the secret data embedding process. (**a**) Embedding Example 1; (**b**) Embedding Example 2.

3.4. Data Extraction and Image Recovery

The data extraction is operated in the reverse embedding order. At the receiver end, the stego-image is first divided into non-overlapping blocks of the same size. For each block, the pixels are sorted to obtain the ordered sequence first. Then, the reverse operations of mini-PEE and max-PEE are executed sequentially to extract the secret data and recover the original pixel values.

The stego-block in Figure 8a is applied as the first example shown in Figure 9a. The pixel sequence is sorted to obtain the minimum-valued pixels in spatial order $(x_1'', x_2'', x_3'') = (191, 192, 192)$ and the triplet $(e_{min}'^1, e_{min}'^2, e_{min}'^3) = (194-191, 194-192, 194-192) = (3,2,2)$. According to the state transition map of the 2-nd layer (see Figure 7e or Equation (23)), $(3,2,2) = (p+1, p, p+0)$ corresponds to the state $(1,0)$ on the map and comes from $(0,0)$ due to embedding of $b_1 b_0 = 01$. Therefore, the original prediction error triplet is $(2+0, 2, 2+0)$ and the pixel values are $(x_1', x_2', x_3') = (192, 192, 192)$. Then, the sequence is sorted again to obtain the maximum-valued pixels $(x_2', x_3', x_4') = (192, 192, 194)$ and the prediction error triplet $(e_{max}'^1, e_{max}'^2, e_{max}'^3) = (192-192, 192-192, 194-192) = (0,0,2)$. According to the state transition map of the 0-th layer (see Figure 6e or Equation (19)), the triplet $(0,0,2)$ corresponds to $(0,2)$ on the map and comes from $(0,1)$ due to embedding of $b = 1$. Therefore, the original triplet is $(0,0,1)$ and the cover pixel values are $(x_2, x_3, x_4) = (192, 192, 193)$. The second stego-block is shown in Figure 9b. The pixel sequence is sorted to obtain the minimum-valued pixels in spatial order $(x_1'', x_3'', x_4'') = (194, 191, 193)$ and the prediction error triplet $(e_{min}'^1, e_{min}'^2, e_{min}'^3) = (196-194, 196-191, 196-193) = (2,5,3)$. According to the state transition map of the 2-nd layer (see Figure 7f or Equation (24)), $(2,5,3) = (p, p+3, p+1)$ corresponds to the state $(3,1)$ on the map and comes from $(2,1)$ due to embedding of $b = 1$. Therefore, the original prediction error triplet is $(2, 2+2, 2+1)$ and the pixel values are $(x_1', x_2', x_3') = (194, 192, 193)$. Then, the sequence is sorted again to obtain the maximum-valued pixels $(x_1', x_2', x_4') = (194, 196, 193)$ and the triplet $(e_{max}'^1, e_{max}'^2, e_{max}'^3) = (194-192, 196-192, 193-192) = (2,4,1)$. According to the state transition map of the 1-st layer (see Figure 7d or Equation (22)), the triplet $(2,4,1)$ corresponds to $(1,3)$ on the map and comes from $(1,2)$ due to expansion. Therefore, the original triplet is $(2,3,1)$, and the cover pixel values are $(x_1, x_2, x_4) = (194, 195, 193)$.

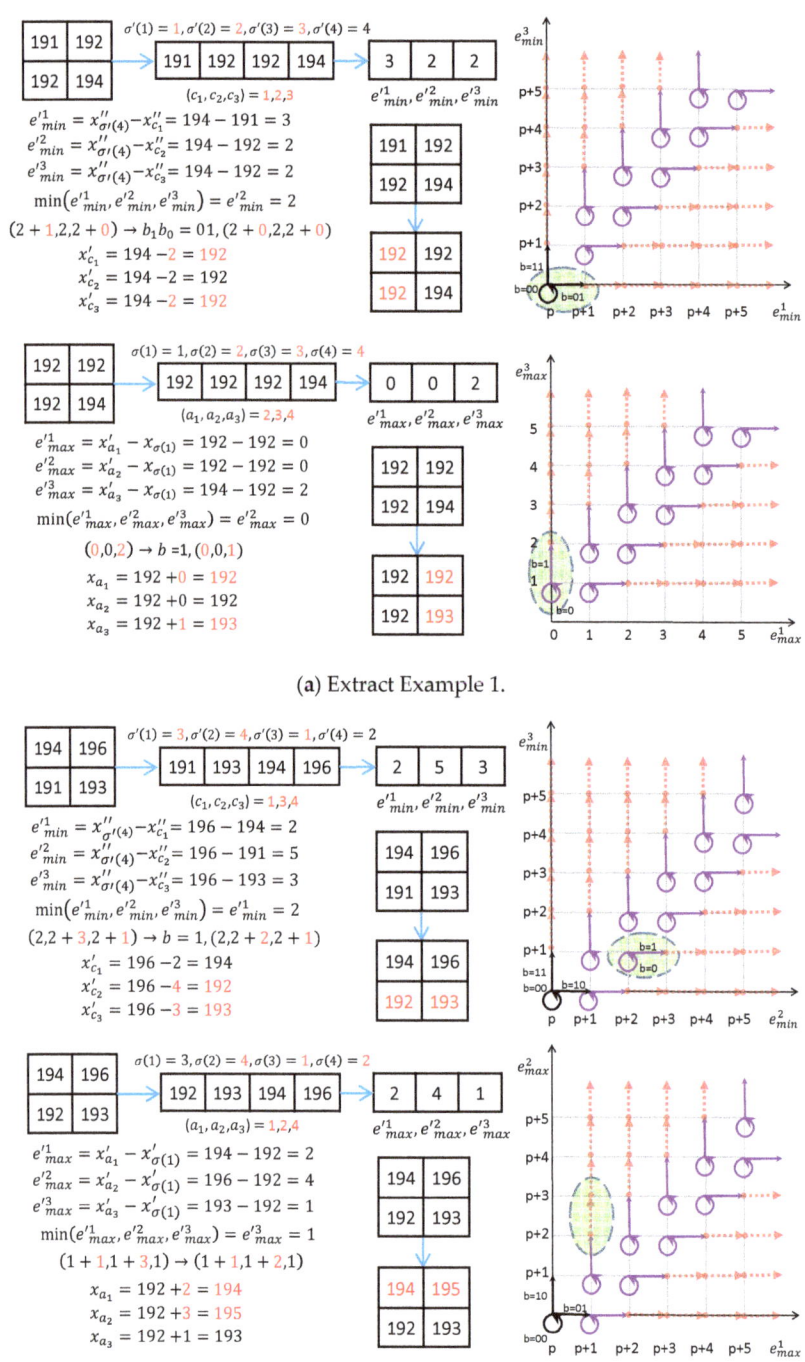

Figure 9. Two examples of the secret data extraction and block recovery process. (**a**) Extract Example 1; (**b**) Extract Example 2.

3.5. Complex Block Exclusion

Since the embeddable states are aligned on two diagonal lines of each quarter plane in the layered structure, at least two pixel-values in a block should be equal or very close to each other to make it embeddable. Complex blocks are non-embeddable, and pixel value expansion is required without any contribution to the embedding capacity.

All PVO-based schemes introduced in the related works include a complexity measure of blocks and skip the complex blocks when embedding. In our scheme, the complexity measure of blocks proposed by Ou et al. in [26] was adopted. The noise level (NL) of a pixel block is evaluated through its context. When the size of the pixel block is $n_1 \times n_2$, referring to Figure 10, the two columns of pixels on the right and the two rows of pixels below the pixel block are regarded as the context of the current block. Calculating the sum of the absolute difference between every two consecutive pixels in the context can obtain the complexity NL of the current pixel block. The formula is given by

$$NL = \sum d_{ver} + \sum d_{hor}, \qquad (25)$$

where d_{ver} denotes an absolute difference of two consecutive pixels in the vertical direction, and d_{hor} denotes an absolute difference of two pixels in the horizontal direction.

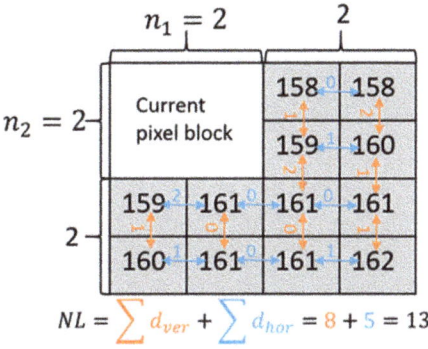

Figure 10. A 2 × 2 sized block and its context (gray pixels), where NL is the noise level.

The pairwise-PVO [24], POV-k [26], k-pass PVO [27], and improved k-pass PVO [28] all classify the image blocks into three types and process them with hybrid schemes. In our work, the proposed single scheme was applied. The complexity measure was just used to exclude the non-embeddable blocks when NL exceeds a given threshold T.

4. Experimental Results and Comparisons

The proposed data hiding scheme is implemented using MATLAB language on the Windows PC environment. Eight standard grayscale test images sized 512 × 512 shown in Figure 11 are applied. The binary secret data S is produced by a random number generator. The performance is mainly evaluated through two indicators, the peak signal-to-noise ratio (PSNR) and the payload. Let W and H be the width and height of the cover image. The PSNR defined by Equation (26) evaluates the visual quality of a stego image.

$$PSNR = 10\log_{10}\left(\frac{H \times W \times (255)^2}{\sum_{i=1}^{H}\sum_{j=1}^{W}\left(G_{ij} - G'_{ij}\right)^2}\right), \qquad (26)$$

where G_{ij} and G'_{ij} are the pixel values in the i-th row and the j-th column of the cover image and the stego-image, respectively. In general, we think that if the PSNR of the hidden image is greater than 30, then the difference between it and the original image is already invisible. Of course, the higher the PSNR, the smaller the difference between the hidden image and the original image, and the less likely it is to discover the secret data on the hidden image. A stego image of a high PSNR value can be produced by minimizing the required modification of pixel values during data embedding. A major objective of data hiding is to resemble the original image as much as possible. Therefore, an excellent data hiding scheme should embed a satisfactory amount of secret data with a high PSNR value.

Figure 11. Eight gray level standard test images applied in our experiments. (**a**) Lena; (**b**) Baboon; (**c**) Barbara; (**d**) Elaine; (**e**) Airplane; (**f**) Peppers; (**g**) Lake; (**h**) Boat.

The payload is the valid part of the data we embed in the stego image, i.e., the secret data. In fact, the data we embed in the stego image consists of two parts: the payload and the auxiliary information. The bigger the payload, the more secret data we can embed.

4.1. Experimental Results

There are two adaptive parameters in our proposed scheme, which are the block size $n_1 \times n_2$ and the threshold of complexity T. In general, larger block size or a smaller threshold value can produce a stego image with a high PSNR value. However, both strategies lead to the reduction of payloads. A larger block size reduces the total number of blocks, while a smaller threshold value reduces the number of applicable smooth blocks.

In our experiments, the influence of the block size was investigated first. The block sizes of $1 \times 4, 2 \times 2, 4 \times 1, 2 \times 3, 3 \times 2$, and 3×3 were tested, and the results are listed in Table 1. As shown in the table, the visual quality of the stego images improves with the expansion in block size. However, among different shapes of the same size, 2×2 and 3×2 outperform the others.

Table 1. PSNR values under different sizes (payload = 10,000 bits).

Image	1×4	2×2	4×1	2×3	3×2	3×3
Lena	59.51	60.26	60.20	61.05	61.18	61.42
Baboon	55.33	55.84	55.33	56.89	56.99	56.72
Barbara	59.65	60.01	59.68	60.97	60.98	61.28
Elaine	58.03	58.52	57.85	59.19	59.29	59.30
Airplane	62.63	63.07	62.97	63.73	63.80	63.63
Peppers	58.30	58.55	58.48	59.75	59.90	60.40
Lake	59.72	59.92	59.39	60.88	60.76	60.72
Boat	58.22	58.51	58.49	59.50	59.52	59.81

By taking both the block size and the threshold value into consideration, Table 2 lists the best block size and the complexity threshold to obtain the best PSNR for different test images under a payload of 10,000 bits. As shown in the table, 3×2 is the most frequent optimal solution and is the smallest size among all the sizes, which is advantageous when the application requires a high payload.

Table 2. PSNR values under different sizes (payload = 10,000 bits).

Image	PSNR	Block Size	T
Airplane	63.80	3×2	20
Baboon	56.99	3×2	223
Barbara	61.29	3×3	65
Boat	59.82	2×4	106
Elaine	59.29	3×2	97
Lake	60.88	2×3	68
Lena	61.57	3×4	70
Peppers	60.55	3×4	105

4.2. Comparisons

In this subsection, the performance of our proposed scheme is compared with the typical PVO-based schemes, namely, PVO [21], IPVO [22], pairwise PVO [24], and the improved k-pass PVO [28]. PSNR values under different payloads for different test images are plotted in Figure 12, where the block size of 3×2 is adopted. The payload starts with 5000 bits, and the step length is 5000 bits, except for the cover image 'Baboon'. Due to the image's special features, the initial and step sizes of the payload are set differently. The results show that, for all test images, the PSNR of the proposed scheme outperforms the other schemes under the same payload. As the amount of payload increases, the PSNR improvement of the proposed scheme is more obvious. Due to the high embedding capacity and the low pixel value distortion during embedding and expansion, the proposed data hiding scheme provides a significant improvement for test images of high complexity such as 'Baboon'. This further confirms the superiority of the proposed 3D state transition map.

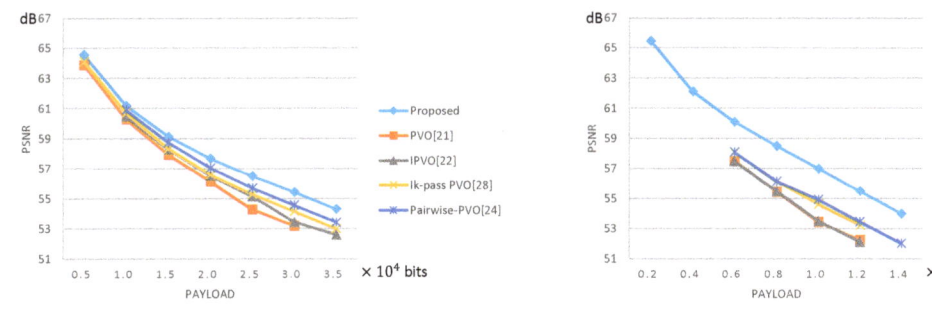

(a) Lena (b) Baboon

Figure 12. *Cont.*

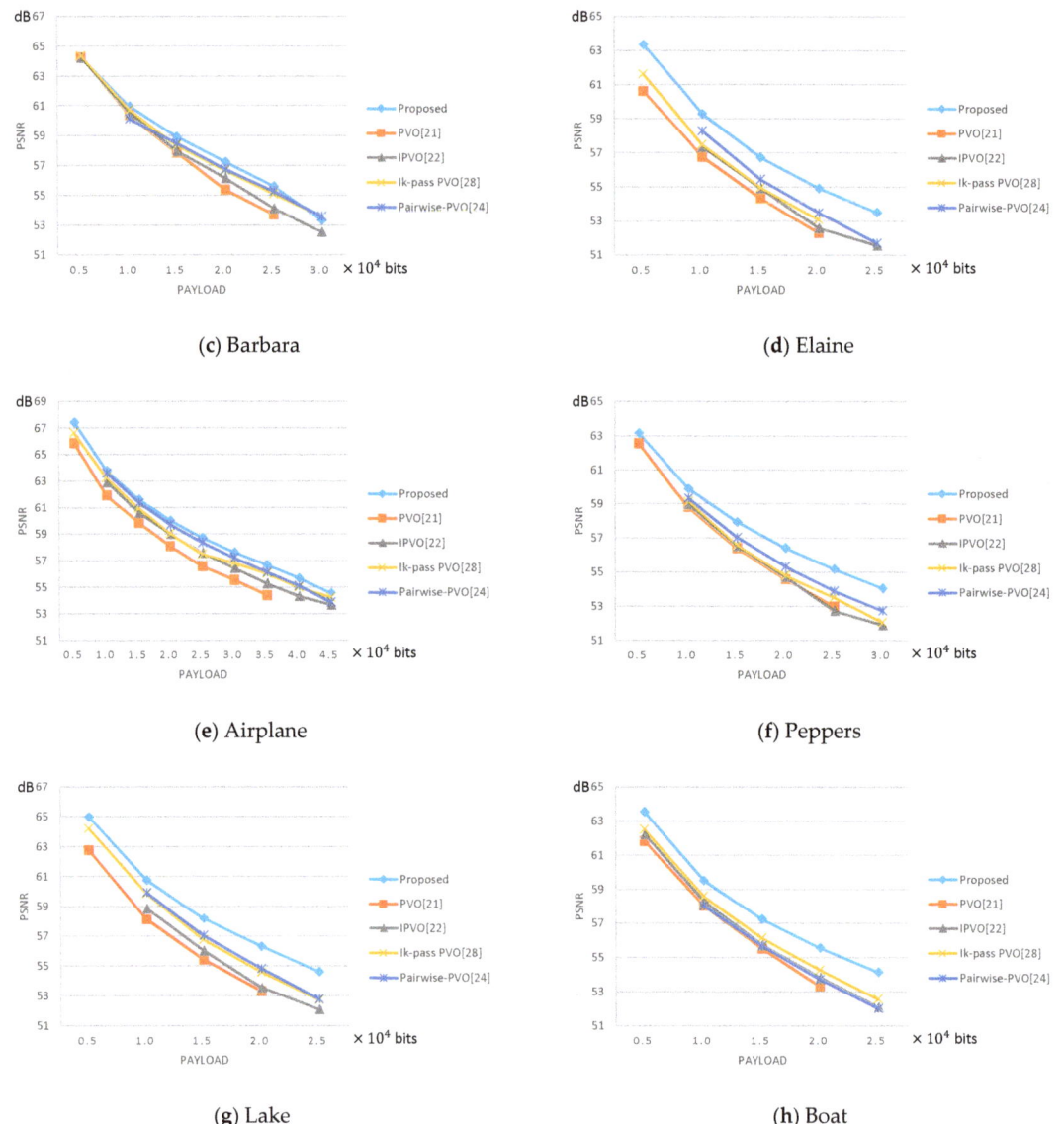

Figure 12. The PSNR values under different payloads. (**a**) Lena; (**b**) Baboon; (**c**) Barbara; (**d**) Elaine; (**e**) Airplane; (**f**) Peppers; (**g**) Lake; (**h**) Boat.

Tables 3 and 4 list the PSNR values of the stego images for related works under the payloads of 10,000 bits and 20,000 bits, where the block size is 3 × 2. The embedding capacity of the test image 'Baboon' cannot achieve 20,000 bits for all schemes, so its corresponding row in Table 4 is empty.

Table 3. Comparison of PSNR values when the pixel block is 3 × 2 (payload = 10,000 bits).

Image	Proposed	[21]	[22]	[24]	[27]	[28]
Lena	61.18	60.28	60.47	60.90	60.64	60.68
Baboon	56.99	53.43	53.49	54.94	54.00	54.60
Barbara	60.98	60.39	60.48	60.14	60.37	60.72
Elaine	59.29	56.79	57.34	58.29	57.67	57.49
Airplane	63.80	61.95	62.90	63.63	63.45	63.28
Peppers	59.90	58.83	58.97	59.36	59.29	59.14
Lake	60.76	58.13	58.85	59.94	59.71	59.86
Boat	59.52	58.05	58.25	58.05	58.28	58.61

Table 4. Comparison of PSNR values when the pixel block is 3 × 2 (payload = 20,000 bits).

Image	Proposed	[21]	[22]	[24]	[27]	[28]
Lena	57.67	56.14	56.51	57.04	56.81	56.67
Baboon	—	—	—	—	—	—
Barbara	57.27	55.40	56.13	55.88	56.09	56.74
Elaine	54.93	52.31	52.58	53.50	53.08	53.14
Airplane	60.04	58.09	58.99	59.73	59.59	59.18
Peppers	56.42	54.61	54.71	55.34	55.10	54.97
Lake	56.31	53.32	53.54	54.84	54.53	54.66
Boat	55.57	53.34	53.81	53.72	54.07	54.27

5. Conclusions

A new 3D state transition map for the PVO-based RDH scheme was proposed. The newly defined prediction error triplet and a sophisticatedly devised 3D state transition map were applied to guide the hiding of secret data in an image. The peak state in the 3D prediction error histogram was efficiently exploited to embed two bits of secret data each. All states, either embeddable or non-embeddable, were processed so that only a single entry of the triplet was modified during the embedding of secret data or pure expansion.

The experimental results showed that the proposed scheme could efficiently embed secret data with very low distortion to the cover image. The PSNR of the proposed scheme significantly outperforms the existing PVO-based schemes. Our scheme is especially advantageous for images with complex textures. As the amount of payload increases, the improvement in the visual quality of stego images becomes more obvious. In the future, a PVO scheme based on a state space of prediction errors with even higher dimensions is promising.

Author Contributions: Conceptualization, H.-X.C. and J.-H.H.; methodology, J.-H.H.; validation, H.-X.C.; writing—original draft preparation, H.-X.C.; writing—review and editing, J.-H.H. and C.-C.C. All authors have read and agreed to the published version of the manuscript.

Funding: This research was funded by the Ministry of Science and Technology of Taiwan, grant number MOST 110-2221-E-507-003.

Institutional Review Board Statement: Not applicable.

Informed Consent Statement: Not applicable.

Data Availability Statement: Not applicable.

Conflicts of Interest: The authors declare no conflict of interest.

References

1. Chang, C.-C. Adversarial Learning for Invertible Steganography. *IEEE Access* **2020**, *8*, 198425–198435. [CrossRef]
2. Chang, C.-C.; Li, C.-T.; Shi, Y.-Q. Privacy-Aware Reversible Watermarking in Cloud Computing Environments. *IEEE Access* **2018**, *6*, 70720–70733. [CrossRef]

3. Chi, H.; Chang, C.-C.; Liu, Y. An SMVQ Compressed Data Hiding Scheme Based on Multiple Linear Regression Prediction. *Connect. Sci.* **2020**, 1–20. [CrossRef]
4. Chen, K.-M. High Capacity Reversible Data Hiding Based on the Compression of Pixel Differences. *Mathematics* **2020**, *8*, 1435. [CrossRef]
5. Yu, C.; Ye, C.; Zhang, X.; Tang, Z.; Zhan, S. Separable Reversible Data Hiding in Encrypted Image Based on Two-Dimensional Permutation and Exploiting Modification Direction. *Mathematics* **2019**, *7*, 976. [CrossRef]
6. Sun, Y.; Lu, Y.; Chen, J.; Zhang, W.; Yan, X. Meaningful Secret Image Sharing Scheme with High Visual Quality Based on Natural Steganography. *Mathematics* **2020**, *8*, 1452. [CrossRef]
7. Chang, C.C.; Liu, Y.; Nguyen, T.S. A Novel Turtle Shell Based Scheme for Data Hiding. In Proceedings of the Tenth International Conference on Intelligent Information Hiding and Multimedia Signal Processing, Kitakyushu, Japan, 27–29 August 2014; pp. 89–93. [CrossRef]
8. Qin, J.; Wang, J.; Tan, Y.; Huang, H.; Xiang, X.; He, Z. Coverless Image Steganography Based on Generative Adversarial Network. *Mathematics* **2020**, *8*, 1394. [CrossRef]
9. Alattar, A.M. Reversible Watermark Using the Difference Expansion of a Generalized Integer Transform. *IEEE Trans. Image Process.* **2004**, *13*, 1147–1156. [CrossRef]
10. Hu, Y.; Lee, H.-K.; Li, J. DE-Based Reversible Data Hiding With Improved Overflow Location Map. *IEEE Trans. Circuits Syst. Video Technol.* **2009**, *19*, 250–260. [CrossRef]
11. Tian, J. Reversible Data Embedding Using a Difference Expansion. *IEEE Trans. Circuits Syst. Video Technol.* **2003**, *13*, 890–896. [CrossRef]
12. Li, X.; Li, B.; Yang, B.; Zeng, T. General Framework to Histogram-Shifting-Based Reversible Data Hiding. *IEEE Trans. Image Process.* **2013**, *22*, 2181–2191. [CrossRef]
13. Ni, Z.; Shi, Y.-Q.; Ansari, N.; Su, W. Reversible Data Hiding. *IEEE Trans. Circuits Syst. Video Technol.* **2006**, *16*, 354–362. [CrossRef]
14. Tsai, P.; Hu, Y.-C.; Yeh, H.-L. Reversible Image Hiding Scheme Using Predictive Coding and Histogram Shifting. *Signal Process.* **2009**, *89*, 1129–1143. [CrossRef]
15. Dragoi, I.-C.; Coltuc, D. Local-Prediction-Based Difference Expansion Reversible Watermarking. *IEEE Trans. Image Process.* **2014**, *23*, 1779–1790. [CrossRef]
16. Dragoi, I.-C.; Coltuc, D. Adaptive Pairing Reversible Watermarking. *IEEE Trans. Image Process.* **2016**, *25*, 2420–2422. [CrossRef]
17. He, W.; Xiong, G.; Weng, S.; Cai, Z.; Wang, Y. Reversible Data Hiding Using Multi-Pass Pixel-Value-Ordering and Pairwise Prediction-Error Expansion. *Inf. Sci.* **2018**, *467*, 784–799. [CrossRef]
18. Sachnev, V.; Kim, H.J.; Nam, J.; Suresh, S.; Shi, Y.Q. Reversible Watermarking Algorithm Using Sorting and Prediction. *IEEE Trans. Circuits Syst. Video Technol.* **2009**, *19*, 989–999. [CrossRef]
19. Luo, L.; Chen, Z.; Chen, M.; Zeng, X.; Xiong, Z. Reversible Image Watermarking Using Interpolation Technique. *IEEE Trans. Inf. Forensics Secur.* **2010**, *5*, 187–193. [CrossRef]
20. Ou, B.; Li, X.; Zhao, Y.; Ni, R.; Shi, Y.-Q. Pairwise Prediction-Error Expansion for Efficient Reversible Data Hiding. *IEEE Trans. Image Process.* **2013**, *22*, 5010–5021. [CrossRef] [PubMed]
21. Li, X.; Li, J.; Li, B.; Yang, B. High-Fidelity Reversible Data Hiding Scheme Based on Pixel-Value-Ordering and Prediction-Error Expansion. *Signal Process.* **2013**, *93*, 198–205. [CrossRef]
22. Peng, F.; Li, X.; Yang, B. Improved PVO-Based Reversible Data Hiding. *Digit. Signal Process.* **2014**, *25*, 255–265. [CrossRef]
23. He, W.; Cai, Z.; Wang, Y. Flexible Spatial Location-Based PVO Predictor for High-Fidelity Reversible Data Hiding. *Inf. Sci.* **2020**, *520*, 431–444. [CrossRef]
24. Ou, B.; Li, X.; Wang, J. High-Fidelity Reversible Data Hiding Based on Pixel-Value-Ordering and Pairwise Prediction-Error Expansion. *J. Vis. Commun. Image Represent.* **2016**, *39*, 12–23. [CrossRef]
25. Zhang, T.; Li, X.; Qi, W.; Guo, Z. Location-Based PVO and Adaptive Pairwise Modification for Efficient Reversible Data Hiding. *IEEE Trans. Inf. Forensics Secur.* **2020**, *15*, 2306–2319. [CrossRef]
26. Ou, B.; Li, X.; Zhao, Y.; Ni, R. Reversible Data Hiding Using Invariant Pixel-Value-Ordering and Prediction-Error Expansion. *Signal Process. Image Commun.* **2014**, *29*, 760–772. [CrossRef]
27. He, W.; Zhou, K.; Cai, J.; Wang, L.; Xiong, G. Reversible Data Hiding Using Multi-Pass Pixel Value Ordering and Prediction-Error Expansion. *J. Vis. Commun. Image Represent.* **2017**, *49*, 351–360. [CrossRef]
28. Weng, S.; Chen, Y.; Ou, B.; Chang, C.-C.; Zhang, C. Improved K-Pass Pixel Value Ordering Based Data Hiding. *IEEE Access* **2019**, *7*, 34570–34582. [CrossRef]

Article

A Novel LSB Matching Algorithm Based on Information Pre-Processing

Yongjin Hu [1], Xiyan Li [1,2,*] and Jun Ma [1]

[1] Department of Cryptogram Engineering, Information Engineering University, Zhengzhou 450001, China; hu_yongjin@126.com (Y.H.); sijunhan@163.com (J.M.)
[2] School of Information Science and Technology, Hainan Normal University, Haikou 571158, China
* Correspondence: xiyanli2006@163.com

Abstract: This paper analyzes random bits and scanned documents, two forms of secret data. The secret data were pre-processed by halftone, quadtree, and S-Box transformations, and the size of the scanned document was reduced by 8.11 times. A novel LSB matching algorithm with low distortion was proposed for the embedding step. The golden ratio was firstly applied to find the optimal embedding position and was used to design the matching function. Both theory and experiment have demonstrated that our study presented a good trade-off between high capacity and low distortion and is superior to other related schemes.

Keywords: data hiding; halftone; quadtree; LSB matching; golden ratio

Citation: Hu, Y.; Li, X.; Ma, J. A Novel LSB Matching Algorithm Based on Information Pre-Processing. *Mathematics* 2022, 10, 8. https://doi.org/10.3390/math10010008

Academic Editor: Radi Romansky

Received: 18 November 2021
Accepted: 16 December 2021
Published: 21 December 2021

Publisher's Note: MDPI stays neutral with regard to jurisdictional claims in published maps and institutional affiliations.

Copyright: © 2021 by the authors. Licensee MDPI, Basel, Switzerland. This article is an open access article distributed under the terms and conditions of the Creative Commons Attribution (CC BY) license (https://creativecommons.org/licenses/by/4.0/).

1. Introduction

With the development of the internet, the transmission and sharing of information have become increasingly convenient. However, with this convenience, criminals may tamper with or intercept information on the internet. To solve the apparently conflicting open access of the network and information security, many privacy protection methods have been studied [1–4]. Encryption can protect privacy, but the spread of encrypted files on the internet easily attracts the attention of attackers. Information hiding technology, which hides secret information in the carrier, emerged in the 1990s. After more than 20 years of research and development, the technology has gained a measure of maturity, although it is still the focus of research in network security.

According to whether an embedded image can be reconstructed, information hiding is divided into two types, reversible and irreversible. Reversible information hiding is usually divided into four categories: lossless compression [5–37], difference expansion [8–10], prediction error expansion [11–13], and histogram shifting [14–16]. All reversible information-hiding schemes can extract secret information and restore the original image; however, the hiding capacity is not high. Most of the time, we need to embed a large volume of information with low distortion, and it does not matter whether the original image can be reconstructed entirely. The least significant bit (LSB) algorithm is a classic spatial information-hiding algorithm. The secret data are embedded into the least significant bit of the pixel value. The LSB algorithm has low complexity, simple operation, and greater hiding capacity, but its robustness is poor. Today, there are many LSB matching algorithms with low distortion.

There are two major concerns when selecting a gray image as the carrier to convey information. The first relates to the high capacity of its pixel modification: if the payload of each pixel for a cover image is less than 3 bpp, human vision is not able to detect the visual artifacts of a steganographic image. An LSB++ scheme was developed to improve the power of LSB-based algorithms. Generally, all these methods have tried to use the reductant space in the cover image more fully. The second concern is the quality of the steganographic image: Digital gray images are widespread on the internet. In many cases, secret data are embedded into cover images without noticeable visual artifacts. However, a high embedding capacity can distort the image, so the transfer is not secure.

With the digital development of life and office, the secure transfer of documents and mail through the internet became necessary. Although current steganography methods send information as random bits, few people have embedded scanned documents into cover images to transmit them safely [17–20]. The scanned documents were pre-processed and embedded into the cover image, so people could share more information with the same capacity. The earliest steganography method was a simple LSB (least-significant-bit) substitution [21]. In many images, differences in the least significant bits of a pixel are imperceptible, so they seem suitable for embedding sensitive information into a cover image. To hide greater volumes of data, many improved methods have been proposed [22–26]. The authors of [22–24] improved the visual quality of the simple LSB methods with low complexity; however, they were ineffective when the embedding rate was 1 bpp [25,26] designed embedding unit consists not only one pixel, and the distortion was better than [22–24]. Refs. [36,37] proposed dual-layer LSB matching algorithms with high embedding efficiency, and the cover image can be reconstructed completely.

There are three problems associated with current methods. The embedding method of the scanned document was rarely specified; high capacity and low distortion could not be achieved together, and a completely reconstructed high-capacity image could not be achieved. The method proposed to improve the LSB matching algorithms by embedding the secret data in the optimal position based on the golden ratio. The major improvements of the proposed scheme are outlined below:

1. The secret data included random bits and scanned document, and they were pre-processed by halftone, quadtree, and S-Box transformations, and the size of the scanned document was reduced by 8.11 times.
2. The golden ratio was applied to find the optimal embedding position and design the matching function.
3. This study got a good trade-off between high capacity and low distortion.

This paper presents our solution to the three obstacles and proposes a new LSB matching algorithm based on scanned document pre-processing. Section 2 introduces related work, including data-hiding schemes based on random bit streams and scanned document images. In Section 3, we describe details of the proposed method, including secret data pre-processing, scanned-document hiding, data extraction, and image recovery. Our study investigated three candidates for pre-processing secret data: the halftone, quadtree, and simple substitution. A novel LSB matching algorithm with low distortion and based on the golden ratio is proposed for the embedding step. Pre-processing provides a steganographic image with low distortion and more transformed secret information than current methods offer. Our LSB data hiding method guarantees approximate cover image reconstruction. In Section 4, we report the experimental results and analysis. In Section 5, our conclusions are presented, and future work is proposed.

2. Related Work

The following methods were evaluated for their hiding capacity of two types of information related to this paper. The main ideas, hiding capacity, and image quality are briefly discussed.

In 2017, Soleymani et al. [17] proposed high-capacity image data hiding on a sparse message of a scanned document image. They compressed the scanned document image by halftone technology and converted the binary strings to their equivalent decimal values. Then, they embedded this information into the cover image using 3-LSB. The average payload was 5.43 bpp, and the quality of the steganographic image was 36 dB. However, this method also coded the background area of the binary image. In 2018, Soleymani et al. [18] improved [17] by using a more effective quadtree algorithm to code only the content of the binary image. The average payload was 7.98 bpp, the PSNR (peak signal to noise ratio) was

38.83 dB, and the SSIM (structural similarity index) was 0.93. Generally, for a high-quality visual image, the PSNR was greater than 50 dB.

Unlike [17,18], which tried to improve embedding capacity using the vacated room of the information and the cover image, Ref. [20] hid secret data in a gray image with the mapping method. The binary values of each pixel image and character were divided into four parts. After that, they selected two bits of the secret data, searched for a two-bit similarity in the image pixels, and saved the location of the match. This approach tried to leave the cover image unchanged and send the matches to the receiver secretly. However, when the message capacity was high, the data could not be embedded completely, and it was hard to recover the original information.

In [19], a high-capacity embedding technique and high-quality encoded image were proposed. The secret data were first converted to their equivalent decimal values then into binary strings. They hid the secret data in the edges of four similar gray images using LSB. In this approach, the PSNR of each encoded image was equal to 81.23 dB. However, the receiver needed to obtain the four images simultaneously to extract all the information.

The earliest steganography method for grayscale images was proposed in [21], which offered a simple method for embedding data in cover images. This scheme embedded information by replacing the LSB plane of the gray-level pixel value; it was invisible. The main disadvantages of this scheme were its low capacity and poor security. When the volume of secret data was high, so was the distortion of the cover image. To reduce the distortion of the LSB algorithm, in [22–24], they proposed the optimal LSB method. The optimal LSB algorithm could generate three steganographic pixel values by the remainder operator, in which one of them had the least distortion. The simple LSB method or the optimal LSB method considered one pixel as an embedding unit. The LSB matching revisited scheme [25,26] considered more than one pixel as an embedding unit. In [25], the cover image was divided into non-overlapping pixel pairs, and two bits of secret information were embedded into the first pixel and a binary function. In [26], three pixels of the cover image were considered as the embedding unit. This scheme utilized the first and second most significant bits; then, the remaining six bits were XORed. The secret data were embedded by comparing the result of XOR with three bits of the secret information. The revisited LSB matching scheme minimized the image distortion, but the embedding capacity was limited, and the original image could not be recovered completely.

3. Proposed Method

Current data-hiding methods try to provide high embedding capacity with low distortion. We propose a novel LSB matching algorithm with low distortion that embeds high-capacity data in the cover images. The constructions of this paper are as follows: (1) the scanned document was pre-processed by halftone, quadtree, decimal coding, and S-Box; (2) a novel LSB matching algorithm with the lowest distortion was applied, based on the golden ratio.

3.1. Pre-Processing Step

3.1.1. S-Box

We examined the DES [27] algorithm, a classic encryption algorithm. The S-Box is a non-linear structure and, for any S-Box, the substitution mapping listed in eight S-Boxes is such that, according to the values of rows and columns, its input is mapped to a compressed equivalent decimal value. For any S-Box, assuming $I = i_1 i_2 i_3 i_4 i_5 i_6$, let $k = i_2 i_3 i_4 i_5$ and $h = i_1 i_6$. According to the values k and h, we could look up the Box value in row h and column k: $O = o_1 o_2 o_3 o_4$, a compressed decimal value. It can be seen that the secret data were compressed from 6 to 4. For example, consider $I = 111{,}000$, and let k = 12 and h = 2. In row 2 and column 12 of the S8-Box in Table 1, the number $O = (15)_{10} = (1111)_2$ was found. The size of the secret data was reduced by a factor of 1.5. In this study, to make good use of the working principle of the S-Box, secret information in a bitstream was divided into 6-bit groups, then compressed by a substitution operator.

Table 1. An example for S8-Box.

R. \ Col.	0	1	2	3	4	5	6	7	8	9	10	11	12	13	14	15
0	13	2	8	4	6	15	11	1	10	9	3	14	5	0	12	7
1	1	15	13	8	10	3	7	4	12	5	6	11	0	14	9	2
2	7	11	4	1	9	12	14	2	0	6	10	13	15	3	5	8
3	2	1	14	7	4	10	8	13	15	12	9	0	3	5	6	11

3.1.2. Halftone and Quadtree

When secret information was scanned in our study, it was converted to embeddable bits by halftone and quadtree techniques. The halftone method was divided into the error-diffusion [28–30] and dither types [31,32]. The halftone image generated by the dither method usually contains an artificial periodic texture; thus, we used the error-diffusion method in our study. By considering the correlation between proximate pixels, the halftone scheme converted each pixel to 0 or 1. Thus, the size of the secret information was reduced by 8 times. The halftone image of a scanned document usually includes signs and white backgrounds, shown with 0 and 1 bits, respectively. People are mainly concerned only with the document content; thus, it is necessary to separate the content from the background with a quadtree algorithm (applicable to any image dimensions). The error-diffusion method consists of three steps:

Step 1: For any scanned document, the integer matrix is converted into a real matrix B by dividing the pixel value by 255.

Step 2: Assume that the threshold t is 1/2 and real matrix B is accessed in raster scan order. If the element of the real matrix is less than t, the halftone pixel value $I(i,j)$ is 0, or 1 otherwise.

Step 3: Here, we defined one value $wc(i,j)$, and $wc = B(i,j) - I(i,j)$. The error of the current pixel is transferred in a ratio of 7:3:5:1 and superimposed on four adjacent pixels. When all the pixels were processed, we obtained the halftone image I.

The quadtree method also consists of three steps:

Step 1: The matrix of the halftone image I was divided into four sub-rectangles. If the size of the sub-rectangle was larger than 1 × 1, the sub-rectangles were divided until the size of all the sub-rectangles was 1 × 1.

Step 2: Some sub-rectangles did not contain information, so only the content and coordinates of sub-rectangles that contain information were kept.

Step 3: All sub-rectangles that contain content are merged into larger rectangles.

Figure 1 shows the process of scanning a document. As seen in Figure 1c, not all sub-rectangles contained a message. Figure 1d shows that it was necessary to save only the content and coordinates of the sub-rectangles that contained the message. The more sub-rectangles there were, the more content and coordinates needed to be saved. As in Figure 1e, to reduce the number of coordinates, all the sub-rectangles that contained messages were merged by scanning neighbor rectangles horizontally and vertically.

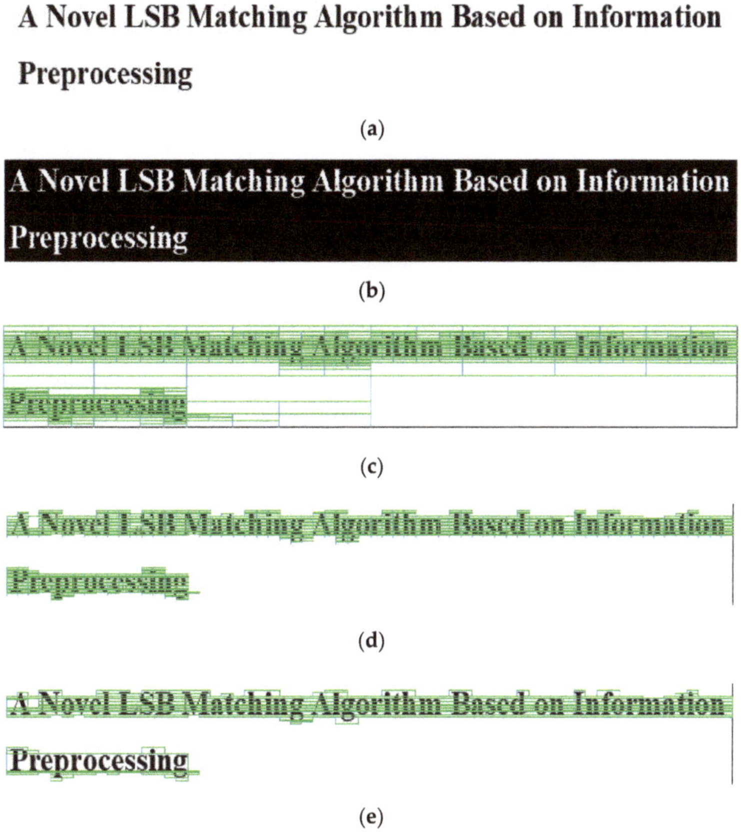

(a)

(b)

(c)

(d)

(e)

Figure 1. (a) Secret document; (b) halftone process; (c) sub-rectangles; (d) content sub-rectangles; (e) content sub-rectangles merging.

3.1.3. Decimal Coding

Usually, zeros on the left side of a binary string do not affect the size of the value. In our study, the content and the merged coordinate were processed by decimal coding and S-Box substitution. In the first step, the bit string of the content and the coordinates were converted to decimal values. In the second step, the values were divided into 6-bit groups then compressed into 4-bit groups by S-Box substitution. In Figure 1, the title of the paper was tested, and the size of the original scanned document image was 17.6 KB (18,106 B). After the above steps, the size of the results was reduced to 1953 B. According to the result, we can see the secret data were compressed by 9.27 times.

3.2. Data Embedding

Mielikainen [25] proposed a simple LSB matching algorithm by modifying the pixel ±1, and two pixels as an embedding unit. The embedding and extraction procedure of Milelikainen's scheme was illustrated as follows:

Set p and q are the cover pixels pair, and c_1 and c_2 are two bits of secret data, respectively. The embedding equation is given in Equation (1). After embedding, the stego image is obtained, and p' and q' are the modified pixels pair. The secret data c_1 can be extracted from the least significant bit of p'. The secret data c_2 can be extracted according to Equation (2).

$$(p',q') = \begin{cases} (p,q), LSB(p) = c_1 \text{ and } LSB(\lfloor \frac{p}{2} \rfloor + q) = c_2 \\ (p,q+1), LSB(p) = c_1 \text{ and } LSB(\lfloor \frac{p}{2} \rfloor + q) \neq c_2 \\ (p-1,q), LSB(p) \neq c_1 \text{ and } LSB(\lfloor \frac{p-1}{2} \rfloor + q) = c_2 \\ (p+1,q), LSB(p) \neq c_1 \text{ and } LSB(\lceil \frac{p-1}{2} \rceil + q) \neq c_2 \end{cases} \quad (1)$$

$$c_2 = LSB(\lfloor \frac{p}{2} \rfloor + q) \quad (2)$$

In this section, the information compressed by halftone, quadtree, decimal coding, and S-Box substitution was embedded into a cover image by a novel revisited LSB matching method. To improve the capacity of data hiding and transmission security, the secret data were compressed then embedded into the cover image by an LSB matching algorithm based on the golden ratio. For the first time, the golden ratio point was used to find the best embedding position and applied as the basic criterion to design the mapping function. First, because the output of the S-Box was 4 bits, the cover image was divided into non-overlapping pixel pairs, and every four pixels were defined as a group. Second, the optimal embedding positions were found according to the golden ratio. Finally, the XOR operation assembled the eight least-significant bits to yield four original bits from the embedding unit. Our new scheme is described below:

① In raster scan order, the cover image was divided into non-overlapping pixel pairs, each pair including four pixels. Assuming the four pixels P_i, P_{i+1}, P_{i+2} and P_{i+3} comprise a hiding unit, the four bits of secret information were $S_1 S_2 S_3 S_4$.

② Each pixel was converted into eight binary bits, and the embedding positions were found according to the calculations $8 \times (1 - 0.618) \approx 3$. Normally, the change of the lowest three significant bits of the pixel value does not affect human vision. To get better visual quality, the optimal embedding position was found according to the calculations $3 \times (1 - 0.618) \approx 1$. The least significant bit can be used to embed information. Assuming $P_i = a_8 a_7 a_6 a_5 a_4 a_3 a_2 a_1$, $P_{i+1} = b_8 b_7 b_6 b_5 b_4 b_3 b_2 b_1$, $P_{i+2} = c_8 c_7 c_6 c_5 c_4 c_3 c_2 c_1$, $P_{i+3} = d_8 d_7 d_6 d_5 d_4 d_3 d_2 d_1$, the four bits of secret data are embedded into the exact location. Here, we defined four values A, B, C, and D, and they were obtained according to Equation (3):

$$\begin{cases} A = a_1 \oplus a_2 \oplus b_1 \\ B = b_1 \oplus b_2 \oplus c_1 \\ C = c_1 \oplus c_2 \oplus d_1 \\ D = d_1 \oplus d_2 \oplus a_1 \end{cases} \quad (3)$$

As shown in Equation (1), the values of A and D were controlled by changing a_1 of p_i. Similarly, the values of A and B were controlled by the least significant bit b_1 of p_{i+1}. B and C were controlled by the least significant bit c_1 of p_{i+2}. C and D were controlled by the least significant bit d_1 of p_{i+3}. When the pixel p_{i+1} was an odd number, A was controlled by modifying bit b_1 and b_2 by $P_{i+1} + 1$. When the pixel was an even number, A was controlled by modifying bit b_1 and b_2 by $P_{i+1} - 1$. Similarly, B, C, and D were controlled by modifying the least significant bit and the second least significant bit of p_{i+2}, p_{i+3}, and p_i.

③ We compared four secret data with four values to see whether they were the same. The four pixels did not need to be altered in the data-hiding process if they were equal. Otherwise, we needed to modify the four pixels until they were equal. We describe the scheme in detail as follows:

Step 1: If there was $(s_1 = A)\&\&(s_2 = B)\&\&(s_3 = C)\&\&(s_4 = D)$, the four pixels did not need to be altered in the data-hiding process.

Step 2: If only $(s_1 \neq A)$ or $(s_2 \neq B)$ or $(s_3 \neq C)$ or $(s_4 \neq D)$, and the pixel p_{i+1} was an odd number, we needed to control it with $P_{i+1} + 1$; otherwise, we controlled it with $P_{i+1} - 1$, so that $S_1 = A$. In the same way, if the pixel p_{i+2} was an odd number, we needed to control it with $P_{i+2} + 1$; otherwise, we controlled it with $P_{i+2} - 1$, so that $S_2 = B$. If the pixel p_{i+3} was an odd number, we needed to control it with $p_{i+3} + 1$; otherwise, we controlled it with $p_{i+3} - 1$, so that $S_3 = C$. If the pixel p_i was an odd number, we needed to control it with $P_i + 1$; otherwise, we controlled it with $P_i - 1$, so that $S_4 = D$.

Step 3: If only $(s_1 \neq A)\&\&(s_2 \neq B)$ or $(s_1 \neq A)\&\&(s_3 \neq C)$ or $(s_1 \neq A)\&\&(s_4 \neq D)$ or $(s_2 \neq B)\&\&(s_3 \neq C)$ or $(s_2 \neq B)\&\&(s_4 \neq D)$ or $(s_3 \neq C)\&\&(s_4 \neq D)$, if the pixel p_{i+1} was an odd number, we needed to control it with $P_{i+1} - 1$, otherwise, we controlled it with $P_{i+1} + 1$, so that $(s_1 = A)\&\&(s_2 = B)$. In the same manner, if the pixels p_{i+1} and p_{i+3} were odd numbers, we needed to control them with $P_{i+1} + 1$, $P_{i+3} + 1$, otherwise, we controlled them with $P_{i+1} - 1$, $p_{i+3} - 1$, so that $(s_1 = A)\&\&(s_3 = C)$. If the pixel p_i was an odd number, we needed to control it with $P_i - 1$; otherwise, we controlled it with $P_i + 1$, so that $(s_1 = A)\&\&(s_4 = D)$. If the pixel p_{i+2} was an odd number, we needed to control it with $P_{i+2} - 1$; otherwise, we controlled it b with y $P_{i+2} + 1$, so that $(s_2 = B)\&\&(s_3 = C)$. If the pixel p_i, p_{i+2} were odd numbers, we needed to control them with $P_i + 1$, $P_{i+2} + 1$; otherwise, we controlled them with $P_i - 1$, $P_{i+2} - 1$, so that $(s_2 = B)\&\&(s_4 = D)$. If the pixel p_{i+3} was an odd number, we needed to control it with $p_{i+3} - 1$; otherwise, we controlled it with $p_{i+3} + 1$, so that $(s3 = C)\&\&(s4 = D)$.

Step 4: If $(s_1 \neq A)\&\&(s_2 \neq B)\&\&(s_3 \neq C)$ or $(s_1 \neq A)\&\&(s_2 \neq B)\&\&(s_4 \neq D)$ or $(s_1 \neq A)\&\&(s_3 \neq C)\&\&(s_4 \neq D)$ or $(s_2 \neq B)\&\&(s_3 \neq C)\&\&(s_4 \neq D)$. If p_{i+1} was an odd number, we needed to control it with $P_{i+1} + 1$; otherwise, we controlled it with $P_{i+1} - 1$. If p_{i+2} was an odd number, we needed to control it with $P_{i+2} - 1$; otherwise, we controlled it with $P_{i+2} + 1$, so that $(s_1 = A)\&\&(s_2 = B)\&\&(s_3 = C)$. In the same manner, we modified the other pixels and obtained $(s_1 = A)\&\&(s_2 = B)\&\&(s_4 = D)$, $(s_1 = A)\&\&(s_3 = C)\&\&(s_4 = D)$, $(s_2 = B)\&\&(s_3 = C)\&\&(s_4 = D)$.

Step 5: If $(s_1 \neq A)\&\&(s_2 \neq B)\&\&(s_3 \neq C)\&\&(s_4 \neq D)$, when p_i was an odd number, we needed to control it with $P_i + 1$; otherwise, we controlled it with $P_i - 1$. If p_{i+1} was an odd number, we needed to control it with $P_{i+1} - 1$; otherwise, we controlled it with $P_{i+1} + 1$. If p_{i+3} was an odd number, we needed to control it with $p_{i+3} + 1$; otherwise, we controlled it with $p_{i+3} - 1$. Lastly, we obtained $(s_1 = A)\&\&(s_2 = B)\&\&(s_3 = C)\&\&(s_4 = D)$.

According to the scheme above, four bits of the secret data, s_1, s_2, s_3 and s_4, were ensured to be embedded into the pixel pairs p_i, p_{i+1}, p_{i+2} and p_{i+3} respectively.

For example, as Table 2 shows, s_1, s_2, s_3 and s_4 represent any four bits of secret information. When $p_i = (101)_{10} = (01100101)_2$, $p_{i+1} = (50)_{10} = (00110010)_2$, $p_{i+2} = (213)_{10} = (11010101)_2$, $p_{i+3} = (210)_{10} = (11010010)_2$, we obtained $A = 1$, $B = 0$, $C = 1$, and $D = 0$ according to Equation (1). We adjusted the pixel values by the above rule and let p_i, p_{i+1}, p_{i+2}, p_{i+3} denote the adjusted pixel values.

Table 2. Pixel variation using the LSB algorithm after data hiding. LSB—least significant bit.

Secret Data	q_i	q_{i+1}	q_{i+2}	q_{i+3}	Secret Data	q_i	q_{i+1}	q_{i+2}	q_{i+3}
$(0000)_2$	$101-1$	50	$213-1$	210	$(1000)_2$	101	50	$213-1$	210
$(0001)_2$	$101-1$	50	$213-1$	$210+1$	$(1001)_2$	101	50	$213-1$	$210+1$
$(0010)_2$	$101-1$	50	213	210	$(1010)_2$	101	50	213	210
$(0011)_2$	$101-1$	50	213	$210+1$	$(1011)_2$	101	50	213	$210+1$
$(0100)_2$	$101-1$	$50+1$	$213-1$	210	$(1100)_2$	101	$50+1$	$213-1$	210
$(0101)_2$	$101-1$	$50+1$	$213-1$	$210+1$	$(1101)_2$	101	$50+1$	$213-1$	$210+1$
$(0110)_2$	$101-1$	$50+1$	213	210	$(1110)_2$	101	$50+1$	213	210
$(0111)_2$	$101-1$	$50+1$	213	$210+1$	$(1111)_2$	101	$50+11$	213	$210+1$

As seen from Table 1, the probability of four pixels that needed to be modified was 1/16, the probability of three pixels that need to be modified was 4/16, the probability of two pixels that needed to be modified was 6/16, the probability of one pixel that needed to be modified was 4/16, and the probability of the preserved original pixels was 1/16. The expected value of the changed pixels of the proposed algorithm was:

$$(1/16) \times 4 + (4/16) \times 3 + (6/16) \times 2 + (4/16) \times 1 + (1/16) \times 0 = 29/16$$

The expected number of modifications per pixel was: $(29/16) \div 4 \approx 0.453$.

As Table 3 shows, one of the most important factors of the proposed LSB matching revisited scheme was that at most, only one pixel at a time can be modified by +1 or −1 when carrying four bits of secret information. Changing four pixels at the same time does not occur. The probability of two pixels needing modification was 7/16, the probability of one pixel needing modification was 8/16, and the probability of the preserved original pixels was 1/16. The expected value of the changed pixels of the proposed algorithm was $(7/16) \times 2 + (8/16) \times 1 + (1/16) \times 0 = 22/16$. The expected number of modifications per pixel was $(22/16) \div 4 \approx 0.344$. The secret data were pre-processed: when the secret data were a bit stream, the expected number of modifications per pixel was $(22/16) \div 6 \approx 0.229$. When the secret data in the document were scanned, the expected number of modifications per pixel was $(22/16) \div 32 \approx 0.0430$. This result demonstrates that the proposed approach effectively prevents pixel distortion after data hiding.

Table 3. Pixel variation using the proposed LSB matching revisited after data hiding. LSB—least significant bit.

Secret Data	q_i	q_{i+1}	q_{i+2}	q_{i+3}	Secret Data	q_i	q_{i+1}	q_{i+2}	q_{i+3}
$(0000)_2$	101	50 − 1	213	210 − 1	$(1000)_2$	101	50	213	210 − 1
$(0001)_2$	101	50 − 1	213	210 + 1	$(1001)_2$	101	50	213	210 + 1
$(0010)_2$	101	50 − 1	213	210	$(1010)_2$	101	50	213	210
$(0011)_2$	101 − 1	50	213	210	$(1011)_2$	101 + 1	50	213	210
$(0100)_2$	101	50	213 − 1	210−1	$(1100)_2$	101	50	213 − 1	210
$(0101)_2$	101 − 1	50	213 − 1	210	$(1101)_2$	101 + 1	50	213 − 1	210
$(0110)_2$	101	50 + 1	213	210	$(1110)_2$	101	50	213 + 1	210
$(0111)_2$	101	50 + 1	213 + 1	210	$(1111)_2$	101 + 1	50	213 + 1	210

Figure 2 shows the comparison of the probability of modifying pixels of the three methods. Mielikainen [25] proposed an LSB matching revisited scheme and groups two pixels as an embedding unit. For every four bits of data embedded, the pixel modification probability of the LSB method and Mielikainen's scheme. However, the LSB matching scheme has low computation complexity. It can be seen that our proposed method modified at most two pixels every four pixels, and the magnitude of the modification was 1. The LSB scheme and Mielikainen's approach modified more pixel values. Our study set every four pixels as a unit, and the computational complexity was lower.

3.3. Extraction

During extraction, the receiver can acquire secret data without any knowledge of the cover image. There are two steps:

(1) Reading the steganographic image: the steganographic image was divided in raster scan order into non-overlapping pixel pairs, and each pair included four pixels.
(2) Extracting the secret data: The four bits of embedded information can be extracted using Equation (1) without knowing the original image information. If the secret data were in a scanned image, the coordinates and S-Box were used to recover the secret information according to content.

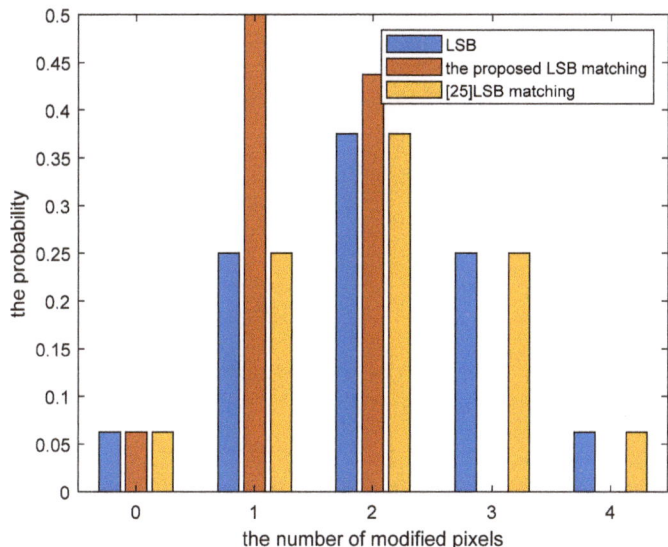

Figure 2. Relationship between the number of modified pixels and the probability.

4. Experimental Results and Comparisons

This section presents the results obtained from our study of the proposed LSB matching algorithm, using 20 standard images from the USC-SIPI image database. PSNR and SSIM were used to evaluate the image; Section 1 gives a detailed example. Our aim was to discover a general method to improve the hiding capacity of images, and we found an effective trade-off between high capacity and low distortion. In part (2), we compare the efficiency of our scheme with other schemes and discuss its implications.

4.1. A Detailed Example

Eight scanned documents of [26,33] were used as secret data. Table 4 lists eight pages of scanned documents. Figure 3 shows the relation between segment size and compression ratio. It can be seen that, for the same scanned document, the segment sizes were 1×1, 4×4, 8×8, 16×16, and 32×32, and the compression ratios for five different thresholds were 8.110523, 4.573963, 2.051653, 2.051653, and 1.665751, respectively. Figure 4 lists the relation between minimum rectangular size and the mean embedding capacity for the Lena image. The mean embedding capacities for five different thresholds were 1.66186 bpp, 2.940742 bpp, 4.494556 bpp, 6.567377 bpp, and 8.084202 bpp. Figures 3 and 4 show that when the segment size was 1×1, the compression ratio was the best, and the volume of secret data transmitted was the highest. In Figure 5, the PSNR values of the steganographic image for five different thresholds were 44.35711 dB, 44.16443 dB, 44.16444 dB, 44.16445 dB, and 44.16446 dB. When the segment size was 1×1, we determined that the visual artifacts were the best.

Table 4. Eight scanned documents and their sizes.

Page Number	Size (B)
1	308,002
2	507,020
3	524,171
4	467,128
5	419,473
6	436,539
7	492,878
8	378,691

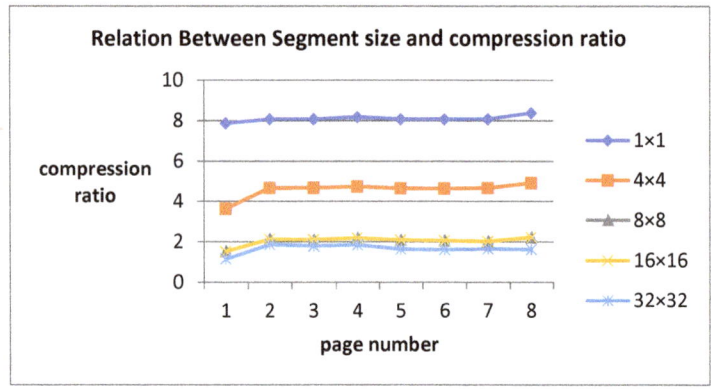

Figure 3. Relationship between segment size and compression ratio.

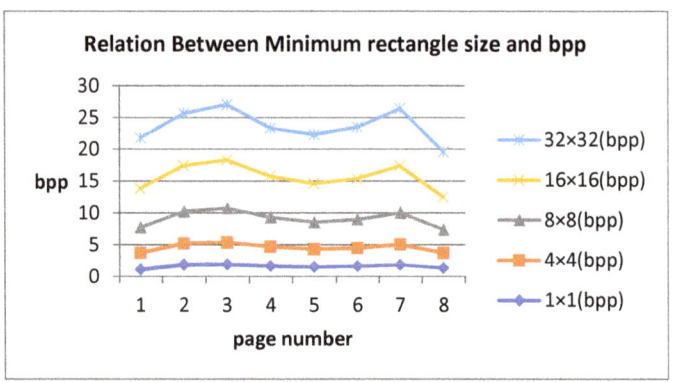

Figure 4. Relationship between segment size and bpp.

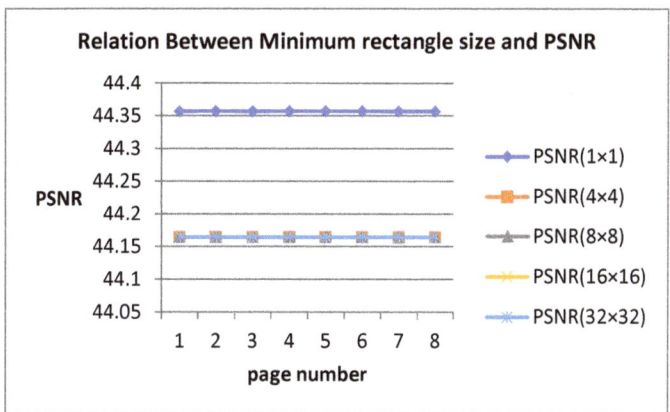

Figure 5. Relationship between segment size and PSNR. PSNR—peak signal to noise ratio.

Using the other algorithms, the 32 KB scanned document needed 262,144 bits of secret information to be embedded. In our study, we had to embed only 32,324 bits. Usually, for a small rectangle, the smaller the divided area was, the greater the time cost. It was confirmed that the larger the segmentation area, the rougher it is, and the lower the cost time. Figure 6 shows two scanned documents of 3 KB and 35 KB. Table 5 lists the actual embedding amounts and the times from embedding to complete extraction for two differently sized scanned documents. The smaller the segmentation size was, the more accurate and the smaller the time cost. The fastest processing time for the 3 KB scanned document was 1 s, and the slowest processing time was 3 s. For the 35 KB scanned document, the fastest processing time was 6 s, and the slowest processing time was 48 s. The larger the document, the longer the processing time, especially with the 32 × 32 block size, which exceeded the user's time limit.

Abstract

(a)

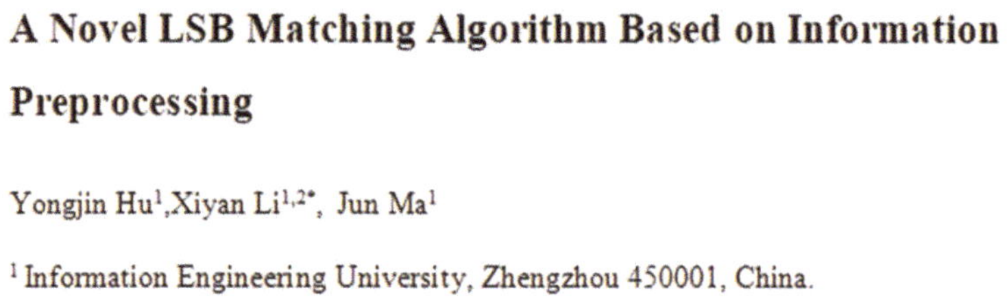

A Novel LSB Matching Algorithm Based on Information Preprocessing

Yongjin Hu[1], Xiyan Li[1,2,*], Jun Ma[1]

[1] Information Engineering University, Zhengzhou 450001, China.

(b)

Figure 6. Scanned documents. (**a**) Scanned document in 3 KB; (**b**) Scanned document in 35 KB.

Table 5. The relationship between block size, embedding amount, and time.

Scanned Document	Norm	1×1	4×4	8×8	16×16	32×32
(a)	Embedding amount (bits)	1460	1972	2588	5148	5148
	time (s)	3	1	2	2	2
(b)	Embedding amount (bits)	24,828	42,068	82,036	82,036	115,780
	time (s)	6	10	27	27	48

Table 6 compares the actual embedding amount and PSNR. When the segmentation size is 1 × 1, the actual embedding amount of the two documents is the smallest, and the image quality is also the best. The values of PSNR were 69.547 and 57.4617. The distortion rate of the image increases as the amount of embedding increases. For the same document, the larger the segmentation area, the more redundant the messages and, therefore, the greater the distortion rate of the steganographic image. For the five segmentation sizes of 35 KB documents, background redundancy was eliminated to varying degrees, but the values of PSNR were all above 50 dB, which shows that the information pre-processing and matching mapping function of this algorithm is sophisticated and practical. Figure 7 shows the images and their histogram, where (a) is the cover image and its histogram, (b) is embedded in document (a) and its histogram, and (c) is embedded in the document (b) and its histogram. Visually, it is impossible to distinguish the difference between the images. The proposed algorithm has good visibility, and the PSNR values are all greater than 57 dB. Because the distortion rate is relatively low, it is not easy to attract the attention of a third party when transmitting on an open channel.

Table 6. The relationship between block size, embedding amount, and PSNR.

Scanned Document	Norm	1 × 1	4 × 4	8 × 8	16 × 16	32 × 32
(a)	Embedding amount (bits)	1460	1972	2588	5148	5148
	PSNR (dB)	69.547	68.2919	67.1127	64.1924	64.1924
(b)	Embedding amount (bits)	24,828	42,068	82,036	82,036	115,780
	PSNR (dB)	62.7946	55.168	52.254	52.254	50.7378

Taking Figure 6 as the secret document, we evaluated our approach against attacks like cropping, rotate, Gaussian noise, pepper, and salt noise. The results of the experiment are in Table 7, which is under extraction accuracy as well.

Table 7. PSNR and accuracy under attacks.

Attack	PSNR	Accuracy
No attack	62.7946	100%
Cropping (1:128,1:128)	17.5888	93.6695%
Rotate (3°)	16.3833	93.7371%
Salt&pepper (0.01)	25.3582	98.9409%
Salt&pepper (0.03)	20.6751	97.1126%
Gaussian noise (0.01)	20.0709	93.0112%
Gaussian noise (0.03)	15.5579	91.4116%

4.2. Comparisons with Related Studies and Discussion

We compared our study to nine state-of-the-art schemes for hiding capacity and image distortion. Table 8 shows the PNSR comparison results for the same scanned document (262,144 bits), and the visual metric PSNR of the LSB scheme [22–24] was 51.154 dB. However, the revisited LSB matching method [25,26] can raise the PSNR to 1.247 dB and 1.763 dB, separately. Lu [36] proposed a dual image based on reversible data-hiding algorithm by improving the LSB matching scheme of [25]. Because there were two stego images, the embedding capacity was 524288 bits, and the average of PSNR was 49.24 dB. Sahu [37] improved Lu's scheme by using a dual-layer LSB matching algorithm. The secret data were embedded into four stego images, and the PSNR and embedding capacity were 46.51 dB and 1572864 bits separately. Our study was also a revisited LSB matching method, but we can embed bit stream and scanned document images into the cover image with an average PSNR of 53.025 dB and 65.55372 dB. It can be seen that Lu and Sahu's schemes with higher embedding capacity and low distortion. However, our study can embed two forms of secret data. We believe that our study demonstrates a significant improvement. Tables 9 and 10 compare our study with similar work. In the comparisons, the same cover images were processed [18] with the quadtree and LSB algorithm, which significantly improved the embedding amount and image quality over [34]. The average PSNR of our study was 44.44 dB, and the value of SSIM was closer to 1. Table 11 summarizes the proposed scheme's average quality and data hiding capacity for comparison with [17,18,34–37]. In our study, information was pre-processed, and the matching function makes the distortion rate small. This gives us information hiding with high embedding capacity and a low distortion rate.

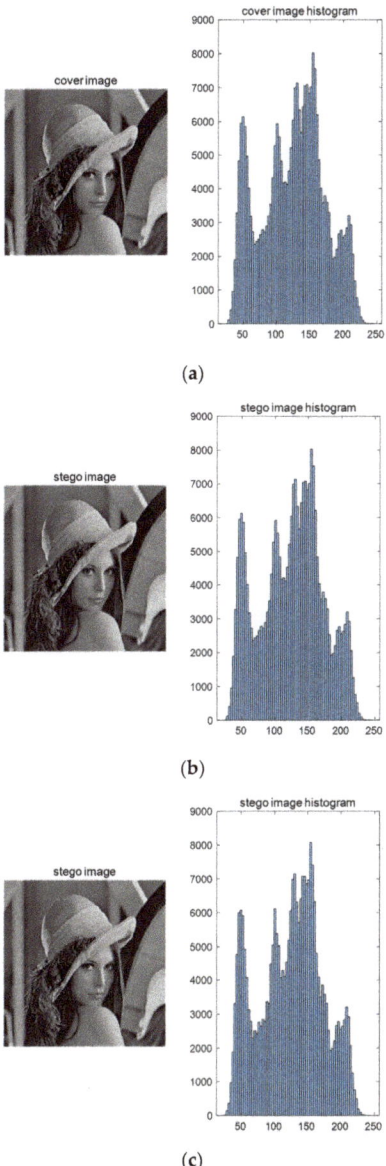

Figure 7. Images and their histograms. (**a**) cover image and histogram; (**b**) stego image and histogram of Figure 6a; (**c**) stego image and histogram of Figure 6b.

Table 8. Comparison between the method proposed and [22–26,36,37].

Cover Image	[22–24]	[25]	[26]	[36]	[37]	Proposed Method	
						Bit Stream	Scanned Document
Lena	51.156	52.404	52.916	49.25	46.50	53.021	65.5538
Airplane	51.143	52.4	52.925	49.22	46.49	53.043	65.5541
Baboon	51.161	52.405	52.917	49.26	46.51	53.022	65.5538
Elaine	51.17	52.407	52.914	49.27	46.52	53.014	65.5536
Man	51.138	52.39	52.911	49.22	46.48	53.025	65.5533
Average	51.154	52.401	52.917	49.24	46.51	53.025	65.55372

Table 9. Comparison between the method proposed and [18,34].

Image	Proposed Method		[18]		[34]	
	PSNR	bpp	PSNR	bpp	PSNR	bpp
Pepper	44.29	15.90	37.48	9.41	34.93	3.95
Lena	44.36	10.73	37.71	6.35	N/A	N/A
Aerial	44.31	11.77	37.66	6.97	N/A	N/A
Jetplane	44.78	12.69	38.14	7.51	34.67	3.95
Average	44.44 (4)	12.77	37.74	7.56	34.8	3.95

Table 10. Comparison between the method proposed and [17,18,35].

Cover Image	Proposed Method		[18]		[17]		[35]	
	PSNR	bpp	PSNR	bpp	PSNR	bpp	PSNR	bpp
Blonde	44.35	15.98	37.48	9.46	35.23	5.65	37.31	3.04
Pepper	44.29	15.90	37.48	9.41	36.19	5.65	37.27	3.05
Jetplane	44.78	12.69	38.14	7.51	36.84	4.77	33.85	3.91
Boat	44.30	16.25	37.46	9.62	37.00	5.70	33.57	3.91
Average	44.43	15.20	37.64	9.00	36.31	5.43	35.50	3.47

Table 11. Comparison between proposed method and [17,18,34–37].

Method	PSNR	Embedding Rate (bpp)
[17]	36.31	5.43
[18]	37.83	7.98
[34]	34.8	3.95
[35]	35.50	3.47
[36]	49.24	4
[37]	46.51	6
Proposed method	44.35	13.48

5. Discussion

In our study, we proposed a novel LSB matching algorithm based on information pre-processing. In the experiments, we proved that our scheme with high capacity and low distortion. To the best of our knowledge, it is the first information pre-processing for a novel LSB matching algorithm. Furthermore, we want to discuss two issues:

(1) Application: In our opinion, our study is most suitable for a digital office because with the digital development of life and office, the secure transfer of documents and mail through the internet became necessary.

(2) Future work: Because the authors did not evaluate our study against the most common attacks, it is just a data-hiding scheme for pre-processed secret data. In the future, we plan to strengthen the study of robustness.

6. Conclusions

We present in this paper a novel, efficient LSB matching algorithm. Experiments showed that it had the lowest distortion, outperforming other related schemes. Before embedding secret data, the information was pre-processed by halftone, quadtree, decimal coding, and substitution treatment, and the size was reduced by at least a factor of eight. In the data hiding step, the cover image was divided into 1×1 sub-blocks. The compressed information was inserted into pixels by a new revisited LSB matching scheme based on the golden ratio. The receiver can extract the information without any knowledge. Therefore, our method has general applicability and provides the best trade-off between capacity and PSNR.

In our study, we saved the additional information and sent it to the receiver secretly. In future work, we plan to improve the speed of pre-processing and reconstruct the cover image completely. Therefore, it is suggested that a more efficient scheme for text documents should be developed.

Author Contributions: Conceptualization, Y.H. and X.L.; methodology, X.L. and J.M.; validation, X.L. and Y.H.; writing—review and editing, X.L., Y.H., and J.M. All authors have read and agreed to the published version of the manuscript.

Funding: This work were supported by the Foundation of Science and Technology on Information Assurance Laboratory (No. KJ-15-108) and Hainan Provincial Reform in Education Project of China (No. Hnjg2020-31).

Institutional Review Board Statement: Not applicable.

Informed Consent Statement: Not applicable.

Data Availability Statement: The corresponding author can provide the data sets utilized in this work upon reasonable request.

Acknowledgments: The authors thank the review of Yang for the deep and constructive comments on the first version of the paper.

Conflicts of Interest: The authors declare no conflict of interest.

References

1. Liu, X.M.; Choo, K.K.R.; Deng, R.H.; Lu, R.X.; Weng, J. Efficient and Privacy-Preserving Outsourced Calculation of Rational Numbers. *IEEE Trans. Dependable Secur. Comput.* **2018**, *15*, 27–39. [CrossRef]
2. Xiong, J.B.; Ma, R.; Chen, L.; Tian, Y.L.; Li, Q.; Liu, X.M.; Yao, Z.Q. A personalized privacy protection framework for mobile crowdsensing in IIoT. *IEEE Trans. Ind. Inform.* **2020**, *16*, 4231–4241. [CrossRef]
3. Chen, Z.; Tian, Y.; Peng, C. An incentive-compatible rational secret sharing scheme using blockchain and smart contract. *Sci. China Inf. Sci.* **2021**, *64*, 202301. [CrossRef]
4. Liu, X.M.; Deng, R.H.; Choo, K.K.R.; Yang, Y. Privacy-Preserving Outsourced Support Vector Machine Design for Secure Drug Discovery. *IEEE Trans. Cloud Comput.* **2020**, *8*, 610–622. [CrossRef]
5. Fridrich, J.; Goljan, M.; Du, R. Invertible authentication. In Proceedings of the Security and Watermarking of Multimedia Contents III, San Jose, CA, USA, 20 January 2001. [CrossRef]
6. Fridrich, J.; Goljan, M.; Du, R. Lossless data embedding for all image formats. In Proceedings of the Security and Watermarking of Multimedia Contents IV, San Jose, CA, USA, 29 April 2002. [CrossRef]
7. Celik, M.U.; Sharma, G.; Tekalp, A.M.; Saber, E. Lossless generalized-LSB data embedding. *IEEE Trans. Image Process.* **2005**, *14*, 253–266. [CrossRef] [PubMed]
8. Jun, T. Reversible data embedding using a difference expansion. *IEEE Trans. Circuits Syst. Video Technol.* **2003**, *13*, 890–896. [CrossRef]
9. Alattar, A.M. Reversible watermark using the difference expansion of a generalized integer transform. *IEEE Trans. Image Process.* **2004**, *13*, 1147–1156. [CrossRef]
10. Thodi, D.M.; Rodriguez, J.J. Expansion embedding techniques for reversible watermarking. *IEEE Trans. Image Process.* **2007**, *16*, 721–730. [CrossRef]
11. Li, X.L.; Li, J.; Li, B.; Yang, B. High-fidelity reversible data hiding scheme based on pixel-value-ordering and prediction-error expansion. *Signal Process.* **2013**, *93*, 198–205. [CrossRef]
12. Ou, B.; Li, X.L.; Zhao, Y.; Ni, R.R. Reversible data hiding using invariant pixel-value-ordering and prediction-error expansion. *Signal Process. Image Commun.* **2014**, *29*, 760–772. [CrossRef]
13. Qu, X.C.; Kim, H.J. Pixel-based pixel value ordering predictor for high-fidelity reversible data hiding. *Signal Process.* **2015**, *111*, 249–260. [CrossRef]
14. Ni, Z.C.; Shi, Y.Q.; Ansari, N.; Su, W. Reversible data hiding. *IEEE Trans. Circuits Syst. Video Technol.* **2006**, *16*, 354–362. [CrossRef]
15. Lin, C.C.; Hsueh, N.L. A lossless data hiding scheme based on three-pixel block differences. *Pattern Recognit.* **2008**, *41*, 1415–1425. [CrossRef]

16. Tsai, P.; Hu, Y.C.; Yeh, H.L. Reversible image hiding scheme using predictive coding and histogram shifting. *Signal Process.* **2009**, *89*, 1129–1143. [CrossRef]
17. Soleymani, S.H.; Taherinia, A.H. High capacity image steganography on sparse message of scanned document image (SMSDI). *Multimed. Tools Appl.* **2017**, *76*, 20847–20867. [CrossRef]
18. Soleymani, S.H.; Taherinia, A.H. High capacity image data hiding of scanned text documents using improved quadtree. *arXiv* **2018**, arXiv:1803.11286.
19. Basheer, N.M.; Aaref, A.M.; Ayyed, D.J. Proposed method of text hiding in image edges. *Int. J. Comput. Appl.* **2015**, *126*, 33–37. [CrossRef]
20. Hussein, H.L.; Abbass, A.A.; Naji, S.A.; Al-Augby, S.; Lafta, J.H. Hiding text in gray image using mapping technique. *J. Phys. Conf. Ser.* **2018**, *1003*, 012032. [CrossRef]
21. Cox, I.J.; Kilian, J.; Leighton, T.; Shamoon, T. A secure, robust watermark for multimedia. In *Information Hiding*; Springer: Berlin/Heidelberg, Germany, 1996.
22. Chan, C.K.; Cheng, L.M. Hiding data in images by simple LSB substitution. *Pattern Recognit.* **2004**, *37*, 469–474. [CrossRef]
23. Thien, C.C.; Lin, J.C. A simple and high-hiding capacity method for hiding digit-by-digit data in images based on modulus function. *Pattern Recognit.* **2003**, *36*, 2875–2881. [CrossRef]
24. Wang, S.J. Steganography of capacity required using modulo operator for embedding secret image. *Appl. Math Comput.* **2005**, *164*, 99–116. [CrossRef]
25. Mielikainen, J. LSB matching revisited. *IEEE Signal Process. Lett.* **2006**, *13*, 285–287. [CrossRef]
26. Wu, N.I.; Hwang, M.S. A novel LSB data hiding scheme with the lowest distortion. *Imaging Sci. J.* **2017**, *65*, 371–378. [CrossRef]
27. Chen, L.S.; Shen, S.Y. *Modern Cryptography*, 2nd ed.; Science Press: Beijing, China, 2008.
28. Liu, L.Y.; Chen, W.; Zheng, W.T.; Geng, W.D. Structure-aware error-diffusion approach using entropy-constrained threshold modulation. *Vis. Comput.* **2014**, *30*, 1145–1156. [CrossRef]
29. Li, X. Edge-directed error diffusion halftoning. *IEEE Signal Process. Lett.* **2006**, *13*, 688–690. [CrossRef]
30. Singh, Y.K. Generalized error diffusion method for halftoning. In Proceedings of the IEEE International Conference on Electrical, Computer and Communication Technologies (ICECCT), Tamil Nadu, India, 5–7 March 2015. [CrossRef]
31. Zhou, Z.; Arce, G.R.; Crescenzo, G.D. Halftone visual cryptography. *IEEE Trans. Image Process.* **2006**, *15*, 2441–2453. [CrossRef]
32. Alasseur, C.; Constantinides, A.G.; Husson, L. Colour quantisation through dithering techniques. In Proceedings of the International Conference on Image Processing (Cat. No.03CH37429), Barcelona, Spain, 14–17 September 2003. [CrossRef]
33. Li, X.Y.; Zhou, X.B.; Zhou, Q.L.; Han, S.J.; Liu, Z. High-capacity reversible data hiding in encrypted images by information preprocessing. *Complexity* **2020**, *2020*, 6989452. [CrossRef]
34. Jana, B. High payload reversible data hiding scheme using weighted matrix. *Optik* **2016**, *127*, 3347–3358. [CrossRef]
35. Bai, J.L.; Chang, C.C.; Nguyen, T.S.; Zhu, C.; Liu, Y.J. A high payload steganographic algorithm based on edge detection. *Displays* **2017**, *46*, 42–51. [CrossRef]
36. Lu, T.C.; Tseng, C.Y.; Wu, J.H. Dual imaging-based reversible hiding technique using LSB matching. *Signal Process.* **2015**, *108*, 77–89. [CrossRef]
37. Aditya, K.S.; Gandharba, S. Reversible Image Steganography Using Dual-Layer LSB Matching. *Sens. Imaging* **2020**, *21*, 1. [CrossRef]

Article

Stochastic Approximate Algorithms for Uncertain Constrained K-Means Problem

Jianguang Lu [1,2], Juan Tang [3,4,*], Bin Xing [2,5] and Xianghong Tang [1]

[1] State Key Laboratory of Public Big Data, Guizhou University, Guiyang 550025, China; jglu@gzu.edu.cn (J.L.); xhtang@gzu.edu.cn (X.T.)
[2] Chongqing Innovation Center of Industrial Big-Data Co., Ltd., Chongqing 400707, China; bingxcq@outlook.com
[3] School of Computer Science and Cyber Engineering, Guangzhou University, Guangzhou 510006, China
[4] Institute of Computing Science and Technology, Guangzhou University, Guangzhou 510006, China
[5] National Engineering Laboratory for Industrial Big-Data Application Technology, Chongqing 400707, China
* Correspondence: tangjn16@gzhu.edu.cn

Abstract: The k-means problem has been paid much attention for many applications. In this paper, we define the uncertain constrained k-means problem and propose a $(1+\epsilon)$-approximate algorithm for the problem. First, a general mathematical model of the uncertain constrained k-means problem is proposed. Second, the random sampling properties of the uncertain constrained k-means problem are studied. This paper mainly studies the gap between the center of random sampling and the real center, which should be controlled within a given range with a large probability, so as to obtain the important sampling properties to solve this kind of problem. Finally, using mathematical induction, we assume that the first $j-1$ cluster centers are obtained, so we only need to solve the j-th center. The algorithm has the elapsed time $O((\frac{1891ek}{\epsilon^2})^{8k/\epsilon}nd)$, and outputs a collection of size $O((\frac{1891ek}{\epsilon^2})^{8k/\epsilon}n)$ of candidate sets including approximation centers.

Keywords: stochastic approximate algorithms; uncertain constrained k-means; approximation centers

1. Introduction

The k-means problem has received much attention in the past several decades. The k-means problems consists of partitioning a set P of points in d-dimensional space $\mathbb{R}^d$ into k subsets $P_1,\ldots,P_k$ such that $\sum_{i=1}^{k}\sum_{p\in P_i}||p-c_i||^2$ is minimized, where c_i is the center of P_i, and $||p-q||$ is the distance between two points of p and q. The k-means problem is one of the classical NP-hard problems, and has been paid much attention in the literature [1–3].

For many applications, each cluster of the point set may satisfy some additional constraints, such as chromatic clustering [4], r-capacity clustering [5], r-gather clustering [6], fault tolerant clustering [7], uncertain data clustering [8], semi-supervised clustering [9], and l-diversity clustering [10]. The constrained clustering problems was studied by Ding and Xu, who presented the first unified framework in [11]. Given a point set $P \subseteq \mathbb{R}^d$, and a positive integer k, a list of constraints $\mathbb{L}$, the constrained k-means problem is to partition P into k clusters $\mathbb{P}=\{P_1,\ldots,P_k\}$, such that all constraints in $\mathbb{L}$ are satisfied and $\sum_{P_i\in\mathbb{P}}\sum_{x\in P_i}||x-c(P_i)||^2$ is minimized, where $c(P_i) = \frac{1}{|P_i|}\sum_{x\in P_i}x$ denotes the centroid of P_i.

In recent years, particular research has been focused on the constrained k-means problem. Ding and Xu [11] showed the first polynomial time approximation scheme with running time $O(2^{poly(k/\epsilon)}(\log n)^k nd)$ for the constrained k-means problem, and obtained a collection of size $O(2^{poly(k/\epsilon)}(\log n)^{k+1})$ of candidate approximate centers. The existing fastest approximation schemes for the constrained k-means problem takes $O(2^{O(k/\epsilon)}nd)$ time [12,13], which was first shown by Bhattacharya, Jaiswai, and Kumar [12]. Their algorithm gives a collection of size $O(2^{O(k/\epsilon)})$ of candidate approximate centers. In this paper, we propose the uncertain constrained k-means problem, which supposes that all points are random variables with probabilistic distributions. We present a stochastic approximate algorithm for the uncertain constrained k-means problem. The uncertain constrained k-means problem can be regarded as a generalization of the constrained k-means problem. We prove the random sampling properties of the uncertain constrained k-means problem, which are fundamental for our proposed algorithm. By applying random sampling and mathematical induction, we propose a stochastic approximate algorithm with lower complexity for the uncertain constrained k-means problem.

This paper is organized as follows. Some basic notations are given in Section 2. Section 3 provides an overview of the new algorithm for the uncertain constrained k-means problem. In Section 4, we discuss the detailed algorithm for the uncertain constrained k-means problem. In Section 5, we investigate the correctness, success probability, and running time analysis of the algorithm. Section 6 concludes this paper and gives possible directions for future research.

2. Preliminaries

Definition 1 (Uncertain constrained k-means problem). *Given a random variable set $\mathcal{X} \subseteq \mathbb{R}^d$, the probability density function $f_X(s)$ for every random variable $X \in \mathcal{X}$, a list of constraints $\mathbb{L}$, and a positive integer k, the uncertain constrained k-means problem is to partition $\mathcal{X}$ into k clusters $\mathbb{X} = \{\mathcal{X}_1, \ldots, \mathcal{X}_k\}$, such that all constraints in $\mathbb{L}$ are satisfied and $\sum_{\mathcal{X}_i \in \mathbb{X}} \sum_{X \in \mathcal{X}_i} \int^{\mathbb{R}^d} ||s - c(\mathcal{X}_i)||^2 f_X(s) ds$ is minimized, where $c(\mathcal{X}_i) = \frac{1}{|\mathcal{X}_i|} \sum_{X \in \mathcal{X}_i} \int^{\mathbb{R}^d} s f_X(s) ds$ denotes the centroid of $\mathcal{X}_i$.*

Definition 2 ([13]). *Let $\mathcal{X}$ be a set of random variables in $\mathbb{R}^d$, $f_X(s)$ be probability density function for every random variable $X \in \mathcal{X}$, and $q \in \mathbb{R}^d$ and P be a set of points in $\mathbb{R}^d$, $p \in P$.*

- *Define $f_2(q, \mathcal{X}) = \sum_{X \in \mathcal{X}} \int^{\mathbb{R}^d} ||s - q||^2 f_X(s) ds$.*
- *Define $c(\mathcal{X}) = \frac{1}{|\mathcal{X}|} \sum_{X \in \mathcal{X}} \int^{\mathbb{R}^d} s f_X(s) ds$.*
- *Define $dist(X, P) = \min_{p \in P} \int^{\mathbb{R}^d} ||s - p|| f_X(s) ds$.*

Definition 3 ([13]). *Let $\mathcal{X}$ be a set of random variables in $\mathbb{R}^d$, $f_X(s)$ be the probability density function for every random variable $X \in \mathcal{X}$, and $\mathcal{X}_1, \ldots, \mathcal{X}_k$ be a partition of $\mathcal{X}$.*

- *Define $m_j = c(\mathcal{X}_j)$.*
- $\beta_j = \frac{|\mathcal{X}_j|}{|\mathcal{X}|}$.
- *Define $\sigma_j = \sqrt{\frac{f_2(m_j, \mathcal{X}_j)}{|\mathcal{X}_j|}}$.*
- *Define*
  $OPT_k(\mathcal{X}) = \sum_{j=1}^k \sum_{X \in \mathcal{X}_j} \int^{\mathbb{R}^d} ||s - c(\mathcal{X}_j)||^2 f_X(s) ds = \sum_{j=1}^k f_2(m_j, \mathcal{X}_j)$.
- *Define $\sigma_{opt} = \sqrt{\frac{OPT_k(\mathcal{X})}{|\mathcal{X}|}} = \sqrt{\sum_{i=1}^k \beta_i \sigma_i^2}$.*

Lemma 1. *For any point $x \in \mathbb{R}^d$ and a random variable set $\mathcal{X} \subseteq \mathbb{R}^d$, $f_2(x, \mathcal{X}) = f_2(c(\mathcal{X}), \mathcal{X}) + |\mathcal{X}| ||c(\mathcal{X}) - x||^2$.*

Proof. Let $f_X(s)$ be the probability density function for every random variable $X \in \mathcal{X}$.

$$f_2(x, \mathcal{X}) = \sum_{X \in \mathcal{X}} \int^{\mathbb{R}^d} ||s - x||^2 f_X(s) ds \tag{1}$$

$$= \sum_{X \in \mathcal{X}} \int^{\mathbb{R}^d} ||s - c(\mathcal{X}) + c(\mathcal{X}) - x||^2 f_X(s) ds \tag{2}$$

$$= \sum_{X \in \mathcal{X}} \int^{\mathbb{R}^d} ||s - c(\mathcal{X})||^2 f_X(s) ds + \sum_{X \in \mathcal{X}} \int^{\mathbb{R}^d} ||c(\mathcal{X}) - x||^2 f_X(s) ds \tag{3}$$

$$= f_2(c(\mathcal{X}), \mathcal{X}) + ||c(\mathcal{X}) - x||^2 \sum_{X \in \mathcal{X}} \int^{\mathbb{R}^d} f_X(s) ds \tag{4}$$

$$= f_2(c(\mathcal{X}), \mathcal{X}) + |\mathcal{X}| ||c(\mathcal{X}) - x||^2. \tag{5}$$

The (3) equality follows from the fact that $\sum_{X \in \mathcal{X}} \int^{\mathbb{R}^d} (s - c(\mathcal{X})) f_X(s) ds = 0$. □

Lemma 2. *Let $\mathcal{X}$ be a set of random variables in $\mathbb{R}^d$ and $f_X(s)$ be the probability density function for every random variable $X \in \mathcal{X}$. Assume that $\mathcal{T}$ is a set of random variables obtained by sampling random variables from $\mathcal{X}$ uniformly and independently. For $\forall \delta > 0$, we have:*

$$Pr(||c(\mathcal{T}) - c(\mathcal{X})||^2 > \frac{1}{\delta |\mathcal{T}|} \sigma^2) < \delta, \tag{6}$$

where $\sigma^2 = \frac{1}{|\mathcal{X}|} \sum_{X \in \mathcal{X}} \int^{\mathbb{R}^d} ||s - c(\mathcal{X})||^2 f_X(s) ds$.

Proof. First, observe that

$$E(c(\mathcal{T})) = c(\mathcal{X}), \quad E(||c(\mathcal{T}) - c(\mathcal{X})||^2) = \frac{1}{|\mathcal{T}|} \sigma^2 \tag{7}$$

where $\sigma^2 = \frac{1}{|\mathcal{X}|} \sum_{X \in \mathcal{X}} \int^{\mathbb{R}^d} ||s - c(\mathcal{X})||^2 f_X(s) ds$. Then apply the Markov inequality to obtain the following.

$$Pr(||c(\mathcal{T}) - c(\mathcal{X})||^2 > \frac{1}{\delta |\mathcal{T}|} \sigma^2) < \delta. \tag{8}$$

□

Lemma 3. *Let $\mathcal{Q}$ be a set of random variables in $\mathbb{R}^d$, $f_X(s)$ be the probability density function for every random variable $X \in \mathcal{Q}$, and $\mathcal{Q}_1$ be an arbitrary subset of $\mathcal{Q}$ with $\alpha |\mathcal{Q}|$ random variables for some $0 < \alpha \le 1$. Then $||c(\mathcal{Q}) - c(\mathcal{Q}_1)|| \le \sqrt{\frac{1-\alpha}{\alpha}} \sigma$, where $\sigma^2 = \frac{1}{|\mathcal{Q}|} \sum_{X \in \mathcal{Q}} \int^{\mathbb{R}^d} ||s - c(\mathcal{Q})||^2 f_X(s) ds$.*

Proof. Let $\mathcal{Q}_2 = \mathcal{Q} \setminus \mathcal{Q}_1$. By Lemma 1, we have the following two equalities.

$$f_2(c(\mathcal{Q}), \mathcal{Q}_1) = f_2(c(\mathcal{Q}_1), \mathcal{Q}_1) + |\mathcal{Q}_1| ||c(\mathcal{Q}_1) - c(\mathcal{Q})||^2, \tag{9}$$

$$f_2(c(\mathcal{Q}), \mathcal{Q}_2) = f_2(c(\mathcal{Q}_2), \mathcal{Q}_2) + |\mathcal{Q}_2| ||c(\mathcal{Q}_2) - c(\mathcal{Q})||^2. \tag{10}$$

Let $L = ||c(\mathcal{Q}_1) - c(\mathcal{Q}_2)||$. By the definition of the mean point, we have:

$$c(\mathcal{Q}) = \frac{1}{|\mathcal{Q}|} \sum_{X \in \mathcal{Q}} \int^{\mathbb{R}^d} s f_X(s) ds = \frac{1}{|\mathcal{Q}|} (|\mathcal{Q}_1| c(\mathcal{Q}_1) + |\mathcal{Q}_2| c(\mathcal{Q}_2)). \tag{11}$$

Thus, the three points $\{c(\mathcal{Q}), c(\mathcal{Q}_1), c(\mathcal{Q}_2)\}$ are collinear, while $||c(\mathcal{Q}_1) - c(\mathcal{Q})|| = (1 - \alpha) L$ and $||c(\mathcal{Q}_2) - c(\mathcal{Q})|| = \alpha L$. Meanwhile, by the definition of σ, we have $\sigma^2 =$

$\frac{1}{|\mathcal{Q}|}(\sum_{X \in \mathcal{Q}_1} \int^{\mathbb{R}^d} ||s - c(\mathcal{Q})||^2 f_X(s) ds + \sum_{X \in \mathcal{Q}_2} \int^{\mathbb{R}^d} ||s - c(\mathcal{Q})||^2 f_X(s) ds)$. Combining Equality (9) and Equality (10), we have:

$$\sigma^2 \geq \frac{1}{|\mathcal{Q}|}(|\mathcal{Q}_1|||c(\mathcal{Q}_1) - c(\mathcal{Q}||^2 + |\mathcal{Q}_2|||c(\mathcal{Q}_2) - c(\mathcal{Q}||^2) \tag{12}$$

$$= \alpha((1-\alpha)L)^2 + (1-\alpha)(\alpha L)^2 \tag{13}$$

$$= \alpha(1-\alpha)L^2. \tag{14}$$

Thus, we have $L \leq \frac{\sigma}{\sqrt{\alpha(1-\alpha)}}$, which means that $||c(\mathcal{Q}) - c(\mathcal{Q}_1)|| = (1-\alpha)L \leq \sqrt{\frac{1-\alpha}{\alpha}}\sigma$. □

Lemma 4 ([12]). *For any $x, y, z \in \mathbb{R}^d$, then $||x - z||^2 \leq 2||x - y||^2 + 2||y - z||^2$.*

Theorem 1 ([14]). *Let $X_1, \ldots, X_s$ be s, an independent random $0 - 1$ variable, where X_i takes 1 with a probability of at least p for $i = 1, \ldots, s$. Let $X = \sum_{i=1}^{s} X_i$. Then, for any $\delta > 0$, $Pr(X < (1-\delta)ps) < e^{-\frac{1}{2}\delta^2 ps}$.*

3. Overview of Our Method

In this section, we first introduce the main idea of our methodology to solve the uncertain constrained k-means problem.

Considering the optimal partition $\mathbb{X} = \{\mathcal{X}_1, \ldots, \mathcal{X}_k\}(|\mathcal{X}_1| \geq \ldots \geq |\mathcal{X}_k|)$ of $\mathcal{X}$, since $|\mathcal{X}_1|/|\mathcal{X}| \geq 1/k$, if we could sample a set $\mathcal{S}$ of size $O(k/\epsilon)$ from $\mathcal{X}$ uniformly and independently, then at least $O(1/\epsilon)$ random variables in $\mathcal{S}$ are from $\mathcal{X}_1$ with a certain probability. All subsets of $\mathcal{S}$ of size $O(1/\epsilon)$ could be enumerated to discover the approximate center of $\mathcal{X}_1$.

We assume that $C_{j-1} = \{c_1, \ldots, c_{j-1}\}$ is the set including approximate centers of the $\mathcal{X}_1, \ldots, \mathcal{X}_j$. Let $\mathcal{B}_j = \{X \in \mathcal{X} | dist(X, C_{j-1}) = min_{c \in C_{j-1}} \int^{\mathbb{R}^d} ||s - c|| f_X(s) ds \leq r_j\}$, where $r_j = \sqrt{\frac{\epsilon}{40\beta_j k}}\sigma_{opt}$. The set $\mathcal{X}_j$ is divided into two parts: $\mathcal{X}_j^{out}$ and $\mathcal{X}_j^{in}$, where $\mathcal{X}_j^{out} = \mathcal{X}_j \setminus \mathcal{B}_j$ and $\mathcal{X}_j^{in} = \mathcal{X}_j \cap \mathcal{B}_j$. For each random variable X, let $\widetilde{X}$ be the nearest point (particular random variable) in C_{j-1} to X. Let $\widetilde{\mathcal{X}}_j^{in} = \{\widetilde{X} | X \in \mathcal{X}_j^{in}\}$, and $\widetilde{\mathcal{X}}_j = \widetilde{\mathcal{X}}_j^{in} \cup \mathcal{X}_j^{out}$.

If most of the random variables of $\mathcal{X}_j$ are in $\mathcal{X}_j^{in}$, our idea is to use the center of $\widetilde{\mathcal{X}}_j^{in}$ to approximate the center of $\mathcal{X}_j$. The center of $\widetilde{\mathcal{X}}_j^{in}$ is found based on C_{j-1}. If most of the random variables of $\mathcal{X}_j$ are in $\mathcal{X}_j^{out}$, our ideal is to replace the center of $\mathcal{X}_j$ with the center of $\widetilde{\mathcal{X}}_j$. For seeking out the approximate center of $\widetilde{\mathcal{X}}_j$, we should find out a subset $\mathcal{S}'$ by uniformly sampling from $\widetilde{\mathcal{X}}_j$. However, the set $\mathcal{X}_j^{out}$ is unknown. We need to find the set $\mathcal{S}' \cap \mathcal{X}_j^{out}$. We apply a branching strategy to find a set $\mathcal{Q}$ such that $\mathcal{X} \setminus \mathcal{B}_j \subseteq \mathcal{Q}$, and $|\mathcal{Q}| < 2|\mathcal{X} \setminus \mathcal{B}_j|$. Then, a random variables set $\mathcal{S}$ is obtained by sampling random variables from $\mathcal{Q}$ independently and uniformly. And the set $\mathcal{X} \setminus \mathcal{B}_j \subseteq \mathcal{Q}$ can be replaced by a subset $\mathcal{S}^*$ of $\mathcal{S}$ from $\mathcal{X}_j^{out}$. Based on $\mathcal{S}^*$ and $\widetilde{\mathcal{X}}_j^{in}$, the approximation center of $\widetilde{\mathcal{X}}_j$ could be obtained. Therefore, the algorithm presented in this paper outputs a collection of size $O((\frac{1891ek}{\epsilon^2})^{8k/\epsilon}n)$ of candidate sets containing approximation centers, and has the running time $O((\frac{1891ek}{\epsilon^2})^{8k/\epsilon}nd)$.

4. Our Algorithm cMeans

Given an instance $(\mathcal{X}, k, \mathbb{L})$ of the uncertain constrained k-means problem, $\mathbb{X} = \{\mathcal{X}_1, \ldots, \mathcal{X}_k\}$ denotes an optimal partition of $(\mathcal{X}, k, \mathbb{L})$. There exist six parameters (ϵ, $\mathcal{Q}$, g, k, C, U) in our **cMeans**, where $\epsilon \in (0, 1]$ is the approximate factor, $\mathcal{Q}$ is the input random variable set, g is the number of centers, k is the number of the clusters, C is the set of approximate cluster centers, and U is a collection of candidate sets including the approximate center. Let $M = \frac{6}{\epsilon}$, $N = \frac{79,380k}{\epsilon^3}$, where M is the size of subsets of the sampling set and N is the size of the sampling set. Without loss of generality, assume that values of M and N are integers.

We use the branching strategy to seek out the approximate centers of clusters in $\mathbb{X}$. There exist two branches in our algorithm **cMeans**, which can be seen in Figure 1. On one branch, a size N set $\mathcal{S}_1$ is obtained by sampling from $\mathcal{Q}$ uniformly and independently; $\mathcal{S}_2$ is constructed by $\mathcal{S}_1$ and M copies of each point in C. Moreover, we consider each subset $\mathcal{S}'$ of size M of $\mathcal{S}_2$, and the centroid c of $\mathcal{S}'$ is solved to represent the approximate center of $\mathcal{X}_{k-g+1}$, and our algorithm **cMeans**$(\epsilon, \mathcal{Q}, g-1, k, C \cup \{c\}, U)$ is used to obtain the remaining $g-1$ cluster centers.

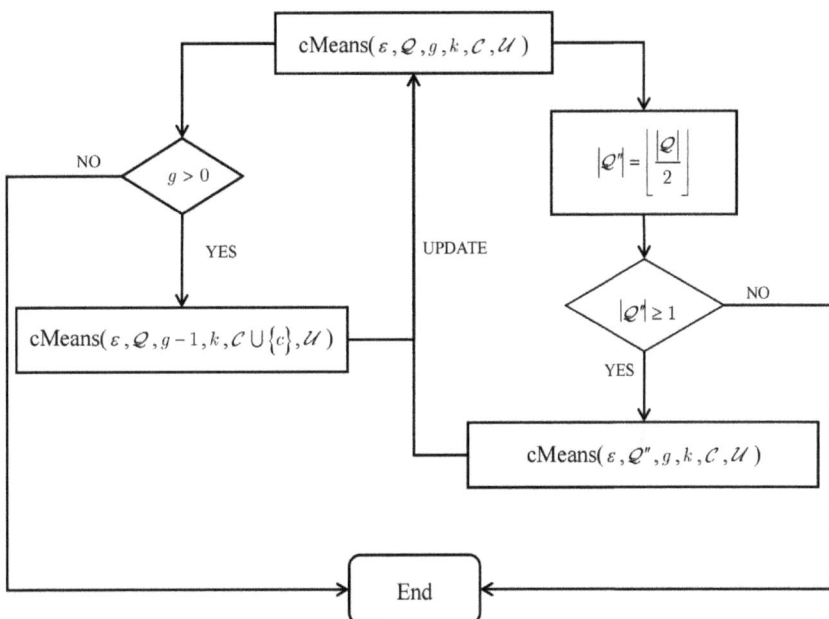

Figure 1. Flow chart of our algorithm **cMeans**.

On the other branch, for each random variable $X \in \mathcal{Q}$, we calculate the distance between X and C first. H denotes the set of all distances of random variables in $\mathcal{X}$ to C, where H is a multi-set. We should obtain the median value m for all values in H, which is the $\lfloor |H|/2 \rfloor$-th element if all of the values in H are sorted. In the second branch, $\mathcal{Q}$ is divided into two parts, $\mathcal{Q}'$ and $\mathcal{Q}''$, based on m such that for $\forall X' \in \mathcal{Q}'$, $X'' \in \mathcal{Q}''$, $dist(X', C) \leq dist(X'', C)$, where $|\mathcal{Q}'| = \lceil \frac{|\mathcal{Q}|}{2} \rceil$, $|\mathcal{Q}''| = \lfloor \frac{|\mathcal{Q}|}{2} \rfloor$. Subroutine **cMeans**$(\epsilon, \mathcal{Q}'', g, k, C, U)$ is used to obtain the remaining g cluster centers. Therefore, we present the specific algorithm for seeking out a collection of candidate sets in the Algorithm 1.

Algorithm 1: cMeans($\epsilon, \mathcal{Q}, g, k, C, U$)

Input: ($\epsilon, \mathcal{Q}, g, k, C, U$)
Output: a collection of candidate sets

1. $M = \frac{6}{\epsilon}, N = \frac{79380k}{\epsilon^3}, \mathcal{S}_1 = \mathcal{S}_2 = H = \emptyset$;
2. **if** $g = 0$ **then**
3.   add C to the collection U;
4. **end**
5. sample a set $\mathcal{S}_1$ of size N from $\mathcal{Q}$ independently and uniformly;
6. **if** $C = \emptyset$ **then**
7. $\mathcal{S}_2 = \mathcal{S}_1$;
8. **end**
9. **else**
10. $\mathcal{S}_2 = \mathcal{S}_1 \cup \{M \text{ copies of each point in } C\}$;
11. **end**
12. **for** each subset $\mathcal{S}'$ of size M of $\mathcal{S}_2$ **do**
13.   compute the centroid c of $\mathcal{S}'$;
14.   cMeans($\epsilon, \mathcal{Q}, g-1, k, C \cup \{c\}, U$);
15. **end**
16. **for** each random variable $X \in \mathcal{Q}$ **do**
17.   compute $dist(X, C)$, and add $dist(X, C)$ to H;
18.   obtain the median value m of all values in H, which is the $\lfloor \frac{|H|}{2} \rfloor$-th element if all the values in H are sorted;
19.   divide $\mathcal{Q}$ into $\mathcal{Q}'$ and $\mathcal{Q}''$ by m such that for $\forall X' \in \mathcal{Q}', X'' \in \mathcal{Q}''$, $dist(X', C) \leq dist(X'', C)$, where $|\mathcal{Q}'| = \lceil \frac{|\mathcal{Q}|}{2} \rceil, |\mathcal{Q}''| = \lfloor \frac{|\mathcal{Q}|}{2} \rfloor$;
20.   **if** $|\mathcal{Q}''| \geq 1$ **then**
21.   cMeans($\epsilon, \mathcal{Q}'', g, k, C, U$);
22.   **end**
23. **end**

5. Analysis of Our Algorithm cMeans

We investigate the success probability, correctness, and time complexity analysis of the algorithm **cMeans** in this section.

Lemma 5. *There exists a candidate set, with a probability of at least $1/12^k$, including the approximate center $C_k = \{c_1, \ldots, c_k\}$ in U satisfying $||m_j - c_j||^2 \leq \frac{9}{10}\epsilon\sigma_j^2 + \frac{1}{10\beta_j k}\epsilon\sigma_{opt}^2 (1 \leq j \leq k)$.*

The following Lemmas from Lemma 6 to 16 are used to prove Lemma 5. We prove Lemma 5 via induction on j. For $j = 1$, we can obtain $\beta_1 \geq 1/k$ easily, and prove the success probability first.

Lemma 6. *In the process of finding c_1 in our algorithm cMeans, by sampling a set of $79{,}380k/\epsilon^3$ random variables from $\mathcal{X}$ independently and uniformly, denoted by $\mathcal{S}_1$, the probability that at least $6/\epsilon$ random variables in $\mathcal{S}_2$ are from $\mathcal{X}_1$ is at least $1/2$.*

Proof. In our algorithm **cMeans**, we assume that $\mathcal{S}_1 = S_1, \ldots, S_N$, where $N = 79{,}380k/\epsilon^3$. Let $x'_1, \ldots, x'_N$ be the corresponding random variables of elements in $\mathcal{S}_1$. If $S_i \in \mathcal{X}_1$, then

$x'_i = 1$. Otherwise $x'_i = 0$. It is known easily that $Pr[S_i \in \mathcal{X}_1] \geq \frac{1}{k}$. Let $x = \sum_{i=1}^{N} x'_i$, $u = \sum_{i=1}^{N} E(x'_i)$. We obtain that $u \geq 79{,}380k/\epsilon^3$. Then,

$$Pr[x > \frac{6}{\epsilon}] = 1 - Pr[x \leq \frac{6}{\epsilon}] \tag{15}$$

$$= 1 - Pr[x \leq \frac{6\epsilon^2}{79{,}380} \frac{79{,}380}{\epsilon^3}] \tag{16}$$

$$\geq 1 - Pr[x \leq \frac{\epsilon^2}{13{,}230} u] \tag{17}$$

$$\geq 1 - e^{-\frac{(1-\frac{\epsilon^2}{13{,}230})^2 u}{2}} \tag{18}$$

$$\geq 1 - e^{-\frac{(1-\frac{\epsilon^2}{13{,}230})^2 \frac{79{,}380}{\epsilon^3}}{2}} \tag{19}$$

$$\geq 1 - e^{-\frac{(1-\frac{1}{13{,}230})^2 \cdot 79{,}380}{2}} \tag{20}$$

$$\geq \frac{1}{2}. \tag{21}$$

□

From Lemma 6, an $\mathcal{S}^*$ with size $6/\epsilon$ of $\mathcal{S}_2$ can be obtained, and the probability that all points in $\mathcal{S}^*$ are from $\mathcal{X}_1$ is at least $1/2$. Let c_1 denote the centroid of $\mathcal{S}^*$, and $\delta = 5/6$. For $|\mathcal{S}^*| = 6/\epsilon$, by Lemma 2, we conclude that $||m_1 - c_1||^2 \leq \frac{1}{5}\epsilon\sigma_1^2$ holds with a probability of at least $1/6$. Then, the probability that a subset $\mathcal{S}^*$ of size $6/\epsilon$ of $\mathcal{S}_2$ can be found such that $||m_1 - c_1||^2 \leq \frac{1}{5}\epsilon\sigma_1^2 \leq \frac{9}{10}\epsilon\sigma_1^2 + \frac{1}{10\beta_1 k}\epsilon\sigma_{opt}^2$ holds is at least $1/12$. Therefore, we conclude that Lemma 5 holds for $j = 1$.

Moreover, we assume that for $j \leq j_0 (1 \leq j_0)$, Lemma 5 holds with a probability of at least $1/12^j$. Considering the case $j = j_0 + 1$, we prove Lemma 5 by the following two cases: (1) $|\mathcal{X}_j^{out}| \leq \frac{\epsilon}{49}\beta_j n$; (2) $|\mathcal{X}_j^{out}| > \frac{\epsilon}{49}\beta_j n$.

5.1. Analysis for Case 1: $|\mathcal{X}_j^{out}| \leq \frac{\epsilon}{49}\beta_j n$

Since $|\mathcal{X}_j^{out}| \leq \frac{\epsilon}{49}\beta_j n$, most of the random variables of $\mathcal{X}_j$ are in $\mathcal{B}_j$. Our idea is to replace the center of $\mathcal{X}_j$ with the center of $\tilde{\mathcal{X}}_j^{in}$. Thus, we need to find the approximate center c_j of $\tilde{\mathcal{X}}_j^{in}$ and the bound distance $||m_j - c_j||$. We divide the distance $||m_j - c_j||$ into the following three parts: $||m_j - m_j^{in}||$, $||m_j^{in} - \tilde{m}_j^{in}||$, and $||\tilde{m}_j^{in} - c_j||$. We first study the distance between m_j and m_j^{in}.

Lemma 7. $||m_j - m_j^{in}|| \leq \sqrt{\frac{\epsilon}{48}}\sigma_j$.

Proof. Since $|\mathcal{X}_j| = \beta_j n$ and $|\mathcal{X}_j^{out}| \leq \frac{\epsilon}{49}\beta_j n$, the proportion of $\mathcal{X}_j^{in}$ in $\mathcal{X}_j$ is at least $1 - \frac{\epsilon}{49}$. By Lemma 3, $||m_j - m_j^{in}|| \leq \sqrt{\frac{\epsilon/49}{1-\epsilon/49}}\sigma_j \leq \sqrt{\frac{\epsilon}{48}}\sigma_j$. □

Lemma 8. $||m_j^{in} - \tilde{m}_j^{in}|| \leq r_j$.

Proof. Since $m_j^{in} = \frac{1}{|\mathcal{X}_j^{in}|}\sum_{X \in \mathcal{X}_j^{in}} \int_{\mathbb{R}^d} s f_X(s) ds$, and $\widetilde{m}_j^{in} = \frac{1}{|\mathcal{X}_j^{in}|} \sum_{X \in \mathcal{X}_j^{in}} \widetilde{X}$, we can obtain the following:

$$||m_j^{in} - \widetilde{m}_j^{in}|| = ||\frac{1}{|\mathcal{X}_j^{in}|}\sum_{X \in \mathcal{X}_j^{in}} \int_{\mathbb{R}^d} s f_X(s) ds - \frac{1}{|\mathcal{X}_j^{in}|}\sum_{X \in \mathcal{X}_j^{in}} \widetilde{X}|| \quad (22)$$

$$= \frac{1}{|\mathcal{X}_j^{in}|}||\sum_{X \in \mathcal{X}_j^{in}} \int_{\mathbb{R}^d} (s - \widetilde{X}) f_X(s) ds|| \quad (23)$$

$$\leq \frac{1}{|\mathcal{X}_j^{in}|} \sum_{X \in \mathcal{X}_j^{in}} \int_{\mathbb{R}^d} ||s - \widetilde{X}|| f_X(s) ds \quad (24)$$

$$\leq \frac{1}{|\mathcal{X}_j^{in}|} \sum_{X \in \mathcal{X}_j^{in}} r_j \quad (25)$$

$$= r_j. \quad (26)$$

□

Lemma 9. $f_2(\widetilde{m}_j^{in}, \widetilde{\mathcal{X}}_j^{in}) \leq 2|\mathcal{X}_j^{in}|r_j^2 + 2f_2(m_j, \mathcal{X}_j^{in}) - |\mathcal{X}_j^{in}|||m_j - \widetilde{m}_j^{in}||^2$.

Proof. Since $|\widetilde{\mathcal{X}}_j^{in}| = |\mathcal{X}_j^{in}|$, by 1, we have $f_2(m_j, \widetilde{\mathcal{X}}_j^{in}) = f_2(\widetilde{m}_j^{in}, \widetilde{\mathcal{X}}_j^{in}) + |\mathcal{X}_j^{in}|||\widetilde{m}_j^{in} - m_j||$. Then,

$$f_2(\widetilde{m}_j^{in}, \widetilde{\mathcal{X}}_j^{in}) = f_2(m_j, \widetilde{\mathcal{X}}_j^{in}) - |\mathcal{X}_j^{in}|||\widetilde{m}_j^{in} - m_j||^2 \quad (27)$$

$$= \sum_{X \in \mathcal{X}_j^{in}} ||\widetilde{X} - m_j||^2 - |\mathcal{X}_j^{in}|||m_j - \widetilde{m}_j^{in}||^2 \quad (28)$$

$$= \sum_{X \in \mathcal{X}_j^{in}} \int_{\mathbb{R}^d} ||\widetilde{X} - m_j||^2 f_X(s) ds - |\mathcal{X}_j^{in}|||m_j - \widetilde{m}_j^{in}||^2 \quad (29)$$

$$= \sum_{X \in \mathcal{X}_j^{in}} \int_{\mathbb{R}^d} ||\widetilde{X} - s + s - m_j||^2 f_X(s) ds - |\mathcal{X}_j^{in}|||m_j - \widetilde{m}_j^{in}||^2 \quad (30)$$

$$\leq \sum_{X \in \mathcal{X}_j^{in}} \int_{\mathbb{R}^d} (2||\widetilde{X} - s||^2 + 2||s - m_j||^2) f_X(s) ds - |\mathcal{X}_j^{in}|||m_j - \widetilde{m}_j^{in}||^2 \quad (31)$$

$$\leq 2|\mathcal{X}_j^{in}|r_j^2 + 2\sum_{X \in \mathcal{X}_j^{in}} \int_{\mathbb{R}^d} ||s - m_j||^2 f_X(s) ds - |\mathcal{X}_j^{in}|||m_j - \widetilde{m}_j^{in}||^2 \quad (32)$$

$$= 2|\mathcal{X}_j^{in}|r_j^2 + 2f_2(m_j, \mathcal{X}_j^{in}) - |\mathcal{X}_j^{in}|||m_j - \widetilde{m}_j^{in}||^2 \quad (33)$$

□

Lemma 10. *In the process of finding c_j in our algorithm **cMeans**, for the set $\mathcal{S}_2$ in step 5, a subset $\mathcal{S}^*$ of size $6/\epsilon$ of $\mathcal{S}_2$ can be obtained such that all random variables in $\mathcal{S}^*$ are from $\widetilde{\mathcal{X}}_j^{in}$. Let c_j be the centroid of $\mathcal{S}^*$. Then, the inequality $||\widetilde{m}_j^{in} - c_j||^2 \leq \frac{2}{5}\epsilon r_j^2 + \frac{49}{120}\epsilon \sigma_j^2 - \frac{1}{5}\epsilon||m_j - \widetilde{m}_j^{in}||^2$ holds with a probability of at least $1/6$.*

Proof. For each point $p \in C_{j-1}$, $6/\epsilon$ copies of p are added to $\mathcal{S}_2$ in step 9 in our algorithm **cMeans**. Thus, a subset $\mathcal{S}^*$ of size $6/\epsilon$ of $\mathcal{S}_2$ can be obtained such that all random variables in $\mathcal{S}^*$ are from $\widetilde{\mathcal{X}}_j^{in}$. Let $\delta = 5/6$. Since $|\mathcal{S}^*| = 6/\epsilon$, by Lemma 2, $||\widetilde{m}_j^{in} - c_j||^2 \leq \frac{\epsilon}{5} \frac{f_2(\widetilde{m}_j^{in}, \widetilde{\mathcal{X}}_j^{in})}{|\mathcal{X}_j^{in}|}$ holds with a probability of at least $1/6$. Assume that $||\widetilde{m}_j^{in} - c_j||^2 \leq \frac{\epsilon}{5} \frac{f_2(\widetilde{m}_j^{in}, \widetilde{\mathcal{X}}_j^{in})}{|\mathcal{X}_j^{in}|}$. Then,

$$||\widetilde{m}_j^{in} - c_j||^2 \leq \frac{\epsilon}{5} \frac{f_2(\widetilde{m}_j^{in}, \widetilde{\mathcal{X}}_j^{in})}{|\mathcal{X}_j^{in}|} \tag{34}$$

$$\leq \frac{1}{5}\epsilon \frac{2|\mathcal{X}_j^{in}|r_j^2 + 2f_2(m_j, \mathcal{X}_j^{in}) - |\mathcal{X}_j^{in}|||m_j - \widetilde{m}_j^{in}||^2}{|\mathcal{X}_j^{in}|} \tag{35}$$

$$= \frac{2}{5}\epsilon r_j^2 + \frac{2}{5}\epsilon \frac{f_2(m_j, \mathcal{X}_j^{in})}{|\mathcal{X}_j^{in}|} - \frac{1}{5}\epsilon ||m_j - \widetilde{m}_j^{in}||^2 \tag{36}$$

$$\leq \frac{2}{5}\epsilon r_j^2 + \frac{2}{5}\epsilon \frac{f_2(m_j, \mathcal{X}_j)}{|\mathcal{X}_j| - |\mathcal{X}_j^{out}|} - \frac{1}{5}\epsilon ||m_j - \widetilde{m}_j^{in}||^2 \tag{37}$$

$$\leq \frac{2}{5}\epsilon r_j^2 + \frac{2}{5}\epsilon \frac{\beta_j n \sigma_j^2}{(1 - \epsilon/49)\beta_j n} - \frac{1}{5}\epsilon ||m_j - \widetilde{m}_j^{in}||^2 \tag{38}$$

$$\leq \frac{2}{5}\epsilon r_j^2 + \frac{49}{120}\epsilon \sigma_j^2 - \frac{1}{5}\epsilon ||m_j - \widetilde{m}_j^{in}||^2. \tag{39}$$

□

Lemma 11. *If c_j satisfies $||\widetilde{m}_j^{in} - c_j||^2 \leq \frac{2}{5}\epsilon r_j^2 + \frac{49}{120}\epsilon \sigma_j^2 - \frac{1}{5}\epsilon ||m_j - \widetilde{m}_j^{in}||^2$, then $||m_j - c_j||^2 \leq \frac{9}{10}\epsilon \sigma_j^2 + \frac{1}{10\beta_j k}\epsilon \sigma_{opt}^2$.*

Proof. Assume that c_j satisfies $||\widetilde{m}_j^{in} - c_j||^2 \leq \frac{2}{5}\epsilon r_j^2 + \frac{49}{120}\epsilon \sigma_j^2 - \frac{1}{5}\epsilon ||m_j - \widetilde{m}_j^{in}||^2$. Then,

$$||m_j - c_j||^2 = ||m_j - \widetilde{m}_j^{in} + \widetilde{m}_j^{in} - c_j||^2 \tag{40}$$

$$\leq 2||m_j - \widetilde{m}_j^{in}||^2 + 2||\widetilde{m}_j^{in} - c_j||^2 \tag{41}$$

$$\leq (2 - \frac{2}{5}\epsilon)||m_j - \widetilde{m}_j^{in}||^2 + \frac{4}{5}\epsilon r_j^2 + \frac{49}{60}\epsilon \sigma_j^2 \tag{42}$$

$$\leq (2 - \frac{2}{5}\epsilon)||m_j - m_j^{in} + m_j^{in} - \widetilde{m}_j^{in}||^2 + \frac{4}{5}\epsilon r_j^2 + \frac{49}{60}\epsilon \sigma_j^2 \tag{43}$$

$$\leq (2 - \frac{2}{5}\epsilon)(2||m_j - m_j^{in}||^2 + 2||m_j^{in} - \widetilde{m}_j^{in}||^2) + \frac{4}{5}\epsilon r_j^2 + \frac{49}{60}\epsilon \sigma_j^2 \tag{44}$$

$$\leq (2 - \frac{2}{5}\epsilon)(\frac{1}{24}\epsilon \sigma_j^2 + 2r_j^2) + \frac{4}{5}\epsilon r_j^2 + \frac{49}{60}\epsilon \sigma_j^2 \tag{45}$$

$$\leq \frac{9}{10}\epsilon \sigma_j^2 + 4r_j^2 \tag{46}$$

$$= \frac{9}{10}\epsilon \sigma_j^2 + \frac{1}{10\beta_j k}\epsilon \sigma_{opt}^2. \tag{47}$$

□

5.2. Analysis for Case 2: $|\mathcal{X}_j^{out}| > \frac{\epsilon}{49}\beta_j n$

Let $\widetilde{\mathcal{X}}_j = \mathcal{X}_j^{in} \cup \mathcal{X}_j^{out}$, and $\widetilde{m}_j$ denote the centroid of $\widetilde{\mathcal{X}}_j$. Our idea is to replace the center of $\mathcal{X}_j$ with the center of $\widetilde{\mathcal{X}}_j$. But it is difficult to seek out the center of $\widetilde{\mathcal{X}}_j$. Thus, we try to find an approximate center c_j of $\widetilde{\mathcal{X}}_j$.

Lemma 12. $\frac{|\mathcal{X}_j^{out}|}{|\mathcal{X} \backslash \mathcal{B}_j|} \geq \frac{\epsilon^2}{3969k}$.

Proof.

$$\frac{|\mathcal{X}_j^{out}|}{|\mathcal{X} \setminus \mathcal{B}_j|} = \frac{|\mathcal{X}_j^{out}|}{\sum_{i=1}^{j-1} |\mathcal{X}_i \setminus \mathcal{B}_j| + |\mathcal{X}_j^{out}| + \sum_{i=j+1}^{k} |\mathcal{X}_i \setminus \mathcal{B}_j|} \quad (48)$$

$$\geq \frac{|\mathcal{X}_j^{out}|}{\sum_{i=1}^{j-1} \frac{f_2(c_i, \mathcal{X}_i)}{r_j^2} + |\mathcal{X}_j^{out}| + \sum_{i=j+1}^{k} |\mathcal{X}_i|} \quad (49)$$

$$\geq \frac{|\mathcal{X}_j^{out}|}{\sum_{i=1}^{j-1} \frac{f_2(m_i, \mathcal{X}_i) + |\mathcal{X}_i|\|m_i - c_i\|^2}{r_j^2} + |\mathcal{X}_j^{out}| + \sum_{i=j+1}^{k} |\mathcal{X}_i|} \quad (50)$$

$$\geq \frac{|\mathcal{X}_j^{out}|}{\frac{(1+\epsilon)n\sigma_{opt}^2}{r_j^2} + |\mathcal{X}_j^{out}| + \sum_{i=j+1}^{k} |\mathcal{X}_i|} \quad (51)$$

$$\geq \frac{|\mathcal{X}_j^{out}|}{\frac{40(1+\epsilon)k\beta_j n}{\epsilon} + |\mathcal{X}_j^{out}| + (k-j)\beta_j n} \quad (52)$$

$$\geq \frac{\frac{\epsilon}{49}\beta_j n}{\frac{40(1+\epsilon)k\beta_j n}{\epsilon} + \frac{\epsilon}{49}\beta_j n + (k-j)\beta_j n} \quad (53)$$

$$\geq \frac{\epsilon^2}{(80k+k)49 + (\epsilon - 49j)\epsilon} \quad (54)$$

$$\geq \frac{\epsilon^2}{3969k} \quad (55)$$

□

Lemma 13. $\|m_j - \widetilde{m}_j\| \leq r_j$.

Proof.

$$\|m_j - \widetilde{m}_j\| = \|\frac{1}{|\mathcal{X}_j|} \sum_{X \in \mathcal{X}_j} \int^{\mathbb{R}^d} s f_X(s) ds - \frac{1}{|\mathcal{X}_j|}(\sum_{X \in \mathcal{X}_j^{in}} \widetilde{X} + \sum_{X \in \mathcal{X}_j^{out}} \int^{\mathbb{R}^d} s f_X(s) ds)\| \quad (56)$$

$$= \frac{1}{|\mathcal{X}_j|} \|\sum_{X \in \mathcal{X}_j^{in}} \int^{\mathbb{R}^d} (s - \widetilde{X}) f_X(s) ds\| \quad (57)$$

$$= \frac{1}{|\mathcal{X}_j|} \sum_{X \in \mathcal{X}_j^{in}} \int^{\mathbb{R}^d} \|s - \widetilde{X}\| f_X(s) ds \quad (58)$$

$$\leq \frac{1}{|\mathcal{X}_j|} \sum_{X \in \mathcal{X}_j^{in}} r_j \quad (59)$$

$$= \frac{|\mathcal{X}_j^{in}|}{|\mathcal{X}_j|} r_j \quad (60)$$

$$\leq r_j \quad (61)$$

□

Lemma 14. $f_2(\widetilde{m}_j, \widetilde{\mathcal{X}}_j) \leq 2 f_2(m_j, \mathcal{X}_j) + 4\beta_j n r_j^2$.

Proof.

$$f_2(\widetilde{m}_j, \widetilde{\mathcal{X}}_j) = \sum_{X \in \mathcal{X}_j^{in}} ||\widetilde{X} - \widetilde{m}_j||^2 + \sum_{X \in \mathcal{X}_j^{out}} \int^{\mathbb{R}^d} ||s - \widetilde{m}_j||^2 f_X(s) ds \tag{62}$$

$$= \sum_{X \in \mathcal{X}_j^{in}} \int^{\mathbb{R}^d} ||\widetilde{X} - \widetilde{m}_j||^2 f_X(s) ds + \sum_{X \in \mathcal{X}_j^{out}} \int^{\mathbb{R}^d} ||s - \widetilde{m}_j||^2 f_X(s) ds \tag{63}$$

$$= \sum_{X \in \mathcal{X}_j^{in}} \int^{\mathbb{R}^d} ||\widetilde{X} - s + s - \widetilde{m}_j||^2 f_X(s) ds + \sum_{X \in \mathcal{X}_j^{out}} \int^{\mathbb{R}^d} ||s - \widetilde{m}_j||^2 f_X(s) ds \tag{64}$$

$$\leq \sum_{X \in \mathcal{X}_j^{in}} \int^{\mathbb{R}^d} (2||\widetilde{X} - s||^2 + 2||s - \widetilde{m}_j||^2) f_X(s) ds + \sum_{X \in \mathcal{X}_j^{out}} \int^{\mathbb{R}^d} ||s - \widetilde{m}_j||^2 f_X(s) ds \tag{65}$$

$$\leq 2 \sum_{X \in \mathcal{X}_j^{in}} \int^{\mathbb{R}^d} ||\widetilde{X} - s||^2 f_X(s) ds + 2 \sum_{X \in \mathcal{X}_j^{out}} \int^{\mathbb{R}^d} ||s - \widetilde{m}_j||^2 f_X(s) ds \tag{66}$$

$$\leq 2|\mathcal{X}_j^{in}|r_j^2 + 2f_2(\widetilde{m}_j, \mathcal{X}_j) \tag{67}$$

$$= 2|\mathcal{X}_j^{in}|r_j^2 + 2f_2(m_j, \mathcal{X}_j) + 2|\mathcal{X}_j| ||m_j - \widetilde{m}_j||^2 \tag{68}$$

$$\leq 2f_2(m_j, \mathcal{X}_j) + 4\beta_j n r_j^2 \tag{69}$$

□

Lemma 15. *In the process of finding c_j in our algorithm **cMeans**, we assume that $\mathcal{Q}$ satisfies $\mathcal{X} \setminus \mathcal{B}_j \subseteq \mathcal{Q}$ and $|\mathcal{Q}| < 2|\mathcal{X} \setminus \mathcal{B}_j|$. For the set $\mathcal{S}_2$ in step 5, a subset $\mathcal{S}^*$ of size $6/\epsilon$ of $\mathcal{S}_2$ can be obtained such that all random variables in $\mathcal{S}^*$ are from $\widetilde{\mathcal{X}}_j^{in}$ with a probability of $1/2$. Let c_j denotes the centroid of $\mathcal{S}^*$. Then, the inequality $||\widetilde{m}_j - c_j||^2 \leq \frac{4}{5}\epsilon r_j^2 + \frac{2}{5}\epsilon \sigma_j^2$ holds with a probability of at least $1/6$.*

Proof. In our algorithm **cMeans**, we assume that $\mathcal{S}_1 = S_1, \ldots, S_N$, where $N = 79380k/\epsilon^3$. Let $x_1', \ldots, x_N'$ be the corresponding random variables of elements in $\mathcal{S}_1$. If $S_i \in \mathcal{X}_j^{out}$, obtain $x_i' = 1$, or else $x_i' = 0$. It is known easily that $Pr[S_i \in \mathcal{X}_j^{out}] \geq \frac{\epsilon^2}{7938k}$ by Lemma 12. Let $x = \sum_{i=1}^N x_i'$, $u = \sum_{i=1}^N E(x_i')$. We obtain that $u \geq 10/\epsilon$, and

$$Pr[x > \frac{6}{\epsilon}] = 1 - Pr[x \leq \frac{6}{\epsilon}] \tag{70}$$

$$\geq 1 - Pr[x \leq \frac{3}{5}u] \tag{71}$$

$$\geq 1 - e^{-\frac{(1-\frac{3}{5})^2 u}{2}} \tag{72}$$

$$\geq 1 - e^{-\frac{(1-\frac{3}{5})^2 \frac{10}{\epsilon}}{2}} \tag{73}$$

$$\geq 1 - e^{-\frac{4}{5}} \tag{74}$$

$$\geq \frac{1}{2}. \tag{75}$$

Then, the probability that at least $6/\epsilon$ random variables in $\mathcal{S}_1$ are from $\mathcal{X}_j^{out}$ is at least $1/2$. Since $\mathcal{S}_2 = \mathcal{S}_1 \cup \{6/\epsilon$ copies of each point in $C\}$, a subset $\mathcal{S}^*$ of size $6/\epsilon$ of $\mathcal{S}_2$ can be obtained, and the probability that all random variables in $\mathcal{S}^*$ are from $\widetilde{\mathcal{X}}_j^{in}$ is at least $1/2$. Let c_j denote the centroid of $\mathcal{S}^*$ and $\delta = 5/6$. For $|\mathcal{S}^*| = 6/\epsilon$ and $|\widetilde{\mathcal{X}}_j| = |\mathcal{X}_j|$, by Lemma 2, $||\tilde{m}_j - c_j||^2 \leq \frac{\epsilon}{5}\frac{f_2(\tilde{m}_j, \tilde{\mathcal{X}}_j)}{|\tilde{\mathcal{X}}_j|} = \frac{\epsilon}{5}\frac{f_2(\tilde{m}_j, \tilde{\mathcal{X}}_j)}{|\mathcal{X}_j|}$ holds with a probability of at least 1/6. Assume that $||\tilde{m}_j - c_j||^2 \leq \frac{\epsilon}{5}\frac{f_2(\tilde{m}_j, \tilde{\mathcal{X}}_j)}{|\mathcal{X}_j|}$. Then,

$$||\tilde{m}_j - c_j||^2 \leq \frac{\epsilon}{5}\frac{f_2(\tilde{m}_j, \tilde{\mathcal{X}}_j)}{|\mathcal{X}_j|} \leq \frac{\epsilon}{5}\frac{2f_2(m_j, \mathcal{X}_j) + 4\beta_j n r_j^2}{|\mathcal{X}_j|} \leq \frac{4}{5}\epsilon r_j^2 + \frac{2}{5}\epsilon \sigma_j^2. \tag{76}$$

□

Lemma 16. *If c_j satisfies $||\tilde{m}_j - c_j||^2 \leq \frac{4}{5}\epsilon r_j^2 + \frac{2}{5}\epsilon\sigma_j^2$, then $||m_j - c_j||^2 \leq \frac{9}{10}\epsilon\sigma_j^2 + \frac{1}{10\beta_j k}\epsilon\sigma_{opt}^2$.*

Proof. Assume that c_j satisfies $||\tilde{m}_j - c_j||^2 \leq \frac{4}{5}\epsilon r_j^2 + \frac{2}{5}\epsilon\sigma_j^2$. Then,

$$||m_j - c_j||^2 = ||m_j - \tilde{m}_j + \tilde{m}_j - c_j||^2 \tag{77}$$
$$\leq 2||m_j - \tilde{m}_j||^2 + 2||\tilde{m}_j - c_j||^2 \tag{78}$$
$$\leq 2r_j^2 + \frac{8}{5}\epsilon r_j^2 + \frac{4}{5}\epsilon\sigma_j^2 \tag{79}$$
$$= \frac{4}{5}\epsilon\sigma_j^2 + (2 + \frac{8}{5}\epsilon)r_j^2 \tag{80}$$
$$\leq \frac{9}{10}\epsilon\sigma_j^2 + \frac{1}{10\beta_j k}\epsilon\sigma_{opt}^2. \tag{81}$$

□

Lemma 17. *Given an instance $(\mathcal{X}, k, \mathbb{L})$ of the uncertain constrained k-means problem, where the size of $\mathcal{X}$ is n, for $\forall \epsilon \in (0,1], k \geq 2$, we assume that by using our algorithm cMeans(ϵ, $\mathcal{X}$, k, C,U) (C and U are initialized as empty sets), a collection U of candidate sets including approximate centers is obtained. If there exists a set $C_k = \{c_1, \ldots, c_k\}$ in U satisfying that $||m_j - c_j||^2 \leq \frac{9}{10}\epsilon\sigma_j^2 + \frac{1}{10\beta_j k}\epsilon\sigma_{opt}^2 (1 \leq j \leq k)$, then C_k is a $(1+\epsilon)$-approximation for the uncertain constrained k-means problem.*

Proof. Assume that $C_k = c_1, \ldots, c_k$ is a set in U satisfying that $||m_j - c_j||^2 \leq \frac{9}{10}\epsilon\sigma_j^2 + \frac{1}{10\beta_j k}\epsilon\sigma_{opt}^2 (1 \leq j \leq k)$. Then,

$$\sum_{j=1}^{k} f_2(c_j, \mathcal{X}_j) = \sum_{j=1}^{k}(f_2(m_j, \mathcal{X}_j) + |\mathcal{X}_j|||m_j - c_j||^2) \tag{82}$$
$$\leq \sum_{j=1}^{k}(f_2(m_j, \mathcal{X}_j) + \beta_j n(\frac{9}{10}\epsilon\sigma_j^2 + \frac{1}{10\beta_j k}\epsilon\sigma_{opt}^2)) \tag{83}$$
$$\leq \sum_{j=1}^{k}(f_2(m_j, \mathcal{X}_j) + \frac{9}{10}\epsilon n\sum_{j=1}^{k}\beta_j\sigma_j^2 + \frac{1}{10}\epsilon n\sigma_{opt}^2 \tag{84}$$
$$\leq \sum_{j=1}^{k}(f_2(m_j, \mathcal{X}_j) + \frac{9}{10}\epsilon n\sigma_{opt}^2 + \frac{1}{10}\epsilon n\sigma_{opt}^2 \tag{85}$$
$$= (1+\epsilon) \cdot OPT_k(P). \tag{86}$$

□

5.3. Time Complexity Analysis

We analyze the time complexity for our algorithm **cMeans** in this section.

Lemma 18. *The time complexity of our algorithm cMeans is $O(4^k(\frac{13231\epsilon k}{\epsilon^2})^{6k/\epsilon}\frac{1}{\epsilon}nd)$.*

Proof. Let $a = C^M_{N+kM}$, which $N = \frac{79380k}{e^3}$, $M = \frac{6}{\epsilon}$. By the Stirling formula,

$$C^M_{N+kM} \leq \frac{(N+kM)^M}{M!} \approx O((e\frac{N+kM}{M})^M) = O((\frac{13231ek}{\epsilon^2})^{\frac{6}{\epsilon}}).$$

In our algorithm **cMeans**, steps 5–9 have a run time of $O(k/\epsilon^3)$, step 11 have a run time of $O(d/\epsilon)$, and steps 13–16 have a run time of $O(knd)$. Let $T(n,g)$ denote the time complexity of algorithm **cMeans**, where g is the number of cluster centers, and n is the size of Q.

If $g = 0$, $T(n,0) = O(1)$. When $n = 1$, $T(1,g) = a(T(1,g-1) + O(d/\epsilon)) + O(k/\epsilon^3)$. Because $a > k/\epsilon^3$, $T(1,g) = a(T(1,g-1) + O(d/\epsilon)) \leq a^g \cdot T(1,0) + g \cdot a^g \cdot O(d/\epsilon) = O(g \cdot a^g \cdot d/\epsilon)$. Therefore, $T(1,g) \leq O(4^g(\frac{13231ek}{\epsilon^2})^{6g/\epsilon})\frac{1}{\epsilon}d$, where $e = 2.7183$.

For $\forall n \geq 2$ and $g \geq 1$, the recurrence of $T(n,g)$ could be obtained as follows:

$$T(n,g) = a \cdot T(n,g-1) + T(\lfloor\frac{n}{2}\rfloor,g) + a \cdot O(\frac{d}{\epsilon}) + O(\frac{k}{\epsilon^3}) + O(knd).$$

Because $a > k/\epsilon^3$, two constants b_1 and b_2 with $b_1 \geq 1$ and $b_2 \geq 1$ could be obtained to arrive at the following recurrence.

$$T(n,g) \leq a \cdot T(n,g-1) + T(\lfloor\frac{n}{2}\rfloor,g) + a \cdot b_1 \cdot \frac{d}{\epsilon} + b_2 \cdot knd.$$

Now we claim that $T(n,g) \leq b_1 \cdot b_2 \cdot \frac{1}{\epsilon} \cdot a^g \cdot 2^{2g} \cdot nd - b_1 \cdot \frac{d}{\epsilon}$. If $g = 0$, then $T(n,0) = O(1)$. If $g \geq 1, n = 1$, then $T(1,g) \leq O(4^g(\frac{13231ek}{\epsilon^2})^{6g/\epsilon})\frac{1}{\epsilon}d$, and the claim holds. Suppose that if $\forall n_1 \geq 0, \forall g > g_1$, the claim holds for $T(n_1,g_1)$, and if $\forall 0 < n_2 < n, \forall g_2$, the claim holds for $T(n_2,g_2)$. We need to prove that:

$$b_1 \cdot b_2 \cdot \frac{1}{\epsilon} \cdot a^g \cdot 2^{2g} \cdot nd - b_1 \cdot \frac{d}{\epsilon} \geq a(b_1 \cdot b_2 \cdot \frac{1}{\epsilon} \cdot a^{(g-1)} \cdot 2^{2(g-1)} \cdot nd - b_1 \cdot \frac{d}{\epsilon})$$
$$+ b_1 \cdot b_2 \cdot \frac{1}{\epsilon} \cdot a^g \cdot 2^{2g} \cdot \lfloor\frac{n}{2}\rfloor d - b_1 \cdot \frac{d}{\epsilon} + a \cdot b_1 \cdot \frac{d}{\epsilon} + b_2 \cdot knd.$$

The above formula can be simplified as $\frac{1}{4\epsilon} \cdot b_1 \cdot a^g 2^{2g} \geq k$, which holds for $\forall g \geq 1$. For $a = (\frac{13231ek}{\epsilon^2})^{6/\epsilon}$, $T(n,k) = O(4^k(\frac{13231ek}{\epsilon^2})^{6k/\epsilon}\frac{1}{\epsilon}nd)$. □

Thus, we can obtain the following Theorem 2.

Theorem 2. *Given an instance $(\mathcal{X},k,\mathbb{L})$ of the uncertain constrained k-means problem, where the size of $\mathcal{X}$ is n, for $\forall \epsilon \in (0,1], k \geq 2$, by using our algorithm cMeans$(\epsilon,\mathcal{X},k,C,U)$, a collection U of candidate sets including approximate centers can be obtained with a probability of at least $1/12^2$ such that U includes at least one candidate set including approximate centers that is a $(1+\epsilon)$-approximation for the uncertain constrained k-means problem, and the time complexity of our algorithm cMeans is $O(4^k(\frac{13231ek}{\epsilon^2})^{6k/\epsilon}\frac{1}{\epsilon}nd)$.*

6. Conclusions

In this paper, we defined the uncertain constrained k-means problem first, and then presented a stochastic approximate algorithm for the problem in detail. We proposed a general mathematical model of the uncertain constrained k-means problem, and studied the random sampling properties, which are very important to deal with the uncertain constrained k-means problem. By applying a random sampling technique, we obtained a $(1+\epsilon)$-approximate algorithm for the problem. Then, we investigated the success probability, correctness and time complexity analysis of our algorithm **cMeans**, whose running time is $O(4^k(\frac{13231ek}{\epsilon^2})^{6k/\epsilon}\frac{1}{\epsilon}nd)$. However, there also exists a big gap between the current algorithms for the uncertain constrained k-means problem and the practical algorithms for the problem, which has been mentioned in [13] similarly.

We will try to explore a much more practical algorithm for the uncertain constrained k-means problem in future. It is known that the 2-means problem is the smallest version of the k-means problem, and remains NP-hard. The approximation schemes for the 2-means problem can be generalized to solve the k-means problem. Due to the particularity of the uncertain constrained 2-means problem, we will study approximation schemes for the uncertain constrained 2-means problem and reduce the algorithm complexity of approximation schemes for the uncertain constrained k-means problem through approximation schemes of the uncertain constrained 2-means problem. Additionally, we will apply the proposed algorithm to some practical problems in the future.

Author Contributions: J.L. and J.T. contributed to supervision, methodology, validation and project administration. B.X. and X.T. contributed to review and editing. All authors have read and agreed to the published version of the manuscript.

Funding: This research was funded in part by the Science and Technology Foundation of Guizhou Province ([2021]015), in part by the Open Fund of Guizhou Provincial Public Big Data Key Laboratory (2017BDKFJJ019), in part by the Guizhou University Foundation for the introduction of talent ((2016) No. 13), in part by the GuangDong Basic and Applied Basic Research Foundation (No. 2020A1515110554), and in part by the Science and Technology Program of Guangzhou (No. 202002030138), China.

Institutional Review Board Statement: Not applicable.

Informed Consent Statement: Not applicable.

Data Availability Statement: Not applicable.

Conflicts of Interest: The authors declare no conflict of interest.

References

1. Feldman, D.; Monemizadeh, M.; Sohler, C. A PTAS for k-means clustering based on weak coresets. In Proceedings of the 23rd ACM Symposium on Computational Geometry, SoCG, Gyeongju, Korea, 6–8 June 2007; pp. 11–18.
2. Ostrovsky, R.; Rabani, Y.; Schulman, L.J.; Swamy, C. The effectiveness of lloyd-type methods for the k-means problem. *J. ACM* **2012**, *59*, 28:1–28:22. [CrossRef]
3. Jaiswal, R.; Kumar, A.; Sen, S. A simple D^2-sampling based PTAS for k-means and other clustering problems. *Algorithmica* **2014**, *71*, 22–46. [CrossRef]
4. Arkin, E.M.; Diaz-Banez, J.M.; Hurtado, F.; Kumar, P.; Mitchell, J.S.; Palop, B.; Perez-Lantero, P.; Saumell, M.; Silveira, R.I. Bichromatic 2-center of pairs of points. *Comput. Geom.* **2015**, *48*, 94–107. [CrossRef]
5. Yhuller, S.; Sussmann, Y.J. The capacitated k-center problem. *SIAM J. Discrete Math.* **2000**, *13*, 403–418.
6. Har-Peled, S.; Raichel, B. Net and prune: A linear time algorithm for Euclidean distance problems. *J. ACM* **2015**, *62*, 4401–4435. [CrossRef]
7. Swamy, C.; Shmoys, D.B. Fault-tolerant facility location. *ACM Trans. Algorithms* **2008**, *4*, 1–27. [CrossRef]
8. Xu, G.; Xu, J. Efficient approximation algorithms for clustering point-sets. *Comput. Geom.* **2010**, *43*, 59–66. [CrossRef]
9. Valls, A.; Batet, M.; Lopez, E.M. Using expert's rules as background knowledge in the clusdm methodology. *Eur. J. Oper. Res.* **2009**, *195*, 864–875. [CrossRef]
10. Li, J.; Yi, K.; Zhang, Q. Clustering with deversity. In Proceedings of the 37th International Colloquium on Automata, Languages and Programming, ICALP, Bordeaux, France, 6–10 July 2010; pp. 188–200.
11. Ding, H.; Xu, J. A unified framework for clustering constrained data without locality property. In Proceedings of the 26th Annual ACM-SIAM Symposium on Discrete Algorithms, SODA, San Diego, CA, USA, 4–6 January 2015; pp. 1471–1490.
12. Bhattacharya, A.; Jaiswal, R.; Kumar, A. Faster algorithms for the constrained k-means problem. *Theory Comput. Syst.* **2018**, *62*, 93–115. [CrossRef]
13. Feng, Q.; Hu, J.; Huang, N.; Wang, J. Improved PTAS for the constrained k-means problem. *J. Comb. Optim.* **2019**, *37*, 1091–1110. [CrossRef]
14. Hoeffding, W. Probability inequalities for sums of bounded random variables. *J. Am. Stat. Assoc.* **1963**, *58*, 13–30. [CrossRef]

Article

A (k, n)-Threshold Secret Image Sharing Scheme Based on a Non-Full Rank Linear Model

Ji-Hwei Horng [1], Si-Sheng Chen [2,3,*] and Chin-Chen Chang [3,*]

1. Department of Electronic Engineering, National Quemoy University, Kinmen 89250, Taiwan; horng@email.nqu.edu.tw
2. School of Big Data and Artificial Intelligence of Fujian Polytechnic Normal University, Fuzhou 350030, China
3. Department of Information Engineering and Computer Science, Feng Chia University, Taichung 40724, Taiwan
* Correspondence: sschen358@mail.fcu.edu.tw (S.-S.C.); ccc@o365.fcu.edu.tw (C.-C.C.)

Abstract: Secret image sharing is a hot issue in the research field of data hiding schemes for digital images. This paper proposes a general (k, n) threshold secret image sharing scheme, which distributes secret data into n meaningful image shadows based on a non-full rank linear model. The image shadows are indistinguishable from their corresponding distinct cover images. Any k combination of the n shares can perfectly restore the secret data. In the proposed scheme, the integer parameters (k, n), with $k \leq n$, can be set arbitrarily to meet the application requirement. The experimental results demonstrate the applicability of the proposed general scheme. The embedding capacity, the visual quality of image shadows, and the security level are satisfactory.

Keywords: secret image sharing; data hiding; meaningful shadow images; non-full rank linear model

1. Introduction

With the rapid development of portable devices and wireless communication, a huge amount of information is transmitted via the Internet in daily life. To protect the security of private information, encryption techniques are applied [1,2], which transform the private data into a meaningless ciphertext with a secret key. However, the meaningless ciphertext may arouse the eavesdropper's suspicion. Researchers turn to develop some techniques which hide private data into meaningful media such as digital images or videos. The technique of embedding secret data in a digital cover image to produce a stego image is called image steganography. Conventional methods for image steganography include the least significant bits (LSB) substitution [3], the exploiting modifying direction (EMD) method [4], the difference expansion (DE) [5], the histogram shifting (HS) [6], and some other approaches [7,8]. The secret data are transmitted under the cover of a meaningful digital image, without attracting the eavesdropper's suspicion.

The current image steganography techniques suffer from a problem that the stego images are vulnerable to tampering attack. Slight changes to a stego image may completely disrupt the decryption result. To improve the flexibility of decryption, in 1995, Naro and Shamir [9] proposed the visual secret sharing (VSS), also called visual cryptography, in which they encrypted a secret image into n shares and recovered the secret image through stacking not less than t shares. Later, many improved versions of visual secret sharing were proposed [10–13]. The main weakness of such schemes is the low quality of the restored secret image.

As a result, a series of secret image sharing schemes was proposed [14–19] that used mathematical computation to recover the secret image instead of stacking. A common approach is to apply the polynomial-based secret sharing scheme. In a (k, n) polynomial-based secret image sharing scheme, the dealer divides a pixel or a pixel block of the secret image into n shadows via a polynomial function. In such schemes, we can consider that the

secret image is encrypted with polynomial-based secret sharing into n noise-like images. Due to the continuous feature of a polynomial, the reconstructed secret image is distorted by numerical errors.

Another series of secret image sharing schemes focusing on sharing secret into multiple image shadows were proposed [20–22]. The image shadows are indistinguishable from the cover images and the secret can be perfectly recovered. In 2007, Chang et al. [20] introduced the first version of such schemes. The secret message is transmitted through two meaningful image shadows, and it can be recovered only when both image shadows are obtained. Although these schemes distribute the secret data into multiple image shadows, all shadows are required in the secret extraction phase.

Some works on (k, n)-threshold secret image sharing have been proposed [23–26], in which the secret data can be completely recovered by no less than k shares. However, shadow images are vulnerable to the steganalysis because they are generated based on the same cover image. Recently, some secret image sharing schemes using different meaningful cover images have been proposed [27,28]. In these methods, (k, n) is a fixed pair of predefined constants.

The motivation of this research is to find a general secret image sharing scheme, in which parameters (k, n) with $k < n$ can be arbitrarily chosen according to different application requirements, and the n distinct cover images can be arbitrarily assigned too. We first present a (k, n)-threshold secret sharing scheme based on a non-full rank linear model. A secret segment of k entries is used to generate a solution vector of n entries. By using any combination of k entries from the solution vector, the complete solution vector can be recovered and the secret segment can be restored.

Then, this scheme is applied to a digital image transmission system. In the first step, the secret data is divided into secret vectors too. Then, the solution vectors are generated in the same way as the proposed secret sharing scheme. To implement it on the image transmission system, each solution vector is further applied to modulate a vector constituted by pixel values collected from different cover images. In the final step, the resulting modulated vector is recorded to the image shadows. In the recovery phase, only a predefined number of shadows are required to restore the complete secret.

The remainder of this paper is organized as follows. In Section 2, we introduce the (k, n) secret sharing scheme based on a non-full rank linear model. The proposed (k, n)-threshold secret image sharing scheme is described in Section 3. The experimental results and theoretic analysis are given in Section 4. Finally, we conclude this paper in Section 5.

2. (k, n)-Threshold Secret Sharing Scheme Based on Non-Full Rank Linear Model

In this section, we first discuss the solution of a non-full rank linear model over a finite integer field. Then, an application of recovering a solution vector with missing entries is introduced. Based on this mathematical model, we propose a generalized (k, n)-threshold secret sharing scheme based on a non-full rank linear model.

2.1. Non-Full Rank Linear Model over a Finite Integer Field

Assume p is a prime number, z_p is a field of integers modulo p; n and k are two positive integers with $n \geq k$. The equations $\pi_1, \pi_2, \cdots, \pi_{n-k}$ are $(n-k)$ linearly independent equations of n variables over the field z_p, which are formulated as

$$\pi_i: a_{i,1}x_1 + a_{i,2}x_2 + \cdots + \cdots a_{i,n}x_n = b_i \bmod p, \; i = 1, 2, \cdots, n-k. \tag{1}$$

Let

$$A = \begin{pmatrix} a_{1,1} & a_{1,2} & \cdots & a_{i,n} \\ a_{2,1} & a_{2,2} & \cdots & a_{2,n} \\ \vdots & \vdots & \ddots & \vdots \\ a_{n-k,1} & a_{n-k,2} & \cdots & a_{n-k,n} \end{pmatrix}, b = \begin{pmatrix} b_1 \\ b_2 \\ \vdots \\ b_{n-k} \end{pmatrix}. \tag{2}$$

Then, the solution space of the $(n-k)$ linear equations Equation (1) is given by

$$H = \{x \mid x = (x_1, x_2, \cdots, x_n)^T, Ax = b \bmod p\}. \tag{3}$$

This system of linear equations can also be written in matrix form as

$$\begin{pmatrix} a_{1,1} & a_{1,2} & \cdots & a_{i,n} \\ a_{2,1} & a_{2,2} & \cdots & a_{2,n} \\ \vdots & \vdots & \ddots & \vdots \\ a_{n-k,1} & a_{n-k,2} & \cdots & a_{n-k,n} \end{pmatrix} \begin{pmatrix} x_1 \\ x_2 \\ \vdots \\ x_n \end{pmatrix} = \begin{pmatrix} b_1 \\ b_2 \\ \vdots \\ b_{n-k} \end{pmatrix} \bmod p. \tag{4}$$

According to linear algebra, a system of n linearly independent equations with n variables $x = (x_1, x_2, \cdots, x_n)^T$, a unique solution vector x can be determined. The current non-full rank $(n-k < n)$ system of linearly independent equations leads to a solution space of rank $n - (n-k) = k$.

We can manipulate the augmented matrix $(A|b)$ by using elementary row operations over field z_p to obtain the simplest row form as

$$\begin{pmatrix} 1 & 0 & \cdots & 0 & c_{1,n-k+1} & \cdots & c_{1,n+1} \\ 0 & 1 & \cdots & 0 & c_{2,n-k+1} & \cdots & c_{2,n+1} \\ \vdots & \vdots & \ddots & \vdots & \vdots & \ddots & \vdots \\ 0 & 0 & \cdots & 1 & c_{n-k,n-k+1} & \cdots & c_{n-k,n+1} \end{pmatrix}. \tag{5}$$

Then, we obtain an equivalent system of linearly independent equations

$$\begin{cases} x_1 = -c_{1,n-k+1} x_{n-k+1} - c_{1,n-k+2} x_{n-k+2} - \cdots - c_{1,n} x_n + c_{1,n+1} \bmod p \\ x_2 = -c_{2,n-k+1} x_{n-k+1} - c_{2,n-k+2} x_{n-k+2} - \cdots - c_{2,n} x_n + c_{2,n+1} \bmod p \\ \vdots \\ x_{n-k} = -c_{n-k,n-k+1} x_{n-k+1} - c_{n-k,n-k+2} x_{n-k+2} - \cdots - c_{n-k,n} x_n + c_{n-k,n+1} \bmod p \end{cases}. \tag{6}$$

Let $\beta = (\beta_1, \beta_2, \ldots, \beta_{n-k}, 0, 0, \cdots, 0)^T$ be a particular solution for Equation (6). To solve the unknown entries, we substitute β into Equation (6) and obtain

$$\begin{cases} \beta_1 = c_{1,n+1} \\ \beta_2 = c_{2,n+1} \\ \vdots \\ \beta_{n-k} = c_{n-k,n+1} \end{cases}. \tag{7}$$

To solve a set of linearly independent homogeneous solutions of Equation (6), let the k homogeneous solutions be

$$(\alpha_1, \alpha_2, \cdots, \alpha_k) = \begin{pmatrix} \alpha_{1,1} & \alpha_{2,1} & \cdots & \alpha_{k,1} \\ \alpha_{1,2} & \alpha_{2,1} & \cdots & \alpha_{k,2} \\ \vdots & \vdots & \ddots & \vdots \\ \alpha_{1,n-k} & \alpha_{2,n-k} & \cdots & \alpha_{k,n-k} \\ 1 & 0 & \cdots & 0 \\ 0 & 1 & \cdots & 0 \\ \vdots & \ddots & \vdots & 0 \\ 0 & 0 & \cdots & 1 \end{pmatrix}. \tag{8}$$

To solve the unknown entries of each solution α_i, we can substitute them into the homogeneous equation that corresponds to Equation (6) and obtain

$$\begin{cases} \alpha_{i,1} = -c_{1,n-k+j} \mod p \\ \alpha_{i,2} = -c_{2,n-k+j} \mod p \\ \quad\vdots \\ \alpha_{i,n-k} = -c_{n-k,n-k+j} \mod p \end{cases}, i = 1, 2, \ldots, k. \tag{9}$$

The solution space H can be defined by using the homogeneous and particular solutions as

$$H = \left\{ x \,\middle|\, x = \sum_{i=1}^{k} m_i \alpha_i + \beta \mod p \right\}, \text{ where } m_i \in z_p. \tag{10}$$

Suppose a particular solution vector with missing entries $x' = (x'_1, x'_2, \cdots, x'_k)^T$ is given, where $(n - k)$ entries of a solution $x = (x_1, x_2, \cdots, x_n)^T \in H$ are missing. We can recover the missing entries by the following procedures.

Without the loss of generality, let us assume the available entries are the first k entries. We first manipulate the original augmented matrix $(A|b)$ with elementary row operations into the following form

$$\begin{pmatrix} h_{1,1} & \cdots & h_{1,k} & 1 & 0 & \cdots & 0 & h_{1,n+1} \\ h_{2,1} & \cdots & h_{2,k} & 0 & 1 & \cdots & 0 & h_{2,n+1} \\ \vdots & \ddots & \vdots & \vdots & \vdots & \ddots & \vdots & \vdots \\ h_{n-k,1} & \cdots & h_{n-k,k} & 0 & 0 & \cdots & 1 & h_{n-k,n+1} \end{pmatrix}. \tag{11}$$

Then, the missing entries can be obtained by

$$\begin{cases} x_{k+1} = -h_{1,1} x_1 - h_{1,2} x_2 - \cdots - h_{1,k} x_k + h_{1,n+1} \mod p \\ x_{k+2} = -h_{2,1} x_1 - h_{2,2} x_2 - \cdots - h_{2,k} x_k + h_{2,n+1} \mod p \\ \quad\vdots \\ x_n = -h_{n,1} x_1 - h_{n,2} x_2 - \cdots - h_{n,k} x_k + h_{n,n+1} \mod p \end{cases}. \tag{12}$$

Each solution vector can be represented as

$$x = m_1 \alpha_1 + m_2 \alpha_2 + \cdots + m_k \alpha_k + \beta \mod p. \tag{13}$$

By substituting the obtained particular and homogeneous solutions into Equation (13), we can get

$$\begin{pmatrix} x_1 \\ x_2 \\ \vdots \\ x_{n-k} \\ \vdots \\ x_n \end{pmatrix} = m_1 \begin{pmatrix} a_{1,1} \\ a_{1,2} \\ \vdots \\ a_{1,n-k} \\ 1 \\ \vdots \\ 0 \end{pmatrix} + m_2 \begin{pmatrix} a_{2,1} \\ a_{2,2} \\ \vdots \\ a_{2,n-k} \\ 0 \\ \vdots \\ 0 \end{pmatrix} + \cdots + m_k \begin{pmatrix} a_{k,1} \\ a_{k,2} \\ \vdots \\ a_{k,n-k} \\ 0 \\ \vdots \\ 1 \end{pmatrix} + \begin{pmatrix} \beta_1 \\ \beta_2 \\ \vdots \\ \beta_{n-k} \\ 0 \\ \vdots \\ 0 \end{pmatrix} \mod p. \tag{14}$$

By expanding the last k rows, we can also get the coefficients of the given vector x'.

$$\begin{cases} m_1 = x_{n-k+1} \\ m_2 = x_{n-k+2} \\ \quad\vdots \\ m_k = x_n \end{cases}. \tag{15}$$

From the above analysis, Equations (5)–(7) give the solution steps to obtain a particular solution, and Equations (8) and (9) give the solution steps to obtain a set of linearly independent homogeneous solutions. Thus, any solution vector of the given $(n-k)$ linearly independent equations of n variables can be represented with a linear combination of homogeneous and particular solutions as Equation (10). In addition, Equations (11) and (12) give the solution steps to recover the missing $(n-k)$ entries of a solution vector from k available entries; Equations (13)–(15) give a one-to-one mapping between a solution vector and the coefficients of the linear combination. Based on this model, suppose coefficients $(m_1, m_2, \cdots, m_k)$ are the secret, we can produce a vector $(x_1, x_2, \cdots, x_n)^T$, which includes n secret shares, using Equation (13). When k shares among n are available, we can restore the remaining shares and calculate the secret from the restored complete set of shares.

2.2. (k, n). -Threshold Secret Sharing Scheme Based on the Non-Full Rank Linear Model

A general scheme for (k, n) threshold secret sharing based on a non-full rank linear model is proposed in this section. It is divided into three phases: the setup, the share generation, and the secret extraction with authentication.

2.2.1. Setup

The scenario is that a dealer embeds secret data S into n shares $X_1, X_2, \cdots, X_n$ and distributes them to n participants. To recover secret data, at least k participants should cooperate by providing their shares. The dealer first selects $(n-k)$ linearly independent equations with n variables over the field z_p as

$$\pi_i : a_{i,1}x_1 + a_{i,2}x_2 + \cdots + a_{i,n}x_n = b_i \bmod p, \ i = 1, 2, \cdots, n-k. \quad (16)$$

Then, a set of linearly independent homogeneous solutions $\{\alpha_1, \alpha_2, \cdots, \alpha_k\}$ and a particular solution β can be obtained by applying Equations (5)–(9).

2.2.2. Share Generation

The secret data S to be shared is divided into l secret segments of k entries denoted by $m_j = (m_{j,1}, m_{j,2}, \cdots, m_{j,k})$, where $m_{j,r}(1 \leq r \leq k) \in z_p$, $1 \leq j \leq l$. For each secret message segment m_j, a solution vector x_j can be generated by

$$x_j = F(m_j) = (m_{j,1} + \gamma_{j,1})\alpha_1 + (m_{j,2} + \gamma_{j,2})\alpha_2 + \cdots + (m_{j,k} + \gamma_{j,k})\alpha_k + \beta \bmod p, \quad (17)$$

where $\gamma_{j,r}(1 \leq r \leq k)$ is a series of integers over z_p generated by a pre-shared data hiding key. This integer series encrypt each secret entry by adding a random offset. By rearranging the collection of synthesized vectors x_j $(1 \leq j \leq l)$, the dealer generates n secret shares as

$$X_i = (x_1(i), x_2(i), \cdots, x_l(i))^T, 1 \leq i \leq n, \quad (18)$$

where $x_j(i)$ denotes the i-th entry of the j-th synthesized vector x_j. Finally, these shares are distributed to the n participants.

2.2.3. Secret Extraction with Authentication

Suppose k faithful participants provide their shares as $X_1, X_2, \cdots, X_k$. The combiner first rearranges the k shares into l vectors as

$$x'_j = (x'_j(1), x'_j(2), \cdots, x'_j(k))^T, 1 \leq j \leq l, \quad (19)$$

where $x'_j(i)$ denotes the j-th entry of the i-th share. Then, the vector x'_j with missing entries can be restored into the complete solution x_j by using Equations (11) and (12).

To extract secret data, the combiner first reproduces the random sequence $\gamma_{j,r}(1 \le r \le k)$ by the shared data hiding key. Then, the secret segments $m_j(1 \le j \le l)$ can be extracted by substituting the complete solution vectors $x_j(1 \le j \le l)$ back into Equation (17), as

$$\begin{pmatrix} x_j(1) \\ x_j(2) \\ \vdots \\ x_j(n-k) \\ \vdots \\ \vdots \\ x_j(n) \end{pmatrix} = (m_{j,1} + \gamma_{j,1}) \begin{pmatrix} \alpha_{1,1} \\ \alpha_{1,2} \\ \vdots \\ \alpha_{1,n-k} \\ 1 \\ 0 \\ \vdots \\ 0 \end{pmatrix} + \cdots + (m_{j,k} + \gamma_{j,k}) \begin{pmatrix} \alpha_{k,1} \\ \alpha_{k,2} \\ \vdots \\ \alpha_{k,n-k} \\ 0 \\ 0 \\ \vdots \\ 1 \end{pmatrix} + \begin{pmatrix} \beta_1 \\ \beta_2 \\ \vdots \\ \beta_{n-k} \\ 0 \\ 0 \\ \vdots \\ 0 \end{pmatrix} \mod p. \quad (20)$$

By expanding the last k rows, we can get the secret segments

$$\begin{cases} m_{j,1} = x_j(n-k+1) - \gamma_{j,1} \\ m_{j,2} = x_j(n-k+2) - \gamma_{j,2} \\ \quad \vdots \\ m_{j,k} = x_j(n) - \gamma_{j,k} \end{cases}. \quad (21)$$

When additional doubtful shares are available, they can be authenticated by using the restored missing entries based on the trustworthy shares.

2.3. Demonstration

Let us assume $k = 2$, $n = 4$, and $p = 5$. That is, we are going to demonstrate a (2,4)-threshold secret sharing scheme. The dealer selects two linearly independent equations with four variables, as

$$\begin{aligned} \pi_1 &: 1x_1 + 3x_2 + 1x_3 + 2x_4 = 1 \mod 5, \\ \pi_2 &: 2x_1 + 4x_2 + 0x_3 + 1x_4 = 3 \mod 5. \end{aligned} \quad (22)$$

That is, $A = \begin{pmatrix} 1 & 3 & 1 & 2 \\ 2 & 4 & 0 & 1 \end{pmatrix}$ and $b = \begin{pmatrix} 1 \\ 3 \end{pmatrix}$.

2.3.1. Particular and Homogeneous Solutions

Manipulate the augmented matrix with elementary row operations (see Appendix A) over the field Z_p to obtain a row simplest augmented matrix as

$$(A|b) = \begin{pmatrix} 1 & 3 & 1 & 2 & | & 1 \\ 2 & 4 & 0 & 1 & | & 3 \end{pmatrix} \xrightarrow{R_2 = R_2 + 3R_1} \begin{pmatrix} 1 & 3 & 1 & 2 & | & 1 \\ 0 & 3 & 3 & 2 & | & 1 \end{pmatrix}$$
$$\xrightarrow{R_2 = 2R_2} \begin{pmatrix} 1 & 3 & 1 & 2 & | & 1 \\ 0 & 1 & 1 & 4 & | & 2 \end{pmatrix} \xrightarrow{R_1 = R_1 + 2R_2} \begin{pmatrix} 1 & 0 & 3 & 0 & | & 0 \\ 0 & 1 & 1 & 4 & | & 2 \end{pmatrix}. \quad (23)$$

Then, by applying Equation (7), we can get a particular solution $\beta = (0,2,0,0)^T$. By applying Equations (8) and (9), we can get a set of linearly independent homogeneous solutions

$$\alpha_1 = (-3 \mod 5, -1 \mod 5, 1, 0) = (2,4,1,0), \quad (24)$$

$$\alpha_2 = (-0 \mod 5, -4 \mod 5, 0, 1) = (0,1,0,1). \quad (25)$$

2.3.2. Share Generation

For each secret segment $m_j = (m_{j,1}, m_{j,2})$, the solution vector x_j can be generated by

$$x_j = (m_{j,1} + \gamma_{j,1})\alpha_1 + (m_{j,2} + \gamma_{j,2})\alpha_2 + \beta \mod 5. \quad (26)$$

Let the secret data be $m_1 = (4,0)$, $m_2 = (1,1)$, $m_3 = (4,2)$, and the random integer series generated by the data hiding key be $(\gamma_{1,1}, \gamma_{1,2}) = (3, 2)$, $(\gamma_{2,1}, \gamma_{2,2}) = (4, 2)$, $(\gamma_{3,1}, \gamma_{3,2}) = (2, 3)$, then the generated vectors are

$$x_1 = \begin{pmatrix} x_1(1) \\ x_1(2) \\ x_1(3) \\ x_1(4) \end{pmatrix} = (4+3)\begin{pmatrix} 2 \\ 4 \\ 1 \\ 0 \end{pmatrix} + (0+2)\begin{pmatrix} 0 \\ 1 \\ 0 \\ 1 \end{pmatrix} + \begin{pmatrix} 0 \\ 2 \\ 0 \\ 0 \end{pmatrix} = \begin{pmatrix} 4 \\ 2 \\ 2 \\ 2 \end{pmatrix}, \quad (27)$$

$$x_2 = \begin{pmatrix} x_2(1) \\ x_2(2) \\ x_2(3) \\ x_2(4) \end{pmatrix} = (1+4)\begin{pmatrix} 2 \\ 4 \\ 1 \\ 0 \end{pmatrix} + (1+2)\begin{pmatrix} 0 \\ 1 \\ 0 \\ 1 \end{pmatrix} + \begin{pmatrix} 0 \\ 2 \\ 0 \\ 0 \end{pmatrix} = \begin{pmatrix} 0 \\ 0 \\ 0 \\ 3 \end{pmatrix}, \quad (28)$$

$$x_3 = \begin{pmatrix} x_3(1) \\ x_3(2) \\ x_3(3) \\ x_3(4) \end{pmatrix} = (4+2)\begin{pmatrix} 2 \\ 4 \\ 1 \\ 0 \end{pmatrix} + (2+3)\begin{pmatrix} 0 \\ 1 \\ 0 \\ 1 \end{pmatrix} + \begin{pmatrix} 0 \\ 2 \\ 0 \\ 0 \end{pmatrix} = \begin{pmatrix} 2 \\ 1 \\ 1 \\ 0 \end{pmatrix}. \quad (29)$$

The dealer rearranges the vector entries into secret shares and distributes them to the participants.

$$X_1 = (4,\ 0,\ 2)^T, X_2 = (2,\ 0,\ 1)^T, X_3 = (2,\ 0,\ 1)^T, X_4 = (2,\ 3,\ 0)^T. \quad (30)$$

2.3.3. Authentication

At the combiner side, suppose that only shares $X_1 = (4,\ 0,\ 2)^T$ and $X_2 = (2,\ 0,\ 1)^T$ are trustworthy, while X_3 and X_4 are doubtful. The combiner can reproduce the remaining shares and restore the secret data by using the faithful ones. He/she first manipulates $(A|b)$ by using elementary row operations, so that the submatrix constituted by column 3 and 4 becomes an identity matrix as

$$(A|b) = \begin{pmatrix} 1 & 3 & 1 & 2 & | & 1 \\ 2 & 4 & 0 & 1 & | & 3 \end{pmatrix} \xrightarrow{R_1 = R_1 + 3R_2} \begin{pmatrix} 2 & 0 & 1 & 0 & | & 0 \\ 2 & 4 & 0 & 1 & | & 3 \end{pmatrix}. \quad (31)$$

Then, the combiner rearranges the available entries into $x'_1 = (4,2)^T$, $x'_2 = (0,0)^T$, and $x'_3 = (2,1)^T$. Finally, these vectors with missing entries are substituted into Equation (31) as

$$\begin{cases} x_1(3) = -2 \times 4 - 0 \times 2 + 0 \bmod 5 = 2 \\ x_1(4) = -2 \times 4 - 4 \times 2 + 3 \bmod 5 = 2 \end{cases}, \quad (32)$$

$$\begin{cases} x_2(3) = -2 \times 0 - 0 \times 0 + 0 \bmod 5 = 0 \\ x_2(4) = -2 \times 0 - 4 \times 0 + 3 \bmod 5 = 3 \end{cases}, \quad (33)$$

$$\begin{cases} x_3(3) = -2 \times 2 - 0 \times 1 + 0 \bmod 5 = 1 \\ x_3(4) = -2 \times 2 - 4 \times 1 + 3 \bmod 5 = 0 \end{cases}. \quad (34)$$

Therefore, the complete solution vectors are $x_1 = (4,2,2,2)^T$, $x_2 = (0,0,0,3)^T$, $x_3 = (2,1,1,0)^T$, and the remaining shares should be $X_3 = (2,\ 0,\ 1)^T$, $X_4 = (2,\ 3,\ 0)^T$. If a share provided by a suspicious participant does not match the result, then he/she is a cheater.

2.3.4. Secret Recovery

To restore secret data, the combiner first manipulates the given linear equations to obtain the particular and homogeneous solutions as the share generation phase. Thus, the solution vectors should be

$$x_j = (m_{j,1} + \gamma_{j,1}) \begin{pmatrix} 2 \\ 4 \\ 1 \\ 0 \end{pmatrix} + (m_{j,2} + \gamma_{j,2}) \begin{pmatrix} 0 \\ 1 \\ 0 \\ 1 \end{pmatrix} + \begin{pmatrix} 0 \\ 2 \\ 0 \\ 0 \end{pmatrix} \bmod 5. \tag{35}$$

Therefore, the secret segments can be obtained by substituting the restored shares X_3, X_4 and the integer series $\gamma_{j,r}, 1 \leq j \leq 2, 1 \leq r \leq 2$, generated by the shared data hiding key into the last two rows of Equation (35), as

$$\begin{cases} m_{1,1} + \gamma_{1,1} = x_1(3) \\ m_{1,2} + \gamma_{1,2} = x_1(4) \end{cases} \rightarrow \begin{cases} m_{1,1} = x_1(3) - \gamma_{1,1} \bmod 5 = 2 - 3 \bmod 5 = 4 \\ m_{1,2} = x_1(4) - \gamma_{1,2} \bmod 5 = 2 - 2 \bmod 5 = 0 \end{cases}. \tag{36}$$

$$\begin{cases} m_{2,1} = x_2(3) - \gamma_{2,1} \bmod 5 = 0 - 4 \bmod 5 = 1 \\ m_{2,2} = x_2(4) - \gamma_{2,2} \bmod 5 = 3 - 2 \bmod 5 = 1 \end{cases}. \tag{37}$$

$$\begin{cases} m_{3,1} = x_3(3) - \gamma_{3,1} \bmod 5 = 1 - 2 \bmod 5 = 4 \\ m_{3,2} = x_3(4) - \gamma_{3,2} \bmod 5 = 0 - 3 \bmod 5 = 2 \end{cases} \tag{38}$$

The recovered secret segments are $m_1 = (4,0), m_2 = (1,1), m_3 = (4,2)$, which are the same as embedded.

3. (k, n)-Threshold Secret Image Sharing Scheme Based on Linear Model

In this section, the (k, n)-threshold secret sharing scheme discussed above is applied to the platform of digital image transmission. By using the proposed secret sharing scheme, we can hide secret data in three distinct meaningful images and produce three shadows with imperceptible changes. While the shadow images are transmitted to n different participants, the secret data can be recovered only if more than k participants share their shadows. We present our scheme with the following subsections: system overview, setup, shadow image generation, secret data extraction with authentication, and a demonstration.

3.1. System Overview

The flowchart of the proposed scheme is shown in Figure 1. In the proposed scheme, secret data S are converted into a sequence of p-ary digits first. Then, this sequence is divided into segments denoted by $S = \left\{ m_j \middle| m_j = (m_{j,1}, m_{j,2}, \cdots, m_{j,k})^T \in z_p^k, j = 1, 2, \cdots, l \right\}$, where l is the total number of secret segments. We randomly choose n distinct meaningful cover images $I_1, I_2, \ldots, I_n$ with size $w \times h > l$. A vector sequence is produced from the cover images and denoted by $I_{vec} = \left\{ y_j \middle| y_j = (y_j(1), y_j(2), \ldots, y_j(n))^T, j = 1, 2, \cdots, w \times h \right\}$, where each vector y_j is a collection of n pixel values retrieved from corresponding positions of the n images. To embed secret data, we apply the proposed (k, n)-threshold secret sharing scheme to generate a vector $x_j = (x_j(1), x_j(2), \ldots x_j(n))^T$ of n digits using a secret segment m_j of k digits. After all secret segments are converted, the resulting vector sequence $X = \{x_j | j = 1, 2, \cdots, l\}$, is applied to modulate $I_{vec} = \{y_j | j = 1, 2, \cdots, w \times h\}$ and obtain the sequence $\hat{I}_{vec} = \{\hat{y}_j | j = 1, 2, \cdots, w \times h\}$, correspondingly. Finally, the secret image shadows are generated by distributing the modulated sequence back into n meaningful images $\hat{I}_1, \hat{I}_2, \ldots, \hat{I}_n$ sized $w \times h$. In the secret data recovery phase, at least k trustworthy shadows should be available. These k shadows are rearranged into a vector sequence with missing entries $\hat{I}'_{vec} = \left\{ \hat{y}'_j \middle| \hat{y}'_j = (\hat{y}'_j(1), \hat{y}'_j(2), \ldots, \hat{y}'_j(k))^T, j = 1, 2, \cdots, w \times h \right\}$. Then, a sequence of vectors with missing entries $\hat{X}' = \left\{ \hat{x}'_j \middle| \hat{x}'_j = (\hat{x}'_j(1), \hat{x}'_j(2), \ldots, \hat{x}'_j(k))^T, j = 1, 2, \cdots, l \right\}$ are demodulated. The missing entries can be recovered by using Equations (11) and (12). If there are suspicious participants, the one who provides a share that mismatches the reproduced shadow is a cheater. Finally, the secret data can be recovered using Equations (20) and (21).

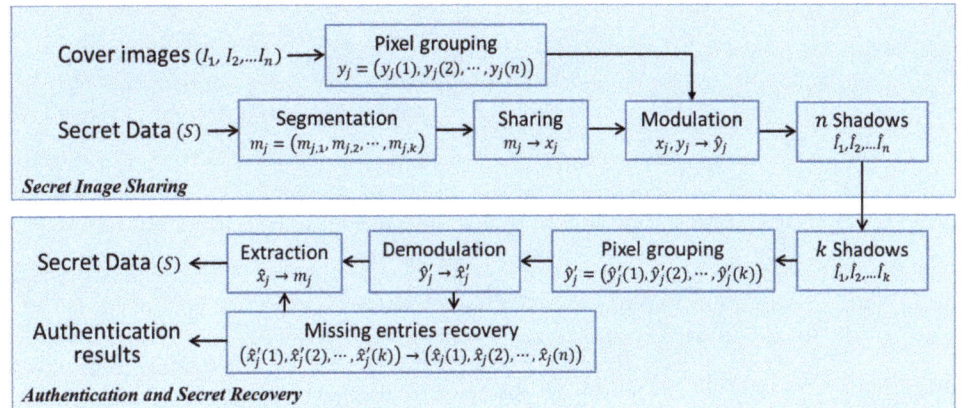

Figure 1. Flowchart of the proposed scheme.

3.2. Setup

The dealer decides the number of the participants n, the threshold k, and the prime number p. He/she selects $(n-k)$ linearly independent equations of n variables over the field z_p

$$\pi_i : a_{i,1}x_1 + a_{i,2}x_2 + \cdots + a_{i,n}x_n = 0 \bmod p, \text{ where } i = 1, 2, \cdots, (n-k). \quad (39)$$

We can rewrite them in matrix form as

$$Ax = b \bmod p. \quad (40)$$

Find a set of linearly independent homogeneous solutions $\{\alpha_1, \alpha_2, \cdots, \alpha_k\}$ and a particular solution β by applying Equations (5)–(9).

3.3. Shadow Image Generation

Let us assume that the secret data to be embedded are denoted as S and the n distinct meaningful cover images with size $w \times h$ are denoted as $I_1, I_2, \cdots, I_n$. The shadow images can be generated by the following steps.

Step 1. Rearrange the cover images $I_1, I_2, \cdots, I_n$ into vector sequence as

$$I_{vec} = \left\{ y_j \middle| y_j = (y_j(1), y_j(2), \ldots y_j(n))^T, j = 1, 2, \cdots, w \times h \right\}. \quad (41)$$

Step 2. Convert the secret data stream S into a sequence of p-ary digits and divide them into segments denoted by $S = \left\{ m_j \middle| m_j = \left(m_{j,1}, m_{j,2}, \cdots, m_{j,k} \right)^T \in z_p^k, j = 1, 2, \cdots, l \right\}$, where $l \leq w \times h$ is the total number of secret segments.

Step 3. Apply $m_j = (m_{j,1}, m_{j,2}, \cdots, m_{j,k})^T, j = 1, 2, \cdots, l$ to generate vectors $x_j = (x_j(1), x_j(2), \ldots x_j(n))^T, j = 1, 2, \cdots, l$ using Equation (17). Compute the residual vectors of I_{vec} by

$$\overline{x}_j = (\overline{x}_j(1), \overline{x}_j(2), \ldots \overline{x}_j(n))^T (y_j(1), y_j(2), \ldots y_j(n))^T \bmod p, \text{ where } j = 1, 2, \cdots, l. \quad (42)$$

by Compute the stego vector sequence $\hat{I}_{vec} = \left\{\hat{y}_j \middle| \hat{y}_j = (\hat{y}_j(1), \hat{y}_j(2), \ldots, \hat{y}_j(n))^T, j = 1, 2, \cdots, l\right\}$

$$\hat{y}_j(i) = \begin{cases} y_j(i) + [(x_j(i) - \bar{x}_j(i)) \bmod p], & \text{if } (x_j(i) - \bar{x}_j(i)) \bmod p < p/2, \\ y_j(i) - [(\bar{x}_j(i) - x_j(i)) \bmod p], & \text{otherwise.} \end{cases} \quad (43)$$

When overflow/underflow is encountered, do

$$\hat{y}_j(i) = \begin{cases} \hat{y}_j(i) + p, & \text{if } \hat{y}_j(i) < 0, \\ \hat{y}_j(i) - p, & \text{if } \hat{y}_j(i) > 255. \end{cases} \quad (44)$$

Append the rest of the unmodulated vectors $y_j, j = l+1, l+2, \cdots, w \times h$ to constitute $\hat{I}_{vec} = \{\hat{y}_j | j = 1, 2, \cdots, w \times h\}$.

Step 4. Distribute the modulated sequence $\hat{I}_{vec} = \{\hat{y}_j | j = 1, 2, \cdots, w \times h\}$ back into n meaningful shadow images $\hat{I}_1, \hat{I}_2, \ldots, \hat{I}_n$ sized $w \times h$.

3.4. Secret Data Extraction with Authentication

Suppose the n meaningful shadow images $\hat{I}_1, \hat{I}_2, \ldots, \hat{I}_n$ sized $w \times h$ are transmitted to n participants and now k faithful participants provide their shadow images to a combiner. The combiner can recover secret data and authenticate the rest shadows by the following steps. Without loss of generality, let us suppose that the k trustworthy shadows are $\hat{I}_1, \hat{I}_2, \ldots, \hat{I}_k$.

Step 1. Convert k shadow images $\hat{I}_1, \hat{I}_2, \ldots, \hat{I}_k$ into vectors of k-tuples as

$$\hat{I}'_{vec} = \left\{\hat{y}'_j \middle| \hat{y}'_j = (\hat{y}'_j(1), \hat{y}'_j(2), \ldots, \hat{y}'_j(k))^T, j = 1, 2, \cdots, w \times h\right\}. \quad (45)$$

Step 2. Compute the residual vectors

$$\hat{x}'_j = \left(\hat{y}'_j(1), \hat{y}'_j(2), \ldots, \hat{y}'_j(k)\right)^T \bmod p, \text{ where } j = 1, 2, \cdots, l. \quad (46)$$

Step 3. Substitute each vector $\hat{x}'_j = \left(\hat{x}'_j(1), \hat{x}'_j(2), \ldots, \hat{x}'_j(k)\right)^T$ into Equations (11) and (12), the missing entries can be recovered to obtain its corresponding complete solution vector $\hat{x}_j = (\hat{x}_j(1), \hat{x}_j(2), \ldots, \hat{x}_j(n))^T$.

Step 4. Convert a doubtful shadow $\hat{I}_r$ into sequence $\hat{y}^*_j(r), j = 1, 2, \ldots, w \times h$. Then, compute its residual sequence $\hat{x}^*_j(r), j = 1, 2, \ldots, l$. If $\hat{x}^*_j(r) = \hat{x}_j(r), j = 1, 2, \ldots, l$, the authentication is passed; else, it is a tampered shadow.

Step 5. Extract the secret data by applying $\hat{x}_j = (\hat{x}_j(n-k+1), \ldots, \hat{x}_j(n))^T$, $j = 1, 2, \ldots, l$ to Equation (21).

3.5. Demonstration

We use the example model given in Section 2.3 to demonstrate how the proposed secret sharing scheme can be applied to image transmission applications. That is, $k = 2$, $n = 4$, $p = 5$, and the two linearly independent equations with four variables are

$$\pi_1 : x_1 + 3x_2 + x_3 + 2x_4 = 1 \bmod 5 \text{ and } \pi_2 : 2x_1 + 4x_2 + 0x_3 + x_4 = 3 \bmod 5. \quad (47)$$

As analyzed in Section 2.3.1, $\alpha_1 = (2, 4, 1, 0)^T$ and $\alpha_2 = (0, 1, 0, 1)^T$ are two linearly independent homogeneous solutions, and $\beta = (0, 2, 0, 0)^T$ is a particular solution.

Assume that $m_1 = (2, 1)$ and $m_2 = (3, 0)$ are two 5-ary secret segments, and the four cover images are $I_1 = (135, 136)$, $I_2 = (161, 162)$, $I_3 = (201, 200)$, and $I_4 = (55, 58)$. Two random segments $\gamma_1 = (4, 0)$ and $\gamma_2 = (1, 2)$ are generated by the data hiding key.

For the secret segments m_1 and m_2, we generate their corresponding solution vectors by using Equation (17) and obtain

$$x_1 = F(m_1) = (2+4)\begin{pmatrix}2\\4\\1\\0\end{pmatrix} + (1+0)\begin{pmatrix}0\\1\\0\\1\end{pmatrix} + \begin{pmatrix}0\\2\\0\\0\end{pmatrix} = \begin{pmatrix}2\\2\\1\\1\end{pmatrix}, \quad (48)$$

$$x_2 = F(m_2) = (3+1)\begin{pmatrix}2\\4\\1\\0\end{pmatrix} + (0+2)\begin{pmatrix}0\\1\\0\\1\end{pmatrix} + \begin{pmatrix}0\\2\\0\\0\end{pmatrix} = \begin{pmatrix}3\\0\\4\\2\end{pmatrix}. \quad (49)$$

The residual vectors are

$$\bar{x}_1 = (135, 161, 201, 55)^T \bmod 5 = (0, 1, 1, 0)^T, \quad (50)$$

$$\bar{x}_2 = (136, 162, 200, 58)^T \bmod 5 = (1, 2, 0, 3)^T. \quad (51)$$

Then, the stego vectors are

$$\hat{y}_1 = \begin{pmatrix}135 + (2-0)\bmod 5\\161 + (2-1)\bmod 5\\201 + (1-1)\bmod 5\\55 + (1-0)\bmod 5\end{pmatrix} = \begin{pmatrix}137\\162\\201\\56\end{pmatrix}, \hat{y}_2 = \begin{pmatrix}136 + (3-1)\bmod 5\\162 - (2-0)\bmod 5\\200 - (0-4)\bmod 5\\58 - (3-2)\bmod 5\end{pmatrix} = \begin{pmatrix}138\\160\\199\\57\end{pmatrix}. \quad (52)$$

Finally, the four shadow images are

$$\hat{I}_1 = (137, 138), \hat{I}_2 = (162, 160), \hat{I}_3 = (201, 199), \hat{I}_4 = (56, 57). \quad (53)$$

The shares $\hat{I}_1, \hat{I}_2, \hat{I}_3, \hat{I}_4$ are distributed to the four participants, respectively.

If a combiner obtains trustworthy shadow images $\hat{I}_1 = (137, 138)$ and $\hat{I}_2 = (162, 160)$, he/she first calculates the residual vectors as

$$\hat{x}'_1 = (137, 162)^T \bmod 5 = (2, 2)^T, \hat{x}'_2 = (138, 160)^T \bmod 5 = (3, 0)^T. \quad (54)$$

Then, the missing entries can be recovered using Equations (11,12). For the current case, manipulations are demonstrated in Equation (31) as

$$\begin{cases} x_1(3) = -2 \times 2 - 0 \times 2 + 0 \bmod 5 = 1 \\ x_1(4) = -2 \times 2 - 4 \times 2 + 3 \bmod 5 = 1 \end{cases}. \quad (55)$$

$$\begin{cases} x_2(3) = -2 \times 3 - 0 \times 0 + 0 \bmod 5 = 4 \\ x_2(4) = -2 \times 3 - 4 \times 0 + 3 \bmod 5 = 2 \end{cases}. \quad (56)$$

To extract secret data, the random segments $\gamma_1 = (4, 0)$ and $\gamma_2 = (1, 2)$ are generated by the shared data hiding key first. The secret data can be extracted using Equation (21) as

$$m_1 = (1 - 4, 1 - 0) = (2, 1), m_2 = (4 - 1, 2 - 2) = (3, 0). \quad (57)$$

4. Experimental Results and Discussions

In this section, we use two secret image sharing schemes with different combinations of (k, n) values to demonstrate the applicability of the proposed approach. Performance evaluation based on the embedding capacity and the visual quality of image shadows are given. The security level of the proposed scheme is also analyzed.

4.1. Demonstration of Applicability

In this subsection, we implement a (2,4)-threshold and a (3,5)-threshold secret image sharing schemes to verify the applicability and the generalizability of the proposed approach.

4.1.1. (2,4)-Threshold Secret Image Sharing Scheme

In our first implementation, the parameter settings are $k = 2$, $n = 4$, $p = 5$, and the two linearly independent equations given in Equation (47) are applied. The secret data are assumed to be a secret image, as shown in Figure 2a, which is a grayscale image sized 384×384. The four distinct cover images are shown in Figure 2b–e, which are all grayscale images sized 512×512. All pixel values in our experiments are recorded in eight bits.

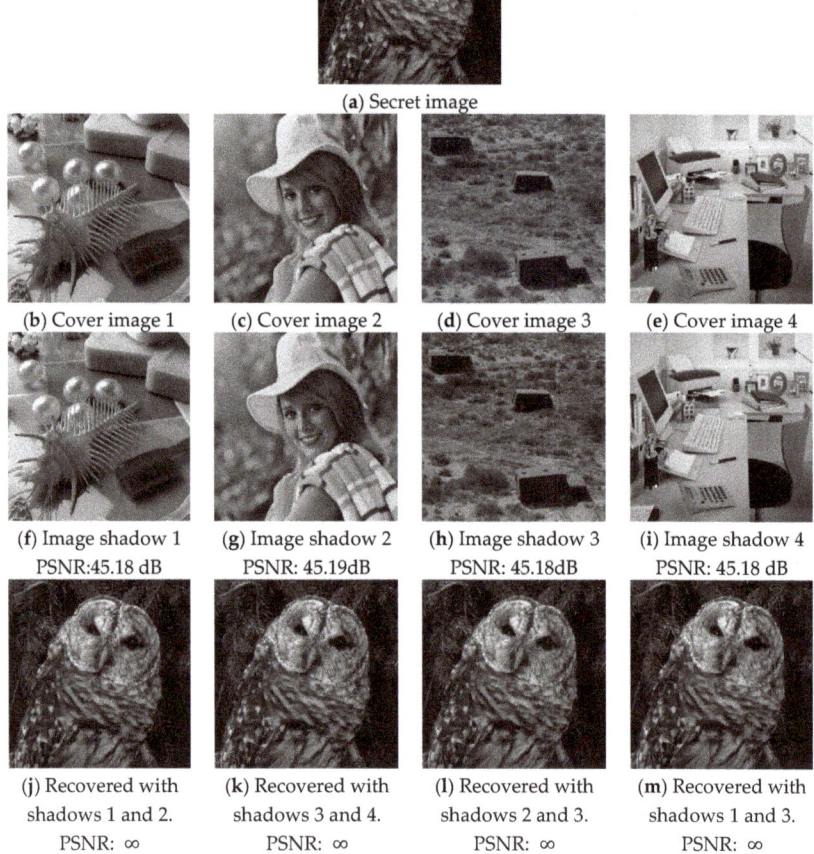

(a) Secret image

(b) Cover image 1   (c) Cover image 2   (d) Cover image 3   (e) Cover image 4

(f) Image shadow 1   (g) Image shadow 2   (h) Image shadow 3   (i) Image shadow 4
PSNR: 45.18 dB   PSNR: 45.19dB   PSNR: 45.18dB   PSNR: 45.18 dB

(j) Recovered with   (k) Recovered with   (l) Recovered with   (m) Recovered with
shadows 1 and 2.   shadows 3 and 4.   shadows 2 and 3.   shadows 1 and 3.
PSNR: ∞   PSNR: ∞   PSNR: ∞   PSNR: ∞

Figure 2. The experimental results of the (2,4)-threshold secret image sharing.

To fit the parameter settings, the pixels of the secret image are divided into groups of four pixels each. Thirty-two bits of each pixel group are converted into fourteen 5-ary digits and then grouped into seven secret segments of two digits. Each secret segment is applied to generate a solution vector of four entries and used to modulate four cover pixels. Therefore, four pixel-values of the secret image are distributed in fourteen pixels for each cover image. The generated image shadows are shown in Figure 2f–i. The changes with respect to their corresponding cover images are imperceptible. The peak-signal-to-noise-ratio (PSNR) given below the figures is defined by

$$\text{PSNR} = 10 \, \log_{10}(\frac{255^2}{e_{mse}}) \, (\text{dB}), \tag{58}$$

where e_{mse} denotes the mean-square-error between the cover image I_j and the shadow image $\hat{I}_j$ defined by

$$e_{mse} = \frac{1}{w \times h} \sum_{j=1}^{w \times h} (\hat{I}_j - I_j)^2. \tag{59}$$

The recovered secret images by using different combinations of image shadow pairs are given in Figure 2j–m. In all cases, the secret image can be perfectly recovered.

4.1.2. (3,5)-Threshold Secret Image Sharing Scheme

In our second implementation, the parameter settings are $k = 3$, $n = 5$, and $p = 5$, and the two linearly independent equations are given by

$$\pi_1 : 2x_1 + 2x_2 + x_3 + 3x_4 + x_5 = 1 \bmod 5. \pi_2 : 3x_1 + 4x_2 + 3x_3 + 4x_4 + x_5 = 3 \bmod 5. \tag{60}$$

The solution space H of π_1 and π_2 over z_5 is formulated as

$$H = c_1 \begin{pmatrix} 1 \\ 0 \\ 0 \\ 4 \\ 1 \end{pmatrix} + c_2 \begin{pmatrix} 0 \\ 1 \\ 0 \\ 3 \\ 4 \end{pmatrix} + c_3 \begin{pmatrix} 0 \\ 0 \\ 1 \\ 3 \\ 0 \end{pmatrix} + \begin{pmatrix} 1 \\ 1 \\ 1 \\ 2 \\ 0 \end{pmatrix} \bmod 5, \tag{61}$$

where $c_1, c_2, c_3 \in z_5$. Then, solution vector generation function is given by

$$x_j = F(m_j) = (m_{j,1} + \gamma_{j,1}) \begin{pmatrix} 1 \\ 0 \\ 0 \\ 4 \\ 1 \end{pmatrix} + (m_{j,2} + \gamma_{j,2}) \begin{pmatrix} 0 \\ 1 \\ 0 \\ 3 \\ 4 \end{pmatrix} + (m_{j,3} + \gamma_{j,3}) \begin{pmatrix} 0 \\ 0 \\ 1 \\ 3 \\ 0 \end{pmatrix} + \begin{pmatrix} 1 \\ 1 \\ 1 \\ 2 \\ 0 \end{pmatrix} \bmod p. \tag{62}$$

The secret image sized 512×438 is given in Figure 3a; the five distinct cover images sized 512×512 are given in Figure 3b–f. To fit the parameter settings, pixels of the secret image are divided into groups of six pixels each. Forty-eight bits of each pixel group are converted into twenty-one 5-ary digits, and then grouped into seven secret segments of three digits. Each secret segment is applied to generate a solution vector of five entries and is used to modulate five cover pixels. Therefore, six pixel-values of the secret image are distributed in thirty-five pixels for each cover image. The generated image shadows are shown in Figure 3g–k. The changes with respect to their corresponding cover images are again imperceptible. The recovered secret images using different combinations of image shadows are given in Figure 3l–p. In all cases, the secret image can be perfectly recovered.

4.2. Performance Evaluation

In our (k, n) threshold secret image sharing scheme, k digits of p-ary numbers are embedded in n pixels of each image shadow. The embedding capacity (EC) can therefore be measured in bits per pixel (bpp) of an image shadow by

$$EC = \log_2 p^k \text{ (bpp)}. \tag{63}$$

When the total number of shares n increases, the total amount of image shadows to be transmitted also increases. However, an increase in the number of shares can improve the flexibility of secret recovery. Recall that any k shares among the n shadows can perfectly recover the secret.

For each cover pixel, Equation (43) always modulates the pixel value with an integer deviation within the range of $[-(p-1)/2 : (p-1)/2]$. Suppose the deviation value is randomly distributed, the mean-square-error e_{mse} of modulation distortion can be estimated by

$$e_{mse} = \frac{1}{p} \sum_{d=-(p-1)/2}^{(p-1)/2} d^2 = \frac{(p-1)(p+1)}{12}. \quad (64)$$

Figure 3. The experimental results of the (3,5)-threshold secret image sharing.

When the pixels of a cover image are not fully exploited to embed secret data, we define the payload ratio as

$$r = \frac{N_e}{N_t}, \quad (65)$$

where N_e and N_t denote the number of pixels exploited and the number of total pixels, respectively. For the two schemes implemented in Section 4.1, the payload ratios can be calculated by

$$r_{(2,4)} = [(384 \times 384)/4(\text{groups}) \times (7 \times 4)(\text{pixels}/\text{group})]/(512 \times 512 \times 4) = 0.9844, \quad (66)$$

$$r_{(3,5)} = [(512 \times 438)/6(\text{groups}) \times (7 \times 5)(\text{pixels}/\text{group})]/(512 \times 512 \times 5) = 0.9980. \quad (67)$$

Under the payload ratio r, the mean-square-error e_{mse} is proportionally corrected to $r \times e_{mse}$. Thus, the expected PNSR value of an image shadow with a payload ratio r is given by

$$\text{PSNR}(r) = 10 \log_{10}\left(\frac{255^2}{r \times e_{mse}}\right) = 10 \log_{10}\left(\frac{12 \times 255^2}{r(p-1)(p+1)}\right) (\text{dB}). \qquad (68)$$

The expected PSNR values with respect to different payload ratios and prime numbers are listed in Table 1. The corresponding evolution curves are plotted in Figure 4, where the curves for four different prime numbers are given. According to the theoretic analysis, the expected PSNR values of the two implemented cases are 45.1889 dB and 45.1290 dB, respectively, which sharply coincide with our experimental values.

Table 1. The expected PSNR value (dB) with specific ratio, r.

					r					
p	0.1	0.2	0.3	0.4	0.5	0.6	0.7	0.8	0.9	1.0
3	59.89	56.88	55.12	53.87	52.90	52.11	51.44	50.86	50.35	49.89
5	55.12	52.11	50.35	49.10	48.13	47.348	46.67	46.09	45.58	45.12
7	52.11	49.10	47.34	46.09	45.12	44.33	43.66	43.08	42.57	42.11
11	48.13	45.12	43.36	42.11	41.14	40.35	39.68	39.10	38.59	38.13

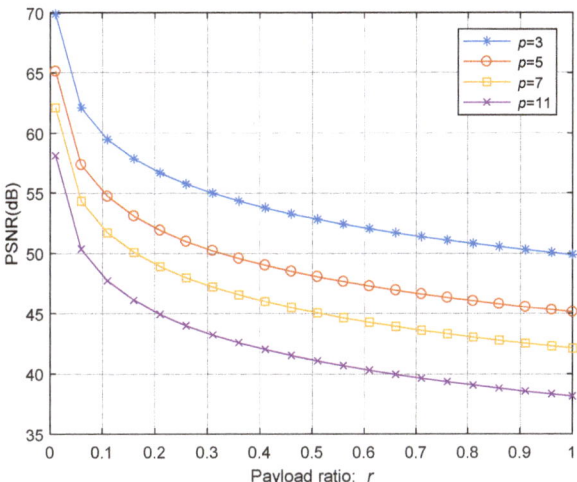

Figure 4. The expected PSNR value of an image shadow with respect to the payload ratio.

4.3. Security Analysis

Various steganalysis techniques [29–32] have been proposed to detect the existence of secret information in a digital image. The general idea of steganalysis is to detect the abnormal statistical feature of a doubtful image. However, there are various types of data hiding methods for images. To successfully detect the embedding of secret, special steganalysis techniques are devised to deal with each target steganography. For example, the RS steganalysis [29] is applied to detect the LSB substitution. For data hiding in encrypted images, people usually use pixel value entropy or gray level histogram to analyze the existence of a secret message.

The data hiding method of the proposed secret sharing scheme is essentially based on the modulus function. Two steganalysis tools, relative entropy [30] and pixel-value differencing [31,32], are suitable for testing the security level of our scheme. The first tool is the relative entropy proposed by Cachin [30]. To measure the difference between cover image I_c and image shadow I_s, we accumulate their probability distributions $P_c(x)$ and $P_s(x)$, respectively. Then, their relative entropy $D(I_c, I_s)$ is calculated by

$$D(I_c, I_s) = \sum_{x=0}^{255} P_c(x) \log_2 \left[\frac{P_c(x)}{P_s(x)} \right]. \tag{69}$$

If $D(I_c, I_s) \leq \varepsilon$, by definition, the data hiding scheme is ε-secure against passive attacking. A smaller value of ε means a better security level. We apply the relative entropy measure to our (3,5)-threshold secret image sharing scheme with $p = 5$. The experimental results are listed in Table 2, where the relative entropy values for half embedded and fully embedded cases are given. All values listed in the table are very close to zero, which implies the image shadows of the proposed scheme are robust under a passive attack.

Table 2. Relative entropy values under half embedded and fully embedded cases.

Cover Images	Half Embedded			Fully Embedded		
	$E(I_c)$	$E(I_s)$	$D(I_c,I_s)$	$E(I_c)$	$E(I_s)$	$D(I_c,I_s)$
Baboon	7.3579	7.3543	0.0049	7.3579	7.3415	0.0185
Boat	7.1914	7.2050	0.0052	7.1914	7.2129	0.0184
Lena	7.4455	7.4482	0.0007	7.4455	7.4510	0.0014
Peppers	7.5944	7.5978	0.0006	7.5944	7.5998	0.0021
Goldhill	7.4778	7.4839	0.0036	7.4778	7.4829	0.0058

The second steganalysis applied is the pixel-value differencing analysis [31,32]. The neighboring pixel-values of a natural image are highly continuous. The continuity is disrupted by most data hiding schemes. If the pixel-value differencing histogram (PDH) of an image is unusually flat, it is highly doubtful. To investigate the security level of the proposed scheme, we apply the PDH analysis to a set of five image shadows produced by our (3,5)-threshold secret image sharing scheme with $p = 5$. The secret image given in Figure 5a is embedded into five distinct cover images. The PDHs of the five pairs of cover images and their corresponding image shadows are plotted in Figure 5b–f. The PDH curves of image shadows are very close to their corresponding cover images, which indicates the proposed scheme is secure under PDH steganalysis.

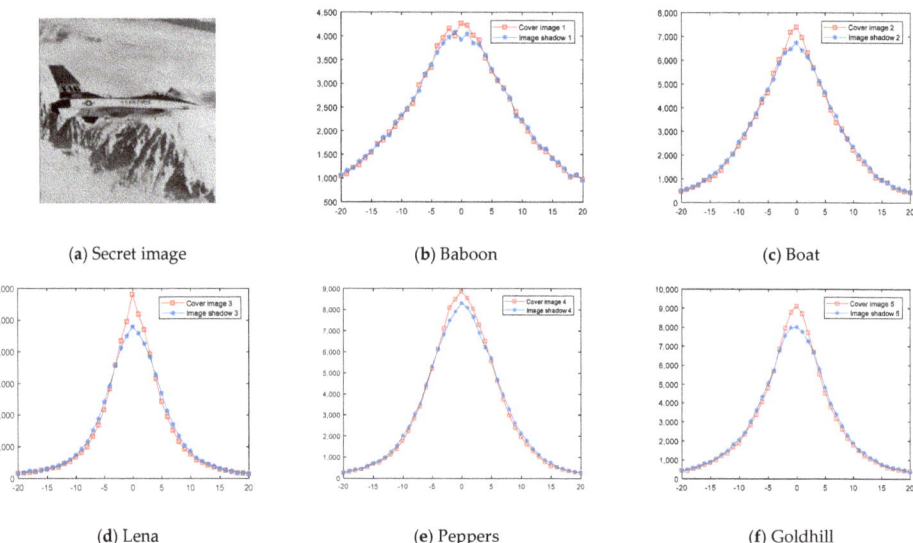

Figure 5. The PVD histogram analysis between the cover images and image shadows.

5. Conclusions

In this paper, we propose a general (k,n)-threshold secret image sharing scheme with meaningful image shadows. We first present a (k,n)-theshold secret sharing scheme based on a non-full rank linear model. It is then applied to the platform of image transmission system. Using n secret shares to modulate n distinct cover images, we can produce n image shadows. A combiner can completely recover the secret message by collecting at least k image shadows.

To demonstrate the applicability to any combination of (k,n) parameter values, we use two example models (2,4) and (3,5) to demonstrate our scheme. Experimental results confirm the applicability of the proposed scheme. Moreover, the embedding capacity and visual quality of image shadows are satisfactory. Embedding capacity and theoretic image quality under different parameter settings are also analyzed. Finally, we use two steganalysis tools to show the security level of our scheme.

The proposed scheme is based on the pixel-value modification in the spatial domain, which is suitable for digital images of a bitmap format. Our future work will focus on the implementation of the general secret sharing scheme to different cover media, such as JPEG images, encrypted images, and QR code images, which are more commonly applied in Internet applications.

Author Contributions: Conceptualization, J.-H.H. and C.-C.C.; methodology, S.-S.C.; software, S.-S.C.; validation, J.-H.H., S.-S.C. and C.-C.C.; formal analysis, S.-S.C. and J.-H.H.; investigation, S.-S.C.; resource, C.-C.C.; data curation, S.-S.C.; writing—original draft preparation, S.-S.C.; writing—review and editing, J.-H.H. and S.-S.C.; visualization, J.-H.H., S.-S.C. and C.-C.C.; supervision, C.-C.C.; project administration, C.-C.C.; funding acquisition, J.-H.H. All authors have read and agreed to the published version of the manuscript.

Funding: This research was funded by the Ministry of Science and Technology of Taiwan, grant number MOST 110-2221-E-507-003.

Data Availability Statement: Not applicable.

Conflicts of Interest: The authors declare no conflict of interest.

Appendix A

The elementary row operations over the field z_p include row switching, row multiplication, and row addition as in conventional linear algebra, except that each resulting integer number should be modulated by p as

$$\forall a, b \in z_p,\ a + ba + b \bmod p \forall a, b \in z_p,\ a \times ba \times b \bmod p \tag{A1}$$

For the addition operation, if $a, b \in z_p$ and $a + b = 0 \bmod p$, then $-a = b \bmod p$; for the multiplication operation, if $a, b \in z_p$ and $a \times b = 1 \bmod p$, then $a^{-1} = b \bmod p$. Next, we use the derivation of Equation (23) in Section 2.3.1 to demonstrate the details of the elementary row operations. The two linearly independent equations are

$$\pi_1 : 1x_1 + 3x_2 + 1x_3 + 2x_4 = 1 \bmod 5, \pi_2 : 2x_1 + 4x_2 + 0x_3 + 1x_4 = 3 \bmod 5. \tag{A2}$$

That is, $A = \begin{pmatrix} 1 & 3 & 1 & 2 \\ 2 & 4 & 0 & 1 \end{pmatrix}$ and $b = \begin{pmatrix} 1 \\ 3 \end{pmatrix}$. The corresponding augmented matrix is

$$(A|b) = \begin{pmatrix} 1 & 3 & 1 & 2 & | & 1 \\ 2 & 4 & 0 & 1 & | & 3 \end{pmatrix} \tag{A3}$$

To transfer the first two columns into an identity matrix, first multiply row 1 by 3 and add to row 2 as

$$\begin{pmatrix} 1 & 3 & 1 & 2 & | & 1 \\ 2 & 4 & 0 & 1 & | & 3 \end{pmatrix} \xrightarrow{R_2 = R_2 + 3R_1} \begin{pmatrix} 1 & 3 & 1 & 2 & | & 1 \\ 5 & 13 & 3 & 7 & | & 6 \end{pmatrix} \bmod 5 = \begin{pmatrix} 1 & 3 & 1 & 2 & | & 1 \\ 0 & 3 & 3 & 2 & | & 1 \end{pmatrix}, \tag{A4}$$

where $R_2 = R_2 + 3R_1$ above the operation arrow denotes the operation detail. Then, scale row 2 by 2 as

$$\begin{pmatrix} 1 & 3 & 1 & 2 & | & 1 \\ 0 & 3 & 3 & 2 & | & 1 \end{pmatrix} \xrightarrow{R_2 = 2R_2} \begin{pmatrix} 1 & 3 & 1 & 2 & | & 1 \\ 0 & 6 & 6 & 4 & | & 2 \end{pmatrix} \bmod 5 = \begin{pmatrix} 1 & 3 & 1 & 2 & | & 1 \\ 0 & 1 & 1 & 4 & | & 2 \end{pmatrix}. \tag{A5}$$

Finally, multiply row 2 by 2 and add to row 1 as

$$\begin{pmatrix} 1 & 3 & 1 & 2 & | & 1 \\ 0 & 1 & 1 & 4 & | & 2 \end{pmatrix} \xrightarrow{R_1 = R_1 + 2R_2} \begin{pmatrix} 1 & 5 & 3 & 10 & | & 5 \\ 0 & 1 & 1 & 4 & | & 2 \end{pmatrix} \bmod 5 = \begin{pmatrix} 1 & 0 & 3 & 0 & | & 0 \\ 0 & 1 & 1 & 4 & | & 2 \end{pmatrix}. \tag{A6}$$

Thus, the final row simplest augmented matrix over the field z_5 is

$$(A|b) \rightarrow \begin{pmatrix} 1 & 0 & 3 & 0 & | & 0 \\ 0 & 1 & 1 & 4 & | & 2 \end{pmatrix}. \tag{A7}$$

References

1. Pareek, N.K.; Patidar, V.; Sud, K.K. Image encryption using chaotic logistic map. *Image Vis. Comput.* **2006**, *24*, 926–934. [CrossRef]
2. Zhu, Z.L.; Zhang, W.; Wong, K.W.; Yu, H. A chaos-based symmetric image encryption scheme using a bit-level permutation. *Inf. Sci.* **2011**, *181*, 1171–1186. [CrossRef]
3. Chan, K.C.; Cheng, L.M. Hiding data in images by simple LSB substitution. *Pattern Recognit.* **2004**, *37*, 469–474. [CrossRef]
4. Zhang, X.; Wang, S. Efficient steganographic embedding by exploiting modification direction. *IEEE Commun. Lett.* **2006**, *10*, 781–783. [CrossRef]
5. Tian, J. Reversible data embedding using a difference expansion. *IEEE Trans. Circuits Syst. Video Technol.* **2003**, *13*, 890–896. [CrossRef]
6. Ni, Z.; Shi, Y.Q.; Ansari, N.; Su, W. Reversible data hiding. *IEEE Trans. Circuits Syst. Video Technol.* **2006**, *16*, 354–361. [CrossRef]
7. Chang, C.C. Neural Reversible steganography with long short-term memory. *Secur. Commun. Netw.* **2021**, *2021*, 5580272. [CrossRef]
8. Chang, C.C.; Li, C.T.; Shi, Y.Q. Privacy-Aware reversible watermarking in cloud computing environments. *IEEE Access* **2018**, *6*, 70720–70733. [CrossRef]
9. Naor, M.; Shamir, A. Visual cryptography. *Lect. Notes Comput. Sci.* **1995**, *950*, 1–12. [CrossRef]
10. Nakajima, M.; Yamaguchi, Y. Extended visual cryptography for natural images. *WSCG* **2002**, *10*, 303–310. [CrossRef]
11. Patil, S.; Rao, J. Extended visual cryptography for color shares using random number generators. *Int. J. Adv. Res. Comput. Commun. Eng.* **2012**, *1*, 399–410.
12. Blundo, C.; De Santis, A.; Naor, M. Visual cryptography for grey level images. *Inf. Process. Lett.* **2000**, *75*, 255–259. [CrossRef]
13. Liu, Z.; Zhu, G.; Wang, Y.G.; Yang, J.; Kwong, S. A Novel (t, s, k, n)-Threshold Visual Secret Sharing Scheme Based on Access Structure Partition. *ACM Trans. Multimed. Comput. Commun. Appl.* **2021**, *16*, 1–21. [CrossRef]
14. Ulutas, M.; Ulutas, G.; Nabiyev, V.V. Medical image security and EPR hiding using Shamir's secret sharing scheme. *J. Syst. Softw.* **2011**, *84*, 341–353. [CrossRef]
15. Charoghchi, S.; Mashhadi, S. Three (t,n)-secret image sharing schemes based on homogeneous linear recursion. *Inf. Sci.* **2021**, *552*, 220–243. [CrossRef]
16. Liu, Y.; Yang, C. Scalable secret image sharing scheme with essential shadows. *Signal Process. Image Commun.* **2017**, *58*, 49–55. [CrossRef]
17. Yan, X.; Li, J.; Pan, Z.; Zhong, X.; Yang, G. Multiparty verification in image secret sharing. *Inf. Sci.* **2021**, *562*, 475–490. [CrossRef]
18. Ding, W.; Liu, K.; Yan, X.; Liu, L. Polynomial-based secret image sharing scheme with fully lossless recovery. *Int. J. Digit. Crime Forensics* **2018**, *10*, 120–136. [CrossRef]
19. Liu, L.; Lu, Y.; Yan, X.; Ding, W.; Xuan, Q. A Lossless Polynomial-Based Secret Image Sharing Scheme Utilizing the Filtering Operation. *Adv. Intell. Syst. Comput.* **2020**, *895*, 129–139. [CrossRef]
20. Chang, C.-C.; Kieu, T.; Chou, Y.-C. Reversible data hiding scheme using two steganographic images. In Proceedings of the TENCON 2007–2007 IEEE Region 10 Conference, Taipei, Taiwan, 30 October–2 November 2007; pp. 1–4. [CrossRef]
21. Chen, S.; Chang, C.C. Reversible data hiding based on three shadow images using rhombus magic matrix. *J. Vis. Commun. Image Represent.* **2021**, *76*, 103064. [CrossRef]
22. Qin, C.; Chang, C.C.; Hsu, T.J. Reversible data hiding scheme based on exploiting modification direction with two steganographic images. *Multimed. Tools Appl.* **2015**, *74*, 5861–5872. [CrossRef]
23. Lin, P.Y.; Lee, J.S.; Chang, C.C. Distortion-free secret image sharing mechanism using modulus operator. *Pattern Recognit.* **2009**, *42*, 886–895. [CrossRef]
24. Lin, P.Y.; Chan, C.S. Invertible secret image sharing with steganography. *Pattern Recognit. Lett.* **2010**, *31*, 1887–1893. [CrossRef]
25. Yadav, M.; Singh, R. Essential secret image sharing approach with same size of meaningful shares. *Multimed. Tools Appl.* **2021**. [CrossRef]

26. Gao, K.; Horng, J.H.; Chang, C.C. A novel (2, 3) reversible secret image sharing based on fractal matrix. *IEEE Access* **2020**, *8*, 174325–174341. [CrossRef]
27. Chang, C.C.; Chen, Y.H.; Wang, H.C. Meaningful secret sharing technique with authentication and remedy abilities. *Inf. Sci.* **2011**, *181*, 3073–3084. [CrossRef]
28. Gao, K.; Horng, J.H.; Chang, C.C. An authenticatable (2, 3) secret sharing scheme using meaningful share images based on hybrid fractal matrix. *IEEE Access* **2021**, *9*, 50112–50125. [CrossRef]
29. Fridrich, J.; Goljan, M.; Du, R. Reliable detection of LSB steganography in color and grayscale images. In Proceedings of the 2001 Workshop on Multimedia and Security: New Challenges, Ottawa, ON, Canada, 5 October 2001; pp. 27–30. [CrossRef]
30. Cachin, C. An information-theoretic model for steganography. *Lect. Notes Comput. Sci.* **1998**, *1525*, 306–318. [CrossRef]
31. Arabia, S. Pixel-Value Differencing Steganography: Attacks and Improvements. In Proceedings of the ICCIT 2012, Chittagong, Bangladesh, 22–24 December 2012; pp. 757–762.
32. Joo, J.C.; Lee, H.Y.; Bui, C.N.; Yoo, W.Y.; Lee, H.K. Steganalytic measures for the steganography using pixel-value differencing and modulus function. *Lect. Notes Comput. Sci.* **2008**, *5353 LNCS*, 476–485. [CrossRef]

Article

A Blockchain-Empowered Arbitrable Multimedia Data Auditing Scheme in IoT Cloud Computing

Shenling Wang, Yifang Zhang and Yu Guo *

School of Artificial Intelligence, Beijing Normal University, Beijing 100875, China; slwang@bnu.edu.cn (S.W.); zyfyydgq@mail.bnu.edu.cn (Y.Z.)
* Correspondence: yuguo@bnu.edu.cn

Abstract: As increasing clients tend to outsource massive multimedia data generated by Internet of Things (IoT) devices to the cloud, data auditing is becoming crucial, as it enables clients to verify the integrity of their outsourcing data. However, most existing data auditing schemes cannot guarantee 100% data integrity and cannot meet the security requirement of practical multimedia services. Moreover, the lack of fair arbitration leads to clients not receiving compensation in a timely manner when the outsourced data is corrupted by the cloud service provider (CSP). In this work, we propose an arbitrable data auditing scheme based on the blockchain. In our scheme, clients usually only need to conduct private audits, and public auditing by a smart contract is triggered only when verification fails in private auditing. This hybrid auditing design enables clients to save audit fees and receive compensation automatically and in a timely manner when the outsourced data are corrupted by the CSP. In addition, by applying the deterministic checking technique based on a bilinear map accumulator, our scheme can guarantee 100% data integrity. Furthermore, our scheme can prevent fraudulent claims when clients apply for compensation from the CSP. We analyze the security strengths and complete the prototype's implementation. The experimental results show that our blockchain-based data auditing scheme is secure, efficient, and practical.

Keywords: data auditing; data integrity; bilinear map accumulator; blockchain; smart contract

MSC: 68P20

1. Introduction

The rapid development of the Internet of Things (IoT) and intelligent multimedia has led to the explosive growth of massive amounts of data, which has put tremendous pressure on the entire Internet. To cope with this challenge, storing IoT and intelligent multimedia data with a cloud service provider (CSP) is a common solution [1–4]. Many schemes have been implemented and proved to ensure the security of outsourced data during transmission [5]. However, such a wide attack surface and many recent data breaches have raised concerns about data integrity and availability [6–10]. When sensitive IoT and intelligent multimedia data are outsourced to a CSP, the clients lose control of the data, and the data may be changed or deleted without their permission. To solve this problem, clients need to regularly check the integrity of the outsourced data, and remote data integrity checking is becoming an important issue in cloud computing.

Most existing data integrity checking techniques are probabilistic [11–27]. In this approach, the verifier randomly selects partial data blocks and then performs integrity verification on those chosen data blocks instead of checking the whole dataset, and hence a 100% guarantee for the integrity of the data cannot be provided. However, for massive IoT and intelligent multimedia data, especially sensitive data related to finance, energy, transportation, etc., a probabilistic approach is not enough, since they have strict requirements for data integrity and correctness. Another type of data integrity checking technique is deterministic. In this approach, the verifier examines all data blocks instead of only checking chosen partial data blocks, thus providing 100% assurance of data integrity [28]. However, the deterministic method means higher verification and computational overhead, and hence efficiency is a challenge and must be considered in this approach.

In order to check remote outsourced data integrity, numerous data auditing schemes have been proposed. According to the different roles of verifiers, the existing auditing schemes can be divided into private auditing and public auditing [24]. In private auditing schemes, the role of the verifier is assumed by the client himself, and some important key information used in verification is usually stored by the client instead of the CSP. Therefore, there will be disputes when the verification fails, because if the key information used in the verification is broken by a malicious client, the response of the CSP cannot pass verification. In other words, we cannot determine whether the CSP has damaged the data when verification fails. At this point, fair arbitration is required because the CSP needs to compensate the client for data corruption if verification is not passed. In public auditing schemes, the client usually resorts to a third-party auditor (TPA) to check the integrity of outsourced data. Thus, the audit results completely depend on the TPA. However, this is unrealistic since a fully credible TPA may not always exist. In addition, it should be noted that in these two existing types of auditing schemes, if the auditing results show that the outsourced data are corrupted by the CSP, it is usually difficult for clients to obtain the compensation from the CSP in a timely manner.

In this work, we propose an efficient blockchain-based hybrid auditing scheme with fair arbitration. In our scheme, we use bilinear map accumulators to realize deterministic checking, in which the verifier can check all data blocks, and at the same time, the computational overhead is acceptable. Specifically, for outsourced data $B = \{b_1, \cdots, b_n\}$, the basic idea of an audit is that the verifier uses the random index j to challenge the CSP. Upon receiving the challenge, the CSP needs to compute the corresponding witness wit_{b_j} for the target data block b_j, and all data blocks except b_j are used in the calculation of the witness. The CSP returns both the target data block b_j and the calculated witness as a response, namely (wit_{b_j}, b_j). Thus, even a small change in the outsourced data can cause the generated response to change, and so the generated response cannot pass verification. In other words, a valid response cannot be generated by the CSP if the data are not actually saved or the data are corrupted with the CSP. Therefore, the verifier examines all data blocks instead of only checking partial data blocks, thus providing 100% assurance of data integrity.

Moreover, the client not only holds the data file digest acc_B, which is the key information used in verification by him or herself, but also saves a copy of the digest acc_B to the blockchain simultaneously with the data uploading phase. During the audit, the role of the verifier can be assumed by a client or blockchain smart contract, which means that clients usually only need to conduct private audits, and public auditing by a smart contract is triggered only when verification fails in private auditing because if the data file digest is broken by the client, the CSP's response cannot pass verification even if the data are not corrupted by the CSP, and disputes may arise in this point. In this case, it will trigger the blockchain smart contract to conduct the public auditing for fair judgement, since the data file digest acc_B saved in the blockchain will not be broken by anyone due to the non-tamperability property of the blockchain. Therefore, this blockchain-based hybrid auditing scheme with fair arbitration can solve the problem of distrust between the CSP and the client.

It is worth noting that we replace the TPA with a blockchain smart contract in our public auditing phase, and by using this technology, designing a smart contract with fair arbitration can ensure that the client will be compensated automatically and in a timely manner when the outsourced data are corrupted by the CSP due to the smart contract, which is an automatically executed code running on the blockchain. Furthermore, a dishonest client may falsely claim for compensation from the CSP, and we resort to digital signature technology to prevent dishonest behavior by the client. The contributions of our work are summarized as follows:

- We present an efficient hybrid data auditing scheme for the IoT and intelligent multimedia by using the blockchain. By applying deterministic cryptographic techniques and the blockchain, our proposed design can fairly solve the problem of distrust between the CSP and the client. It also makes the auditing scheme more reliable, because the deterministic methods provide 100% data possession and integrity guarantees.
- We enforce a healthy ecosystem to punish dishonest CSPs automatically and provide timely compensation to the client for data corruption by the CSP in the proposed scheme.
- Our scheme can protect honest CSPs and prevent fraudulent claims by dishonest clients at the same time.
- We use the hybrid auditing design in the proposed scheme. It can also save audit fees and communication costs for the client, because the public auditing phase is triggered only when verification fails in the private auditing phase.
- We not only theoretically prove the correctness and soundness of our scheme but also experimentally verify the feasibility and efficiency of the scheme by the prototype's implementation.

The rest of the paper is structured as follows. Section 2 overviews some related works, and Section 3 introduces the preliminaries used in our scheme. After that, we give the system model of our proposed design, including the architecture overview, threat model, and security goals, in Section 4. Section 5 presents a detailed description of our proposed scheme. In Section 6, we present security analysis and some characteristics of our proposed scheme. We show the performance evaluation in Section 7 and conclude the paper in Section 8.

2. Related Works
2.1. Data Auditing Schemes

With the increase in demand for outsourced data integrity checking, many data auditing schemes have been proposed [29,30]. Ateniese et al. [11] introduced the notion of provable data possession (PDP), which was the first public audit scheme to verify the authenticity of data, in 2007. However, data privacy protection and the full data dynamic operation cannot be supported in this scheme [12]. Then, Erway et al. [13] proposed a PDP scheme supporting full dynamic data updating. Since then, to achieve more functions and improve the efficiency of data auditing for remote data, a lot of research has been conducted in this area. Wang et al. [14] proposed a public data auditing scheme supporting data dynamic operations. In [15], the follow-up work supports privacy-preserving multiple-task auditing. Yuan et al. [16] proposed a public audit scheme for dynamic data sharing with the help of doubly linked information tables. In [17], the authors used the data structure of a Merkle hash tree to devise a public auditing scheme in which the communication overhead and verification efficiency are greatly taken into account. In addition to public auditing, private auditing is necessary in some cases [21–24]. Furthermore, various PDP models have been proposed [25–27]. The PDP method above allows a verifier to verify the remote data integrity without retrieving or downloading all of the data, only randomly selecting a few data blocks and then performing integrity verification on those chosen data blocks instead of checking the whole dataset. Thus, this is a probabilistic method and cannot provide a 100% guarantee for the data's integrity.

Due to the limitations of hardware, few deterministic auditing schemes have been proposed. In [31], the authors proposed the first deterministic public auditing mechanism, but it did not support dynamic data operation. In [32], Deswarte et al. proposed an auditing scheme based on the Diffie–Hellman cryptographic protocol. However, it incurred a high computational overhead, because the CSP must compute the power of the entire file for each auditing verification. Filho et al. [33] proposed a simple deterministic data integrity checking protocol based on a homomorphic RSA-based hash function, but the computation cost remained high and without data dynamic support. In [34], Sebé et al. devised a data possession checking protocol based on the Diffie–Hellman key exchange, which can reduce the computational overhead but without public auditing or data dynamic support. Barsoum [35] proposed a multi-copy provable data possession scheme supporting the public verifiability of multiple replicas of the data. In [36], Hao et al. proposed a privacy-preserving data integrity auditing scheme that supports public auditing and data dynamics.

With the development of the IoT and intelligent multimedia, several data auditing schemes for the IoT and intelligent multimedia services have been proposed. In [28], the authors devised a data audit mechanism by using a bilinear mapping accumulator for sensor data. The proposed design can check all data blocks, thereby eliminating the possibility of any server-side operation. However, existing data auditing solutions cannot solve the trust issue between the data owner and the CSP (or TPA). For private auditing schemes, since the key information used in verification is stored only on the client's side locally, this cannot solve the problem of client fraud. For public auditing schemes, the data owner usually resorts to a TPA to check the outsourced data integrity, but this is unrealistic as a fully trusted TPA may not always exist. As mentioned in [18], the involvement of a TPA may lead to data loss or abuse of authority.

2.2. Blockchain and Smart Contracts

As the core technology of the emerging cryptocurrencies, the blockchain is essentially a distributed database where the transactions are batched into an ordered growing list of blocks which are linked using cryptography. As is well known, the blockchain has the characteristics of decentralization, immutability, and distributed storage. Smart contracts [37] are executable, pre-agreed programs running automatically on the blockchain. Based on the properties and functions of the blockchain, many typical applications such as decentralized storage [38–41], crowdsourcing systems [42–45], medical data management [46,47], and distributed ledger technologies [48,49] have been built.

Recently, Wang et al. [19] leveraged smart contracts to design a blockchain-based fair payment scheme to replace TPAs for public cloud auditing. Yuan et al. [20] proposed a blockchain-based public auditing and secure deduplication scheme which supports automatic compensation of users for data corruption and automatic punishment of malicious CSPs by using a smart contract, but users need to pay an audit fee to the miners of the blockchain in each verification. Wang et al. [24] proposed a blockchain-based private provable data possession scheme which not only saves storage space but also greatly improves efficiency. However, it has no mechanism for automatic punishment and compensation when the outsourced data are corrupted by a CSP. Moreover, theses blockchain-based auditing schemes are all for the probabilistic approach. In light of the previous work, our work used a different auditing design which combines private auditing and public auditing for a deterministic approach. We aim to ensure reliability for data integrity verification and financial fairness in the data auditing scheme so that both the clients and CSPs are incentivized to conduct trustworthy behavior while saving on auditing fees for the clients. Table 1 shows the comparison between our proposed design and some related existing auditing schemes.

Table 1. Comparison with some related existing data integrity auditing schemes.

Scheme	Wang et al. [19]	Yuan et al. [20]	Ren et al. [28]	Wang et al. [24]	Our Scheme
Deterministic audit	×	×	√	×	√
Fair arbitration	√	√	×	√	√
Without third-party auditor	√	√	×	√	√
Data dynamic supporting	×	×	√	×	√
Privacy preserving	√	√	√	√	√
Automatic compensation and punishment mechanism	√	√	×	×	√

3. Preliminaries

3.1. Bilinear Mapping

Let G_1, G_2, and G_T be three cyclic groups of the prime order p. We use g_1 and g_2 to denote the generator of G_1 and G_2, respectively. Bilinear mapping (pairing) is a mapping $e : G_1 \times G_2 \rightarrow G_T$ with the following properties:

- Bilinearity: $\forall\, x, y \in Z_p, e(g_1{}^x, g_2{}^y) = e(g_1, g_2)^{xy} = e(g_1{}^y, g_2{}^x)$;
- Non-degeneracy: $e(g_1, g_2) \neq 1_{G_T}$; that is, $e(g_1, g_2)$ generates G_T;
- Computability: For all $x, y \in Z_p$, there exists an effectively computable algorithm to compute $e(g_1{}^x, g_2{}^y)$.

3.2. q-SDH Assumption

Here we assume that $G_1 = G_2 = G$. Therefore, let G be a finite cyclic group of the order p, where p is a prime number whose length is κ bits. Thus, for a randomly chosen element $\alpha \in Z_p^*$, a random generator g of G, and PPT algorithm A, the following holds:

$$\Pr\left[(c, g^{\frac{1}{\alpha+c}}) \leftarrow A(g, g^\alpha, \cdots\cdots, g^{\alpha^q})\right] \leq \epsilon(\kappa) \text{ for some } c \in Z_p \setminus \{-\alpha\}$$

where $\epsilon(\kappa)$ denotes a negligible function.

The bilinear map accumulator to be used in our data integrity auditing scheme is based on the properties of bilinear mapping and the q-SDH assumption described above. See [28] for details.

3.3. Smart Contract

The concept of a smart contract was first proposed by Nick [37] in 1995. It is an executable pre-agreed program running automatically on the blockchain according to its content. Developers can build distributed applications such as voting, financial transactions, and signing agreements based on smart contracts for Ethereum. When deploying the smart contract, it is necessary to preset the trigger condition and the corresponding response rule. After the smart contract is deployed, once an event triggers the terms of the contract, the code will be executed automatically without central authorization. The relevant details can be found in [37].

4. System Model

We present the system model, threat model, and security goals of our proposed hybrid auditing scheme with fair arbitration for data integrity verification in this section.

4.1. Architecture Overview

The traditional cloud data integrity auditing scheme consists of three roles—the client, verifier, and CSP—as shown in Figure 1. The client is the data owner who wants to outsource their personal data to a CSP, the CSP provides outsourced data storage and management services for the client, and the verifier is in charge of auditing the outsourced data's integrity. The role of the verifier can be performed by a client or a third-party auditor (TPA), which correspond to private auditing and public auditing, respectively. Our proposed blockchain-based hybrid auditing scheme extends the work performed in [20,28]. The integrity verification scheme in [28] meets both private and public auditing, but both of these types of audits have some defects: (1) In private auditing, when verification fails, we cannot determine whether the CSP has damaged the data because the file digest acc_B used in verification is stored on the client's side locally. If the file digest is broken by the client, the CSP's response cannot pass verification. At this point, fair arbitration is required, because the CSP needs to compensate the client for data corruption in this case. (2) In public auditing, the client resorts to a TPA to audit the data's integrity. However, it is unrealistic that the correctness of the auditing results depends entirely on the TPA.

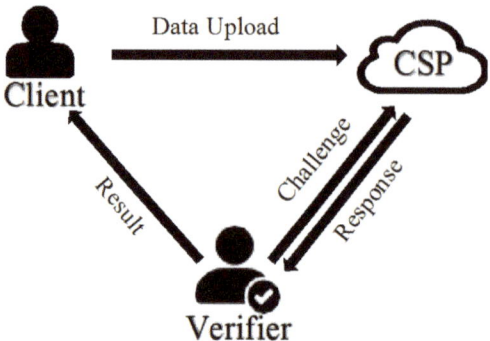

Figure 1. Overview of data integrity auditing.

Based on the defects in above two types of auditing in [28], we propose an arbitrable hybrid auditing scheme based on the blockchain. In this scheme, the client first conducts a private audit, and in case verification fails, it will trigger the blockchain to perform a public audit for fair judgement. It is worth noting that the TPA is replaced by the blockchain in public audits in our scheme, and we designed a smart contract with fair arbitration for the client. Using this smart contract, the client can be compensated automatically when data are broken by the CSP. Our scheme includes three different roles: the client, CSP, and blockchain. As shown in Figure 2, the interactions among them are described as follows:

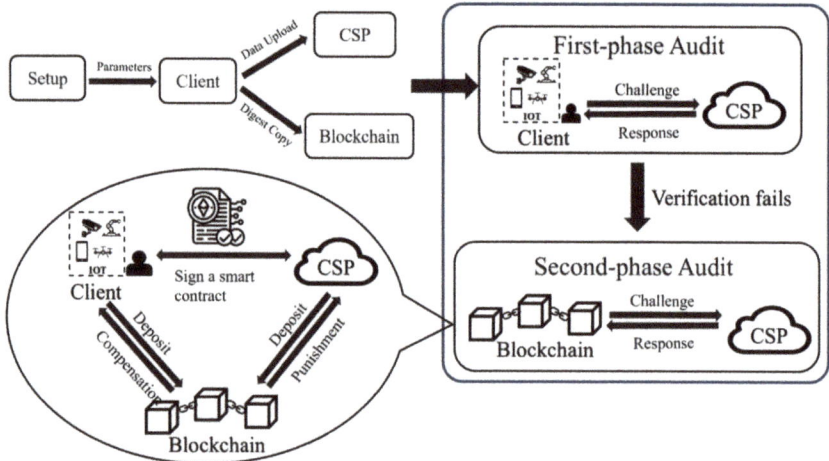

Figure 2. Architecture of our two-phase data auditing scheme.

1. The client has a large amount of data and needs to outsource this data to the CSP for maintenance and computation but does not save the copy locally. It also stores a file digest copy on the blockchain. Then, the client challenges the CSP and verifies the response coming from the CSP. If the response from the CSP passes verification, the outsourced data are considered complete; otherwise, they are considered incomplete. This case will trigger the blockchain to perform public auditing for fair judgement.
2. The CSP has huge storage space and computation resources to provide outsourced data storage and management services for the client. Upon receiving the client's (or blockchain's) challenge, the CSP sends the generated response to the client (or blockchain).
3. The blockchain stores copies of the file digests for the client. When the blockchain is triggered to perform public auditing for fair judgement, the blockchain will challenge

the CSP and then verify the response coming from the CSP. If the response can pass verification, the remote data are complete; otherwise, they are determined to be incomplete, since the data file digest acc_B saved in the blockchain will not be broken by anyone due to the non-tamperability property of the blockchain. Therefore, the failure of verification must be due to damage to the outsourced data by the CSP, and the client obtains compensation from the CSP automatically through a smart contract.

4.2. Threat Model and Design Goals

Both the CSP and the clients can be dishonest in our scheme. It is assumed that the CSP has no motivation to disclose managed data to others and also has no motivation to drop the managed data. However, the data stored on the CSP may be damaged due to software, hardware bugs, or hacker attacks. The CSP may conceal data corruption to avoid compensation. For the clients, they may modify the file digests used in private auditing, which leads to a failed verification result for obtaining compensation from the CSP. Moreover, one may pass him or herself off as a real client (i.e., real data owner) to obtain compensation from the CSP.

In this scheme, we will achieve the following security goals:

- Correctness: If the outsourced data have not been broken by the CSP, and if the client and CSP execute the proposed scheme honestly, then the response from the CSP can pass verification;
- Soundness: Only when the data are complete can they pass verification;
- Privacy preserving: The entire auditing process will not disclose any data privacy in-formation;
- Dynamic operations support: This supports that the client can insert, delete, and update the data outsourced to the CSP, and after dynamic operations, the auditing scheme remains applicable;
- Timely compensation: The client can obtain compensation from the CSP in a timely manner when the outsourced data are damaged by the CSP.

In order to better understand our audit scheme's construction, the major notations and their meanings in this paper are listed in Table 2.

Table 2. Notations.

Notation	Meaning
e	A bilinear pairing
G, G_1, G_2, G_T	Cyclic groups with order p
g	Generator of group G
F	The original data file to be divided into n segments $f_1, \cdots, f_n$
c_i	The ciphertext of segment f_i
τ_i	The tag of segment c_i, i.e., $\tau_i = H(c_i)$
H	A cryptographic hash function
B	The processed data file $B = (b_1, \cdots, b_n)$ with $b_i = c_i \| \tau_i$
acc_B	The accumulated value of data file B by the bilinear pair accumulator
wit_{b_j}	The witness calculated by the CSP
σ	The signature of file B
ssk, spk	The private key ssk and public key spk for a digital signature algorithm
sk_{acc}, pk_{acc}	The secret key sk_{acc} and public key pk_{acc} for a bilinear pair accumulator

5. Scheme Construction

We first give the main idea of our design and then show the auditing scheme in detail.

5.1. Main Idea

Our proposed blockchain-based hybrid auditing scheme extends the work in [20] and [28], but the difference is that the role of the verifier can be the client or blockchain smart contract, which enables our scheme to audit with fair arbitration and timely compensation, saving audit fees and communication costs for the client.

In our proposed blockchain-based hybrid auditing scheme, to save audit fees and communication costs for the client, the audit phase is executed by the client first (i.e., the client assumes the role of the verifier for the audit). If verification is passed, then the outsourced data are complete; otherwise, the outsourced data are possibly incomplete. At this point, the blockchain smart contract is triggered for fair arbitration; that is, the blockchain smart contract assumes the role of the verifier for auditing again. Meanwhile, both the client and CSP send deposits to the smart contract, and then client signs a smart contract with the CSP. First, the smart contract submits the deposit of the client to the miners as an audit fee. Secondly, if verification is passed, the CSP's deposit is returned; otherwise, the smart contract sends the CSP's deposit to the client as compensation. Note that if verification is passed, then the outsourced data are complete, and thus the CSP's deposit is returned. If the auditing verification is not correct, then the outsourced data are incomplete, and the verification result must be incurred by the CSP since the file digest acc_B used for verification is stored on the blockchain, and the blockchain has the property of non-tamperability.

5.2. A Concrete Scheme

The outsourced data are assumed to be static in our scheme. Our hybrid auditing scheme consists of three phases—the set-up phase, the data upload phase, and the audit phase—which extends Ren et al.'s construction [28] as follows:

- Set-up phase: The algorithm of the bilinear pairing instance generator is used to generate cyclic groups G_1, G_2, and G_T with prime order p, a bilinear map $e : G_1 \times G_2 \to G_T$, and $s \xleftarrow{R} Z_p^*$. For simplicity, we assume $G_1 = G_2 = G$, but this is not essential. The generator of G is denoted by g. Let $sk_{acc} = s$ be the secret key and $pk_{acc} = \left(g, g^s, \cdots, g^{s^n}\right)$ be the public key, where n is the upper bound on the number of elements to accumulate. Each client generates the private key ssk and public key spk for a digital signature algorithm. Then sk_{acc} and ssk are the secret parameters, and the public parameters of our scheme are pk_{acc}, spk, e, and g. Let H be a cryptographic hash function.

- Data upload phase: The client divides the file F into n segments with l_1 bits (i.e., $F = (f_1, \cdots, f_n)$) and then performs the following procedure:

  (1) Each segment is encrypted separately using asymmetric encryption techniques such that $c_i = E(f_i)$ for $i = 1, \cdots, n$.

  (2) An l_2-bit tag τ_i is generated for each segment c_i such that $\tau_i = H(c_i)$ for $i = 1, \cdots, n$. The tags are saved in the tag index table (TIT).

  (3) Each tag is put at the end of its corresponding segment and generates a data block $b_i = c_i \parallel \tau_i$ such that $B = \{b_1, \cdots, b_n\}$.

  (4) The accumulated value of the processed file set B is calculated with the bilinear pair accumulator (i.e., $acc_B = g^{\prod_{i=1}^n (b_i + s)}$), and the signature $\sigma = Sig_{ssk}(name)$ is computed, where the name $\in Z_p$ is the identifier of file B, which is uniformly and randomly chosen by the client.

  (5) The client stores the copies of the TIT, the signature σ, and the auxiliary value $aux = (acc_B, e, g, pk_{acc})$ on the blockchain.

  (6) The processed data file B, the signature σ, and $pk_{acc} = \left(g, g^s, \cdots, g^{s^n}\right)$ are uploaded to the CSP.

- First-phase audit: The client interacts with the CSP as follows:

  (1) The client uses the random index j to challenge the CSP.

  (2) Upon receiving the challenge, the CSP needs to calculate the witness $wit_{b_j} = acc_B^{(b_j+s)^{-1}}$ of element b_j, but the witness cannot be calculated directly since s is unknown.

However, the CSP can express the witness as $wit_{b_j} = \prod_{i=0}^{n-1}(g^{s^i})^{a_i}$ using $pk_{acc} = (g, g^s, \cdots, g^{s^n})$, where $\{a_0, \cdots, a_{n-1}\}$ is the coefficient of s in polynomial $f(s) = \prod_{b \in B \setminus \{b_j\}}(b+s)$. Note that the CSP uses all elements in B except b_j to compute wit_{b_j}.

(3) The CSP returns (wit_{b_j}, b_j) as a response to the client.

(4) After receiving (wit_{b_j}, b_j), the client checks whether $e(acc_B, g) = e\left(wit_{b_j}, g^{b_j}g^s\right)$ holds. Meanwhile, the client extracts the corresponding segment c_j^* and its tag τ_j^* from the block b_j returned by the CSP and compares whether the extracted tag τ_j^* and the original τ_j stored in the TIT are equal. If they are, then $\tau_j' = H(c_j^*)$ is calculated using the extracted data segment c_j^*, and it is determined whether the calculated tag τ_j' and the original tag τ_j are equal.

If verification is passed, output "1" is determined, meaning the outsourced data are complete; otherwise, output "0" is assigned, which triggers the blockchain's smart contract to perform a second-phase audit for fair arbitration.

- Second-phase audit: The blockchain smart contract interacts with the CSP as follows:
    (1) The blockchain smart contract uses the random index j to challenge the CSP.
    (2) Upon receiving the challenge, the CSP calculates the witness $wit_{b_j} = \prod_{i=0}^{n-1}(g^{s^i})^{a_i}$ of the element b_j by $pk_{acc} = (g, g^s, \cdots, g^{s^n})$.
    (3) The CSP sends (wit_{b_j}, b_j) as a response to the blockchain smart contract.
    (4) After receiving (wit_{b_j}, b_j), the blockchain smart contract checks whether $e(acc_B, g) = e\left(wit_{b_j}, g^{b_j}g^s\right)$ holds. Meanwhile, it extracts the corresponding segment c_j^* and its tag τ_j^* from the block b_j returned by the CSP and compares whether the extracted tag τ_j^* and the original τ_j stored in the TIT are equal. If they are, then it calculates $\tau_j' = H(c_j^*)$ using the extracted data segment c_j^*, and determines whether the calculated tag τ_j' and the original tag τ_j are equal.

If verification is passed, output "1" is reached, meaning the outsourced data are complete, and the smart contract automatically returns the CSP's deposit and submits the deposit of the client to the miner as an audit fee; otherwise, output "0" is reached, meaning the outsourced data are not complete. In this case, the CSP verifies the signature σ by public parameter spk, the smart contract submits the CSP's deposit to the client as compensation only if the outsourced data belong to the client, and then the smart contract submits the deposit of the client to the miners as an audit fee.

In order to better understand the caculations of digest acc_B and the witness in the above audit scheme construction, an illustrative example is given below in Figure 3.

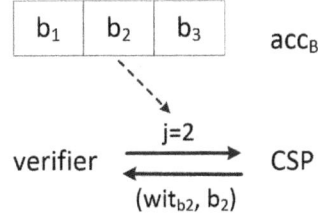

Figure 3. An illustrative example.

Suppose the data processed by the client are $B = \{b_1, b_2, b_3\}$. The client first calculates the digest $acc_B = g^{\prod_{i=1}^{3}(b_i+s)}$. In the audit phase, upon receiving the challenge index j (suppose j = 2) from the verifier (which can be the client or blockchain smart contract), the CSP needs to calculate the witness $wit_{b_2} = g^{\prod_{i=1, i\neq 2}^{3}(b_i+s)}$, but the witness cannot be calculated directly since s is unknown. Let $f(s) = \prod_{i=1, i\neq 2}^{3}(b_i+s) = (b_1+s)(b_3+s) = s^2 + (b_1+b_3)s + b_1b_3$. The CSP can express the witness as $wit_{b_2} = \prod_{i=0}^{2}(g^{s^i})^{a_i} = (g)^{b_1b_3} \cdot (g^s)^{b_1+b_3} \cdot (g^{s^2})^1$ using $pk_{acc} = (g, g^s, \cdots, g^{s^n})$, where $\{a_0 = b_1b_3, a_1 = b_1+b_3, a_2 = 1\}$ is the coefficient of s in polynomial $f(s)$. The CSP sends (wit_{b_2}, b_2) as a response to the verifier. We can see that the CSP needs to use all elements in B except b_j to compute the witness wit_{b_j}.

6. Analysis of Our Design

In this section, we analyze the security and characteristics of our scheme. It is assumed that the underlying cryptographic tools such as the bilinear pairing instance generator algorithm, bilinear pair accumulator, one-way hash function, asymmetric encryption algorithm, and digital signature algorithm are secure.

6.1. Security Analysis

We should ensure the correctness and soundness requirements in our scheme. Correctness means that the response provided by the CSP can pass verification if the outsourced data on the CSP are not corrupted. Soundness means that verification can be passed only if the outsourced data on the CSP is not broken. We give the following theorems to prove these requirements can be satisfied in our proposed scheme:

Theorem 1. *For correctness, suppose that both the CSP and client execute the proposed scheme honestly. If the outsourced data on the CSP are not broken, then the CSP's response can pass verification.*

Proof. Suppose that both the CSP and client execute the proposed scheme honestly. As described in our scheme, the CSP's response (wit_{b_j}, b_j) can pass verification only when the following two conditions are met:

(1) $e(acc_B, g) = e(wit_{b_j}, g^{b_j}g^s)$.

(2) By extracting the data segment c_j^* and its corresponding tag τ_j^* from the target block b_j returned by the CSP, the extracted tag τ_j^* and the original τ_j stored in the TIT are equal. By calculating $\tau_j' = H(c_j^*)$ using the extracted data segment c_j^*, the calculated tag τ_j' and the original tag τ_j are equal.

If the outsourced data on the CSP are not broken, then the first condition is met since the following equations hold due to the properties of bilinear mapping:

$$e(acc_B, g) = e(g^{\prod_{i=1}^{n}(b_i+s)}, g)$$

$$= e(g, g)^{\prod_{i=1}^{n}(b_i+s)}$$

$$= e(g^{\prod_{b_i \in B \setminus \{b_j\}}(b_i+s)}, g^{(b_j+s)})$$

$$= e(wit_{b_j}, g^{b_j}g^s)$$

where for the data file digest $acc_B = g^{\prod_{i=1}^{n}(b_i+s)} = g^{\prod_{b_i \in B}(b_i+s)}$, the witness response by the CSP is $wit_{b_j} = g^{\prod_{b_i \in B \setminus \{b_j\}}(b_i+s)}$.

Meanwhile, the client extracts the corresponding segment c_j^* and its tag τ_j^* from the target block b_j returned by the CSP. If the outsourced data are complete, then the extracted tag τ_j^* and the original τ_j stored in the TIT must be equal, and the calculated $\tau_j' = H(c_j^*)$ using the extracted data segment c_j^* must be equal to the original tag τ_j stored in the TIT, so the second condition is met. Therefore, if the outsourced data on the CSP are not broken, then the CSP's response can pass verification. □

Theorem 2. *Regarding soundness, verification is only possible if the outsourced data on the CSP are not corrupted. In other words, if the outsourced data are not complete, then verification cannot be passed.*

Proof. In our proposed scheme, verification can be passed in either the first-phase auditing or the second-phase auditing. In both cases, after receiving (wit_{b_j}, b_j) from the CSP, verification can be passed only when the following two conditions are met:

(1) $e(acc_B, g) = e\left(wit_{b_j}, g^{b_j} g^s\right)$.
(2) When extracting the data segment c_j^* and its corresponding tag τ_j^* from the target block b_j returned by the CSP, the extracted tag τ_j^* and the original τ_j stored in the TIT are equal, and by calculating $\tau_j' = H(c_j^*)$ using the extracted data segment c_j^*, the calculated tag τ_j' and the original tag τ_j are equal.

Upon receiving the challenge, the CSP needs to compute the corresponding witness wit_{b_j} for the target data block b_j, and all data blocks except b_j must be used in the calculation of the witness. Thus, even a small change in the outsourced data can cause the generated witness to change. Moreover, the CSP returns both the target data block and the calculated witness as a response. If the target data block b_j is corrupted, then either the extracted tag τ_j^* is not equal to the original τ_j stored in the TIT or the calculated $\tau_j' = H(c_j^*)$ using the extracted data segment c_j^* is not equal to the original tag τ_j stored in the TIT. In other words, due to the security of the hash algorithm, it is almost impossible to generate the same tags using other data blocks. Thus, a valid response cannot be generated by the CSP if the data are not actually saved or the data are corrupted on the CSP. Therefore, if the outsourced data are not complete, then verification cannot be passed. □

6.2. Other Characteristics

Our scheme has the following properties:

- Privacy preservation: Before uploading the data, the client divides the data file F into n segments with l_1 bits; that is, $F = (f_1, \cdots, f_n)$, and then each segment is encrypted separately using asymmetric encryption techniques such that $c_i = E(f_i)$ for $i = 1, \cdots, n$. Note that the client does not disclose the key for the encrypted data to others in the whole auditing process so no one can access the outsourced data except the client him or herself;
- Dynamic operations support: Our proposed scheme also supports the dynamic operations of data such as inserting, deleting, and updating by using the tag index table (TIT) similar to the method in [28], ensuring that after dynamic operations, the auditing scheme remains applicable;
- Timely compensation: As described in our scheme, the blockchain smart contract must be triggered for fair arbitration if the outsourced data are corrupted by the CSP. The client signs a smart contract with the CSP, and both the client and CSP send deposits to the smart contract. First, the smart contract submits the deposit of the client to the miners as an audit fee. Secondly, if verification is passed, it returns the CSP's deposit; otherwise, the deposit of the CSP is sent to the client as compensation via the smart contract. Thus, if the outsourced data are corrupted by the CSP, then verification cannot be passed, so the smart contract submits the deposit to the client as compensation automatically after the CSP verifies the signature σ; that is, the client can obtain compensation from the CSP in a timely manner.

7. Performance Evaluation

We implemented our system prototype of our proposed auditing scheme model via Python code. In this scheme, we used Solidity 0.8.11 to build an Ethereum smart contract and used Go Ethereum (Geth) 1.10.16 as the Ethereum client. The smart contract was deployed to the Ethereum test network.

The overhead of the smart contract comes from the posting parameter and on-chain verification. In this scheme, there is just one parameter named acc_B which is used for on-chain verification. Figure 4 measures the gas costs of different sizes of files that were used in our auditing scheme. It is shown that the cost of our contract implemented on Ethereum was a constant value. The gas cost was fixed at 4.2216×10^4. The total cost of ether could be calculated by the Ethereum gas rule: gasCost × gasPrice. The average gas price was about 45 Gwei, and 1 Gwei is 10^{-9} ether. The current exchange rate is 1 ether = USD 2500. As shown in Figure 4, our cost for deploying the auditing scheme model was about USD 4.7493. The results confirm that this was not a huge cost for the client.

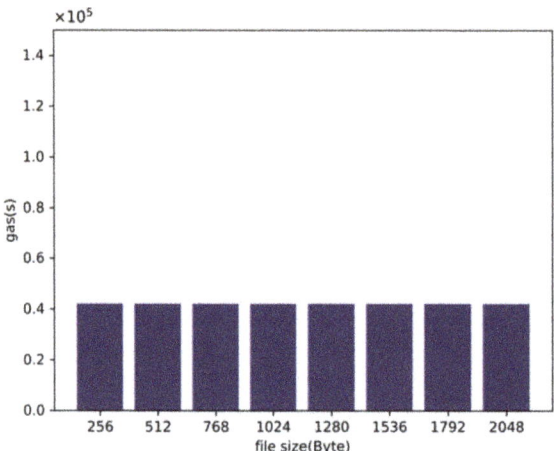

Figure 4. Storage overhead required for blockchain verification based on different file sizes.

In order to execute the polynomial operations in a bilinear map accumulator, we introduced the PBC library in the implementation. The PBC library is an open-source C library built on the GMP library that performs the mathematical operations underlying pairing-based cryptosystems. In the data upload phase, the client encrypts the data blocks which need to be outsourced by RSA, a kind of asymmetric encryption algorithm. Then, the client generates conflict-free 20-bit tags using a hash algorithm. To evaluate the performance of our model, we used the following set-up. The server proxy of the client was collocated with the CSP server on 8 cores of a machine with 2.60 GHz Intel i7-6700 HQ processors and 12 GB of RAM running Ubuntu Linux.

The upload time of the client, the witness computation time of the CSP, and the verification time cost of the verifier should be considered. First, we fixed the size of the data file to 2 MB. The data file was generated randomly from 0–9, a–z, and A–Z in our testing. Both the base size of the data blocks and the size of each increment were designed to be 256 bytes. When the block size was increased to 2 KB, the experiment would be stopped. For each round of experiments, we ran 100 tests with the same data and took the average as the result to reduce the error effect of a single experiment. Note that the larger the data block size, the fewer segments were divided, and the fewer labels were generated since the size of the data file was fixed. The final experimental results are shown in Figure 5a,b. It is not hard to observe that the upload time and the generation time of the witness were inversely proportional to the block size, and the time required for the verifier to conduct verification was fixed at 0.002 s, which conformed to our expectations. We can see that as the block size increased, the time required to calculate acc_B and wit decreased correspondingly, as shown in Figure 5c. Additionally, the order of magnitude of these parameters was about 0.01, well below the upload time. For the client, most of the time the cost was spent on encrypting the data file. Moreover, the calculation overhead of the parameters b (i.e., data segment) and τ (i.e., tag) was independent of the block size.

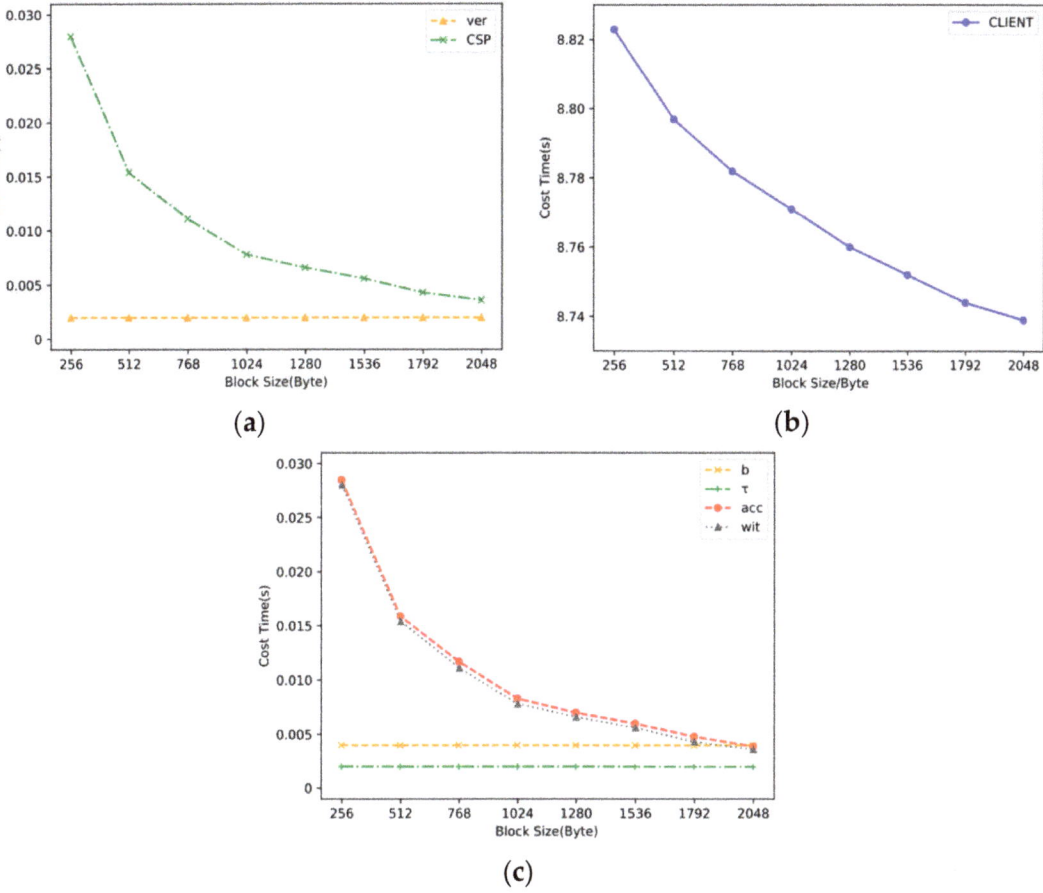

Figure 5. Computing overhead based on different block sizes. (**a**) Computing overhead of audit participants. (**b**) Computing overhead of the client. (**c**) Computing overhead of the parameters.

In addition, if the block size was fixed at 256 bytes, we increased the data file size from 256 KB to 2 MB in increments of 256 KB. Figure 6a,b shows that most of the computing overhead was spent on the data upload phase, and the vast majority of this time was used to encrypt the data as mentioned above. As shown in Figure 6c, both the time required for generating acc_B by the client and the computational overhead for calculating the witness by the CSP were proportional to the size of the outsourced data file. The results show that the computational overhead of the verifier was a constant value regardless of the data file size and the data block size. Therefore, the experimental results show that our proposed auditing scheme was very effective.

To measure the distribution trend of the computing overhead with different parameters, we fixed the size of the data file at 2 MB and the block size at 256 bytes. Then, we repeated the experiment 100 times and recorded the computing overhead of the parameters for each experiment. The distribution trend of the computing overhead is shown in Figure 7. The computing overhead of all parameters was according to Gaussian distribution.

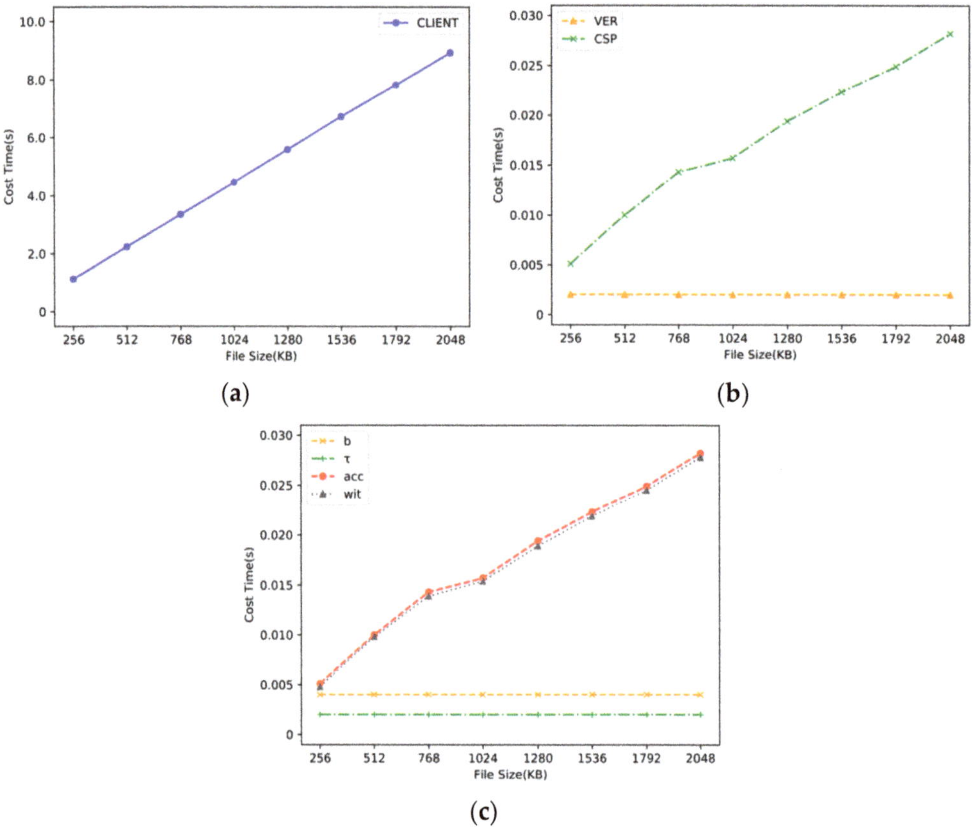

Figure 6. Computing overhead based on different file sizes. (**a**) Computing overhead of audit participants. (**b**) Computing overhead of the client. (**c**) Computing overhead of the parameters.

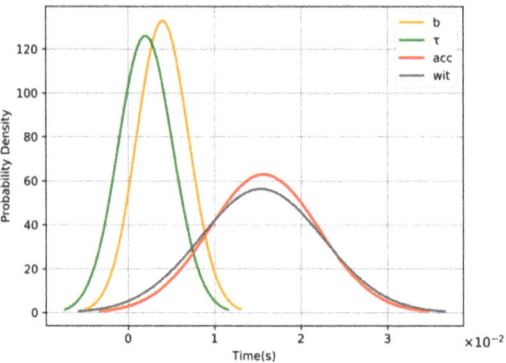

Figure 7. The distribution trend of computing overhead with different parameters.

8. Conclusions and Future Work

In this paper, we designed a novel and efficient two-phase arbitrable hybrid auditing scheme based on the blockchain. By using a bilinear map accumulator and blockchain smart contract, our scheme not only realizes deterministic checking, which provides 100% data possession and integrity guarantees, but also enables a healthy ecosystem between the client and the CSP. That aside, when the outsourced data are lost or corrupted by the CSP, our scheme can compensate the client in a timely manner and punish the dishonest CSP automatically with a smart contract. Meanwhile, our scheme also protects the honest CSP and prevents dishonest behavior from the client. Furthermore, we designed hybrid auditing in our scheme instead of conducting public auditing through the blockchain. The hybrid auditing design not only provides fair judgment but also saves audit fees for the client, because the public auditing phase by the blockchain is triggered only when verification fails in the private auditing phase. Through theoretical and experimental analysis, it was verified that our design was feasible and efficient, and it achieved the desired security goals. Of course, our scheme still has some limitations to be improved upon. For example, it can only check whether the outsourced data are corrupted and cannot determine which data blocks are corrupted or how to repair the corrupted data blocks. In future works, we will enhance more functions of our auditing scheme, such as the location and repair of corrupted data blocks.

Author Contributions: Conceptualization, S.W. and Y.G.; methodology, S.W. and Y.G.; validation, Y.Z. and Y.G.; writing—original draft preparation, S.W.; writing—review and editing, S.W., Y.Z. and Y.G. All authors have read and agreed to the published version of the manuscript.

Funding: This work was supported by the Fundamental Research Funds for the Central Universities under Grants 2020NTST32 and National Natural Science Foundation of China under Grants 62102035.

Data Availability Statement: The data used to support the findings of this study are available from the authors upon request.

Conflicts of Interest: The authors declare no conflict of interest.

References

1. Zheng, X.; Cai, Z. A Private and Efficient Mechanism for Data Uploading in Smart Cyber-Physical Systems. *IEEE Trans. Netw. Sci. Eng.* **2020**, *7*, 766–775.
2. Cai, Z.; He, Z. Trading Private Range Counting over Big IoT Data. In Proceedings of the 2019 IEEE 39th International Conference on Distributed Computing Systems (ICDCS), Dallas, TX, USA, 31 October 2019.
3. Zheng, X.; Cai, Z. Privacy-Preserved Data Sharing towards Multiple Parties in Inxdustrial IoTs. *IEEE J. Sel. Areas Commun.* **2020**, *38*, 968–979. [CrossRef]
4. Cai, Z.; Shi, T. Distributed Query Processing in the Edge Assisted IoT Data Monitoring System. *IEEE Internet Things J.* **2021**, *8*, 12679–12693. [CrossRef]
5. Dragulinescu, A.-M.; Constantin, F.; Orza, O.; Bosoc, S.; Streche, R.; Negoita, A.; Osiac, F.; Balaceanu, C.; Suciu, G. Smart Watering System Security Technologies using Blockchain. In Proceedings of the 2021 13th International Conference on Electronics, Computers and Artificial Intelligence (ECAI), Pitesti, Romania, 1–3 July 2021.
6. Cai, Z.; He, Z.; Guan, X.; Li, Y. Collective Data-Sanitization for Preventing Sensitive Information Inference Attacks in Social Networks. *IEEE Trans. Dependable Secur. Comput.* **2018**, *15*, 577–590. [CrossRef]
7. Miao, Y.; Ma, J.; Liu, X.; Weng, J.; Li, H.; Li, H. Lightweight fine-grained search over encrypted data in fog computing. *IEEE Trans. Serv. Comput.* **2018**, *12*, 772–785. [CrossRef]
8. Ong, Q.; Miao, Y.; Li, H.; Liu, X.; Deng, R. Privacy-Preserving Ranked Spatial Keyword Query in Mobile Cloud-Assisted Fog Computing. *IEEE Trans. Mob. Comput.* **2021**. [CrossRef]
9. Xie, H.; Guo, Y.; Jia, X. Privacy-preserving Location-based Data Queries in Fog-enhanced Sensor Networks. *IEEE Internet Things J.* **2021**. [CrossRef]
10. Guo, Y.; Xie, H.; Wang, C.; Jia, X. Enabling privacy-preserving geographic range query in fog-enhanced iot services. *IEEE Trans. Dependable Secur. Comput.* **2021**. [CrossRef]
11. Ateniese, G.; Burns, R.; Curtmola, R.; Herring, J.; Kissner, L.; Peterson, Z.; Song, D. Provable data possession at untrusted stores. In Proceedings of the 14th ACM Conference on Computer and Communications Security, New York, NY, USA, 2 November 2007–31 October 2007; pp. 598–609.
12. Ateniese, G.; Di Pietro, R.; Mancini, L.V.; Tsudik, G. Scalable and efficient provable data possession. In Proceedings of the 4th International Conference on Security and Privacy in Communication Networks, New York, NY, USA, 22–25 September 2008.
13. Erway, C.C.; Kupcu, A.; Papamanthou, C.; Tamassia, R. Dynamic provable data possession. *ACM Trans. Inf. Syst. Secur.* **2015**, *17*, 1–29. [CrossRef]
14. Wang, Q.; Wang, C.; Ren, K.; Lou, W.; Li, J. Enabling public auditability and data dynamics for storage security in cloud computing, IEEE Trans. *Parallel Distrib. Syst.* **2011**, *22*, 847–859. [CrossRef]
15. Wang, C.; Chow, S.S.M.; Wang, Q.; Ren, K.; Lou, W. Privacy-preserving public auditing for secure cloud storage. *IEEE Trans. Comput.* **2013**, *62*, 362–375. [CrossRef]

16. Yuan, J.; Yu, S. Public integrity auditing for dynamic data sharing with multiuser modification. *IEEE Trans. Inf. Forensics Secur.* **2015**, *10*, 1717–1726. [CrossRef]
17. Liu, C.; Ranjan, R.; Yang, C.; Zhang, X.; Wang, L.; Chen, J. MuR-DPA: Top-down levelled multi-replica Merkle hash tree based secure public auditing for dynamic big data storage on cloud. *IEEE Trans. Comput.* **2014**, *64*, 2609–2622. [CrossRef]
18. Yu, Y.; Li, Y.; Ni, J.; Yang, G.; Mu, Y.; Susilo, W. Comments on 'public integrity auditing for dynamic data sharing with multiuser modification'. *IEEE Trans. Inf. Forensics Secur.* **2015**, *11*, 658–659. [CrossRef]
19. Wang, H.; Qin, H.; Zhao, M.; Wei, X.; Shen, H.; Susilo, W. Blockchain-based fair payment smart contract for public cloud storage auditing. *Inform. Sci.* **2020**, *519*, 348–362. [CrossRef]
20. Yuan, H.; Chen, X.; Wang, J.; Yuan, J.; Yan, H.; Susilo, W. Blockchain-based public auditing and secure deduplication with fair arbitration. *Inf. Sci.* **2020**, *541*, 409–425. [CrossRef]
21. Wang, H.; Li, K.; Ota, K.; Shen, J. Remote data integrity checking and sharing in cloud-based health internet of things. *IEICE Trans. Inf. Syst.* **2016**, *99*, 1966–1973. [CrossRef]
22. Wang, H.; He, D.; Yu, J.; Wang, Z. Incentive and unconditionally anonymous identity-based public provable data possession. *IEEE Trans. Serv. Comput.* **2019**, *12*, 824–835. [CrossRef]
23. Wang, H. Proxy provable data possession in public clouds. *IEEE Trans. Serv. Comput.* **2013**, *6*, 551–559. [CrossRef]
24. Wang, H.; Wang, Q.; He, D. Blockchain-based private provable data possession. *IEEE Trans. Dependable Secur. Comput.* **2021**, *18*, 2379–2389. [CrossRef]
25. Wang, H.; He, D.; Fu, A.; Li, Q.; Wang, Q. Provable data possession with outsourced data transfer. *IEEE Trans. Serv. Comput.* **2019**, *14*, 1929–1939. [CrossRef]
26. Kuang, B.; Fu, A.; Yu, S.; Yang, G.; Su, M.; Zhang, Y. ESDRA: An efficient and secure distributed remote attestation scheme for IoT swarms. *IEEE Internet Things J.* **2019**, *6*, 8372–8383. [CrossRef]
27. Zhang, Y.; Yu, J.; Hao, R.; Wang, C.; Ren, K. Enabling efficient user revocation in identity-based cloud storage auditing for shared big data. *IEEE Trans. Dependable Secur. Comput.* **2018**, *17*, 608–619. [CrossRef]
28. Ren, Y.; Qi, J.; Liu, Y.; Wang, J.; Kim, G.-J. Integrity verification mechanism of sensor data based on bilinear map accumulator. *ACM Trans. Internet Technol.* **2021**, *21*, 1–19. [CrossRef]
29. Zafar, F.; Khan, A.; Malik, S.U.R.; Ahmed, M.; Anjum, A.; Khan, M.I.A. 2017. Survey of cloud computing data integrity schemes: Design challenges, taxonomy and future trends. *Comput. Security.* **2017**, *65*, 29–49. [CrossRef]
30. Du, Y.; Duan, H.; Zhou, A.; Wang, C.; Au, M.; Wang, Q. Enabling Secure and Efficient Decentralized Storage Auditing with Blockchain. *Proc. IEEE Trans. Dependable Secur. Comput* **2021**. [CrossRef]
31. Caronni, G.; Waldvogel, M. Establishing trust in distributed storage providers. In Proceedings of the Third International Conference on Peer-to-Peer Computing (P2P2003), Linköping, Sweden, 1–3 September 2003; pp. 128–133.
32. Deswarte, Y.; Quisquater, J.-J.; Saïdane, A. *Remote Integrity Checking, in Integrity and Internal Control in Information Systems VI*; Springer: Berlin, Germany, 2004; pp. 1–11.
33. Filho, D.L.G.; Barreto, P.S.L.M. Demonstrating Data Possession and Uncheatable Data Transfer. Cryptology ePrint Archive: Report 2006/150. Available online: https://eprint.iacr.org/2006/150 (accessed on 12 December 2021).
34. Sebe, F.; Domingo-Ferrer, J.; Martinez-balleste, A.; Deswarte, Y.; Quisquater, J. Efficient remote data possession checking in critical information infrastructures. *IEEE Trans. Knowl. Data Eng.* **2008**, *20*, 1034–1038. [CrossRef]
35. Barsoum, A.F.; Hasan, M.A. *Provable Possession and Replication of Data over Cloud Servers*; University Waterloo: Waterloo, ON, Canada, 2010.
36. Hao, Z.; Zhong, S.; Yu, N. A privacy-preserving remote data integrity checking protocol with data dynamics and public verifiability. *IEEE Trans. Knowl. Data Eng.* **2011**, *23*, 1432–1437.
37. Buterin, V. Ethereum White Paper. Available online: https://www.mendeley.com (accessed on 12 December 2021).
38. The Storj Project, [Online]. Available online: https://storj.io/storj.pdf (accessed on 12 December 2021).
39. Guo, Y.; Zhang, C.; Jia, X. Verifiable and forward-secure encrypted search using blockchain techniques. In Proceedings of the IEEE International Conference on Communications, Dublin, Ireland, 7–11 June 2020.
40. Guo, Y.; Wang, S.; Huang, J. A blockchain-assisted framework for secure and reliable data sharing in distributed systems. *EURASIP J. Wirel. Commun. Netw.* **2021**, *2021*, 1–19. [CrossRef]
41. Tong, W.; Dong, X.; Shen, Y.; Jiang, X. A hierrchical sharding protocol for multi-domain IoT blockchains. In Proceedings of the ICC 2019—2019 IEEE International Conference on Communications, Shanghai, China, 20–24 May 2019.
42. Zhu, S.; Cai, Z.; Hu, H.; Li, Y.; Li, W. zkCrowd: A Hybrid Blockchain-based Crowdsourcing Platform. *IEEE Trans. Ind. Inform.* **2019**, *16*, 4196–4205. [CrossRef]
43. Guo, Y.; Xie, H.; Miao, Y.; Wang, C.; Jia, X. FedCrowd: A federated and privacy-preserving crowdsourcing platform on blockchain. In Proceedings of the IEEE Transactions on Services Computing, 14 October 2020.
44. Li, C.; Qu, X.; Guo, Y. TFCrowd: A blockchain-based crowdsourcing framework with enhanced trustworthiness and fairness. *EURASIP J. Wirel. Commun. Netw.* **2021**. [CrossRef]
45. Zhang, C.; Guo, Y.; Jia, X.; Wang, C.; Du, H. Enabling Proxy-Free Privacy-Preserving and Federated Crowdsourcing by Using Blockchain. *IEEE Internet Things J.* **2021**, *8*, 6624–6636. [CrossRef]
46. Wang, M.; Guo, Y.; Zhang, C.; Wang, C.; Huang, H.; Jia, X. MedShare: A Privacy-Preserving Medical Data Sharing System by Using Blockchain. *IEEE Trans. Serv. Comput.* **2021**. [CrossRef]

47. The MedRec Project. Available online: https://www.pubpub.org/pub/medrec (accessed on 28 December 2021).
48. Silvano, F.W.; Marcelino, R. Iota Tangle: A cryptocurrency to communicate Internet-of-Things data—ScienceDirect. *Future Gener. Comput. Syst.* **2020**, *112*, 307–319. [CrossRef]
49. Suciu, G.; Nadrag, C.; Istrate, C.; Vulpe, A.; Ditu, M.-C.; Subea, O. Comparative Analysis of Distributed Ledger Technologies. In Proceedings of the 2018 Global Wireless Summit (GWS), Chiang Rai, Thailand, 25–18 November 2018.

Article

Toward Prevention of Parasite Chain Attack in IOTA Blockchain Networks by Using Evolutionary Game Model

Yinfeng Chen [1,2], Yu Guo [1], Yaofei Wang [1,2] and Rongfang Bie [1,*]

[1] School of Artificial Intelligence, Beijing Normal University, Beijing 100875, China; chenyf@mail.bnu.edu.cn or 201931210002@mail.bnu.edu.cn (Y.C.); yuguo@bnu.edu.cn (Y.G.); yfwang@mail.bnu.edu.cn (Y.W.)
[2] School of Computer Information Management, Inner Mongolia University of Finance and Economics, Hohhot 010070, China
* Correspondence: rfbie@bnu.edu.cn

Abstract: IOTA is a new cryptocurrency system designed for the Internet of Things based on directed an acyclic graph structure. It has the advantages of supporting high concurrency, scalability, and zero transaction fees; however, due to the particularity of the directed acyclic graph structure, IOTA faces more complex security threats than the sequence blockchain, in which a parasite chain attack is a common double-spending attack. In this work, we propose a scheme that can effectively prevent parasite chain attacks to improve the security of the IOTA ledger. Our main idea is to analyze the behavior strategies of IOTA nodes based on evolutionary game theory and determine the key factors affecting the parasite chain attack and the restrictive relationship between them. Based on the above research, we provide a solution to resist the parasite chain attack and further prove the effectiveness of the scheme by numerical simulation. Finally, we propose the parasite chain attack prevention algorithms based on price splitting to effectively prevent the formation of the parasite chain.

Keywords: IOTA; parasite chain attack; the tangle; evolutionary game; security

MSC: 68Q01; 68W01; 68U01; 68R01; 68V99

Citation: Chen, Y.; Guo, Y.; Wang, Y.; Bie, R. Toward Prevention of Parasite Chain Attack in IOTA Blockchain Networks by Using Evolutionary Game Model. *Mathematics* **2022**, *10*, 1108. https://doi.org/10.3390/math10071108

Academic Editors: Ximeng Liu, Yinbin Miao and Zuobin Ying

Received: 17 February 2022
Accepted: 25 March 2022
Published: 30 March 2022

Publisher's Note: MDPI stays neutral with regard to jurisdictional claims in published maps and institutional affiliations.

Copyright: © 2022 by the authors. Licensee MDPI, Basel, Switzerland. This article is an open access article distributed under the terms and conditions of the Creative Commons Attribution (CC BY) license (https://creativecommons.org/licenses/by/4.0/).

1. Introduction

The rapid development of blockchain technology has accelerated the popularization of the Internet of Things (IoT). Along with the increasing scale of IoT, the blockchain technology based on directed acyclic graph (DAG) structure has attracted more and more attention in IoT with its high concurrency and high scalability. At present, the most representative one is IOTA (Internet of Things application) [1–3].

IOTA is a revolutionary new cryptocurrency system specially designed for IoT. It overcomes the inefficiency in the existing blockchain design by replacing the sequence distributed ledger with the distributed ledger based on the DAG structure, named the Tangle, and creates a new method for reaching the consensus of the decentralized P2P system. IOTA realizes zero transaction fees, high concurrency, and unlimited scalability to complete the free transaction between machines and provide the underlying public chain technology for IoT. IoT architecture based on IOTA Tangle is shown in Figure 1. The left part in the figure is the IoT device layer (composed of sensors, bar codes and radio frequency electronic tags, etc.), which is responsible for receiving user requests and collecting information in real-time and transmitting them to the client layer (composed of IOTA wallets or applications running on computers or smartphones). After a transaction is packaged and generated by the client, it is sent to the IOTA node (composed of the IoT device with a node software to read and write access to the Tangle) for processing. If the transaction is valid and follows the protocol standards, the IOTA node first updates the local ledger (the right part in the figure) after verification and then broadcasts the updated ledger to other IOTA nodes through P2P protocol to complete the consensus process [4].

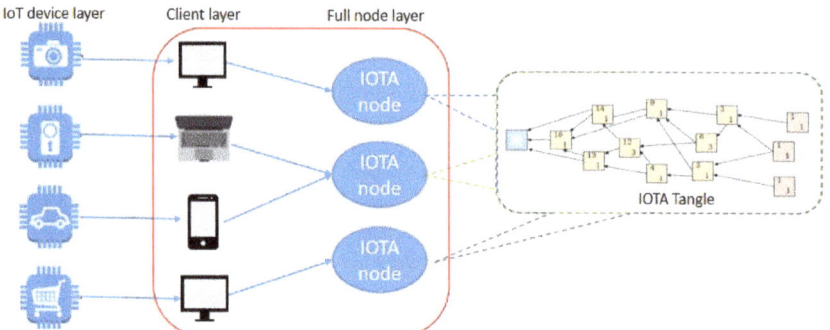

Figure 1. IoT Architecture based on IOTA Tangle.

However, due to the particularity of the DAG structure, the security of IOTA will face major challenges. IOTA is subject to a variety of attacks [1], among which the parasite chain (PC) attack is the most common. If the attack is successful, Tangle's historical records will be tampered with, and the attacker will realize double-spending. In this paper, we focus on the PC attack. Similar to selfish mining by nodes in the single-chain architecture [5–8], malicious nodes privately create parasite chains and broadcast them when the opportunities are ripe, in order to replace the corresponding legal branches in the main tangle; however, so far, few people look for the cause of PC attacks from IOTA nodes themselves. There is an obvious game relationship between IOTA nodes. As a player, each node will choose its strategy to maximize its utility when given the strategies of other players. It should be noted that the cost of launching a PC attack is an important part of building a game revenue matrix; a survey found that there is no expression to calculate the cost of the PC attack directly now [9–13]. In addition, in the actual scenario of IoT, the node's malicious behavior is studied through the classical game theory based on the assumption of "complete rationality" [14–17], but the static results cannot meet the actual needs of IOTA, nor can they reflect the dynamic change of IOTA node's strategic behavior and the evolution process that eventually tends to be stable; therefore, it is necessary to analyze PC attacks using game theory, but it is particularly important to find a game method more suitable for IOTA scenarios. In light of the above observations and given literature [1], we study what circumstances IOTA nodes actively launch PC attacks; therefore, we should design a scheme that can effectively detect and prevent parasite chain attacks.

It is challenging to achieve the above goal in that: (1) Nodes can join or exit the IOTA network at any time. We must ensure that enough nodes can synchronize the Tangle, but it is difficult to determine the number of effective working nodes. (2) The distributed ledger based on the DAG structure solves the problems of high concurrency and high scalability of IoT and increases the growth randomness of the ledger with time. The randomness raises the complexity of the cost of PC attacks launched by computing nodes. (3) Affected by the dynamic change of the Tangle, the initial behavior choices of nodes are not necessarily optimal, so it is hard to analyze and obtain the final evolutionary stability strategies of nodes.

In this paper, for the first time, we solve the problem of PC attacks in IOTA blockchain networks by introducing epidemic dynamics models and evolutionary game theory. With the help of the improved epidemic model, our proposed scheme can determine the number of nodes that synchronize the Tangle, and provide a guarantee for the normal operation of IOTA by monitoring the change of the number of nodes in real-time. Evolutionary game theory is a combination of game theory analysis and dynamic evolutionary process analysis. It studies how bounded rational individuals evolve in dynamic processes, how to learn adaptively in repeated games, and choose the optimal strategy to maximize their interests [18]. In this study, the dynamic evolution process of IOTA nodes' behavior strategies was analyzed through evolutionary game, and the key factors inducing nodes to launch PC attacks were found. To realize this scheme, the main contributions of this paper are as follows:

(1) We introduce an improved epidemic model TG_SEI. IOTA can effectively synchronize the number of nodes in the Tangle estimated by using the TG_SEI model, which is not only an important indicator to measure whether IOTA is running normally, but also an important part of the PC attack cost.
(2) We propose a computational expression for the PC attack cost. The transaction involves multiple key links, from creation to issuance. If a malicious node wants to successfully launch a PC attack, an additional cost must be paid. We used the method of dividing the time according to the key points of events to complete the cost accounting of each stage.
(3) We designed the parasite chain attack prevention algorithms based on price splitting. Using evolutionary game theory to analyze the behaviors of IOTA nodes, it was found that the commodity prices are the main factor that triggers PC attacks. Moreover, we predicted the concentrated time slot of PC attacks, which makes it more efficient to resist PC attacks.

The rest of this paper is organized as follows. Section 2 describes the related work. Section 3 presents the background. Section 4 introduces the improved epidemic model TG_SEI. Section 5 gives the details of the evolution game analysis of nodes in IOTA, followed by the proposed algorithm in Section 6. Section 7 concludes the whole paper.

2. Related Work

The emergence of blockchain technology has accelerated the development of decentralization, privacy protection, and encrypted search of IoT [19–23], especially in crowdsensing systems [24], fog computing [25,26], privacy protection [27–29], and crowdsourcing [30–32]. On this basis, the blockchain system based on DAG provides a guarantee for the high concurrency, high scalability, and zero handling fee of IoT. The most representative is IOTA.

After the IOTA project was launched in 2015, Serguei Popov [1] explained the working principle of the Tangle in the relevant white paper, proposed an MCMC algorithm to provide an attachment strategy for new transactions arriving, and finally listed a variety of possible attack scenarios. Among them, the PC attack, as a common double-spending attack, has attracted extensive attention.

2.1. PC Attack

In [1], the authors first described the formation and attack principle of the parasite chain. Cai, D [9] pointed out that the coordinator still played a major role in IOTA. Once removed, it would face security problems caused by parasite chain attacks. In the parasite chain attack scenario, Yixin Li et al. [10] used the Markov chain model to describe the consistency process behavior of the DAG ledger under dynamic load and tested the probability of a successful attack under different network load modes. Philip Staupe [11] studied the method to reduce the risk of a double-spending attack by analyzing the probability absorbed by the parasite chain in the MCMC random walk. A. Cullen et al. [12] analyzed the effectiveness of the Markov chain Monte Carlo (MCMC) algorithm by using a matrix model and proposed an extended MCMC algorithm to improve the resistance of the distributed ledger to these attacks. Andreas Penzkofer et al. [13] proposed a detection mechanism for parasite chain attacks. Honest nodes improved the tip selection algorithm by detecting the structure of the parasite chain to prevent the parasite chain from successfully launching attacks. The above studies fully show that the parasite chain attack is one of the major security risks of IOTA and show that further research on the parasite chain attack has practical significance. Observing these studies, it is found that no one has analyzed the impact of node behavior strategies on PC attacks from the perspective of the IOTA nodes themselves.

2.2. Blockchain and Game Theory

At present, game theory is mainly used to analyze the mining behaviors of nodes in the blockchain, the computing power competition between mining pools, and the blockchain consensus and incentive mechanisms. Liu Z et al. [14] summarized the application of game theory in blockchain and pointed out that game theory was a mathematical model for studying the strategic interaction between rational decision makers, which was naturally applicable to the decision making of all consensus nodes in the blockchain network. Changbing Tang et al. [15] understood and analyzed the PoW consensus algorithm from the perspective of game theory, providing new ideas and methods for further designing consensus algorithms based on game theory. Lihua Song et al. [16] analyzed some problems in the design of the bitcoin incentive mechanism and used the idea of game theory to design an anti-collusion smart contract for clients in cloud computing. Shi H et al. [17] gave the mining pool the power to unilaterally control the miners' income using the zero-determinant theory and stimulated the miners' cooperation through the proposed zero determinant incentive mechanism. Xuan S et al. [33] proposed a data-sharing incentive model of smart contract blockchain based on evolutionary game theory. Their model was proposed to solve the challenges of establishing mutual trust and improving user participation in data sharing. According to the increasing demand for blockchain scalability and sustainability in various fields, Shashank Motepalli et al. [34] proposed a reward mechanism framework. Then, they further analyzed how participants' behavior evolved with the reward mechanism by using evolutionary game theory.

The above research shows that it is feasible and a research hotspot to analyze the behavior of blockchain nodes through game theory, but IOTA, as a blockchain based on the DAG structure, is rarely involved in game methods. Serguei Popov et al. [35] have proved that there is a Nash equilibrium in IOTA, but it is necessary to conduct in-depth analysis on the malicious behavior of nodes in IOTA to resist attacks.

However, the current literature has not paid too much attention to the impact of IOTA nodes' own behaviors on IOTA security, and no one has analyzed IOTA nodes' behavior strategies through evolutionary game theory. Under the premise of "bounded rationality" of participants, we put forward the cost calculation method of launching a PC attack, construct the payoff matrix to analyze the dynamic behaviors of IOTA nodes, calculate the evolutionary stable strategy, and finally find an effective algorithm to prevent PC attacks.

3. Background

3.1. IOTA

IOTA does not charge transaction fees, and each node maintains the update of the ledger by contributing its own computing power to confirm the two existing transactions in the Tangle. Figure 2a shows the DAG structure of the Tangle. The rectangle represents a transaction. On the left is the genesis transaction, and the unconfirmed transactions on the right are called tips. To avoid malicious competition between nodes caused by not charging transaction fees, the concept of weight is introduced into the IOTA system. Each transaction has weight, which is divided into cumulative weight and own weight (shown in Figure 2b. The number in the upper left corner of transaction A is cumulative weight, and the number in the lower right corner is own weight). The transaction with a large cumulative weight in the Tangle is more "important", and its own weight is proportional to the amount of work that the issuing node invested into it. To ensure the effectiveness of transactions in the Tangle, we propose approval rate (AR) and tangle robustness level σ.

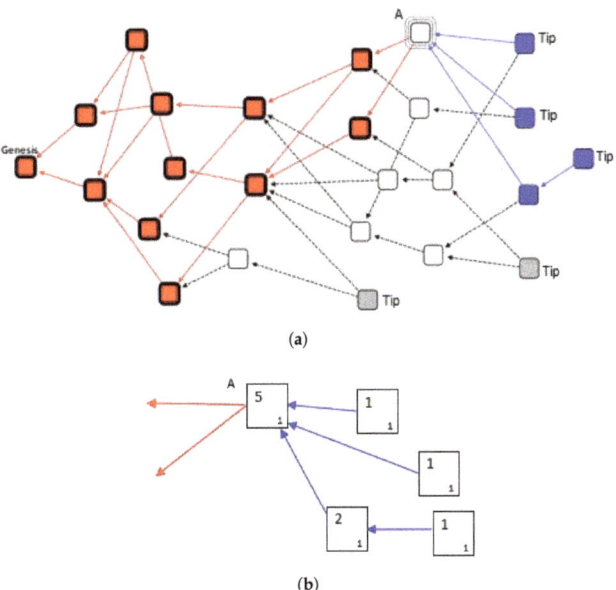

Figure 2. IOTA's distributed ledger—the Tangle diagram. (**a**) DAG structure of the Tangle. (**b**) Example of cumulative weight and own weight of transaction A.

Definition 1. *Approval rate AR: The ratio of the number of tips directly or indirectly pointing to the transaction at a certain time to the total number of tips at that time. As shown in Figure 2, the AR of transaction A is 0.6. The greater the AR, the greater the possibility that the transaction cannot be tampered with.*

Definition 2. *Tangle robustness level σ: When AR meets certain conditions, additional cumulative weight is required to ensure the confirmation of existing transactions to offset the difference between the cumulative weight achieved by malicious nodes and honest nodes.*

3.2. Epidemic Model

The epidemic model can reflect the dynamic characteristics of infectious diseases. Through the qualitative and quantitative analysis and numerical simulation of the epidemic model, we can reveal the epidemic law of diseases and predict their change trend, so as to provide a theoretical and quantitative basis for disease prevention and control. The iterative form of the SI model is as follows:

$$\begin{cases} \frac{dS(t)}{dt} = \alpha M - \beta S(t)I(t) - \alpha S(t) \\ \frac{dI(t)}{dt} = \beta S(t)I(t) - \alpha I(t) \end{cases}, \quad (1)$$

where $S(t)$ represents the susceptible population at time t, $I(t)$ represents the infected population at time t, β represents the transmission coefficient of S and I, M represents the total population at time t, and α represents the natural mortality of S and I at time t. This paper mainly improves the SI model. The information transmission between nodes has a similar dynamic evolution process with virus infection, so the mathematical model based on the epidemic is also suitable for the field of network information transmission [36,37]. Based on the dynamic evolution model of infectious disease transmission, we put forward a calculation method for estimating the number of nodes in the actual synchronous Tangle.

3.3. Evolutionary Game Theory

In evolutionary game theory, evolutionary stable strategy (ESS) and replication dynamics are two core concepts. ESS refers to that, in the process of the game, due to the limited rationality of both sides in the game, the game side cannot find the optimal strategy and the optimal equilibrium point at the beginning; therefore, the game player needs to constantly learn in the process of the game. If the player has made strategic mistakes, they will gradually correct them, and constantly imitate and improve towards the most favorable strategies for themselves and others in the past. After a period of imitation and error correction, all players will tend to a stable strategy. Replication dynamics is actually a dynamic differential equation that describes the frequency of a specific strategy adopted in a population, which can be expressed by the following formula:

$$\frac{dx_i}{dt} = x_i[(u_{s_i}, x) - u(x, x)], \qquad (2)$$

where x_i is the proportion or probability of adopting pure strategy s_i in a population, which represents the fitness when adopting the pure strategy and the average fitness.

4. Improved Epidemic Model TG_SEI

The number of effective nodes in the synchronous ledger (hereinafter referred to as the number of synchronous nodes) reaches a certain threshold (below the threshold, IOTA cannot operate normally. The threshold is set according to the actual situation of IOTA), that can ensure the normal operation of IOTA. Monitoring the number of synchronization nodes in IOTA regularly can reflect the service level of the network to a certain extent. If the synchronization node is seriously missing, the service quality of IOTA will be reduced; therefore, regular monitoring, timely warning, and troubleshooting must be carried out. In addition, the number of synchronization nodes is also an important part of calculating the attack cost; therefore, it is very important to find a method to solve the number of synchronization nodes. The process of the IOTA node synchronizing to the Tangle is very similar to the spread of some viruses in the infectious disease model [38–40]; therefore, we adopt the improved epidemic model TG_SEI to estimate the number of synchronization nodes at any time period. IOTA nodes have three statuses: invalid synchronization status S, the Tangle synchronization delay status E, and effective synchronization status I. Nodes in the S status have not synchronized the Tangle yet. The nodes in the E status synchronize the Tangle but fail to forward it to other nodes in time due to delay. The delay is generally related to the actual network delay threshold. For example, if it is greater than 50 ms, the E status will appear. Nodes in the I status synchronize the Tangle and immediately forward it to other nodes. Assuming that the nodes in the S status connect the nodes in the I status, the Tangle is synchronized.

In the beginning, only one node G is in the I status (that is, the node issuing the Genesis transaction) while the other IOTA nodes are in the S status. After node G issues the transaction, it starts broadcasting the Tangle to the whole network. The nodes directly connecting to node G to synchronize the Tangle will change status S to status I or E. Due to network delay, some of the nodes that synchronized the Tangle are temporarily in the E status. When the delay is alleviated, the nodes in the E status will continue to forward the Tangle to other nodes. With the continuous spread of the Tangle ledger, the connectivity scale between nodes will gradually expand until the whole IOTA network. Most of the nodes that finally synchronized the Tangle are in the I status. In this spreading process, due to natural disasters, equipment failures, crashes, and other factors, a few nodes will not keep the ledger synchronized with node G's and they are removed from the network.

Suppose that at any time t, $S(t)$ denotes the number of nodes that have not synchronized the Tangle (also known as the number of invalid synchronization nodes). The movement of invalid synchronization nodes is random. During this period, very few nodes may not work or crash and be removed from the network. $E(t)$ denotes the number of delayed nodes synchronizing the Tangle. Due to the uncertainty in the network link, there will be a certain delay in forwarding the Tangle. During this period, very few nodes may not work or crash and be removed from the network. $I(t)$ denotes the number of nodes that fully synchronize to the Tangle and forward it (also known as the number of effective synchronization nodes). During this period, very few nodes may not work or crash and be removed from the network.

Let M denote the total number of nodes in the IOTA at time t. To simplify the calculation, the rate at which new nodes join or exit the IOTA is α; therefore, $M = S(t) + E(t) + I(t)$ is constant. β represents the average spreading rate of the IOTA Tangle, which is related to the average degree of the network. δ represents the average delay rate of the synchronizing Tangle and meets $0 < \delta < 1$. δ is related to the actual situation of the network. The greater the network delay, the larger the value of δ. γ indicates the conversion rate from status E to status I. Most nodes will synchronize the Tangle after delay. The improved epidemic model TG_SEI iteration form is as follows,

$$\begin{cases} \frac{dS(t)}{dt} = \alpha M - \beta S(t)I(t) - \alpha S(t) \\ \frac{dE(t)}{dt} = \beta \delta S(t)I(t) - (\gamma + \alpha)E(t) \\ \frac{dI(t)}{dt} = \beta(1-\delta)S(t)I(t) + \gamma E(t) - \alpha I(t) \end{cases} \quad (3)$$

The evolution process of the synchronous nodes' number is the same as that of $I(t)$, that is, the final result of $I(t)$ evolution is the number of synchronous nodes in IOTA denoted as X,

$$\begin{cases} \frac{dI(t)}{dt} = \beta(1-\delta)S(t)I(t) + \gamma E(t) - \alpha I(t) \\ I(0) = 1 \end{cases} \quad (4)$$

According to Equation (3), two groups of possible equilibrium points of the equations are obtained, which are $E_1^*(M,0,0)$ and $E_2^*(\frac{\alpha(\gamma+\alpha)}{\beta(\gamma+\alpha-\alpha\delta)}, \frac{\alpha\delta(M\beta(\gamma+\alpha-\alpha\delta)-\alpha(\gamma+\alpha))}{\beta(\gamma+\alpha-\alpha\delta)(\gamma+\alpha)}, \frac{M\beta(\gamma+\alpha-\alpha\delta)-\alpha(\gamma+\alpha)}{\beta(\gamma+\alpha)})$. Because only when the basic reproduction number $R_0 > 1$, the Tangle of node G can be synchronized and forwarded by most other nodes; therefore, the equilibrium point E_2^* is the only asymptotically stable equilibrium point. When $t \to \infty$ and $M\beta(\gamma+\alpha-\alpha\delta) - \alpha(\gamma+\alpha) > 0$, $I(t) \to \frac{M\beta(\gamma+\alpha-\alpha\delta)-\alpha(\gamma+\alpha)}{\beta(\gamma+\alpha)}$, we can obtain

$$X = \lfloor \frac{M\beta(\gamma+\alpha-\alpha\delta) - \alpha(\gamma+\alpha)}{\beta(\gamma+\alpha)} \rfloor, \quad (5)$$

where parameters α, β, δ, and γ are greater than 0 and less than 1. For example, when $M = 10{,}000$, $\alpha = 0.005$, $\beta = 0.2$, $\delta = 0.8$, and $\gamma = 0.2$, the probability curve of the number of synchronization nodes with time evolution based on the TG_SEI model is shown in Figure 3. The red point line indicates the changing trend of the number of invalid synchronization nodes with time, which is decreasing. The blue dotted line indicates the changing trend of the number of effective synchronization nodes with time, which is increasing. The solid line indicates the changing trend of the number of synchronization delay nodes. After a certain delay, most of the nodes in E status will become nodes in I status.

To simplify the calculation, we set the number of nodes joining and exiting IOTA per unit time equal. In a real scenario, they may not be equal. The values of α, β, δ, and γ in the TG_SEI model can be obtained by (1) prediction of supervised learning model in machine learning or (2) analysis of the propagation mechanism and dynamics of the complex network [41,42].

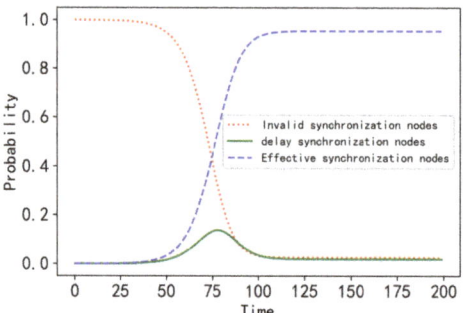

Figure 3. Probability curve of the number of synchronous nodes with time evolution based on the TG_SEI model.

5. Evolution Game Analysis of Nodes in IOTA

In IOTA, all nodes form a node group. Each node has an initial strategy about whether to choose a parasite chain attack. Nodes repeatedly randomly select other nodes from the group to play the game. In this process, nodes with a low payoff will change the strategy to imitate the high-payoff nodes, while low-payoff strategies will be gradually eliminated. After such continuous learning and adjustment, the node group will eventually reach an equilibrium state, which is that all nodes in the group will choose the ESS.

Creating transactions to issuing the transactions to the Tangle is a complex process. In this process, the Tangle is vulnerable to malicious attacks. One of the most-common attacks is PC attacks. In Figure 4, a parasite chain is "generated" under a transaction in the Tangle where the red site is a conflict transaction. The parasite chains formed in the actual scene have different shapes and sizes, and the attacker can freely choose the number of transfers of the PC and decide which transfers the attacker confirms; therefore, this paper makes some restrictions on the PC. We only study the simple PC because it does not affect the generality.

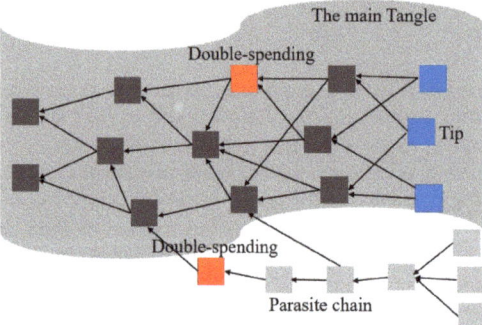

Figure 4. The Tangle with a parasite chain.

5.1. Research Hypothesis and Parameter Description

We make the following assumptions.

Assumption 1. *IOTA nodes are bounded rationality, that is, they cannot find the optimal strategy at the beginning of the game. It needs to learn constantly in the process of the game.*

Assumption 2. *The computational power cost consumed by node attack is large enough to enable the successful completion of the attack; the computational power cost of two nodes is the same.*

Assumption 3. *Each node purchases the same commodity at the same price.*

Assumption 4. *The change of node payoff caused by the change of market price of the currency is not considered.*

Since the payoff matrix of the repeated game model is closely related to the specific payoff parameters of each game participant, the parameters are described as shown in Table 1.

Table 1. Description of parameters.

Parameter	Description
i, j	Node number, representing node i and node j
S_i, S_j	Strategies adopted by node i and node j respectively, $S_i, S_j \in \{Attack, No\ attack\}$
$x (0 \leq x \leq 1)$	Probability of selecting attack strategy
C_1	Cost of node successfully launching PC attack
C_2	Cost of node not launching attack
U_i, U_j	Represent the expected returns of both parties respectively
Pri	Commodity price
w_{ini}	The node issues the initial weight of a transaction (recorded as tran1) in the main tangle
w_0	The merchant agrees to the cumulative weight threshold of the transaction (tran1)
t_0	The time when the node issues a transaction tran1 to the merchant in main tangle and also the starting time of the private PC chain
t_1	The time when the cumulative weight of transaction tran1 reaches the merchant weight threshold and the merchant accepts the transaction
t	The time after the node implements the PC attack, the cumulative weight of the double-spending transaction generated on the PC exceeds the cumulative weight time of the legal transaction in main tangle
S_h	The sum of cumulative weights of transaction tran1 in main Tangle at time t
S_m	The sum of cumulative weights corresponding to the double-spending transaction in the parasite chain at time t
λ	Average transaction arrival rate of the node no launching PC attacks (i.e., an honest node), $\lambda > 0$
μ	Average transaction arrival rate of nodes launching PC attacks (i.e., a malicious node), $\mu > 0$
w_h	The average weight of transactions generated by honest nodes
w_m	The average weight of transactions generated by malicious nodes

5.2. Transaction Number, Cumulative Weight, Time to Successfully Launch Parasite Chain Attack, and Its Cost Function

Let A be any node in IOTA. Node A may launch a parasite chain attack. If node A has a parasite chain at time t, before node A broadcasts the parasite chain to IOTA, the average rate of new transactions reaching the main Tangle is λ and the average rate of new transactions arriving at the parasite chain is μ.

(1) If node A launches a parasite chain attack successfully, the number of transactions issued is

$$N_1 = (\lambda + \mu)(t_1 - t_0) + \mu(t - t_1). \tag{6}$$

If node A does not launch a parasite chain attack, the number of transactions issued is

$$N_2 = \lambda(t - t_0). \tag{7}$$

(2) Cumulative weight

Suppose that node A issues a transaction tran1 to the main Tangle at time t_0 and waits for the merchant's confirmation. At the same time, node A starts to build a parasite chain privately and generates a transaction tran2. Node A transfers the money used to transaction tran1 to the corresponding account of transaction tran2 in the parasite chain.

That is, transaction tran1 and transaction tran2 have the same money but correspond to different accounts of node A. When the cumulative weight of tran1 reaches the merchant's weight threshold w_0 at t_1, the merchant accepts the transaction and delivers the goods. Once the difference between the cumulative weights of transaction tran2 and transaction tran1 is greater than σ, that is, $S_m - S_h >= \sigma$, then node A can successfully launch a parasite chain attack and realize double spending. σ is the Tangle robustness level, which is related to AR. σ reflects the difficulty of the node to implement the malicious attack successfully. For S_m and S_h, see below for details.

At time t_1, the merchant accepts the cumulative weight threshold expression of transaction tran1 issued by node A in the main Tangle is

$$w_0 = w_{ini} + \lambda(t_1 - t_0)w_h. \tag{8}$$

At time t, the cumulative weight of transaction tran1 in the main Tangle is

$$\begin{aligned} S_h &= w_0 + (1 - p_m)\lambda(t - t_1)w_h \\ &= w_{ini} + \lambda(t_1 - t_0)w_h + (1 - p_m)\lambda(t - t_1)w_h. \end{aligned} \tag{9}$$

where P_m is the probability that the transaction is absorbed by the parasite chain after the honest node runs the MCMC algorithm [11], $0 < P_m < 1$. It is worth noting that after the parasite chain is broadcast to the whole network, the parasite chain can no longer reference the transactions in the main Tangle. Because the honest node will check the historical consistency and will not accept the double-spending transaction as a valid transaction. At time t, node A issues the cumulative weight of the corresponding double-spending transaction in the parasite chain as follows

$$S_m = w_{ini} + \mu(t - t_0)w_m + p_m\lambda(t - t_1)w_h. \tag{10}$$

(3) Time of successful parasite chain attack

$$S_m - S_h \geq \sigma. \tag{11}$$

Combined with Equations (8)–(10), the relationship expression of time t is

$$t \geq \frac{\sigma + (\mu w_m - \lambda w_h)t_0 + 2p_m\lambda w_h t_1}{\mu w_m - \lambda w_h + 2p_m\lambda w_h}. \tag{12}$$

Let $T_1 = \frac{\sigma + (\mu w_m - \lambda w_h)t_0 + 2p_m\lambda w_h t_1}{\mu w_m - \lambda w_h + 2p_m\lambda w_h}$; $t \geq T_1$ is obtained by simplification.

(4) Cost function

Assuming that the actual number of effective synchronization nodes in IOTA at time t is X and the number of malicious nodes is n, the cost function required for node A to successfully launch a parasite chain attack is expressed as

$$C_1 = [(\lambda + \mu)(t_1 - t_0) + \mu(t - t_1)]q_0 + (X - 1)\lambda(t_1 - t_0)q_1 + (n - 1)\mu(t - t_1)q_1. \tag{13}$$

If the node does not launch an attack, the cost function is

$$C_2 = \lambda(t - t_0)q_0 + (X - 1)\lambda(t_1 - t_0)q_1 + (X - n - 1)\lambda(t - t_1)q_1, \tag{14}$$

where q_0 is the average cost of generating and issuing a transaction for the node and q_1 is the average cost of verifying and disseminating an incoming transaction, and $q_0 > 0$, $q_1 > 0$.

5.3. Constructing Evolutionary Game Model and Results

The following two cases are discussed. One is that malicious nodes conspire to create the PC, and the attack cost is halved after malicious nodes cooperate. The other is that malicious nodes create PCs alone.

5.3.1. Nodes Conspire to Create the Parasite Chain

Analyze the payoff of node i and node j at time t to construct the payoff matrix of the evolutionary game model shown in Table 2.

Table 2. Payoff matrix.

		Node j	
		Attack(y)	No Attack(1 − y)
Node i	Attack(x)	$Pri - C_1/2, Pri - C_1/2$	$Pri - C_1, -C_2$
	No attack(1 − x)	$-C_2, Pri - C_1$	$-C_2, -C_2$

For node i (Note: the analysis method of node j is the same as that of node i, which will not be repeated later), the expected payoff of adopting the "attack" strategy is

$$U_{i1} = x(Pri - C_1/2) + (1-x)(Pri - C_1) = (C_1/2)x + Pri - C_1. \tag{15}$$

Take the "no attack" strategy and the expected payoff is

$$U_{i2} = -C_2. \tag{16}$$

The overall average expected payoff of node i is

$$\begin{aligned} U &= xU_{i1} + (1-x)U_{i2} \\ &= (C_1/2)x^2 + x(Pri - C_1 + C_2) - C_2. \end{aligned} \tag{17}$$

From Equations (15)–(17), the replicator dynamics equation of the subject proportion of actors adopting the "attack" strategy is

$$\begin{aligned} F(x) &= dx/dt \\ &= x(U_{i1} - U) \\ &= x(1-x)[(C_1/2)x + Pri - C_1 + C_2]. \end{aligned} \tag{18}$$

When $F(x) = 0$, we can obtain three stable states

$$x_1^* = 0, x_2^* = 1, x_3^* = \frac{2(C_1 - C_2 - Pri)}{C_1}. \tag{19}$$

According to the value of x_3^*, the ESS is discussed in three cases below.

(1) The ESS when $x_3^* \leq 0$

The condition of $x_3^* = \frac{2(C_1 - C_2 - Pri)}{C_1} \leq 0$ is

$$Pri \geq C_1 - C_2. \tag{20}$$

Because of $0 \leq x \leq 1$, the replicator dynamics at this time only have two stable states $x_1^* = 0$ and $x_2^* = 1$. The ESS x^* has the characteristics of resisting small interference. When the interference makes $x < x^*$, there is $F(x) = dx/dt > 0$. When the interference makes $x > x^*$, there is $F(x) = dx/dt < 0$. In the phase diagram of the replicator dynamics equation, the curve intersects the abscissa at several points. If the tangent slope at the intersection is negative, it is the ESS of the replicator dynamics in the evolutionary game;

therefore, according to the above conditions, $F'(0) \geq 0$ and $F'(1) < 0$, its ESS $x^* = 1$. The replicator dynamics equation phase diagram is shown in Figure 5. Nodes tend to launch parasite chain attacks.

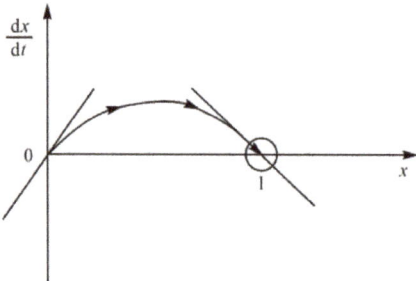

Figure 5. Replicator dynamics equation phase diagram when $x_3^* \leq 0$.

(2) The ESS when $x_3^* \geq 1$

The condition of $x_3^* = \frac{2(C_1 - C_2 - Pri)}{C_1} \geq 1$ is

$$Pri \leq C_1/2 - C_2. \tag{21}$$

At this time, the replicator dynamics only have two stable states $x_1^* = 0$ and $x_2^* = 1$. Since $F'(0) < 0$ and $F'(1) \geq 0$, its ESS is $x^* = 0$. The replicator dynamics equation phase diagram is shown in Figure 6. Nodes tend not to launch parasite chain attacks.

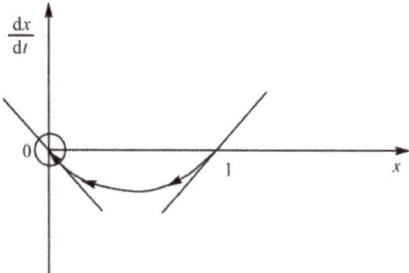

Figure 6. Replicator dynamics equation phase diagram when $x_3^* \geq 1$.

(3) The ESS when $0 < x_3^* < 1$

The condition of $0 < \frac{2(C_1 - C_2 - Pri)}{C_1} < 1$ is

$$C_1/2 - C_2 < Pri < C_1 - C_2. \tag{22}$$

At this time, the replicator dynamics have three stable states. Since $F'(0) < 0$ and $F'(1) < 0$, the corresponding replicator dynamics phase diagram is shown in Figure 7.

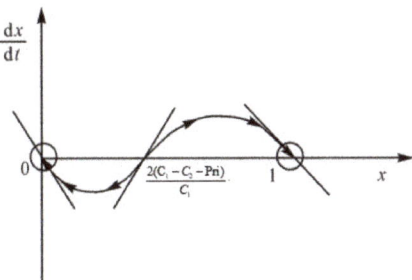

Figure 7. Replicator dynamics equation phase diagram when $0 < x_3^* < 1$.

When $0 < x_3^* < \frac{2(C_1 - C_2 - Pri)}{C_1}$, its ESS is $x^* = 0$.

When $\frac{2(C_1 - C_2 - Pri)}{C_1} < x_3^* < 1$, its ESS is $x^* = 1$.

The analysis shows that when the commodity price provided by the merchant is satisfied $Pri \geq C_1 - C_2$, that is, the commodity price is higher than the difference between the cost paid by the node to launch a parasite chain attack and the cost paid by not launching an attack, the node will choose to launch a parasite chain attack, because, compared with the original, the node will increase revenue and be profitable. When the commodity price provided by the merchant is satisfied $Pri \leq C_1/2 - C_2$, the node will not launch a parasite chain attack, because the attack cost is higher than the payoff, which will damage its interests and outweigh the loss. When the commodity price provided by the merchant is satisfied $C_1/2 - C_2 < Pri < C_1 - C_2$, if x_3^* is included in $(0, \frac{2(C_1 - C_2 - Pri)}{C_1})$, the node chooses not to attack because the probability of successfully launching a parasite chain attack is small. If x_3^* falls in $(\frac{2(C_1 - C_2 - Pri)}{C_1}, 1)$, the node will choose to launch an attack because the probability of successfully launching a parasite chain attack increases. Next, Matlab 2020a was used to simulate the above evolutionary game process.

(1) Assuming $C_2 = 1$, $Pri = 2$, and C_1 takes 2, 4, and 6, respectively, the strategy selection of node i changes as shown in Figure 8.
(2) Assuming $C_2 = 1$, $C_1 = 2$, and Pri takes 2, 0.5, and 0.1, respectively, the strategy selection of node i changes as shown in Figure 9.

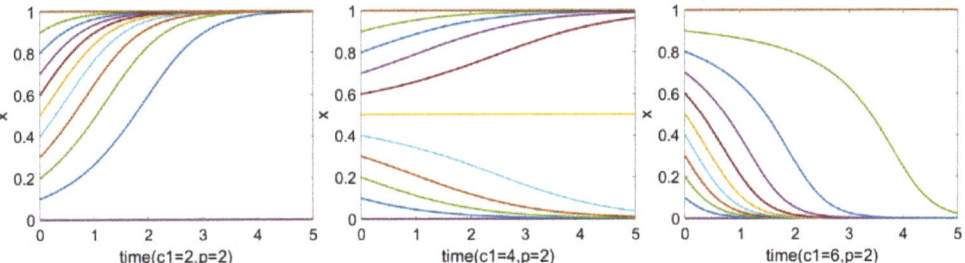

Figure 8. The evolution process of node i's strategy selection when C_1 value increases.

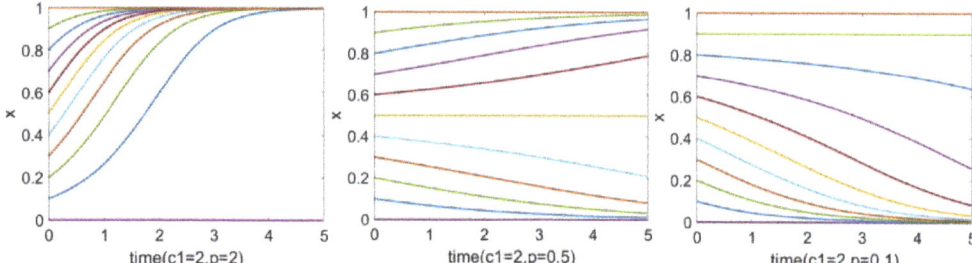

Figure 9. The evolution process of node i's strategy selection when Pri value decreases.

Figure 8 shows the evolution trend of probability x with C_1 when Pri and C_2 remain unchanged. Figure 9 shows the evolution trend of probability x with Pri when C_1 and C_2 remain unchanged. The analysis shows that if other conditions are certain, increasing the attack cost will reduce the probability of nodes choosing parasite chain attacks. Similarly, other conditions are certain, the lower the commodity price, the lower the probability of nodes successfully launching parasite chain attacks.

5.3.2. Each Node Will Make Its Parasite Chain

If a node launches a PC attack, it needs to create a parasite chain alone. The payoff matrix of the evolutionary game model is shown in Table 3.

Table 3. Payoff matrix.

		Node j	
		Attack(y)	No Attack(1 − y)
Node i	Attack(x)	$Pri − C_1$, $Pri − C_1$	$Pri − C_1$, $−C_2$
	No attack(1 − x)	$−C_2$, $Pri − C_1$	$−C_2$, $−C_2$

Moreover, $Pri1$ and $Pri2$ represent the price of goods purchased by node i and node j, respectively. The analysis process is the same as Section 5.3.1, and two stable states $x_1^* = 0$ and $x_2^* = 1$ are obtained. The analysis results also reflect the relationship between commodity price and cost. For node i, when $Pri1 \geq C_1 − C_2$, the node will launch a parasite chain attack. When $Pri1 < C_1 − C_2$, the node will not launch an attack. The analysis method of node j is the same as that of node i and will not be repeated.

6. The Proposed Algorithms

It can be seen from the previous section that the lower the commodity price in the transaction, the less likely it is to be attacked by PC; therefore, we can effectively resist PC attacks by splitting large transaction prices into small ones. At the same time, it also further proves the applicability of micropayments in IOTA. With the continuous expansion of the scale of IoT, if we can further predict the concentrated time slot of many PC attacks and strengthen prevention, we can also effectively resist PC attacks.

6.1. Concentrated Time Slot of PC Attacks

According to the analysis results in Section 5, we can further determine the concentrated time slot for nodes to launch PC attacks. This section only focuses on the situation that satisfied $Pri \geq C_1 − C_2$. When ESS is 1, nodes will launch PC attacks to increase their interests; therefore, Equation (20) is deformed to

$$C_1 \leq Pri + C_2. \tag{23}$$

By substituting Equation (14) into (23), we obtain

$$C_1 \leq Pri + \lambda(t - t_0)q_0 + (X - 1)\lambda(t_1 - t_0)q_1 + (X - n - 1)\lambda(t - t_1)q_1, \quad (24)$$

According to Equation (24), the cost of an IOTA node launching a parasite chain attack successfully depends on many factors, such as commodity price, the number of IOTA synchronization nodes, the number of malicious nodes, the time issuing transaction, the time transacting with merchants, the time it takes for a parasite chain to attack successfully, the arrival rate of transactions, the average cost of issuing a transaction, the average verification and dissemination cost of a transaction, etc.

As shown in Figure 10, solid line a and dotted line b represent the cost threshold varying with time t and the cost paid by the node when successfully launching a parasite chain attack, respectively. Assuming $(\mu - \lambda)q_0 - (X\lambda - n\lambda - \lambda - n\mu + \mu)q_1$, the time at the intersection of the two lines is

$$T_2 = \frac{Pri - (\lambda t_1 - \mu t_0)q_0 - (X\lambda - n\lambda - \lambda - n\mu + \mu)t_1 q_1}{(\mu - \lambda)q_0 - (X\lambda - n\lambda - \lambda - n\mu + \mu)q_1}. \quad (25)$$

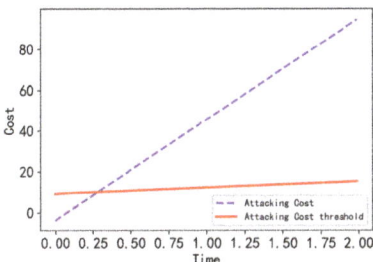

Figure 10. Cost function of launching a parasite chain attack diagram.

In Equation (12), when $T_1 > T_2, T_1 > 0$ and $T_2 > 0$, that is, $t \in [T_2 + t_1, T_1]$, the probability of a node successfully launching a parasite chain attack will increase. To prevent nodes from launching parasite chain attacks, it is important to strengthen prevention during this time slot as shown in Algorithm 1.

Algorithm 1 Algorithm for determining the concentrated time slot of PC attacks.

Input: Commodity price Pri; The average transaction arrival rate of an honest node λ; The average transaction arrival rate of a malicious node μ; The average cost of generating and issuing a transaction q_0; The average cost of verifying and disseminating a transaction q_1; Actual number of synchronized ledger nodes X; Number of malicious nodes n; The time when the node issues a transaction to the merchant in the main Tangle t_0; The time when the cumulative weight of transaction reaches the merchant weight threshold w_0 and the merchant accepts the transaction t_1.
Output: The concentrated time slot.
$t \leftarrow t_0$;
Calculate the time points T_1 and T_2 according to Equations (12) and (25) respectively;
While $t > 0$
    if $t \geq T_1$ and $t \leq T_2$
        Monitor the Tangle in real-time;
        If conflicting transactions are detected, run the tip select algorithm and only retain the legal branch with the largest cumulative weight;
    Endif
    Monitor the Tangle regularly;
    If conflicting transactions are detected, run the tip select algorithm and only retain the legal branch with the largest cumulative weight. Monitor in real-time for some time to ensure the complete elimination of conflicting transactions;

6.2. The Algorithm for Preventing PC Attacks Based on Price Splitting—APS

If the commodity price is low and the payment amount is small, IOTA nodes generally do not launch PC attacks to damage their interests, but prefer to work honestly. If the commodity price is high and the transaction amount is too large, it can be divided into multiple small amounts for payment to avoid PC attacks. There are many ways to split the price, which can be designed according to the needs of the actual IOTA network. For example, the simplest price halving method is used. Since the parasite chain can be generated jointly or independently, the corresponding algorithms are shown in Algorithms 2 and 3, respectively.

Algorithm 2 APS-conspiracy.

Input: Commodity price Pri; PC attack cost C_1; Cost of not launching an attack C_2.
Output: Splitting the price stored in $M[i]$ and the price split copies j.
$M[] \leftarrow 0, i \leftarrow 0, j \leftarrow 0, x \leftarrow 0$;
M.append(Pri);
While $Pri \geq C_1 - C_2$
    $Pri = Pri/2$;
    M.append(Pri);
    $i = i + 1$;
While $C_1/2 - C_2 < Pri < C_1 - C_2$ and $2(C_1 - C_2 - Pri)/C_1 < x < 1$
    $Pri = Pri/2$;
    M.append(Pri);
    $i = i + 1$;
$j = M[0]/M[i]$;
Return $M[i]$ and j;

Algorithm 3 APS-independence.

Input: Commodity price Pri; PC attack cost C_1; Cost of not launching an attack C_2.
Output: Splitting the price stored in $M[i]$ and the price split copies j.
$M[] \leftarrow 0, i \leftarrow 0, j \leftarrow 0, x \leftarrow 0$;
M.append(Pri);
While $Pri \geq C_1 - C_2$
 $Pri = Pri/2$;
 M.append(Pri);
 i = i + 1;
$j = M[0]/M[i]$;
Return $M[i]$ and j;

In addition, IOTA can also add some incentive or punishment mechanisms to further prevent nodes from launching attacks. A reasonable incentive mechanism can make the node offset part of the work cost and reduce the probability of launching a PC attack, while the punishment mechanism can restrain the node from launching attacks via punishment.

7. Conclusions

In this paper, we proposed an effective scheme to prevent parasite attacks. First, we proposed a cost calculation method for parasite chain attacks. Then, the behavior strategies of the IOTA node launching attack were analyzed by evolutionary game theory, the key factors required to successfully launch parasite chain attack were studied, and the numerical simulation was carried out. Finally, the algorithms to prevent parasite chain attacks were proposed, which are based on price segmentation detection to further suppress the formation of parasitic chain attacks. Our proposed scheme is a new exploration and attempts to use the evolutionary game theory based on the bounded rationality of participants to analyze the behavior relationship between IOTA nodes. As future work, we plan to use existing techniques to implement the detection and prevention of PC attacks in IOTA.

Author Contributions: Conceptualization, Y.C.; methodology, Y.C. and R.B.; validation, Y.G. and Y.C.; writing—original draft, Y.C.; writing—review and editing, Y.C., Y.G. and Y.W. All authors have read and agreed to the published version of the manuscript.

Funding: This research is sponsored by the National Natural Science Foundation of China under Grants 62102035, 62177007, 61571049, 71961022, the Fundamental Research Funds for the Central Universities under Grants 2020NTST32, and the Foreign Expert Programs of Ministry of Science and Technology grant number DL2021123002L.

Institutional Review Board Statement: Not applicable.

Informed Consent Statement: Not applicable.

Data Availability Statement: Not applicable.

Conflicts of Interest: The authors declare no conflict of interest.

References

1. Popov, S. The Tangle. Version 1.4.3. 2018. Available online: https://assets.ctfassets.net/r1dr6vzfxhev/2t4uxvsIqk0EUau6g2sw0g/45eae33637ca92f85dd9f4a3a218e1ec/iota1_4_3.pdf (accessed on 16 February 2022).
2. Silvano, W.F.; Marcelino, R. IOTA Tangle: A cryptocurrency to communicate Internet-of-Things data. *Future Gener. Comput. Syst.* **2020**, *112*, 307–319. [CrossRef]
3. Guo, F.; Xiao, X.; Hecker, A.; Dustdar, S. Characterizing IOTA Tangle with Empirical Data. In Proceedings of the GLOBECOM 2020–2021 IEEE Global Communications Conference, Taipei, Taiwan, 7–11 December 2020; pp. 1–6. [CrossRef]
4. Halgamuge, M.N. Optimization framework for best approver selection method (BASM) and best tip selection method (BTSM) for IOTA tangle network: Blockchain-enabled next generation industrial IoT. *Comput. Netw.* **2021**, *199*, 108418. [CrossRef]
5. Eyal, I.; Sirer, E.G. Majority Is Not Enough: Bitcoin mining is vulnerable. *Commun. ACM* **2018**, *61*, 95–102. [CrossRef]

6. Sapirshtein, A.; Sompolinsky, Y.; Zohar, A. Optimal Selfish Mining Strategies in Bitcoin. In *International Conference on Financial Cryptography and Data Security*; Springer: Berlin/Heidelberg, Germany, 2015.
7. Nayak, K.; Kumar, S.; Miller, A.; Shi, E. Stubborn Mining: Generalizing Selfish Mining and Combining with an Eclipse Attack. In Proceedings of the IEEE European Symposium on Security & Privacy, Saarbruecken, Germany, 21–24 March 2016.
8. Niu, J.; Feng, C. Selfish Mining in Ethereum. In Proceedings of the 2019 IEEE 39th International Conference on Distributed Computing Systems (ICDCS), Dallas, TX, USA, 7–10 July 2019.
9. Cai, D. A Parasite Chain Attack in IOTA. Bachelor's Thesis, University of Twente, Enschede, The Netherlands, 2019.
10. Li, Y.; Cao, B.; Peng, M.; Zhang, L.; Zhang, L.; Feng, D.; Yu, J. Direct Acyclic Graph-based Ledger for Internet of Things: Performance and Security Analysis. *IEEE/ACM Trans. Netw.* **2020**, *28*, 1643–1656. [CrossRef]
11. Staupe, P. Quasi-Analytic Parasite Chain Absorption Probabilities in the Tangle. 2017. Available online: https://www.iota.org/foundation/research-papers (accessed on 16 February 2022).
12. Cullen, A.; Ferrar, P.; King, C.; Shorten, R. Distributed Ledger Technology for IoT: Parasite Chain Attacks. 2019. Available online: https://arxiv.org/pdf/1904.00996.pdf (accessed on 16 February 2022).
13. Penzkofer, A.; Kusmierz, B.; Capossele, A.; Sanders, W.; Saa, O. Parasite Chain Detection in the IOTA Protocol. 2020. Available online: https://arxiv.org/abs/2004.13409 (accessed on 16 February 2022).
14. Liu, Z.; Luong, N.C.; Wang, W.; Niyato, D.; Wang, P.; Liang, Y.C.; Kim, D.I. A Survey on Applications of Game Theory in Blockchain. *arXiv* **2019**, arXiv:1902.10865.
15. Tang, C.B.; Yang, Z.; Zheng, Z.L.; Chen, Z.Y.; Li, X. Game Dilemma Analysis and Optimization of PoW Consensus Algorithm. *Acta Autom. Sin.* **2017**, *43*, 1520–1531.
16. Song, L.; Li, T.; Wang, Y. Applications of Game Theory in Blockchain. *J. Cryptologic Res.* **2019**, *6*, 100–111.
17. Shi, H.; Wang, S.; Hu, Q.; Cheng, X.; Yu, J. Fee-Free Pooled Mining for Countering Pool-Hopping Attack in Blockchain. *IEEE Trans. Dependable Secur. Comput.* **2020**, *18*, 1580–1590. [CrossRef]
18. Phelps, S.; Wooldridge, M. Game Theory and Evolution. *Intell. Syst.* **2013**, *28*, 76–81. [CrossRef]
19. Hu, S.; Cai, C.; Wang, Q.; Wang, C.; Luo, X.; Ren, K. Searching an encrypted cloud meets blockchain: A decentralized, reliable and fair realization. In Proceedings of the IEEE INFOCOM 2018—IEEE Conference on Computer Communications, Honolulu, HI, USA, 16–19 April 2018; pp. 792–800.
20. Cai, C.; Weng, J.; Yuan, X.; Wang, C. Enabling reliable keyword search in encrypted decentralized storage with fairness. *IEEE Trans. Dependable Secur. Comput.* **2018**, *18*, 131–144. [CrossRef]
21. Yan, D.; Jia, X.; Shu, J.; Yu, R. A Blockchain-based Database System for Decentralized Information Management. In Proceedings of the 2021 IEEE Global Communications Conference (GLOBECOM), Madrid, Spain, 7–11 December 2021; pp. 1–6.
22. Zhang, Y.; Deng, R.H.; Shu, J.; Yang, K.; Zheng, D. TKSE: Trustworthy keyword search over encrypted data with two-side verifiability via blockchain. *IEEE Access* **2018**, *6*, 31077–31087. [CrossRef]
23. Xu, L.; Xu, C.; Liu, Z.; Wang, Y.; Wang, J. Enabling Comparable Search Over Encrypted Data for IoT with Privacy-Preserving. *Comput. Mater. Contin.* **2019**, *60*, 675–690. [CrossRef]
24. Cai, C.; Zheng, Y.; Du, Y.; Qin, Z.; Wang, C. Towards private, robust, and verifiable crowdsensing systems via public blockchains. *IEEE Trans. Dependable Secur. Comput.* **2019**, *18*, 1893–1907. [CrossRef]
25. Miao, Y.; Ma, J.; Liu, X.; Weng, J.; Li, H.; Li, H. Lightweight fine-grained search over encrypted data in fog computing. *IEEE Trans. Serv. Comput.* **2018**, *12*, 772–785. [CrossRef]
26. Guo, Y.; Xie, H.; Wang, C.; Jia, X. Enabling privacy-preserving geographic range query in fog-enhanced iot services. *IEEE Trans. Dependable Secur. Comput.* **2021**. [CrossRef]
27. Wang, M.; Guo, Y.; Zhang, C.; Wang, C.; Huang, H.; Jia, X. MedShare: A Privacy-Preserving Medical Data Sharing System by Using Blockchain. *IEEE TSC* **2021**. [CrossRef]
28. Zhang, C.; Guo, Y.; Jia, X.; Wang, C.; Du, H. Enabling Proxy-free Privacy-preserving and Federated Crowdsourcing by Using Blockchain. *IEEE IoT-J* **2020**, *8*, 6624–6636. [CrossRef]
29. Yao, J.; Zheng, Y.; Guo, Y.; Cai, C.; Zhou, A.; Wang, C.; Gui, X. A Privacy-preserving System for Targeted Coupon Service. *IEEE Access* **2019**, *7*, 120817–120830. [CrossRef]
30. Miao, Y.; Ma, J.; Liu, X.; Li, X.; Liu, Z.; Li, H. Practical attribute-based multi-keyword search scheme in mobile crowdsourcing. *IEEE Internet Things J.* **2017**, *5*, 3008–3018. [CrossRef]
31. Guo, Y.; Xie, H.; Miao, Y.; Wang, C.; Jia, X. Fedcrowd: A federated and privacy-preserving crowdsourcing platform on blockchain. *IEEE Trans. Serv. Comput.* **2020**. [CrossRef]
32. Li, C.; Qu, X.; Guo, Y. TFCrowd: A blockchain-based crowdsourcing framework with enhanced trustworthiness and fairness. *EURASIP J. Wirel. Commun. Netw.* **2021**, *2021*, 1–20. [CrossRef]
33. Xuan, S.; Zheng, L.; Chung, I.; Wang, W.; Man, D.; Du, X.; Yang, W.; Guizani, M. An incentive mechanism for data sharing based on blockchain with smart contracts. *Comput. Electr. Eng.* **2020**, *83*, 106587. [CrossRef]
34. Motepalli, S.; Jacobsen, H.A. Reward Mechanism for Blockchains Using Evolutionary Game Theory. 2021. Available online: https://arxiv.org/abs/2104.05849 (accessed on 16 February 2022).
35. Popov, S.; Saa, O.; Finardi, P. Equilibria in the tangle. *Comput. Ind. Eng.* **2019**, *136*, 160–172. [CrossRef]
36. Fang, L. The Analysis of SI Group Knowledge Dissemination Model with Expected Effect. *J. Taiyuan Norm. Univ. Sci. Ed.* **2020**, *19*, 9–12.

37. Gong, Y.; Li, F.; Zhou, L.; Hu, F. Global Dissemination of Information Based on Online Social Hypernetwork. *J. Univ. Electron. Sci. Technol. China* **2021**, *50*, 437–444.
38. Feng, L.; Wang, H.; Feng, S. Improved SIR model of computer virus propagation in the network. *J. Comput. Appl.* **2011**, *31*, 1891–1893.
39. Lu, T. Qualitative Analysis of SEI Model with the Impact of Media. *J. Nanjing Norm. Univ. (Nat. Sci. Ed.)* **2011**, *34*, 32–35.
40. Li, G.; Zhen, J. Global stability of an SEI epidemic model with general contact rate. *Chaos Solitons Fractals* **2005**, *23*, 997–1004. [CrossRef]
41. Wang, X.; Chen, G. *Complex Network Theory and Its Application*; Tsinghua University Press: Beijing, China, 2006.
42. Mata, A.S. An overview of epidemic models with phase transitions to absorbing states running on top of complex networks. *Chaos* **2021**, *31*, 012101. [CrossRef]

Article

Efficient Reversible Data Hiding Based on Connected Component Construction and Prediction Error Adjustment

Limengnan Zhou [1,2], Chongfu Zhang [2], Asad Malik [3] and Hanzhou Wu [4,5,*]

1 School of Electronic and Information Engineering, University of Electronic Science and Technology of China, Zhongshan Institute, Zhongshan 528402, China
2 School of Information and Communication Engineering, University of Electronic Science and Technology of China, Chengdu 611731, China
3 Department of Computer Science, Aligarh Muslim University, Aligarh 202002, India
4 School of Communication and Information Engineering, Shanghai University, Shanghai 200444, China
5 Guangdong Provincial Key Laboratory of Information Security Technology, Guangzhou 510006, China
* Correspondence: hanzhou@shu.edu.cn

Abstract: To achieve a good trade-off between the data-embedding payload and the data-embedding distortion, mainstream reversible data hiding (RDH) algorithms perform data embedding on a well-built prediction error histogram. This requires us to design a good predictor to determine the prediction errors of cover elements and find a good strategy to construct an ordered prediction error sequence to be embedded. However, many existing RDH algorithms use a fixed predictor throughout the prediction process, which does not take into account the statistical characteristics of local context. Moreover, during the construction of the prediction error sequence, these algorithms ignore the fact that adjacent cover elements may have the identical priority of data embedding. As a result, there is still room for improving the payload-distortion performance. Motivated by this insight, in this article, we propose a new content prediction and selection strategy for efficient RDH in digital images to provide better payload-distortion performance. The core idea is to construct multiple connected components for a given cover image so that the prediction errors of the cover pixels within a connected component are close to each other. Accordingly, the most suitable connected components can be preferentially used for data embedding. Moreover, the prediction errors of the cover pixels are adaptively adjusted according to their local context, allowing a relatively sharp prediction error histogram to be constructed. Experimental results validate that the proposed method is significantly superior to some advanced works regarding payload-distortion performance, demonstrating the practicality of our method.

Keywords: reversible watermarking; reversible data hiding; graph optimization; prediction error

MSC: 94A08

1. Introduction

As an interdisciplinary research field, information hiding (IH) is generally modeled as a covert communication problem involving three participants: *Alice*, *Bob* and *Eve* [1]. Alice plays the role of the data sender. Bob plays the role of the data receiver. However, Eve serves as the attacker. Given a digital media object such as digital video and image, Alice first embeds a secret message into the digital media object (also called *cover*) by modifying the content of the cover without introducing noticeable artifacts. The resulting object concealing the secret message will be sent to Bob via an insecure channel that will be monitored by Eve. Eve will attempt to detect the existence of the secret message within the conveyed object or alter the conveyed object to remove the possibly embedded information. Once Bob receives the probably altered object containing hidden information, he will try to extract the secret message from the received object. Thus, IH is successfully realized if the secret message can be extracted without error. Otherwise, it is deemed failed. Compared with cryptography that may leave noticeable marks on the encrypted data, IH even conceals the existence of the present communication activity, which has good potential in applications and will become increasingly important in modern information security [2,3].

For IH, one of the most important requirements is that the difference between the cover media and the media containing secret information caused by the data embedding operation should be low so that any adversary will not notice the existence of the secret message within the embedded object [4]. Along this line, many IH algorithms have been introduced in the past two decades [5–8]. Given a secret payload to be embedded, most IH algorithms either embed the secret payload by minimizing a well-designed distortion function or embed the secret payload by preserving the selective model of the cover source [9]. On the other hand, for a pre-specified distortion, we expect to embed as many secret bits as possible. This is typically referred to as the payload-distortion problem. Nevertheless, these algorithms inevitably distort the original cover content. In other words, though the secret message can be successfully extracted without any error, the original cover media cannot be perfectly rebuilt from the object containing the secret message, which is not applicable to sensitive application scenarios that require no degradation of the original cover object [10]. This has motivated researchers to study reversible information hiding (RIH) [11] or say reversible data hiding (RDH) [12], reversible watermarking [13] to ensure that both the secret message and the original cover media can be reconstructed at the receiver side. Many RDH algorithms can be found in the literature such as [13–20].

RDH can be applied to various cover sources. For example, due to the popularity over social networks and the ease of handling, digital imagery is still one of the most popular sources for RDH. Other cover sources such as video sequences [21], speech signals [22] and texts [23] are also of increasing interest to researchers recently due to the fast development of multimedia technologies and social networking services. From the viewpoint of the data embedding mechanism, most advanced RDH algorithms use the so-called prediction errors (PEs) of the elements in the cover to be embedded to realize RDH. There are two main reasons [14]. First, the PEs are noise-like, meaning that modifying them will not produce obvious artifacts of the cover since the prediction process significantly reduces the impact caused by the cover content. Second, the PEs are collected to construct a prediction error histogram (PEH), which is a pooled vector that can be easily handled for RDH based on histogram shifting (HS) [12] or its variants [13,24–27]. In terms of data embedding positions, mainstream RDH works could be roughly divided into spatial domain and transform domain. The former uses the values of spatial pixels to carry secret bits, whereas the latter often uses the transformed values as the cover elements such as discrete cosine transform (DCT) coefficients to carry secret bits. In brief summary, regardless of the data embedding domain, exploiting PEs for RDH is efficient.

From the viewpoint of system design, many existing PE-based works mainly consist of five steps, i.e., *content prediction*, *content selection*, *data embedding*, *data extraction* and *cover reconstruction* [14]. Taking a gray-scale image as the cover for example, content prediction aims to predict the pixels and obtain the PEs. For content selection, its target is to sort the collected PEs by a local complexity function so that smooth pixels are embedded preferentially since smooth pixels have a small PE that can result in superior payload-distortion performance. Thereafter, the aforementioned HS or its variants can be applied to the sorted PE sequence to embed secret bits. Once the secret bits are embedded, the resulting new image (or *marked image*) will be sent to the receiver, who will perform secret data extraction and cover image reconstruction. Extracting the embedded secret data and recovering the original image can be roughly viewed as an inverse process of the data hider. Therefore, it is straightforward to draw out that, in order to provide superior payload-distortion performance, the content prediction, content selection and data embedding procedures can be optimized. For content prediction, it is required for us to design a predictor that can accurately estimate the pixels to be embedded. Since it is hard to model all natural images, even a well-designed predictor cannot predict all pixels accurately, e.g., many existing RDH algorithms use a fixed predictor for content prediction, which does not take into account the statistical characteristics of local context. Therefore, a trade-off strategy is to further select the pixels with a small PE out for data embedding preferentially, which is referred to as content selection. However, during the process of constructing an ordered sequence of PEs, many existing algorithms ignore the fact that adjacent PEs may have the identical priority of data embedding. As a result, there is still room for improving the payload-distortion performance. In addition, for data embedding, once the operation is pre-specified, we should further optimize the data embedding parameters so that the distortion will be low for a given payload.

Motivated by the above analysis, in this article, we are to study the optimization of content prediction and content selection so that the payload-distortion performance can be further improved. Meanwhile, since we use the PEs of image pixels to carry secret data, the optimized HS operation is used. In the proposed work, the pixels are adaptively predicted according to their local context, leading to a sharp prediction error histogram to be embedded. Furthermore, the main idea of content selection is to construct a graph containing multiple connected components for the cover image so that the PEs of the pixels within a connected component are close to each other. Accordingly, the sorted connected components can be used for carrying additional information. Experimental results have demonstrated that the proposed method outperforms a part of advanced works, displaying superiority and applicability of the proposed method.

The remainder of this article is organized as follows. First, we detail the proposed method in Section 2. Experiments and analysis are then provided in Section 3. Finally, we conclude this work and provide discussion in Section 4.

2. Proposed Method

In this section, we first describe the general framework of the proposed method. Then, we will introduce each important part in detail. Before a detailed introduction, we list all the important symbols used in this section and their meaning in Table 1.

Table 1. Important symbols and their meaning.

Symbol	Meaning
x	cover image (gray-scale)
m	secret message
k	secret key
y	marked image
h	the height of the cover image
w	the width of the cover image
$x_{i,j} \in x$	the pixel at position (i,j) whose value is $x_{i,j}$
D	the adjacent set
$\hat{x}_{i,j}$	the prediction value of $x_{i,j} \in x$
$e_{i,j}$	the prediction error of $x_{i,j} \in x$
$G(V,E)$	a non-directed graph whose node-set is V and edge-set is E
T_d	an integer threshold

2.1. General Framework

Throughout this paper, gray-scale images are used to act as the cover image. Figure 1 shows the general technical framework for the proposed algorithm. We describe it as follows. We first pre-process the given cover image adjusting all pixel values into the usable range to avoid the pixel overflow and pixel underflow problem during pixel modification. The modified pixels should be recorded to construct a so-called location map which will be self-embedded into the cover image together with the secret data. Moreover, we self-embed some embedding parameters into the cover image so that the receiver has the ability to extract secret data and recover the original image.

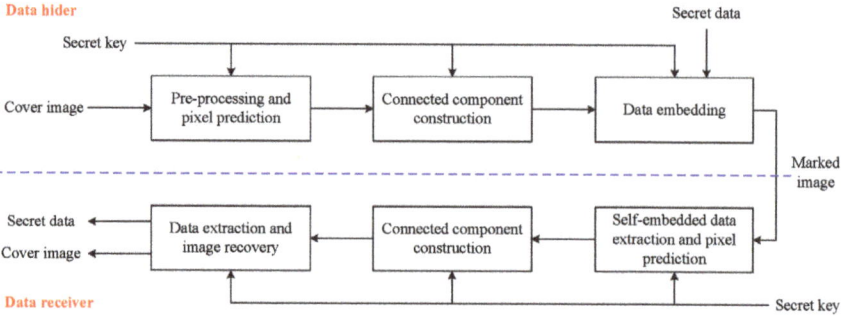

Figure 1. General framework for the proposed method.

After pre-processing, we predict the cover pixels to be embedded based on the local context, by which we can generate a set of PEs that will be used for carrying secret bits. In order to provide good payload-distortion performance, we construct a graph, whose nodes correspond to the pixels to be embedded and edges represent the adjacent relationship between pixels. We sort the PEs by determining the connected components of the graph and a local complexity function. Therefore, by applying optimized HS, we embed the secret data into the sorted PEs. For the data receiver, they first extract the embedding parameters from the marked image and then perform an inverse process of the data hider to reconstruct the embedded information and the original cover content without error. In this way, efficient RDH can be realized. Below, we provide the details.

2.2. Pre-Processing and Pixel Prediction

Let $\mathbf{x}$ denote a gray-scale image whose size is denoted by $h \times w$, where each pixel $x_{i,j} \in \mathcal{I} = \{0, 1, \ldots, 255\}$. Our mission is to embed a secret binary stream $\mathbf{m} \in \{0,1\}^l$ into $\mathbf{x}$ to generate a marked image $\mathbf{y} \in \mathcal{I}^{h \times w}$ such that the distortion between $\mathbf{y}$ and $\mathbf{x}$ is low. In addition, both $\mathbf{m}$ and $\mathbf{x}$ can be reconstructed from $\mathbf{y}$ without any error. Mathematically, we have

$$\mathbf{y} = \mathbf{Embed}(\mathbf{x}, \mathbf{m}, \mathbf{k}) \qquad (1)$$

and

$$\mathbf{m}, \mathbf{x} = \mathbf{Extract}(\mathbf{y}, \mathbf{k}), \qquad (2)$$

where $\mathbf{k}$ represents the secret key shared between the hider and the receiver.

The proposed method modifies the spatial pixels to embed secret data. In order to avoid the above-mentioned pixel underflow and pixel overflow problem, the values of boundary pixels to be embedded should be adjusted into the usable range. Since each pixel is modified by $\{-1, 0, +1\}$ during data embedding, a boundary pixel always has a value of 0 or 255. Therefore, we need to modify each pixel with a value of 0 or 255 as a pixel with a value of 1 or 254 to avoid the pixel underflow and pixel overflow problem. To ensure reversibility, the positions and original values of these boundary pixels are recorded to construct a location map which will be compressed by an efficient lossless compression technique as a binary stream to act as the side information that will be self-embedded into the cover image. This strategy has been applied by many RDH algorithms such as [13,16,17]. The losslessly compressed location map can be considered as a part of the secret message. Since the number of boundary pixels in a natural image is very small, the size of the losslessly compressed location map is also very small. This indicates that the impact of the losslessly compressed location map on the pure embedding payload can be ignored. In addition, the data embedding parameters should be self-embedded into the cover image in advance so that the data receiver is capable of extracting the secret data and reconstructing the original image. This can be achieved by using the least significant bits (LSBs) of some specified pixels to store the parameters. These specified pixels should be unchanged in the subsequent process. The original LSBs of these pixels should be recorded and embedded to ensure reversibility [14].

Given the cover image x, we divide the pixels to be embedded in x into two disjoint sets S_0 and S_1. The pixels in S_0 will be used to predict the pixels in S_1. The pixels in S_1 will be used for embedding secret data. Since the data embedding operation is reversible, once S_1 has been embedded, we can further use the (modified) pixels in S_1 to predict the pixels in S_0. Thus, the pixels in S_0 can be used thereafter for data embedding. Without the loss of generality, in the following, we will use S_0 for pixel prediction and S_1 for data embedding unless otherwise specified. It is noted that when we use S_0 to predict S_1, S_0 should be unchanged during the process of embedding secret data into S_1, and vice versa. We are free to determine S_0 and S_1. In this paper, S_0 and S_1 are determined as:

$$S_b = \{x_{i,j} \in x \mid (i+j) \bmod 2 = b\}. \tag{3}$$

Many existing RDH algorithms use a fixed predictor for pixel prediction, which does not take into account the difference between different local contexts and therefore may not accurately predict the pixels. In this paper, we propose a content-adaptive strategy for pixel prediction. Suppose that the pixels in S_0 are used to predict the pixels in S_1, for each pixel $x_{i,j} \in S_1$, as shown in Figure 2, we determine three candidate prediction values by:

$$\hat{x}_{i,j,0} = \left\lfloor \frac{x_{i,j-1} + x_{i,j+1}}{2} + 0.5 \right\rfloor, \tag{4}$$

$$\hat{x}_{i,j,1} = \left\lfloor \frac{x_{i-1,j} + x_{i+1,j}}{2} + 0.5 \right\rfloor, \tag{5}$$

$$\hat{x}_{i,j,2} = \left\lfloor \frac{x_{i,j-1} + x_{i-1,j} + x_{i,j+1} + x_{i+1,j}}{4} + 0.5 \right\rfloor, \tag{6}$$

where $\lfloor x \rfloor$ returns the largest integer that is no more than x. The operation of "+0.5" is to adjust the prediction value to the corresponding nearest integer. Taking Equation (4) for example, if $(x_{i,j-1} + x_{i,j+1})/2 = 10.7$, then $\hat{x}_{i,j,0}$ will be equal to 11, rather than 10. The final prediction value of $x_{i,j}$, denoted by $\hat{x}_{i,j}$, is selected from the candidate-set $P_{i,j} = \{\hat{x}_{i,j,0}, \hat{x}_{i,j,1}, \hat{x}_{i,j,2}\}$ according to the local context of $x_{i,j}$ which is shown in Figure 3. To this end, we determine a *priority* for each element in $P_{i,j}$. In detail, let $\alpha(\hat{x}_{i,j,k})$ denote the priority of $\hat{x}_{i,j,k}$. We determine $\alpha(\hat{x}_{i,j,k})$ by the following equation:

$$\alpha(\hat{x}_{i,j,k}) = \sum_{(dx,dy) \in D} \delta(|\hat{x}_{i,j,k} - \hat{x}_{i+dx,j+dy,k}|, \min_{r \in \{0,1,2\}} |\hat{x}_{i,j,r} - \hat{x}_{i+dx,j+dy,r}|), \tag{7}$$

where $D = \{(-1,-1), (-1,1), (1,-1), (1,1)\}$, $\delta(x,y) = 1$ if $x = y$, and 0 otherwise. The feasibility of Equation (7) relies on the fact that adjacent pixels in natural images tend to have similar statistical characteristics, which inspires us to use the difference between the prediction values of adjacent pixels to determine which pixels can be embedded preferentially. In this way, $\hat{x}_{i,j}$ can be finally determined by:

$$\hat{x}_{i,j} = \arg\max_{\hat{x}_{i,j,k}} \alpha(\hat{x}_{i,j,k}), \tag{8}$$

where $k \in \{0,1,2\}$. Thus, the PE of $x_{i,j}$ is determined by:

$$e_{i,j} = x_{i,j} - \hat{x}_{i,j}, \tag{9}$$

which will be used for carrying secret data in the subsequent process. It can be concluded that the final prediction value of a pixel is actually selected from multiple candidate values, resulting in that the final PE value of the pixel is essentially selected from multiple candidate PE values as well. It can be said that, as an effective PE adjustment strategy, the proposed method for determining PE is more applicable in practice compared with many existing methods that use a fixed predictor. This is why we term the proposed pixel prediction method as *prediction error adjustment*.

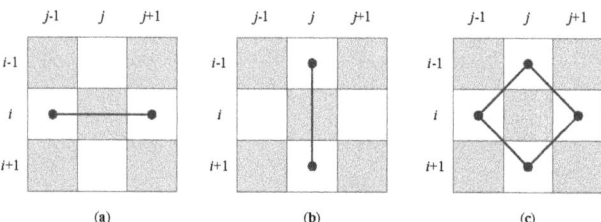

Figure 2. Three prediction modes for the pixel $x_{i,j} \in \mathbf{x}$ to be embedded: (**a**) Horizontal prediction, (**b**) Vertical prediction, (**c**) Four-direction prediction. For example, in (**a**), $x_{i,j}$ will be predicted with $x_{i,j-1}$ and $x_{i,j+1}$, and the prediction equation can be found in Equation (4).

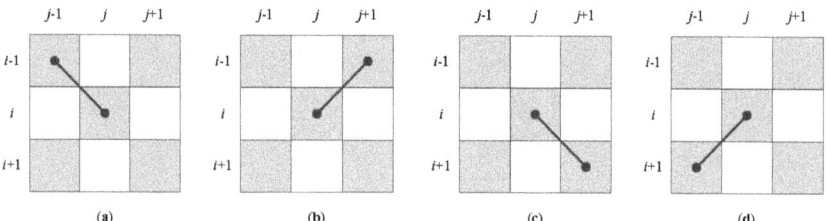

Figure 3. The local context for the pixel $x_{i,j} \in \mathbf{x}$ to be embedded: (**a**) $(dx, dy) = (-1, -1)$, (**b**) $(dx, dy) = (-1, 1)$, (**c**) $(dx, dy) = (1, 1)$, (**d**) $(dx, dy) = (1, -1)$. Namely, four pixels $x_{i-1,j-1}$, $x_{i-1,j+1}$, $x_{i+1,j+1}$ and $x_{i+1,j-1}$ constitute the local context of $x_{i,j}$.

2.3. Connected Component Construction

After pre-processing and pixel prediction, we need to generate an ordered PE sequence that will be used for data embedding. We propose a novel method to construct the PE sequence. Suppose that S_0 is used for pixel prediction and S_1 is used for data embedding, our goal is to sort the pixels in S_1 so that a pixel sequence and the corresponding PE sequence can be determined. We achieve this goal by applying connected component construction. Clearly, for any two different pixels $x_{i,j} \in S_1$ and $x_{i',j'} \in S_1$, they are adjacent to each other if we have

$$(i' - i, j' - j) \in D \text{ and } |\hat{x}_{i,j} - \hat{x}_{i',j'}| \leq T_d, \tag{10}$$

where T_d is a small integer threshold that needs to be pre-determined. If we model every pixel in S_1 as a graph node and the adjacent relationship between two pixels as a graph edge connecting the corresponding two graph nodes, we are able to construct a graph. Without loss of generality, let $G(V, E)$ be the constructed graph, where $V = \{v_1, v_2, \ldots, v_{|V|}\}$ denotes the node set and $E = \{(u_i, v_i) | u_i \in V, v_i \in V, u_i \neq v_i, 1 \leq i \leq |E|\}$ represents the edge set. Clearly, G is a non-directed graph, which means that two edges $(u, v) \in E$ and $(v, u) \in E$ are equivalent to each other. Figure 4 provides an example for constructing $G(V, E)$, from which it is easily inferred that G may contain multiple connected components. A connected component of G is defined as such a subgraph $G'(V', E'), V' \subset V, E' \subset E$ that for any two different nodes $u' \in V'$ and $v' \in V'$, there is at least one *path* between u' and v'. The detailed pseudo-code to collect all the connected components of G is shown in Algorithm 1, which is based on the classical graph search technique called depth-first search (DFS). It can be inferred from Algorithm 1 that the computational complexity of collecting all the connected components given G is $O(|V| + |E|)$, which is very efficient. Clearly, the number of connected components and the number of nodes of a connected component are both affected by T_d. Specifically, a larger T_d

allows more pixels to be adjacent to each other in the graph, resulting in that the number of nodes in a connected component becomes larger, but the number of connected components becomes smaller. A smaller T_d makes the adjacent condition become more strict. As a result, the number of nodes in a connected component becomes smaller, but the number of connected components becomes larger.

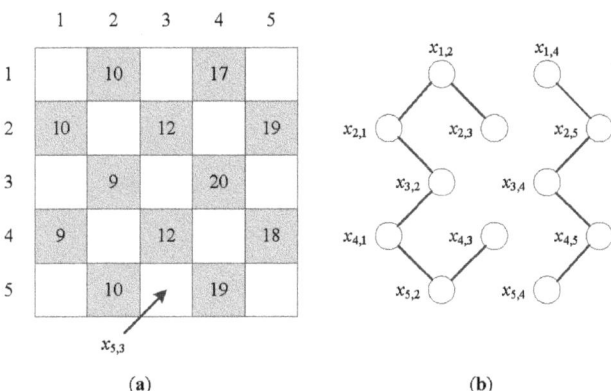

Figure 4. An example for constructing the graph: (**a**) Cover image, (**b**) Constructed graph. The pixels in the gray region are used for data embedding. The displayed values in the gray grids are the prediction values of the corresponding pixels. By setting $T_d = 2$, the corresponding graph is constructed as shown in (**b**).

Algorithm 1 The pseudo-code to collect all the connected components

Input: $G(V, E)$: a non-directed graph.
Output: t: the number of connected components, $G_1(V_1, E_1), G_2(V_2, E_2), \ldots, G_t(V_t, E_t)$: all the connected components.
1: Initialize $t = 0$
2: **for** each node $v \in V$ **do**
3:    **if** v has been previously processed **then**
4:       Continue
5:    **end if**
6:    Set $t = t + 1$
7:    Initialize $G_t(V_t, E_t)$ by $V_t = \{v\}$ and $E_t = \emptyset$
8:    Call $DFS(v, G(V, E), G_t(V_t, E_t))$
9: **end for**
10: **Sub-procedure** $DFS(v, G(V, E), G_t(V_t, E_t))$
11: Mark v as *processed*
12: **for** each $(v, v') \in E$ **do**
13:    **if** v' has been previously processed **then**
14:       Continue
15:    **end if**
16:    Update $V_t = V_t \cup \{v'\}$ and $E_t = E_t \cup \{(v, v')\}$
17:    $DFS(v', G(V, E), G_t(V_t, E_t))$
18: **end for**
19: *End sub-procedure*
20: **return** $t, G_1(V_1, E_1), G_2(V_2, E_2), \ldots, G_t(V_t, E_t)$

By setting a small T_d, the prediction values of most pixels in the same connected component will be close to each other. Based on this, it is reasonable to further assume that the original values of most pixels in the same connected component are close to each other. This indicates that the PEs of most pixels within a connected component are close to each other. Therefore, in order to generate an order PE sequence, it is natural to treat the pixels in the same connected component as equally important. For two different connected components, the one containing more nodes (i.e., pixels) has a higher priority for data embedding since the connected component containing more nodes is likely to have more smooth pixels which is more helpful for data embedding [13,14].

Based on the above analysis, we determine all the connected components of $G(V, E)$, denoted by $\{G_1(V_1, E_1), G_2(V_2, E_2), \ldots, G_t(V_t, E_t)\}$, where t is the total number of connected components. It is required that

$$V = \cup_{i=1}^{t} V_i \text{ and } E = \cup_{i=1}^{t} E_i \tag{11}$$

and

$$V_i \cap V_j = \emptyset \text{ and } E_i \cap E_j = \emptyset, \forall 1 \leq i < j \leq t. \tag{12}$$

We sort the connected components according to the number of nodes of a graph. To this end, we determine a permutation of $\{1, 2, \ldots, t\}$ as $\{r_1, r_2, \ldots, r_t\}$ so that

$$|V_{r_1}| \geq |V_{r_2}| \geq \cdots \geq |V_{r_t}|, \tag{13}$$

where the r_1-th connected component has the maximum number of nodes, whereas the r_t-th connected component has the minimum number of nodes. It is noted that $\{r_1, r_2, \ldots, r_t\}$ can be easily determined by sorting $\{|V_1|, |V_2|, \ldots, |V_t|\}$, whose computational complexity is $O(t \cdot \log_2 t)$. In order to generate the ordered PE sequence, we process each of the sorted connected components in an orderly manner. First of all, we initialize the PE sequence as an empty sequence. Then, for each $1 \leq i \leq t$, we sort all the pixels corresponding to $G_{r_i}(V_{r_i}, E_{r_i})$ according to the local complexity function defined in [13]. After sorting the pixels, we orderly append the corresponding PEs to the end of the above PE sequence. By processing all connected components, we can finally generate an ordered PE sequence. Clearly, during the construction of the PE sequence, for each PE in the sequence, we can easily identify the position of the corresponding pixel, which enables us to modify the corresponding pixel value in the subsequent data embedding procedure. It is worth mentioning that one may not use the local complexity function defined in [13] for sorting the PEs of a connected component. It is free to define other local complexity functions to order the PEs. In summary, sorting the PE sequence in this paper requires us to build a graph and find all connected components. Therefore, we term this process as *connected component construction*.

2.4. Data Embedding

We are now able to embed secret data into the sorted PE sequence by applying HS. Mathematically, we express the sorted PE sequence to be embedded as $\mathbf{e} = \{e_i\}_{i=1}^{n_e}$. Two pairs of peak-zero bins, denoted by (l_p, l_z) and (r_p, r_z), where $l_z < l_p < r_p < r_z$, are used to embed the secret data $\mathbf{m}$ into $\mathbf{e}$ by applying HS as mentioned above. Here, the peak bins l_p and r_p are used to carry secret bits. The bins in range $(l_z, l_p) \cup (r_p, r_z)$ will be shifted to ensure reversibility. The remaining bins will be unchanged. For a given bit $b \in \{0, 1\}$ to be embedded and a PE $e_i \in \mathbf{e}$, the PE carrying secret information $\hat{e}_i$ (also called marked PE) is determined by [28]:

$$\hat{e}_i = \begin{cases} e_i + b, & \text{if } e_i = r_p, \\ e_i - b, & \text{if } e_i = l_p, \\ e_i + 1, & \text{if } r_p < e_i < r_z, \\ e_i - 1, & \text{if } l_z < e_i < l_p, \\ e_i, & \text{otherwise.} \end{cases} \tag{14}$$

The sum of $\hat{e}_i$ and the prediction value of the corresponding pixel will be used as the final value of the marked pixel. We terminate the procedure of embedding secret bits when the secret data $\mathbf{m}$ is entirely embedded. In other words, there must be a PE position $t_s \leq n_e$ where all the PEs $\{e_i \mid i > t_s\}$ are unchanged. It is necessary to optimize the two pairs of peak-zero bins so that the distortion introduced by embedding **m** into $\{e_i\}_{i=1}^{t_s}$ can be kept low. To this end, we apply the optimized method introduced in [16] for determining the near-optimal (l_p, l_z) and (r_p, r_z). It is highlighted that one may exhaust all possible (l_p, l_z) and (r_p, r_z) and find the optimal solution, given sufficient computational resources. Nevertheless, suppose that we have found (l_p, l_z) and (r_p, r_z), as mentioned previously, we should self-embed (l_p, l_z) and (r_p, r_z), as the data embedding parameters, into the cover image so that the data receiver can extract them before extracting secret data and recovering the cover image. In addition, the parameter T_d in Equation (10) should be self-embedded as well.

2.5. Data Extraction and Image Recovery

By extracting the data embedding parameters from the marked image, the data receiver can successfully extract secret data from the marked image and meanwhile recover the original cover image. First of all, the receiver performs pixel prediction and connected component construction in the same way as the data hider, by which a sorted PE sequence carrying the secret information can be obtained. Then, with the data embedding parameters, the secret data can be fully extracted by processing the marked PEs in an orderly manner. In this way, the original secret information and the side information can be retrieved. With the side information, the cover image can be reconstructed without error since the embedding operation is reversible.

2.6. Effectiveness and Complexity Analysis

The technical motivation behind many existing RDH algorithms is that embedding secret bits into smoother pixels will result in better payload-distortion performance. This is based on the fact that smoother pixels are likely to be predicted with a higher prediction accuracy based on their local context. As a result, the prediction error histogram follows a Gaussian-like distribution centered at zero, which is very helpful for data embedding. In this paper, instead of directly exploiting smoother pixels for data embedding, we propose a connected-component-based method to collect the pixels with close PEs for data embedding preferentially. Though the PE values of the pixels in a connected component may not be closer to zero compared with many existing works, the resultant prediction error histogram is still Gaussian-like distributed, meaning that by optimizing the embedding parameters, superior payload-distortion performance can be achieved. In other words, the proposed method has better applicability and generalization ability.

The main contributions of the proposed method include two aspects. One is optimization of the pixel predictor. Unlike many existing methods which use a fixed pixel predictor, the proposed method predicts a pixel in such a way that the final prediction value of a pixel is adaptively adjusted to the most suitable value according to the local context. As a result, the prediction can be more accurate. Since only three prediction modes are used in the proposed method and the local context of a pixel only consists of four neighboring pixels, the complexity to determine the final prediction value for a single pixel is very low. In other words, the overall complexity to determine all the prediction values is linearly proportional to the number of pixels to be predicted, which is very suitable for practice. On the other hand, as mentioned previously, given the graph $G(V, E)$, the procedure of constructing all the connected components requires a complexity of $O(|V| + |E|)$, which is linearly proportional to the size of the node set and the size of the edge set. By using a small T_d, $O(|V| + |E|)$ can be reduced to $O(k \cdot |V|)$, where k is a small coefficient. In other words, the complexity to determine all the connected components is also linearly proportional to the number of pixels to be predicted. Therefore, based on the above analysis, it can be concluded that the time complexity of the proposed method is low.

3. Performance Evaluation and Analysis

In this section, we conduct experiments for evaluating the performance of the proposed method. To this end, we take six standard test images *Airplane, Lena, Tiffany, Peppers, Baboon,* and *Sailboat* shown in Figure 5 varying from smooth to complex for simulation. The test images are all sized at 512 × 512. Furthermore, all values of the pixels are in the range [0, 255]. As described in the previous section, the proposed method divides the cover pixels into two disjoint subsets S_0 and S_1. Both subsets can be used for data embedding. That is, after data embedding with S_1, S_0 can be used for data embedding as well. Therefore, given the secret data **m** (in the form of binary stream), we can use S_1 to carry $|\mathbf{m}|/2$ secret bits. The remaining secret bits can be embedded into S_0. This type of payload partition strategy has been used in existing methods [13,16].

Figure 5. Six standard test images with a size of 512 × 512: (**a**) *Airplane*, (**b**) *Lena*, (**c**) *Tiffany*, (**d**) *Peppers*, (**e**) *Baboon*, and (**f**) *Sailboat*.

In order to demonstrate the superiority of the proposed method, we first show some visual examples for the proposed method. Figure 6 shows the marked images of the test images with an embedding rate of 10,000 bits and 20,000 bits. It can be seen that the proposed method does not introduce noticeable visual artifacts. The reason lies in that the proposed method either keeps the pixels unchanged or modifies the pixels by ±1, which will not introduce significant distortion to the cover image and therefore provides very good visual quality of the marked images. To quantitatively evaluate the payload-distortion performance of the proposed method, we use peak signal-to-noise ratio (PSNR, in dB) to measure the visual quality of the marked image, i.e.,

$$\text{PSNR} = 10 \times \log_{10}\left(\frac{255^2}{\text{MSE}}\right), \tag{15}$$

$$\text{MSE} = \frac{1}{h \times w} \sum_{i=1}^{h} \sum_{j=1}^{w} |x_{i,j} - y_{i,j}|^2, \tag{16}$$

where $x_{i,j}$ and $y_{i,j}$ represent the original value and the marked value of the pixel at position (i, j). It can be seen that PSNR evaluates the difference between the original cover image and the corresponding marked image. A higher PSNR indicates that the difference between the original cover image and the corresponding marked image is lower, accordingly indicating that the marked image is visually better. When the size of the payload is specified, we expect to achieve as high a PSNR value as possible.

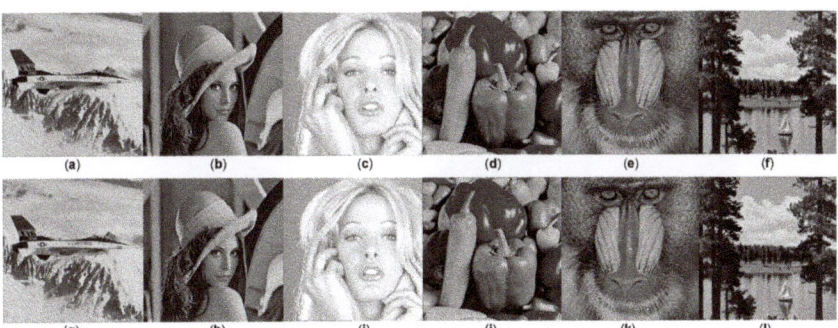

Figure 6. Examples for the marked images: (**a**) *Airplane* with 10,000 bits, (**b**) *Lena* with 10,000 bits, (**c**) *Tiffany* with 10,000 bits, (**d**) *Peppers* with 10,000 bits, (**e**) *Baboon* with 10,000 bits, (**f**) *Sailboat* with 10,000 bits, (**g**) *Airplane* with 20,000 bits, (**h**) *Lena* with 20,000 bits, (**i**) *Tiffany* with 20,000 bits, (**j**) *Peppers* with 20,000 bits, (**k**) *Baboon* with 20,000 bits, and (**l**) *Sailboat* with 20,000 bits.

We use a threshold T_d to control the number of connected components. Since the construction of the sorted PE sequence is dependent on the constructed connected components, we need to analyze the impact of the threshold T_d on the payload-distortion performance. To this end, we take two representative test images *Lena* (smooth image) and *Baboon* (complex image) for necessary analysis. Figure 7 shows the payload-distortion performance for the image *Lena* and the image *Baboon* due to different T_d. The abscissa represents the embedding rate, i.e., the size of the embedded payload, in bits. The ordinate represents the PSNR value. It can be inferred from Figure 7 that different images have different payload-distortion performance and different T_d also result in different payload-distortion performance. For the smooth image *Lena*, a smaller T_d is superior to a larger T_d at a low embedding rate, which is due to the reason that a smoother image enables us to collect more smooth pixels for data embedding by setting a small T_d. In contrast, for the complex image *Baboon*, a relatively smaller T_d is not a good choice for data embedding since the difference between adjacent pixels in *Baboon* is significantly larger than that in *Lena*. As a result, using a relatively larger T_d is a better strategy at a low embedding rate so that the number of relatively smooth pixels in a connected component can be increased, thereby benefiting data embedding. From the overall trend, as the embedding rate increases, the performance difference due to different T_d can be controlled within a small range. This indicates that, from the viewpoint of payload-distortion optimization, we can optimize T_d in a small range so that the payload-distortion performance is superior and the computational complexity is acceptable for practice. To this end, in the following experiments, for all test images, we limit T_d to the range $[0, 8)$ and use the integer resulting in the highest PSNR (for a fixed embedding rate) as the final value of T_d. It is worth mentioning that one may use a very large T_d for RDH. However, this will reduce the performance, as shown in Figure 8. The reason is that, a larger T_d will relax the constraint on the adjacent relationship between pixels, which can be easily inferred from Equation (10). For example, in the extreme case that $T_d = 256$, all the pixels to be embedded will be in the same connected component. In other words, there is only one connected component for $G(V, E)$ and the only one connected component is the graph itself. In this case, the proposed method degenerates to the traditional method. Figure 8 further shows the payload-distortion performance for a large T_d, from which we can infer that it is desirable to use a small T_d. This is why we optimize T_d in range $[0, 8)$ in this paper, which not only provides good payload-distortion performance but also keeps the computational complexity low.

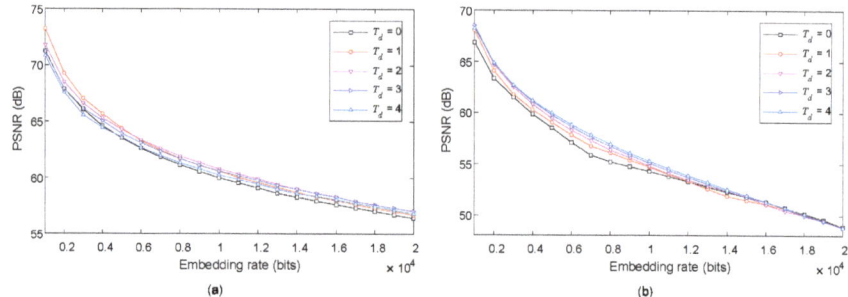

Figure 7. The payload-distortion performance due to small T_d for the images *Lena* and *Baboon*: (**a**) *Lena*, (**b**) *Baboon*.

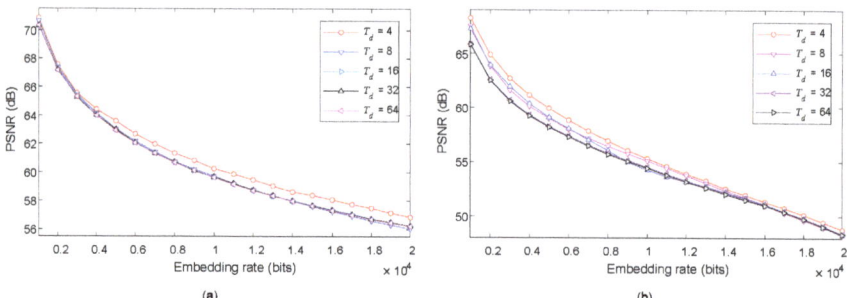

Figure 8. The payload-distortion performance due to large T_d for the images *Lena* and *Baboon*: (**a**) *Lena*, (**b**) *Baboon*.

The above analysis shows that the proposed method has the potential to provide superior payload-distortion performance. To evaluate the payload-distortion performance of the proposed method, we compare the proposed method with some advanced PE-based RDH methods, i.e., DSP [14], PPE [14], GP [29], SP [13], MPE [15] and BFS [28]. Both DSP and PPE are introduced in [14]. It is fair to compare the proposed method with these related works since they all focus on either improving the prediction accuracy or improving the pixel sorting procedure. For comparison, in our experiments, we use a randomly generated binary stream to represent the secret data to be embedded. Figure 9 shows the payload-distortion performance for the proposed method and the related works. It can be seen that different images have different payload-distortion performance, which is reasonable because different images have different statistical characteristics. As the embedding rate increases, the PSNR will decline, which is also reasonable since a larger embedding rate means that more modifications to the pixels will be performed, thereby resulting in a larger distortion between the marked image and the original image. It can be inferred from Figure 9 that the proposed method significantly outperforms the related works in terms of payload-distortion performance for all test images. We explain the reason as follows. DSP [14] uses a dynamic predictor for pixel prediction, which is efficient for smooth images but not suitable for complex images. Moreover, since the prediction mode of one pixel is affected by the prediction mode of the adjacent pixels, the prediction procedure for DSP is time-consuming. PPE [14] exploits the PE of a PE for data embedding, which is efficient for complex images. However, since the predictor is fixed for all pixels to be embedded, there is large room for further performance improvement. GP [29] uses a gradient-based prediction strategy for pixel prediction, which is efficient for RDH. However, processing the pixels from top to bottom and from left to right may result in many pixels not carrying secret bits being modified, accordingly introducing a high distortion of the marked image. Though SP [13] sorts the pixels to be embedded according to a well-designed local complexity function, the used data embedding parameters are not optimal for low embedding rates. Thus, it will introduce large distortion at low embedding rates. Similarly, for MPE [15], the data embedding parameters need to be optimized so as to provide better payload-distortion performance. In BFS [28], the prediction value of a pixel is determined as that of the adjacent pixel, which is not suitable for complex images. Moreover, the BFS method is time-consuming since it needs to optimize many parameters. Therefore, based on our experiments and analysis, it is true that the proposed method achieves better trade-off between embedding payload and embedding distortion compared with related works.

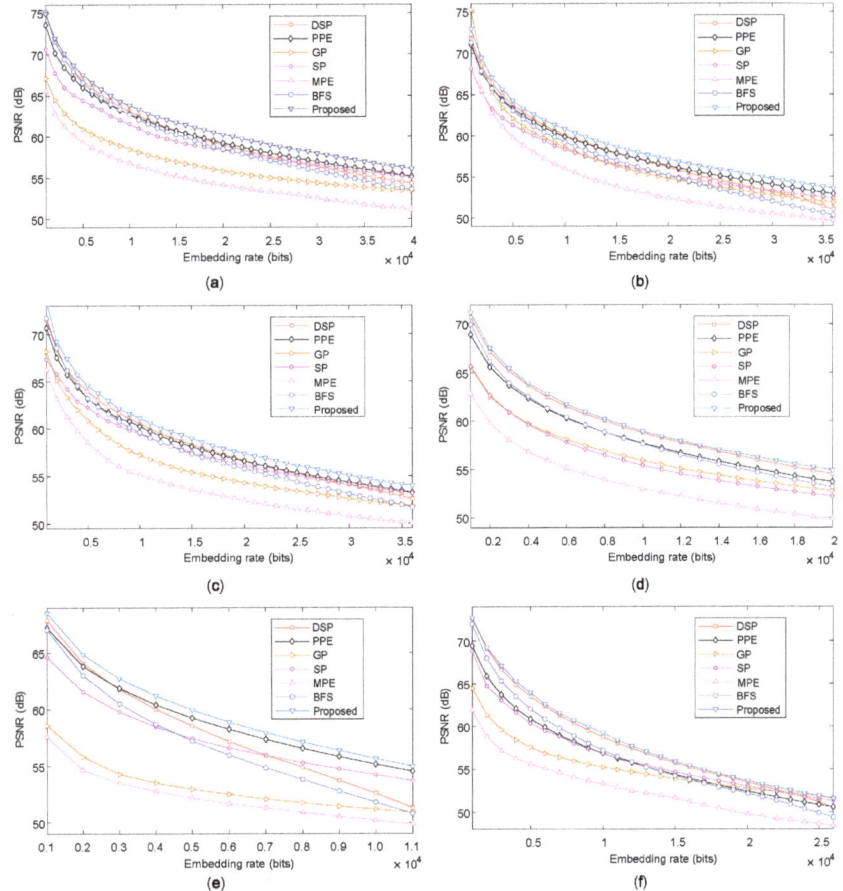

Figure 9. Performance comparison between the proposed method and the methods introduced by DSP [14], PPE [14], GP [29], SP [13], MPE [15] and BFS [28]: (**a**) *Airplane*, (**b**) *Lena*, (**c**) *Tiffany*, (**d**) *Peppers*, (**e**) *Baboon*, (**f**) *Sailboat*.

4. Conclusions

Improving the prediction accuracy of pixels and the embedding order of PEs represents a core problem in prediction-based RDH. This has motivated the authors in this paper to propose a novel strategy based on connected component construction and prediction error adjustment to further improve the prediction accuracy and optimize the embedding order of PEs. On the one hand, compared with previous works, a significantly different insight is that we model the cover pixels on a graph, where the nodes correspond to pixels and the edges represent the adjacent relationship between pixels. Since adjacent pixels have a strong correlation, the PEs of two pixels are close to each other when there is a path between the two pixels. Therefore, it is quite desirable to preferentially use pixels belonging to the same connected component (whose size is large enough) for data embedding. To this end, by determining the connected components of the graph, we propose to sort both the connected components of the graph and the pixels within a connected component for constructing the PE sequence. On the other hand, unlike mainstream methods that use a fixed predictor, we propose to adaptively determine the prediction value of a pixel based on its local context. As a result, the predictors for different pixels can be distinct from each other, which is more helpful for real-world scenarios. Experimental results demonstrate that the payload-distortion performance is significantly improved compared with some advanced methods that use PEs for data embedding. In the future, we will further optimize the proposed method through investigation on the prediction accuracy and the embedding order.

Author Contributions: Conceptualization, L.Z.; methodology, L.Z., A.M. and H.W.; software, L.Z. and H.W.; validation, C.Z. and A.M.; supervision, H.W.; project administration, C.Z. and H.W.; funding acquisition, L.Z., C.Z. and H.W. All authors have read and agreed to the published version of the manuscript.

Funding: This work was partly supported by the National Natural Science Foundation of China (Grant Nos. 61901096 and 61902235), the Shanghai "Chen Guang" Project (Grant No. 19CG46), the National Key Research and Development Program of China (Grant No. 2018YFB1801302), the Science and Technology Foundation of Guangdong Province (Grant No. 2021A0101180005), the Opening Project of Guangdong Province Key Laboratory of Information Security Technology (Grant No. 2020B1212060078), and the CCF-Tencent Rhino-Bird Young Faculty Open Research Fund.

Institutional Review Board Statement: Not applicable.

Informed Consent Statement: Not applicable.

Data Availability Statement: Not applicable.

Conflicts of Interest: The authors declare no conflict of interest.

References

1. Petitcolas, F.A.P.; Anderson, R.J.; Kuhn, M.G. Information hiding-a survey. *Proc. IEEE* **1999**, *87*, 1062–1078. [CrossRef]
2. Ke, Y.; Zhang, M.Q.; Liu, J.; Su, T.T.; Yang, X.Y. Fully Homomorphic Encryption Encapsulated Difference Expansion for Reversible Data Hiding in Encrypted Domain. *IEEE Trans. Circuits Syst. Video Technol.* **2020**, *30*, 2353–2365. [CrossRef]
3. Faheem, Z.B.; Ali, M.; Raza, M.A.; Arslan, F.; Ali, J.; Masud, M.; Shorfuzzaman, M. Image Watermarking Scheme Using LSB and Image Gradient. *Appl. Sci.* **2022**, *12*, 4202. [CrossRef]
4. Qin, J.; Wang, J.; Tan, Y.; Huang, H.; Xiang, X.; He, Z. Coverless Image Steganography Based on Generative Adversarial Network. *Mathematics* **2020**, *8*, 1394. [CrossRef]
5. Atta, R.; Ghanbari, M. A high payload data hiding scheme based on dual tree complex wavelet transform. *Optik* **2021**, *226*, 165786. [CrossRef]
6. Chang, C.C.; Liu, Y.; Nguyen, T.S. A Novel Turtle Shell Based Scheme for Data Hiding. In Proceedings of the Tenth International Conference on Intelligent Information Hiding and Multimedia Signal Processing, Kitakyushu, Japan, 27–29 August 2014; pp. 89–93.
7. Sun, Y.; Lu, Y.; Chen, J.; Zhang, W.; Yan, X. Meaningful Secret Image Sharing Scheme with High Visual Quality Based on Natural Steganography. *Mathematics* **2020**, *8*, 1452. [CrossRef]
8. Chen, Y.; Wang, H.; Wu, H. Data hiding-based video error concealment method using compressed sensing. In Proceedings of the International Conference on Cloud Computing and Security, Nanjing, China, 16–18 June 2017; pp. 28–38.
9. Cox, I.; Miller, M.; Bloom, J.; Fridrich, J.; Kalker, T. *Digital Watermarking and Steganography*, 2nd ed; Morgan Kaufmann: Burlington, MA, USA, 2007.
10. Wu, H.; Shi, Y.; Wang, H.; Zhou, L. Separable reversible data hiding for encrypted palette images with color partitioning and flipping verification. *IEEE Trans. Circuits Syst. Video Technol.* **2017**, *27*, 1620–1631. [CrossRef]
11. Huang, C.-T.; Wang, W.-J.; Yang, C.-H.; Wang, S.-J. A scheme of reversible information hiding based on SMVQ. *Imaging Sci. J.* **2013**, *61*, 195–203. [CrossRef]
12. Ni, Z.; Shi, Y.; Ansari, N.; Su, W. Reversible data hiding. *IEEE Trans. Circuits Syst. Video Technol.* **2006**, *16*, 354–362.
13. Sachnev, V.; Kim, H.J.; Nam, J.; Suresh, S.; Shi, Y. Reversible watermarking algorithm using sorting and prediction. *IEEE Trans. Circuits Syst. Video Technol.* **2009**, *19*, 989–999. [CrossRef]
14. Zhou, L.; Han, H.; Wu, H. Generalized reversible data hiding with content-adaptive operation and fast histogram shifting optimization. *Entropy* **2021**, *23*, 917. [CrossRef] [PubMed]

15. Hong, W.; Chen, T.; Shiu, C. Reversible data hiding for high quality images using modification of prediction errors. *J. Syst. Softw.* **2009**, *82*, 1833–1842. [CrossRef]
16. Wu, H.; Wang, H.; Shi, Y. PPE-based reversible data hiding. In Proceedings of the ACM Workshop on Information Hiding and Multimedia Security, Vigo Galicia, Spain, 20–22 June 2016; pp. 187–188.
17. Wu, H.; Wang, H.; Shi, Y. Dynamic content selection-and-prediction framework applied to reversible data hiding. In Proceedings of the IEEE International Workshop on Information Forensics and Security, Abu Dhabi, United Arab Emirates, 4–7 December 2016; pp. 1–6.
18. Chen, K.-M. High Capacity Reversible Data Hiding Based on the Compression of Pixel Differences. *Mathematics* **2020**, *8*, 1435. [CrossRef]
19. Kaur, G.; Singh, S.; Rani, R. PVO based reversible data hiding technique for roughly textured images. *Multidimens. Syst. Signal Process.* **2021**, *32*, 533–558. [CrossRef]
20. Fragoso-Navarro, E.; Cedillo-Hernandez, M.; Garcia-Ugalde, F.; Morelos-Zaragoza, R. Reversible Data Hiding with a New Local Contrast Enhancement Approach. *Mathematics* **2022**, *10*, 841. [CrossRef]
21. Chen, Y.; Wang, H.; Wu, H.; Liu, Y. Reversible video data hiding using zero QDCT coefficient-pairs. *Multimed. Tools Appl.* **2019**, *78*, 23097–23115. [CrossRef]
22. Nishimura, A. Reversible audio data hiding based on variable error-expansion of linear prediction for segmental audio and G.711 speech. *IEICE Trans. Inf. Syst.* **2016**, *99*, 83–91. [CrossRef]
23. Zheng, X.; Fang, Y.; Wu, H. General framework for reversible data hiding in texts based on masked language modeling. *arXiv* **2022**, arXiv:2206.10112.
24. Tsai, P.; Hu, Y.-C.; Yeh, H.-L. Reversible Image Hiding Scheme Using Predictive Coding and Histogram Shifting. *Signal Process.* **2009**, *89*, 1129–1143. [CrossRef]
25. Coatrieux, G.; Pan, W.; Cuppens-Boulahia, N.; Cuppens, F.; Roux, C. Reversible Watermarking Based on Invariant Image Classification and Dynamic Histogram Shifting. *IEEE Trans. Inf. Forensics Secur.* **2013**, *8*, 111–120. [CrossRef]
26. Chen, H.; Ni, J.; Hong, W.; Chen, T.S. Reversible Data Hiding with Contrast Enhancement Using Adaptive Histogram Shifting and Pixel Value Ordering. Signal Process. *Image Commun.* **2016**, *46*, 1–16.
27. Ying, Q.; Qian, Z.; Zhang, X.; Ye, D. Reversible Data Hiding with Image Enhancement Using Histogram Shifting. *IEEE Access* **2019**, *7*, 46506–46521. [CrossRef]
28. Wu, H. Efficient reversible data hiding simultaneously exploiting adjacent pixels. *IEEE Access* **2020**, *8*, 119501–119510. [CrossRef]
29. Dragoi, I.-C.; Coltuc, D.; Caciula, I. Gradient based prediction for reversible watermarking by difference expansion. In Proceedings of the ACM Workshop on Information Hiding and Multimedia Security, Salzburg, Austria, 11–13 June 2014; pp. 35–40.

Article

A Differential Privacy Budget Allocation Algorithm Based on Out-of-Bag Estimation in Random Forest

Xin Li [1], Baodong Qin [1,*], Yiyuan Luo [2] and Dong Zheng [1,3]

[1] School of Cyberspace Security, Xi'an University of Posts and Telecommunications, Xi'an 710121, China
[2] School of Computer Science and Engineering, Huizhou University, Huizhou 516007, China
[3] School of Computer Science, Qinghai Normal University, Xining 810008, China
* Correspondence: qinbaodong@xupt.edu.cn

Abstract: The issue of how to improve the usability of data publishing under differential privacy has become one of the top questions in the field of machine learning privacy protection, and the key to solving this problem is to allocate a reasonable privacy protection budget. To solve this problem, we design a privacy budget allocation algorithm based on out-of-bag estimation in random forest. The algorithm firstly calculates the decision tree weights and feature weights by the out-of-bag data under differential privacy protection. Secondly, statistical methods are introduced to classify features into best feature set, pruned feature set, and removable feature set. Then, pruning is performed using the pruned feature set to avoid decision trees over-fitting when constructing an ϵ-differential privacy random forest. Finally, the privacy budget is allocated proportionally based on the decision tree weights and feature weights in the random forest. We conducted experimental comparisons with real data sets from Adult and Mushroom to demonstrate that this algorithm not only protects data security and privacy, but also improves model classification accuracy and data availability.

Keywords: differential privacy; machine learning; privacy protection; random forest; out-of-bag estimation

MSC: 68P27

1. Introduction

With the rapid progress of various emerging technologies including the Internet, cloud computing, and computer storage, the era of big data has arrived [1]. Currently, numerous personal privacy data are currently collected by medical, educational, and corporate organizations, such as patient medical records collected by hospital organizations, student learning records collected by educational institutions, and customer location information collected by taxi-hailing platforms [2]. After being collected, these personal privacy data are often used for data analysis, data mining, etc., which will certainly affect the normal life of individuals. For example, the Facebook privacy leakage in 2018 caused significant damage to users. The frequent occurrence of numerous privacy leakage events has made data privacy protection a hot topic for research in the field of information security [3].

At present, data privacy protection methods [4] are mainly based on anonymity technology, encryption technology or noise technology. Privacy protection based on anonymity technology, such as *k*-anonymous algorithms, relies on background knowledge, and privacy protection based on encryption technology, e.g., homomorphic encryption, has a large computational overhead, making it unsuitable for using in massive data environments. In 2006, Dwork et al. [5] presented the noise-based privacy protection technique, i.e., differential privacy, which has been widely applicable to machine learning privacy preservation because of its low computational and transmission costs.

Classification is a very important method in the field of data mining [6]. It uses a large amount of data to build algorithmic models, and uses these models to perform classification operations. There are many algorithms that can be used for classification.

Compared with classification algorithms, such as neural networks, Bayesian and genetic algorithms, decision trees have less algorithmic complexity, are resistant to noise and have strong data scalability [7]. However, traditional single classifier models such as decision trees are single and prone to problems such as overfitting. In order to improve the accuracy of classification prediction, some scholars have proposed integrated methods. Random forest is an algorithm based on decision tree integration, which not only has many advantages of decision tree classification, but also has good tolerance for unbalanced samples, noise and outliers. It has been widely used in many fields such as banking [8], medical [9], e-commerce [10], and finance [11].

In the actual classification process, decision trees, random forest models and their corresponding counting information may leak users' private information, and there is a danger of privacy leakage. Applying differential privacy techniques to random forest models to protect private data is of great importance for data security publication. Current research on this area focuses on the selection and innovation of tree building methods [12,13], the selection of availability functions [14], and methods for pre-processing attribute sets [15–17]. Data protection algorithms based on differential privacy decision trees are mainly classified into interactive framework and non-interactive framework.

In the interactive framework, users can only conduct a limited number of queries through the privacy protection interface, and each query consumes the privacy protection budget. Blum et al. [18] first fused differential privacy with decision trees to obtain the SuLQ-based ID3 algorithm, but the prediction accuracy of the decision tree model was substantially reduced because it added differential privacy noise every time the information gain was calculated. McSherry et al. [19] used the PINQ framework to improve the SuLQ algorithm to obtain the PINQ-based ID3 algorithm. The algorithm partitioned the dataset into multiple disjoint subsets. The disadvantage is that each query consumes the privacy protection budget, many queries resulting in little privacy protection budget allocated for each query, thus adding more noise when dealing with large data sets. Friedman et al. [20] in a further study designed the DiffP-ID3 algorithm, which combines ID3 algorithm with an exponential mechanism to achieve differential privacy protection and effective noise reduction. In the same paper, they proposed the DiffP-C4.5 algorithm by using exponential mechanism to split continuous attributes. However, this method required to invoke the exponential mechanism twice, consuming a disproportionate amount of the privacy protection budget.

In a non-interactive framework, privacy protection algorithms are processed and published to the database, users can process this database for any operation. In this framework, we want to improve the availability of the data publishing by allocating a reasonable privacy protection budget to reduce the overall amount of noise added to the model. Mohammed et al. [21] and Zhu et al. [22] presented the data publishing algorithms DiffGen and DT-Diff under non-interactive, respectively. Both algorithms first generalized the data sets, then performed a subdivision iteration loop, and finally used an exponential mechanism for selection. Generalization replaces calling the exponential mechanism when processing continuous features and saves the privacy protection budget, but such schemes are inefficient when the classification dimension is large. In further research, it was found that decision trees are not stable enough due to their simple structure, and the prediction results are often unsatisfactory when facing high-dimensional data sets, and random forest models were considered to replace single decision trees. Patil et al. [23] combined differential privacy with random forests to build ID3 decision trees for classification and proposed the DiffPRF algorithm, which has the disadvantage that continuous attributes need to be discretized first. Mu et al. [14] improved the DiffPRF algorithm by introducing an exponential mechanism to deal with continuous attributes and proposed the DiffPRFs algorithm. Li et al. [24] proposed the RFDPP-Gini algorithm. Exponential and Laplace mechanisms are used in the selection of split features to deal with continuous and discrete features, respectively, and the Gini index is selected to determine the best splitting feature and the best splitting point using the equivariant privacy budget allocation method.

From the above related studies, it is clear that the current innovations and improvements in this field focus on how to improve the availability of data and the accuracy of model classification. The literature [25] uses out-of-bag estimation to evaluate the classification ability of random forests. Out-of-bag data [26] is an unused asset in random forests, which reflects the classification ability, feature importance, and other data set patterns of random forests. The literature [27] adds differential privacy to the out-of-bag estimation to protect the privacy of the out-of-bag data. In this paper, considering that the importance between trees and features in random forest is not the same, in order to allocate the privacy protection budget in a more targeted way, we need to calculate the solution in advance to obtain the weight sets of tree and feature importance. Choosing out-of-bag data to solve the weight set not only can be used for pruning and preventing overfitting, but also when differential privacy protection is added to it, it does not waste the privacy protection budget and overall reduces the total amount of noise added to the dataset, thus improving the availability of data and the accuracy of model classification. This study provides a more accurate solution for privacy protection in the fields of medical diagnosis, financial decision making, personalized recommendation, and bioinformatics. The main contributions of this paper are summarized as below:

1. We propose a differential privacy budget allocation algorithm based on out-of-bag estimation in random forest.
2. We improve the algorithm for differential privacy out-of-bag estimation to obtain more accurate decision tree weights in out-of-bag forests. We introduce decision tree weights when using the VIM variable importance measure to obtain a more accurate set of feature weights and use statistical methods for classification.
3. We creatively give computational methods to allocate the overall privacy protection budget to each tree in the random forest and to each layer of each tree to achieve a more targeted privacy budget allocation.
4. We conduct a series of experiments on Adult and Mushroom datasets to demonstrate the advantages of the algorithm in this paper.

The remainder of this paper is organized as follows. In Section 2, we introduce differential privacy background knowledge. The proposed method is described in detail in Section 3. The experimental results and analysis are given in Section 4. Finally, we conclude this paper in Section 5.

2. Differential Privacy Background Knowledge

Differential privacy solves the problem of database privacy leakage. With its strict mathematical definition and flexible combination of properties, it is used in all kinds of privacy protection.

Definition 1 (Differential privacy [28]). *For any two neighboring data sets D_1 and D_2, all differences are at most one record. Given a privacy protection algorithm F, Range(F) denotes the set of all possible output ranges of F. If the algorithm F satisfies:*

$$Pr[F(D_1) \in S] \leq e^{\epsilon} Pr[F(D_2) \in S] \tag{1}$$

then it is said that algorithm F provides ϵ-differential privacy protection, where $Pr[E_S]$ denotes the probability of event E_S occurring and ϵ is the privacy protection budget. The value of parameter ϵ should be consistent with the algorithm requirements, so as to obtain a perfect balance between data security and availability.

Definition 2 (Global sensitivity [28]). *Sensitivity is a parameter that measures the magnitude of the joining noise. For any of the functions $Q: D \to R^d$, the global sensitivity of Q is:*

$$\Delta GS = \max_{D_1, D_2} \| Q(D_1) - Q(D_2) \| \tag{2}$$

where R denotes the real number space of the mapping and d denotes the query dimension of the function f.

Definition 3 (Realization mechanism). *The most common implementations of adding differential privacy to the data are the Laplace mechanism and the exponential mechanism.*
1. Laplace mechanism [29–31]. This mechanism is implemented by adding noise satisfying the Laplace distribution to the output result. Given any function $f : D \to R^d$, if the $F(D)$ meets Formula (3), it means that it satisfies ϵ-differential privacy.

$$F(D) = f(D) + (Laplace(\frac{\triangle GS}{\epsilon}))^d \tag{3}$$

where $Laplace(\frac{\triangle GS}{\epsilon})$, beying the Laplace distribution with scale parameter $\frac{\triangle GS}{\epsilon}$.
2. Exponential mechanism [30,31]. Let the input of the randomized algorithm M be a dataset D and the output be an entity object $r \in Range$, $q(D,r)$ is the availability function, $\triangle GS$ is the sensitivity of the function $q(D,r)$. If algorithm M selects and outputs r from Range with probability proportional to $e^{\epsilon q(D,s)/2\triangle GS}$, then algorithm M provides ϵ-differential privacy.

Definition 4 (Combination properties). *In practical scenarios, users may make multiple queries, but the privacy protection budget needs to be kept within a given range. This problem can be cleverly solved by using the differential privacy combination properties.*
1. Sequential composition [32]. Assuming that in a set of mechanisms $A_1, A_2, \ldots, A_n$ provide $(\epsilon_1, \epsilon_2, \ldots, \epsilon_n)$-differential privacy protection respectively, for a same data set D, algorithms $A(A_1(D), A_2(D), \ldots, A_n(D))$ has $(\sum_{i=1}^{n} \epsilon_i)$-differential privacy.
2. Parallel composition [32]. Assuming that in a set of mechanisms $A_1, A_2, \ldots, A_n$ provide $(\epsilon_1, \epsilon_2, \ldots, \epsilon_n)$-differential privacy protection respectively, for the disjoint dataset D, algorithms constitute the combination $A(A_1(D), A_2(D), \ldots, A_n(D))$ with $(\max \epsilon_i)$-differential privacy.

3. Proposed Method

3.1. Solving Decision Tree Weights

In a random forest, each decision tree is generated by randomly selecting samples. When the total number of samples selected is very large, about 1/3 were not selected. These data are out-of-bag data [26]. When these data are applied in decision making on this decision tree, the ratio of forward misclassification to reverse misclassification in the sum of the data of the respective instances is the out-of-bag estimate. Since out-of-bag estimates are closely related to feature importance, forest properties, etc., it is important to incorporate differential privacy to protect out-of-bag data.

Definition 5 (Differential privacy out-of-bag estimation). *For one of the trees, the out-of-bag estimate B is:*

$$B = \frac{1}{2}(\frac{Y}{Y_T} + \frac{N}{N_T})$$

where Y and N represent the number of forward misclassifications and reverse misclassifications. Y_T and N_T indicate the total number of forward and reverse instances.

Differential privacy out-of-bag estimation is defined as:

$$\begin{aligned} B' &= \frac{1}{2}(\frac{Y + N(\epsilon_1)}{Y_T} + \frac{N + N(\epsilon_2)}{N_T}) \\ &= \frac{1}{2}(\frac{(Y \cdot N_T + N \cdot Y_T) + N(\epsilon)}{Y_T \cdot N_T}) \end{aligned} \tag{4}$$

It can be seen from Formula (4) that the noise that we add to the out-of-bag estimated data, which perturbs the true number of data, so that the differential privacy out-of-bag estimation does not lose the dataset regularity and protects the privacy of the data at the same time.

Definition 6 (Decision tree weights). *This paper calculates the decision tree weights with reference to Paul et al. [25]. The weights of the decision tree are defined as:*

$$Q_t = \frac{1}{B'_t} \quad (5)$$

where B'_t is the differentially private out-of-bag estimate of the tree. From Formula (5), we can see that the smaller B'_t is the larger the weight of the tree is, and the better the decision tree classification ability is.

3.2. Feature Weight Calculation and Feature Selection

3.2.1. Feature Weight Calculation

The Gini index is an important method for classifying the purity of attributes. The smaller the Gini index, the better the classification method. The formula for calculating the Gini index G_m is:

$$G_m = \sum_{c=1}^{C} p_{mc}(1 - p_{mc}) \quad (6)$$

where C is the number of features, p_{mc} is the probability of class c at node m.

The importance of node m in feature j_i is:

$$I_{jm} = G_m - w_L G_L - w_R G_R \quad (7)$$

where G_L and G_R are the Gini indices of the left and right nodes after splitting at node m, w_L and w_R are the number of weighted samples.

If the feature j_i is selected n times in the tree T_i, the importance of the feature in this decision tree is:

$$I_{ij} = \sum_{n=1}^{n} I_{jm} \quad (8)$$

The importance I_j of the feature j_i in the random forest is:

$$I_j = \sum_{i=1}^{t} I_{ij} \cdot Q_t / \sum_{j=1}^{k} \sum_{i=1}^{t} I_{ij} \quad (9)$$

where k is the number of input features, and t is the number of decision trees.

If C features are selected to construct t decision trees, the weight W_t of the decision trees in the random forest are:

$$W_t = \sum_{n=1}^{N} I_j / \sum_{t=1}^{t} \sum_{n=1}^{N} I_j \quad (10)$$

3.2.2. Feature Selection

Statistical methods have good results in data pre-processing. In the article, we choose this method to divide the features into Best feature set (BFS), Pruned feature set (PFS) and Removable feature set (RFS).

Definition 7 (Feature selection). *For the set of feature weights, the following conditions are satisfied:*

$$I_j < (\mu - 3\sigma) \quad (11)$$

$$(\mu - 3\sigma) < I_j < (\mu - 1.5\sigma) \quad (12)$$

where μ is the mean of the weight set of R, and σ is the standard deviation. If the weight VIM_j satisfies the Formula (11), the features j are placed into the removable feature set (RFS). If the weight VIM_j satisfies the Formula (12), the features j are placed into the pruned feature set (PFS). The remaining features j are put into the best feature set (BFS). The features in the existing feature weight set are deleted from the removable feature set (RFS) to obtain selected weight set R' with n' features.

3.3. Method for Allocating Privacy Protection Budgets Based on Weights

The reasonable allocation of privacy protection budget has a very important impact on data availability. Previous related works such as MAXGDDP algorithm [16] and AUR-Tree algorithm [17] use class geometry, class equivariance, and equivariance to allocate privacy protection budget during the construction of decision trees. In random forests, such as DiffPRFs algorithm [14] and RFDPP-Gini algorithm [24], it allocates the privacy protection budget equally to each decision tree and then equally to each layer. However, each tree in the random forest has different strengths and weaknesses in classification ability, and each feature in the dataset has different importance in the random forest. The privacy protection budget allocation method designed in this paper is based on adaptive allocation of tree weights and feature weights.

(1) Allocation based on tree weights. The privacy protection budget allocated to each tree ε_t is:

$$\varepsilon_t = \frac{\varepsilon}{T} \cdot W_t \tag{13}$$

where ε is the sum of the privacy protection budget, T is the number of decision trees in the random forest, and W_t is the weight of the decision tree.

(2) Allocation based on tree weights. The privacy protection budget ε_t allocated to each tree is distributed proportionally according to the relative size of the feature weights. After feature selecting to obtain the feature weight set R' with n', follow the random forest principle to randomly select a features ($a < n'$) to get feature set of the tree t and the corresponding feature weight set $R'_t\{I_{j_1}, I_{j_2}, \ldots, I_{j_{n'}}\}$. Calculate the weight ratio S_{j_1} of the features j_1 in this tree:

$$S_{j_1} = \frac{I_{j_1}}{I_{j_1} + I_{j_2} + \cdots + I_{j_{n'}}} \tag{14}$$

The privacy protection budget obtained from the allocation of the decision tree in selecting this feature for splitting is:

$$\varepsilon_{j_1} = \varepsilon_t \cdot S_{j_1} \tag{15}$$

Figure 1 provides an overview of the privacy protection budget allocation.

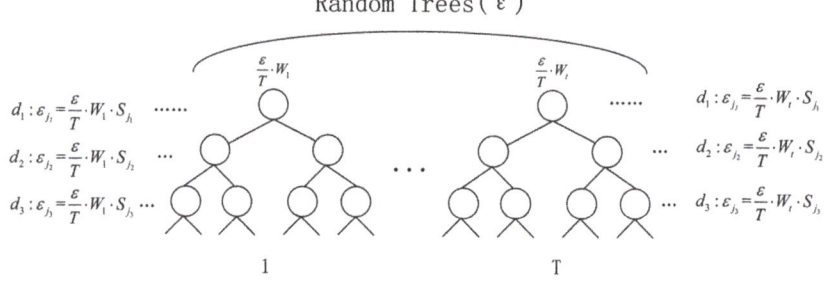

Figure 1. Overview of privacy protection budget allocation.

3.4. Pruning Based on the Divided Set of Attributes

Pruning can simplify the decision tree model in random forests, avoid overfitting, enhance generalization, and improve the accuracy of classification. In this paper, a pre-pruning strategy is used to prune using the pruning feature set (PFS) obtained in Section 3.2.2. In the process of building a tree, the features in order of importance are used as the best splitting features. For the feature set R'_t selected by the tree t, determine whether R'_t has features in the pruned feature set (PFS), and if so, remove them and allocate privacy budget. if not, allocate them according to the original feature set and construct a differential privacy random forest.

3.5. Algorithm Flow

This algorithm process in this paper is to first construct a random forest and extract the out-of-bag dataset, followed by calculating the decision tree weights and feature weights using out-of-bag estimation under differential privacy protection, and the feature weights use statistical methods to classify the features into the best feature set, pruned feature set and removable feature set. When constructing a random forest that satisfies ϵ-differential privacy protection, the randomly selected features are judged using the pruned feature set and the features belonging to the pruned feature set are removed, this method not only saves the privacy protection budget but also prevents the decision tree from overfitting. Then calculate the weights of the trees based on these features, and allocate privacy protection budget to each tree based on the tree weights. In the construction of each tree, the privacy protection budget is allocated and splits are selected sequentially according to the relative size of the feature weights in the feature set. In the construction of each tree, the privacy protection budget is allocated according to the relative size of the feature weights in the feature set and splits are selected sequentially. If continuous features are selected as splitting attributes in the tree building process, the exponential mechanism is invoked to split continuous attributes, and the Laplace mechanism is used to add noise to the count values of the leaf nodes to finally obtain a random forest that satisfies ϵ-differential privacy protection.

3.6. Description

We present a privacy budget allocation algorithm based on tree weights and feature weights in random forest, and the core strategy of the method is to allocate more privacy protection budgets to trees with better classification ability and features with higher importance in the forest.

This paper is divided into three algorithms, Algorithm 1 is the algorithm of extracting out-of-bag data.

Algorithm 1 Extract Out-of-Bag Data Algorithm

Input: Training set D, feature set $J(j_1, j_2, \ldots, j_n)$, number of decision trees t, maximum depth of the decision trees d, number of randomly selected features at splitting a.

Output: Random forest $Trees$, Out-of-bag datasets D_{OOB}.

Stopping condition: All samples on a decision tree node are consistently classified, or the maximum depth of the decision tree is reached d, or the number of features set features less than a.

Step 1. Take out m samples from the training set D with put-back as D_t, and randomly select n ($n < N$) features from J.

Step 2. Calculate the Gini coefficient of each feature, and select the best splitting feature j_n as the splitting feature.

Step 3. According to the different values of feature j_n, the samples on the node are divided into different child nodes, and a decision tree is generated.

Step 4. Repeat steps 1–3 t times to get t decision trees.

Step 5. Put the data in the training set D that was not used to build the decision tree into D_{OOB}.

Step 6. Get random forest $Trees$, out-of-bag datasets D_{OOB}.

Algorithm 2 is a feature weight solving and selection algorithm using out-of-bag estimation. The out-of-bag estimation under differential privacy is used to solve feature weights and decision tree weights, select feature weights, and update the features set.

Algorithm 2 Solving Feature Weights and Selecting Algorithms Using Out-of-Bag Estimation

Input: Out-of-bag datasets D_{OOB}, random forest $Trees$, privacy protection budget ε_{OOB}, feature set $J(j_1, j_2, \ldots, j_n)$.

Output: Selected feature weight set R', selected feature set J', pruned feature set (PFS), best feature set (BFS).

Stopping condition: All features are calculated and screened.

Step 1. For decision tree t, select data containing tree features from out-of-bag data set D_{OOB}, test and count.

Step 2. Add Laplacian noise to all categorical counts for each tree in a random forests, the size of the privacy protection budget for each tree is $\frac{\varepsilon_{OOB}}{t}$.

Step 3. Get the differential privacy out-of-package estimation B' using the Formula (4).

Step 4. Calculate the decision tree weight Q_t using the Formula (5).

Step 5. Repeat steps 1–4 to calculate the weight of each tree in the random forests in turn, and get the weight set $Q(Q_1, Q_2, \ldots, Q_t)$ of the tree.

Step 6. For each tree, use Formulas (6)–(8) to get the importance of the feature in this tree.

Step 7. Calculate the feature weight of this feature in the whole random forest using Formula (9).

Step 8. Repeat steps 6–7 to obtain the feature weight set R of all features.

Step 9. If feature weight set R satisfies Formula (11), put corresponding feature j_n into the removable feature set RFS; if it satisfies Formula (12), put corresponding feature j_n into the pruned feature set (PFS); the remaining features are best feature set (BFS).

Step 10. Delete the features and feature weights in the removable feature set RFS in turn from the initial feature set $J(j_1, j_2, \ldots, j_n)$ and feature weight set R.

Step 11. Get the selected feature weight set R', selected feature set J', pruned feature set (PFS), best feature set (BFS).

Algorithm 3 is a differential privacy budget allocation algorithm based on tree weights and feature weights. The tree weight calculation, pruning and differential privacy budget allocation by randomly selected features in the construction makes the strategy of assigning privacy protection budgets more targeted and reasonable.

Algorithm 3 Differential Privacy Budget Algorithm Based on Tree Weight and Feature Weight

Input: Training set D, selected feature set J', selected feature weight set R', number of decision trees T, maximum depth of the decision trees d, number of features b randomly selected when splitting, privacy protection budget ε, pruned feature set (PFS), best feature set (BFS).

Output: Random forests satisfying ε-differential privacy protection.

Stopping condition: All samples on a decision tree node are consistently classified, or the maximum depth of the decision tree is reached d, or the feature number n' of the filtered feature set is less than b, or the privacy protection budget is exhausted.

Step 1. For decision tree t, b features are randomly selected, the feature set is J'_t, and the corresponding feature weight set calculated by Formula (10) is R'_t.

Step 2. If the feature set J'_t has features belonging to the pruned feature set (PFS), the corresponding feature weight set R'_t removes these feature weights to obtain the feature set R''_t. if the feature set J'_t belongs to the best feature set (BFS), the corresponding feature weight set R'_t does not change.

Step 3. For the feature set J'_t, the weight W_t of the decision tree is obtained according to Formula (13).

Step 4. The privacy budget of the tree is obtained from the weights of the tree as $\varepsilon_t = \frac{\varepsilon}{T} \cdot W_t$.

Step 5. In the feature weight set R'_t, the feature weight ratio S_{j_1} of the feature j_b is calculated according to Formula (14).

Step 6. In the tree t, according to the size of the feature weight set R'_t, the features are sequentially selected from the corresponding feature set J'_t as the best splitting feature.

Step 7. The privacy protection budget allocated by the optimal splitting feature is $\varepsilon_{j_1} = \varepsilon_t \cdot S_{j_1}$

Step 8. Repeat T times to calculate the privacy protection budget required for each feature split on each tree.

Step 9. When constructing the tree to select features, if the best split feature is a continuous feature, an exponential mechanism is invoked to select the best point for splitting:

$$\frac{\exp\left(\frac{\varepsilon}{2\Delta q}q(D_n,j)\right)|R_i|}{\sum_i \exp\left(\frac{\varepsilon}{2\Delta q}q(D_n,j)\right)|R_i|}$$

among them, $q(D_n, j)$ is the Gini index, $|R_i|$ is the size of the interval, and Δq is the sensitivity of the Gini index.

Step 10. If stopping condition is met, the creation of node is stopped, and the node is set as a leaf node.

Step 11. Noise is added to the count value of the leaf nodes of each tree, and the classification with the most samples is selected as the label of the leaf node.

4. Experimental Results and Analysis

4.1. Privacy Analysis

(1) Privacy when computing out-of-bag data. When using the out-of-bag data for each tree calculation, the allocated privacy budget is used to add noise to the counts of the classification results, and thus differential privacy is satisfied.

(2) Privacy of random forests for training sets. There are T trees in this algorithm, and the privacy budget allocated to each tree is $\varepsilon_t = \frac{\varepsilon}{T} \cdot W_t$. The privacy budget divided into each layer according to feature importance is $\varepsilon_{j_1} = \varepsilon_t \cdot S_{j_1}$, for each level of the decision tree, the different nodes are equally divided into $\varepsilon' = \varepsilon_{j_i}/(d+1)$, and the noise is eventually added using Laplace mechanism. Since the samples in each tree in a random forest are randomly selected with a put-back, the data will have crossover. From the sequential composition of differential privacy, it is clear that the consumed privacy budget is the sum of the individual tree consumption, so the training set satisfies ε-differential privacy in the process of constructing the random forest.

Since the two parts of the out-of-bag data and the training set are disjoint and both satisfy ε-differential privacy, the parallel composition of differential privacy shows that the entire process of constructing a differentially private random forest satisfies ε-differential privacy.

4.2. Experimental Design

The hardware environment for the experiments in this paper is Intel(R) Core (TM) i5-5200U CPU @2.20GHz processor and 8GB operating memory. The operating system is Windows 10, the experimental program development tool is Pycharm2021.3 and the programming language is Python.

Two real datasets originating from UCL were used for the experiment: the Adult and Mushroom dataset (Table 1). The Adult dataset contains U.S. Census data with discrete and continuous attributes that determine whether the category is a wage greater than 50k. The Mushroom dataset contains information about mushroom-related species, and the only discrete attributes in this dataset that determine the category is whether a mushroom is edible or not.

Table 1. Dataset Information.

Dataset	Characteristic Number (Discrete/Continuous)	Size	Class Attribute
Adult	14 (8/6)	32,561	1
Mushroom	22 (22/0)	8124	1

To test the effectiveness of Ours' algorithm, multiple sets of comparison experiments are set up in this paper: (1) comparison between different decision tree depths; (2) comparison between different number of decision trees; (3) comparison between different size of privacy budgets; (4) comparison between Ours algorithm, RFDPP-gini [24] algorithm and DiffPRFs [14] algorithms in this paper.

4.3. Experimental Results

For the Adult and Mushroom datasets, a random forest satisfying differential privacy protection is built using this paper's algorithm with different privacy protection budgets and different decision tree depths, and the test datasets are classified to obtain the accuracy of the classification results.

Figure 2 shows the classification accuracy at different tree depths for the Adult dataset with differential privacy noise added and privacy budgets of 0.10, 0.25, 0.50, 0.75, and 1.00, respectively. Figure 3 shows the classification accuracy at different tree depths for the Mushroom dataset with differential privacy noise added and privacy protection budgets of 0.10, 0.25, 0.50, 0.75, and 1.00, respectively.

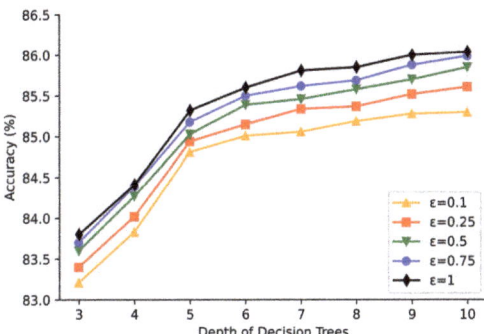

Figure 2. Variation of classification accuracy with tree depth for Adult dataset.

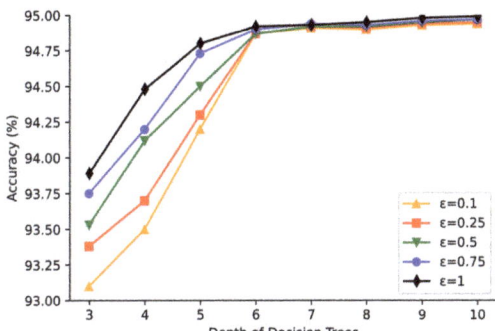

Figure 3. Variation of classification accuracy with tree depth for Mushroom dataset.

Figure 4 shows the classification accuracy for the number of decision trees in the random forest at 10, 30, 50, 70, and 90 for the Adult dataset with differential privacy noise added and privacy budgets of 0.10, 0.25, 0.50, 0.75, and 1.00, respectively. Figure 5 shows the classification accuracy of the Mushroom dataset when the number of decision trees in the random forest is 10, 30, 50, 70, and 90 when differential privacy noise is added and the privacy budget is 0.10, 0.25, 0.50, 0.75, and 1.00, respectively.

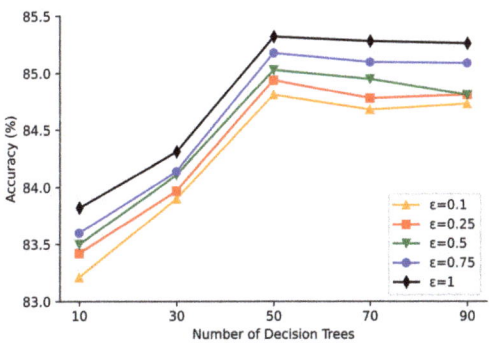

Figure 4. Variation of classification accuracy with the number of decision trees for the Adult dataset.

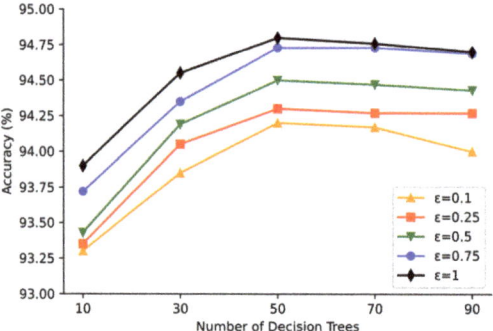

Figure 5. Variation of classification accuracy with the number of decision trees for Mushroom dataset.

To test the performance of the algorithm, the classification accuracy of Ours algorithm is compared with RFDPP-gini and DiffP-RFs algorithms on Adult and Mushroom datasets under the same conditions. Set T = 50, privacy budget to 0.10, 0.25, 0.5, 0.75, 1.00, the depth of the decision tree to 5, and the number of randomly selected features at node splits to 5. The experimental results are shown in Figures 6 and 7.

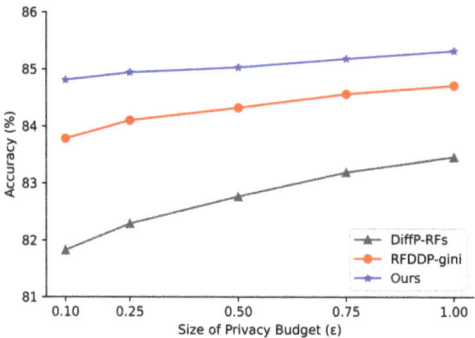

Figure 6. Comparison of classification performance of the three algorithms on Adult dataset.

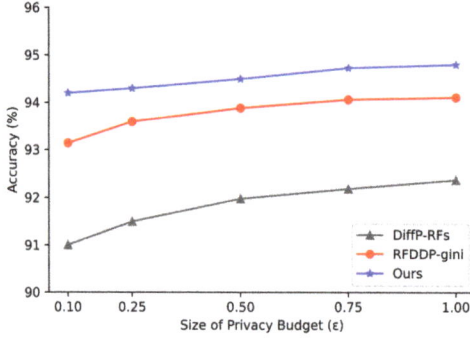

Figure 7. Comparison of classification performance of the three algorithms on Mushroom dataset.

4.4. Comparisons

The privacy budget is a measure of how much noise is added and a measure of the strength of data privacy. As the privacy budget increases, the weaker the privacy of the data, the stronger the classification accuracy of the algorithm. In the decision tree model, as the depth of tree increases, the decision tree becomes more branchy, dividing the dataset to a finer degree, and the division becomes more accurate. The performance of the model is affected by the privacy budget and the depth of the decision tree.

From Figures 2 and 3, it can be seen that when the depth of the tree is 3 and the privacy budget is 0.1, 0.25, 0.5, 0.75, and 1.00, the classification accuracy of the algorithm in this paper 83.21%, 83.40%, 83.60%, 83.70%, and 83.81% for the Adult dataset, respectively, and the accuracy for the Mushroom dataset is 93.1%, 93.38%, 93.53%, 93.75%, and 93.89%, and the accuracy all increase with increasing privacy budget. Similarly, the accuracy of algorithm for two datasets is gradually improved as the depth of the tree increases. From the above experimental results, it is concluded that the higher the depth of the tree, the higher the accuracy when the privacy budget is the same, and the larger the privacy budget, the higher the accuracy when the tree depth is the same.

From Figures 4 and 5, it can be seen that the classification accuracy of the algorithm in this paper for the Adult dataset is 83.50%, 84.11%, 85.03%, 84.95% and 84.81% when the number of decision trees is 50 and the privacy protection budget is 0.1, 0.25, 0.5, 0.75, and 1.00,respectively. The classification accuracies for Mushroom dataset were 93.43%, 94.19%, 94.50%, 94.47% and 94.43%, respectively. And the highest accuracy of classification is achieved when the number of trees is 50. This may be because when the number of trees in the random forest is too small, the generalization ability of the random forest model is poor and the model classification accuracy increases with the number of decision trees. When the number of trees is more than 70, as the privacy budget needs to be allocated to each tree, the more the number of trees the less privacy protection budget on each tree, and at this time it is the privacy budget that constrains the classification accuracy of model. Therefore, the selection of the number of trees to be built in the differential privacy random forest needs to be considered to satisfy the generalization ability of the model while building a small number of trees to improve the overall model classification accuracy.

From Figures 6 and 7 at privacy budgets of 0.1, 0.25, 0.5, 0.75, and 1.00, the classification accuracies of the algorithm in this paper are 84.81%, 84.94%, 85.03%, 85.18% and 85.32% for the Adult dataset and 94.20%, 94.30%, 94.50%, 94.73%, and 94.80% for the Mushroom dataset, respectively. It can be seen from the figure that the classification accuracy of ours, RFDPP-gini and DiffP-RFs algorithms for both Adult and Mushroom datasets increase with increasing privacy protection budget, which is satisfying our expectation. Our algorithm has better classification accuracy than RFDPP-gini and DiffP-RFs algorithms with the same privacy protection budget, which is due to the fact that ours algorithm calculates feature weights and tree weights by differential privacy out-of-bag estimation, which saves privacy budget, while performing feature selecting, etc. to make more important features prominent, and finally allocates privacy budget by feature weights and tree weights, which reduces the effect of noise on important decision trees and important features. In summary, the algorithm presented in this article makes the data more available while satisfying privacy protection.

5. Conclusions

In this paper, we propose a differential privacy budget allocation algorithm based on out-of-bag estimation of random forests, which calculates the weights and feature weights of trees under different datasets to allocate privacy protection budgets by out-of-bag estimation, selects a dynamic balance between the generalization ability of random forests and privacy protection budgets, avoids building decision trees with similar classification performance in random forests, and avoids too many decision trees making the privacy budget on each tree too small. At the same time, this paper improves the method of selecting features for each tree in the random forest, randomly selecting a certain number of features, ranking them according to their importance and selecting splits in turn, and adding differential privacy according to the principle that the higher the importance of features, the more privacy protection budget is allocated, which makes the privacy protection budget have a higher utilization rate. However, in the course of the algorithm, the weights of each tree are found by differential privacy out-of-bag estimation, after which the weights of each tree are found in the construction of a differential privacy random forest. Follow-up consideration is given to how weights under different forests can be linked to simplify the algorithmic process, and further research is conducted to learn how to efficiently allocate differential privacy protection budgets in other models.

Author Contributions: Conceptualization, X.L., B.Q. and D.Z.; methodology, X.L., B.Q. and Y.L.; software, X.L.; validation, B.Q. and Y.L.; writing—original draft preparation, X.L. and B.Q.; writing—review and editing, B.Q. and Y.L.; project administration, B.Q. and D.Z.; funding acquisition, B.Q., Y.L. and D.Z. All authors have read and agreed to the published version of the manuscript.

Funding: This research was funded by the Basic Research Program of Qinghai Province (grant number 2020-ZJ-701) and by the National Natural Science Foundation of China (grant numbers 61872292 and 62072207).

Institutional Review Board Statement: Not applicable.

Informed Consent Statement: Not applicable.

Data Availability Statement: Not applicable.

Conflicts of Interest: The authors declare no conflict of interest.

References

1. Marina, S.; Stan, M. *Challenges in Computational Statistics and Data Mining*; Springer: Cham, Switzerland, 2016; pp. 365–380.
2. Hu, X.Y.; Yuan, M.X.; Yao, J.G.; Deng, Y.; Chen, L.; Yang, Q.; Guan, H.B.; Zeng, J. Differential privacy in telco big data platform. *Proc. VLDB Endow.* **2015**, *24*, 1692–1703. [CrossRef]
3. Abid, M.; Iynkaran, N.; Yong, X.; Guang, H.; Song, G. Protection of big data privacy. *IEEE Access* **2016**, *4*, 1821–1834.
4. Qi, X.J.; Zong, M.K. An overview of privacy preserving data mining. *Procedia Environ. Sci.* **2012**, *12*, 1341–1347. [CrossRef]
5. Dwork, C. Differential privacy. *Lect. Notes Comput. Sci.* **2006**, *10*, 4052.
6. Liu, H.Y.; Chen, J.; Chen, G.Q. A review of data classification algorithms in data mining. *J. Tsinghua Univ. (Nat. Sci. Ed.)* **2002**, *12*, 727–730.
7. Kotsiantis, S.B. Decision trees: A recent overview. *Artif. Intell. Rev.* **2013**, *39*, 261–283. [CrossRef]
8. Peter, A.; Yaw, M.M.; Ussiph, N. Predicting bank operational efficiency using machine learning algorithm: Comparative study of decision tree, random Forest, and neural networks. *Adv. Fuzzy Syst.* **2020**, *2020*, 8581302.
9. Izonin, I.; Tkachenko, R.; Shakhovska, N.; Ilchyshyn, B.; Singh, K.K. A Two-Step Data Normalization Approach for Improving Classification Accuracy in the Medical Diagnosis Domain. *Mathematics* **2022**, *10*, 1942. [CrossRef]
10. Huang, B.; Huang, D.R.; Mi, B. Research on E-Commerce Transaction Payment System Basedf on C4.5 Decision Tree Data Mining Algorithm. *Comput. Syst. Sci. Eng.* **2020**, *35*, 113–121.
11. Sembiring, N.S.B.; Sinaga, M.D.; Ginting, E.; Tahel, F.; Fauzi, M.Y. Predict the Timeliness of Customer Credit Payments at Finance Companies Using a Decision Tree Algorithm. In Proceedings of the 2021 9th International Conference on Cyber and IT Service Management (CITSM), Bengkulu, Indonesia, 22–23 September 2021; pp. 1–4.
12. Zhang, Y.L.; Feng, P.F.; Ning, Y. Random forest algorithm based on differential privacy protection. In Proceedings of the 20th IEEE International Conference on Trust, Security and Privacy in Computing and Communications (TrustCom 2021), Shenyang, China, 20–22 October 2021; pp. 1259–1264.
13. Lv, C.X.; Li, Q.L.; Long, H.Q.; Ren, Y.M.; Ling, F. A differential privacy random forest method of privacy protection in cloud. In Proceedings of the 2019 IEEE International Conference on Computational Science and Engineering (CSE) and IEEE International Conference on Embedded and Ubiquitous Computing (EUC), New York, NY, USA, 1–3 August 2019; pp. 470–475.
14. Mu, H.R.; Ding, L.P.; Song, Y.N.; Lu, G.Q. DiffPRFs: Random forest under differential privacy. *J. Commun.* **2016**, *37*, 175–182.
15. Wang, M.S.; Yao, L.; Gao, F.X.; Xu, J.C. Study on differential privacy protection for medical set-valued data. *Comput. Sci.* **2022**, *49*, 362–368.
16. Fu, J.B.; Zhang, X.J.; Ding, L.P. MAXGDDP: Decision data release with differential privacy. *J. Commun.* **2018**, *39*, 136–146.
17. Zhang, S.Q.; Li, X.H.; Jiang, X.Y.; Li, B. Aur-tree differential privacy data publishing algorithm for medical data. *Appl. Res. Comput.* **2022**, *39*, 2162–2166.

18. Blum, A.; Dwork, C.; McSherry, F.; Nissim, K. Practical privacy: The SuLQ framrk. In Proceedings of the Twenty-Fourth ACM SIGMOD-SIGACT-SIGART Symposium on Principles of Database Systems (PODS'05), Baltimore, MD, USA, 13–15 June 2005; Association for Computing Machinery: New York, NY, USA, 2005; pp. 128–138.
19. McSherry, F.D. Privacy integrated queries: An extensible platform for privacy-preserving data analysis. In Proceedings of the 2009 ACM SIGMOD International Conference on Management of Data (SIGMOD'09), Providence, RI, USA, 29 June–2 July 2009; Association for Computing Machinery: New York, NY, USA, 2009; pp. 19–30.
20. Friedman, A.; Schuster, A. Data mining with differential privacy. In Proceedings of the 16th ACM SIGKDD International Conference on Knowledge Discovery and Data Mining (KDD'10), Washington, DC, USA, 25–28 July 2010; Association for Computing Machinery: New York, NY, USA, 2010; pp. 493–502.
21. Mohammed, N.; Chen, R.; Fung, B.C.M.; Yu, P.S. Data mining with differential privacy. In Proceedings of the 17th ACM SIGKDD International Conference on Knowledge Discovery and Data Mining (KDD'11), San Diego, CA, USA, 21–24 August 2011; Association for Computing Machinery: New York, NY, USA, 2011; pp. 493–501.
22. Zhu, T.Q.; Xiong, P.; Xiang, Y.; Zhou, W.L. An Effective Deferentially Private Data Releasing Algorithm for Decision Tree. In Proceedings of the 2013 12th IEEE International Conference on Trust, Security and Privacy in Computing and Communications, Melbourne, Australia, 16–18 July 2013; pp. 388–395.
23. Patil, A.; Singh, S. Differential private random forest. In Proceedings of the 2014 International Conference on Advances in Computing, Communications and Informatics (ICACCI), Delhi, India, 24–27 September 2014; pp. 2623–2630.
24. Li, Y.H.; Chen, X.L.; Liu, L. Random forest algorithm for differential privacy protection. *Comput. Eng.* **2020**, *46*, 93–101.
25. Paul, A.; Mukherjee, D.P.; Das, P.; Gangopadhyay, A.; Chintha, A.R.; Kundu, S. Improved random forest for classification. *IEEE Trans. Image Process.* **2018**, *27*, 4012–4024. [CrossRef] [PubMed]
26. Truex, S.; Liu, L.; Gursoy, M.E.; Yu, L. Privacy-preserving inductive learning with decision trees. In Proceedings of the 2017 IEEE International Congress on Big Data (BigData Congress), Honolulu, HI, USA, 25–30 June 2017; pp. 57–64.
27. Li, Y.Q.; Chen, Y.H.; Li, Q.; Liu, A.H. Random forest algorithm under differential privacy based on out-of-bag estimate. *J. Harbin Inst. Technol.* **2021**, *53*, 146–154.
28. Dwork, C. A firm foundation for private data analysis. *Commun. ACM* **2011**, *54*, 86–95. [CrossRef]
29. Dwork, C.; McSherry, F.; Nissim, K.; Smith, A. *Theory of Cryptography Conference*; Halevi, S., Rabin, T., Eds.; Springer: Berlin/Heidelberg, Germany, 2006; Volume 3876.
30. Geng, Q.; Viswanath, P. The optimal noise-adding mechanism in differential privacy. *IEEE Trans. Inf. Theory* **2015**, *62*, 925–951. [CrossRef]
31. Mironov, I. Rényi Differential Privacy. In Proceedings of the 2017 IEEE 30th Computer Security Foundations Symposium (CSF), Santa Barbara, CA, USA, 21–25 August 2017; pp. 263–275.
32. Xiong, P.; Zhu, T.Q.; Wang, X.F. Differential privacy protection and its application. *J. Comput. Sci.* **2014**, *37*, 101–122.

Article

DVIT—A Decentralized Virtual Items Trading Forum with Reputation System †

Zuobin Ying [1,*], Wusong Lan [1], Chen Deng [2], Lu Liu [3] and Ximeng Liu [4]

1 Faculty of Data Science, City University of Macau, Macau, China
2 National Institute of Education (NIE), Nanyang Technological University, Singapore 637616, Singapore
3 Faculty of Finance, City University of Macau, Macau, China
4 College of Computer and Data Science, Fuzhou University, Fuzhou 350025, China
* Correspondence: zbying@cityu.mo
† An earlier version of this paper was presented at the Conference on CCNIS2022. Its number is ccnis2022-0053. This article is one of the results of MOST-FDCT Projects (0058/2019/AMJ, 2019YFE0110300) (Research and Application of Cooperative Multi-Agent Platform for Zhuhai-Macao Manufacturing Service).

Abstract: The metaverse provides us with an attractive virtual space in which the value of the virtual property has been increasingly recognized. However, the lack of effective cross-metaverse trading tools and the reputation guarantee makes it difficult to trade items among different metaverses. To this end, a decentralized reputation system for virtual items trading forum named DVIT is devised. To the best of our knowledge, DVIT is the first decentralized cross-metaverse item trading prototype inspired by the online-game trading system. We designed the corresponding transaction function and realized the autonomous governance of the community by introducing the reputation mechanism. An improved election mechanism is proposed to improve efficiency based on Delegated Proof-of-Stake (DPoS). Through token rewards associated with activity levels, users' motivation can be stimulated. The experiments indicate that our proposed scheme could dynamically measure the trustworthiness degree of the users through the dynamic reputation value and thereby exclude malicious users from the blockchain within 20 epochs.

Keywords: metaverse; blockchain; DPoS; video games; virtual economy; virtual worlds

MSC: 68M14

1. Introduction

Metaverse, a digital world parallel to reality, also reckoned as the post-reality universe, integrates a perpetual and persistent multiuser environment with physical reality through digital virtuality, in which each person can have a virtual avatar [1]. In many film and television productions, such as *Ready Player One* (A film Directed by Steven Spielberg in 2018), people have shown a passionate imagination for living in a virtual space called the *Oasis* with advanced devices [2]. Now, our imaginations about the metaverse are no longer illusory. In 2021, Facebook changed its name to Meta, which completely ignited the fever of the metaverse. The company would invest many billions of dollars in the metaverse [3]. According to the survey by Statista, 67.65% of the companies interviewed believe that the metaverse market is going to boom in the next five years [4].

However, to achieve reliability, the metaverse still faces a series of problems. For example, different companies are competing to launch their metaverses. For technical and commercial reasons, these metaverses are not interconnected and will continue to be isolated from each other for the foreseeable future [5]. What if the person from different metaverses wants to exchange stuff or commodities with each other? Take two virtual characters, Alice and Bob, who live in two different metaverses as an example. If Alice has a virtual closet in metaverse α, and now she wants to exchange it with Bob in metaverse β

for a virtual coat. Unless there is already sufficient trust between her and Bob, a trusted third party is needed to go through this transaction. However, introducing a trusted third party would result in a high trading fee and high delay. Moreover, it will also become the bottleneck when cross-metaverse trading increases explosively. To our knowledge, there exists no sufficient solution for trading virtual assets across the metaverses, and in the foreseeable future, due to technical and commercial considerations, metaverses will continue to be independent of each other [6]. Although many metaverse developers have tried to formulate a unified set of guidelines for all metaverses, such as the Web3.0 Open Metaverse Alliance (OMA3) and The Metaverse Standards Forum (MSF), they are still some distance away from being put into use [7,8]. Solving this problem will be beneficial both for the current metaverse market and for the future development of a more complete economy in the metaverse.

Given the fact that we have not entered the metaverse yet, we need to simulate virtual transactions between metaverse by other means. Video games, for example, are a considerable option. First, there is ample precedent for using video games for real-world simulation. In 2005, a virtual plague broke out in *World of Warcraft* (A multiplayer online role-playing game released in 2004 by Blizzard Entertainment). Due to game developers' mistakes, a disease (i.e., Corrupted Blood) could make players lose life continuously and spread among players in the game world. Because of its many similarities to real-world outbreaks of infectious diseases, some infectious disease propagation models were proposed through the inspiration of Role-Playing Games [9]. Secondly, we found that the trading pattern among different metaverses has the most in common with the m in some old video games. Forums are a common form of community on the Internet for enthusiasts to communicate with each other. There is a category of forums where players can trade in-game items with other players. Because it has a wide user base and a mature trading system, we decide to use forums to simulate virtual item trading in the metaverse [10].

In this paper, we introduce DVIT—a decentralized reputation system for virtual item trading forums. The main contributions of this paper are summarized as follows.

- To the authors' knowledge, we are the first to construct a decentralized in-game item-trading forum system. Not only do we design a series of functions to realize the selling and renting of the virtual stuff, but we also put forward a dispute adjudication system for players to resolve the controversy.
- An improved election mechanism is devised to improve efficiency on the basis of Delegated Proof-of-Stake. Through token rewards associated with activity levels, the motivation of users can be increased.
- The simulation experiments indicate that our proposed scheme could dynamically measure the trustworthiness degree of the users through the dynamic reputation value. Therefore, malicious users would be excluded from the blockchain within 20 epochs.

The rest of this paper is organized as follows: Section 2 introduces the preliminaries. Section 3 presents the proposed model. Section 4 presents the model designed in this paper. Section 5 presents simulations. Section 6 presents the performance analysis. Section 7 is the related work, and Section 8 is the conclusion and future work.

2. Preliminaries

In this section, we introduce the building blocks used in our solution, including blockchain consensus algorithms, the reputation value system, and the background knowledge of in-game item-trading platforms.

2.1. Blockchain Consensus Algorithms

The prevailing in-game item-trading forums model has the disadvantage of being too centralized. Therefore, we need to establish trust and consensus among strangers while reducing centralization. Blockchain is a chain of blocks that store all committed transactions using a public ledger [11]. Blockchain has some key characteristics, such as decentralization, transparency, immutability, and audibility [12]. According to different consensus algorithms, blockchains can be classified as Proof-of-Work (PoW), Proof-of-Stake (PoS), and Delegated Proof-of-Stake (DPoS) [13]. DPoS is developed from PoS and is a currently popular consensus algorithm. In DPoS, users will vote and elect delegates (or witnesses) to validate the next block [14]. DPoS is considered by its supporters to be more democratic than PoS. DPoS allows more qualified users to participate in the election process [15]. Further, the speed of block confirmation in DPoS is faster than in PoS [16]. Moreover, DPoS is considered by some scholars to require less energy than PoW [17]. There will be much less tendency to create forks on DPoS [18].

2.2. Reputation Value System

Blockchains may face many security vulnerabilities, such as 51% attack and Double-spending attack [19]. If there is no way to distinguish the evil users who have carried out attacks from normal users, it will pose a risk to the security of the blockchain. In order to improve the security of the blockchain, we introduce a reputation value system. When the node behaves well, it will receive the corresponding reputation value as a reward, and the reputation value will be reduced as punishment when the node misbehaves [20]. DPoS blockchain faces the problem of increasing centralization due to the decreasing motivation of users to participate [21]. Therefore, we combine traditional DPoS with a reputation-based voting mechanism to increase the participation of nodes [16]. On the other hand, to motivate nodes to behave well, we also introduce an incentive system [22].

2.3. Merkle Tree

The Merkle tree is a fundamental part of blockchain technology that realizes data availability and traceability [23]. It is a type of tree where the lower base elements are called leaves while the top element is called the Merkle root. The bottommost leaf node contains the stored data or its hash value, and non-leaf nodes (including intermediate and root nodes) are hashes of the contents of its two child nodes [24]. Merkle trees are formed by repeating pairs of hash nodes until only one hash, the Merkle root remains. The structure is shown in the diagram.

In Figure 1, we show the basic structure of the Merkle tree. First, let $H(.)$ be the hash function. The leaf nodes $Hash_i$ can be calculated by the input data $DATA_i$, such as $Hash_a = H(DATA_a)$. The next layer is donated by leaf nodes $Hash_i$, and the intermediate nodes can be computed by $Hash_{ab} = H(Hash_a, Hash_b)$. Then we repeat the above operation. Finally, we get the root node result by $Hash_{abcd} = H(Hash_{ab}, Hash_{cd})$ [25].

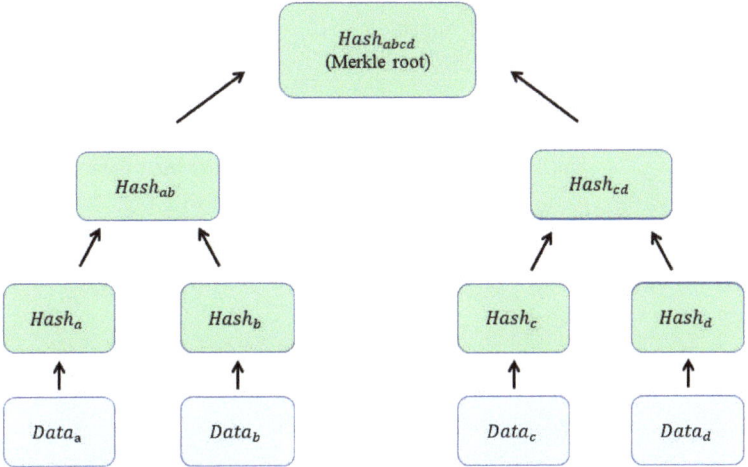

Figure 1. The Merkle Tree.

Merkle trees allow secure, efficient, and consistent validation of large volumes of data. Any changes to the underlying data will be passed to its parent node, layer by layer, to the root node. If attackers tampered with any transactions, the Merkle tree root hash value would be incorrect [26]. Merkle tree can help in improving the efficiency of blockchain verification. It would be cumbersome for nodes to store the full blockchain ledger to verify transactions, but with the Simplified Payment Verification (SPV) technique, verifying the inclusion of transactions would be easy. For each block, a Merkle tree is constructed using the transactions in the block as leaf nodes. Light nodes stored the Merkle root [27]. Merkel tree can also be combined with DPoS. The selected block generators need to prove their identity before generating blocks. They can create a delegated proof with the Merkle root and a Merkle verification path from the Merkle tree. The Merkle root can be used to verify that the block signer used the correct set of delegates and by providing a valid Merkle verification path from their uids to the Merkle root, which means they can prove their identity [28].

2.4. In-Game Item-Trading Platform

Diablo II is a classic action role-playing video game developed by Blizzard North which has developed a mature and complete in-game item-trading ecology. Due to the limitations of Diablo II, players usually choose to use the forum for online item trading. We introduce some of the mainstream trading platforms and their features as follows.

Blizzard has *an official forum* (https://eu.forums.blizzard.com/en/d2r/c/trade/9, accessed on 10 August 2022) for Diablo II which supports trading between players. Except for the official forums, there are a number of third-party trading sites. *Kaienzhijiao* (https://bbs.d.163.com/, accessed on 10 August 2022) is a forum where you can trade with other players. *Traderie* (https://traderie.com/diablo2resurrected, accessed on 10 August 2022) is a website where you can exchange your in-game items with other players. On those websites or forums, real-money trading is not allowed. Players need to swap in-game items with items. When players are desperate for in-game items, they have other options. *Anheihe* (http://d3.17173.com/content/2022-07-18/20220718202629902.shtml, accessed on 10 August 2022) is a mini program based on Wechat where players can trade in-game items of Diablo II. Players can conduct real-money trades in disguise through a kind of token it offers. There is a forum called *d2jsp* (https://www.d2jsp.org/, accessed on 10 August 2022) where users can perform real-money trading by tokens. Due to Diablo II's large player base, it is profitable to engage in-game item trading. Therefore, naturally, some businessmen set their eyes on this place. *DD373* (https://www.dd373.com/s-1psrbm.html, accessed on 10 August 2022) is a professional in-game item-trading platform on which in-game items are sold at the price of CNY.

Most of these platforms are centralized. They are under the control of a small number of administrators, while normal users are not involved in the governance of the community. In some trading platforms, such as Traderie, Anheihe, and DD373, past trading records are not directly disclosed, which has created a barrier for players to understand the correct price. The next part of our work is improving the existing trading platform mechanism.

3. Proposed Model

In this section, we formalize the system model and the threat model. The system definitions and goals of the proposed system will be introduced in this section.

3.1. System Model

Figure 2 depicts the DVIT system architecture. The system has five entities, and the introduction of these entities is as follows:

- Normal Users (**NUs**) are active game players on the forum. They have their nodes on the blockchain. They are honest and want to make transactions with other players.
- The Forum (**TF**) provides a space for users to communicate. Transactions take place between members on **TF**.

- Administrators (**ADM**) on **TF** are responsible for supervising transactions and intervening when players can not resolve problems.
- The blockchain (**BC**) records transactions of **NUs**. Trading between users will be performed on the **BC** by tokens. In addition, the **BC** supports some extended functionality such as in-game item-trading of Non-Fungible Token (NFT).
- Evil Users (**EVs**) are users who would pose a threat to the order of transactions. Some **EVs** try to steal in-game items while trading. Some **EVs** are sent by competing platforms to disrupt the normal functioning of this forum.

3.2. Threaten Model

In our model, **TF** and **BC** need to work together to keep the system running properly. It is assumed that **TF** and **BC** are fully trusted, which means they will follow all protocols and will not collude with **EVs**. **NUs** are assumed to be honest and rational. They will tend to follow the rules. **EVs** are evil. They will break the rules to profit or interfere with the normal order of the system. **EVs** can pose a threat to the system at various points. When trading, **EVs** will induce other players to trade at too high or too low prices. In the block-minting process of DPoS, **EVs** may disrupt the operation of **BC** by deliberately not generating blocks after they are elected.

3.3. System Definitions

1. *Setup*: The *Setup* algorithm is executed by **TF**. The master key MK and public key PK are generated by the **ADM** with a security parameter SP and attributes of the **ADM** AM. SP should be kept confidential. MK and PK will be used to generate their keys for the registered users. The *Setup* process is described as: $(AM, SP) \rightarrow (MK, PK)$.

2. *Keygen*{$(MK, PK, I) \rightarrow k_i, k_{pi}$}: When **NUs** generate nodes on **BC**, they can request the administrators of **TF** to generate keys that belong to them. After administrators receive a request from user i, they will generate a personal secret key k_i and a public key k_{pi} for user i using the user's personal information I, MK, and PK. When users are elected as witnesses, they can use secret keys to sign the blocks generated by them.

3. *Encryption*: When a **NU** i is elected as a witness, i is required to sign the transaction with the personal secret key k_i on the block that i generates. The details of the election process will be described below. It takes i's personal secret key k_i and the details or trading **TD** as input and sig_i, the signature of witness i as output like: $(k_i, TD) \rightarrow (sig_i)$.

4. *Decryption*: When users challenge whether a transaction is recorded by user i, they can verify the sig_i with i's public key k_{pi}. If the transaction was recorded by the correct user, the **TD** that matches the transaction record will be decrypted from sig_i. If the block was produced by an impostor, then the decryption of sig_i will fail. It takes sig_i and k_{pi} as input and **TD** as output, such as $(k_{pi}, sig_i) \rightarrow (TD)$.

3.4. Goals of the Proposed System

The proposed system defines the following design goals:

3.4.1. Security

Given security is the first thing that needs to be ensured in the trading process, we add the **BC** to the original forum mechanism. Tokens for transactions will be transferred on the **BC**, making the process secure. Furthermore, we have added a dispute adjudication mechanism for transactions ensuring controversial transactions will be resolved in time.

3.4.2. Transparency

It is necessary to show the record of transactions in the forum to **NUs** because it will save them from being cheated by **EVs**. Accordingly, we record all transactions and make them available to all players by **BC**.

3.4.3. Decentralization

A **BC** is introduced to avoid the possible tampering and deletion of transaction records in the traditional forum mechanism. Moreover, we set incentives based on reputation value so that **NUs** will spontaneously record transactions and resolve disputes in transactions. Witnesses for generating blocks will be elected by **NUs** themselves.

As Table 1 shows, our DVIT has quite a few improvements over the existing common in-game item-trading platforms. ● in the table indicates that the characteristic is met while ✗ indicates that the characteristic is not met. DVIT provides a decentralized, democratic and transparent trading system. In the next section, we will introduce more details about the construction we proposed.

Table 1. Features of Trading Platforms.

Names of Trading Platforms	Forum	Real-Money Trade	Decentralized	Users Participation in Management	Open Transaction Records
the Offcial Forum	●	✗	✗	✗	●
Kaienzhijiao	●	✗	✗	✗	●
Traderie	✗	✗	✗	✗	✗
Anheihe	✗	●	✗	✗	✗
d2jsp	●	●	✗	✗	●
DD373	✗	●	✗	✗	✗
DVIT	●	●	●	●	●

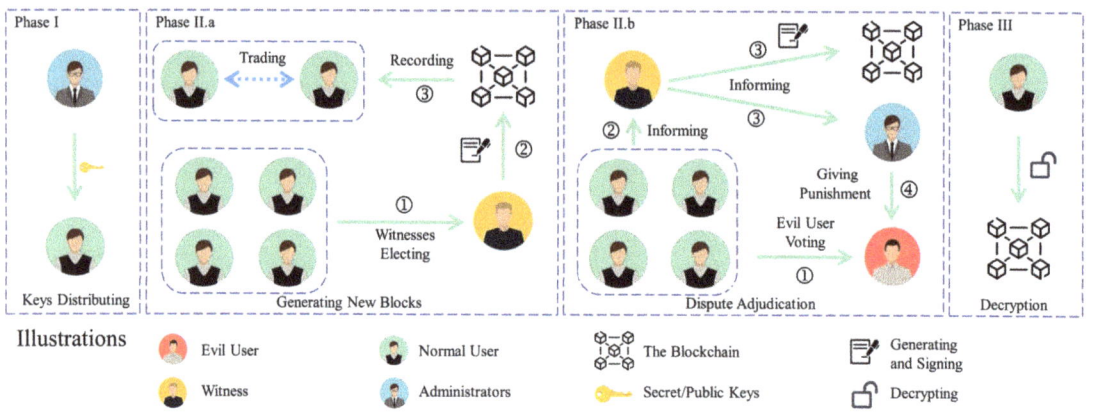

Figure 2. The System Model of DVIT.

4. Detailed DVIT

In this section, we give the concrete construction of the proposed trading system. We present the detail of the reputation value system, the witnesses' election system, and the dispute adjudication system. We also introduce the details of the in-game item-trading forum, such as Trading, Renting, and in-game item-trading NFT.

Our trading system is based on Diablo II, a classic game with a relatively well-developed forum trading mechanism. We will give a brief introduction to how to use the system in the following part. First of all, new users need to register an account. To make themselves trustworthy, they need to pledge some tokens on the chain, which can be exchanged for cryptocurrencies such as Eths.

4.1. Calculation of Reputation Value

After users successfully register on the **BC**, the reputation value of their nodes will be calculated by the following steps.

Step 1: i_{rep0}, which is the fixed reputation value of user i, is calculated based on the number of tokens pledged by i on BC as the initial reputation value. The upper limit of i_{rep0} is 60, and i_{rep0} does not change over time. The reputation value for new participants will generally be designed to be half of the maximum reputation value, and we set the i_{rep0} to fluctuate with the number of pledged tokens to encourage users to pledge more tokens [29].

Step 2: To avoid the disadvantage of not actively voting by nodes in the traditional DPoS consensus, when **NUs** cast a vote in the election of witnesses or dispute adjudication, **NUs** will receive three points of reputation value as a reward [30]. This part of reputation value is called dynamic reputation value, which changes over time. First, calculating i_{repa}, the reputation value user i got in the last 0–10 epochs.

Step 3: Calculating i_{repb}, the reputation value user i got in the last 10–20 epochs.

Step 4: The actual reputation value of user i, i_{rep}, consists of a fixed reputation value and dynamic reputation value. The formula to calculate i_{rep} is as in (1). Weight w in this paper is 1/3. We set the weight to avoid the unlimited accumulation of the reputation value. Their newly acquired reputation value will have a greater weight than the previously acquired one because recent positive behavior will bring more influence [31].

$$i_{rep} = i_{rep0} + i_{repa} + w * i_{repb} \tag{1}$$

4.2. Assessment of Reputation State

According to i_{rep}, we classify users into several reputation states. The notation of the reputation state of user i is i_{rst}. There are four states of i_{rst}: G, W, N, and B, which represent the i's reputation states as "Great", "Well", "Normal", and "Bad". How to calculate i_{rst} is represented in Algorithm 1.

Algorithm 1 Evaluation of i_{rst}.

Input: Reputation value of user i: i_{rep}.
Output: Reputation state of user i: i_{rst}.
   if $i_{rep} > 70$ then
      $i_{rst} = G$ ▷ User i's reputation state is "Great"
   else if $i_{rep} > 50$ then
      $i_{rst} = W$ ▷ User i's reputation state is "Well"
   else if $i_{rep} > 40$ then
      $i_{rst} = N$ ▷ User i's reputation state is "Normal"
   else
      $i_{rst} = B$ ▷ User i's reputation state is "Bad"
   end if

In DPoS, transactions will be recorded by witnesses, and any users registered on **TF** can be nominated as a candidate or participate in a vote if they meet the conditions. To keep the system safe, users must reach the reputation target to participate in the election. When $i_{rst} = N, W$, and G, user i can vote for others; when $i_{rst} = W, G$, user i can be nominated as a candidate. Users can vote for others whether they were nominated as a candidate or not. The specific voting process in an election phase is shown in Algorithm 2. In the following part, we introduce the various features of the forum.

4.3. Witnesses Election

The election of Witnesses will take place by the following steps and will be open to any registered nodes that meet the criteria:

Step 1: The system generates a list of candidates $Candidate[\ ]$. Users whose $i_{rst} = W, G$ will be added to $Candidate[\ ]$.

Step 2: Users whose $i_{rst} = N, W$, and G can vote for users in $Candidate[\ ]$.

Step 3: At the end of the voting phase, users in $Candidate[\ ]$ will be ranked in descending order according to the votes they receive. The top X users in $Candidate[\ ]$ will become witnesses and be included in $Witness[\ ]$. Blocks will be generated by the users in $Witness[\ ]$.

Algorithm 2 Election process.

Input: Reputation value of user i: i_{rst}, Other users' ballots.
Output: Dynamic reputation value of user i: i_{repa}, newly generated blocks, token rewards.
    witnesses voting process
    if $i_{rst} = N$ **then**   ▷ *Determining user i's reputation state*
        user i can vote to others
        if $i_{rst} = W$ **then**   ▷ *Determining user i's reputation state*
            user i can be nominated as a candidate
            if user i being elected as a witness **then**   ▷ *Determining the identity of user i*
                generate a block
                receive handling fee reward by reputation value
            end if
        end if
    end if
    if user i voted in this epoch **then**
        $i_{repa} + 3$ ▷ *Reward for user i's participation in voting*
    end if

4.4. Forum Functions

- *Trading in-game items.* To begin with, seller U_{se} displays the in-game items, I_{it}, to be sold, its price I_{pri}, and seller i's id n_i in a posting (I_{it}, I_{pri}, n_i) on **TF**. Then buyer U_{bu} can initiate trade requests to sellers on **TF**. After U_{bu} and U_{se} confirm the details of the transaction, they can start the transaction on the **BC** through smart contracts.

    Step 1: U_{se} and U_{bu} make the final confirmation about the I_{it} and I_{pri} in the posting on **TF**. After that, the post will be locked.
    Step 2: U_{bu} locks the tokens on the **BC**.
    Step 3: U_{bu} and U_{se} hand over the It in the game.
    Step 4: U_{bu} and U_{se} confirm the transaction on the **BC** by voting; they can choose *yes* or *no* in voting. If the result is $<yes, yes>$, the transaction will complete, and the tokens will be sent to the U_{se}'s account. If either party selects *no* in the confirmation vote, the tokens will be locked on the **BC** and enter the dispute adjudication phase.
    The blockchain has already been introduced into the supply chain to record food safety-related messages [32]. Inspired by this, we will record all transactions on the **BC**. Those recorded messages will be defined as:

$$M_{sellx} = [sig_o || timestamp || n_{Bu} || n_{Se} || TD] \tag{2}$$

    where sig_o, the signature of witness o, is the signature on **TD** using the signing key k_o. The details of sig_o is $hash(timestamp || n_{Bu} || n_{Se} || TD)$. n_{Se} is the U_{se}'s node id, n_{Bu} is the U_{bu}'s node id, and **TD** is the details about this trade. This information is non-falsifiable and publicly available.

- *Renting in-game items.* The process of renting is similar to buying and selling in-game items. First, lessees U_{le} initiate lease requests by posting on **TF** and lock the deposit Dep and rents Ren on **BC**. The posting (I_{it}, Dep, Ren) is about the I_{it} that U_{le} wants and Dep and Ren that U_{lo} would give. Then, lessors U_{lo} should send It to U_{le}. When the lease period is over, the U_{le} needs to return the I_{it} in time. If any dispute occurs during the transaction, it could be resolved by the dispute adjudication mechanism. The details are as follows:

Step 1: U_{le} locks tokens as Dep and Ren on the **BC** and posts lease requests. After communication, U_{le} and U_{lo} make the final confirmation about the I_{it}, Dep, and Ren in the posting on **TF**. Afterward, the post will be locked.

Step 2: U_{le} and U_{lo} hand over the I_{it} in the game, U_{le} should return It in time.

Step 3: When the lease expires, U_{lo} and U_{le} confirm the transaction on **BC** by voting. They can choose yes or no in voting. If the result is $<yes, yes>$, the transaction completes, and Ren will be transferred to U_{lo}'s account while Dep will be returned to U_{le}'s account. If either party selects no in the confirmation vote, the token will be locked on **BC** and enters the dispute adjudication phase. If the U_{le} defaults on the contract, Dep may be given to the U_{lo} as compensation.

Messages of the lease process will be recorded on the chain like:

$$M_{rentx} = [sig_o || timestamp || n_{Lo} || n_{Le} || TD] \tag{3}$$

where sig_o is the signature of witness o, its detail is $hash(timestamp || n_{Lo} || n_{Le} || TD)$. n_{Lo} is U_{lo}'s node id, n_{Le} is the U_{le}'s node, and **TD** means the details about this trading of in-game item information and rental date.

- *In-game item-trading NFT.* For players to buy in-game items in bulk, we introduce the in-game item-trading NFT **iNFT**. Players who $i_{rst} = G$ can submit a request for minting **iNFT** to the forum administrators. After verifying that the players have a sufficient number of in-game items, administrators will mint an **iNFT** for players, and the following information will be recorded in the **iNFT**:

$$Mnft_x = [sig_a || timestamp || in || n_i] \tag{4}$$

where sig_a is the signature of administrator a, and the detail of sig_a is $hash(timestamp || n_i || n_a || in)$. in is the information about the in-game items, such as names and amounts, and n_i is the id of U_{is}, the player who submits the mint request. n_a is the id of the administrator a. An **iNFT** can be traded on the **BC** as the equivalent of a specified number of in-game items. The user who holds the **iNFT** can send a redemption request to U_{is}. The redemption process is as follows:

1. The holder initiates a redemption transaction with U_{is}.
2. U_{is} delivers in-game items to the holder according to n_i.
3. U_{is} and the holder confirm the transaction, and if either party does not confirm, the transaction proceeds to the dispute adjudication stage. If both parties confirm that the transaction is correct, a request is sent to the administrator to burn the **iNFT**.
4. Administrator burns the **iNFT** after confirming the request.

The trading processes and the delivery processes of **iNFTs** will be recorded on the **BC** too. Users can also use in-game items from other games to mint an **iNFT** for trading.

- *Handling fees system.* After recording tradings, witnesses will receive a pro-rate handling fee. To ensure the security of transactions and to increase the motivation of users to maintain a high reputation value, the distribution of transactions between witnesses is by the reputation value. All witnesses will be ranked in order of reputation value from highest to lowest. The witness with the highest reputation value will be responsible for recording transactions with the highest value, and so on. There is often a big price gap between different in-game items. In Table 2, we show the difference in item prices in Diablo II on a trading forum by fg (The token used in the forums). The in-game items on the game forums usually consist of a large number of low-value in-game items and a small number of high-value in-game items, which means the handling fees will have a big difference between transactions.

- *Dispute adjudication system.* When a dispute arises during users' trading on the forum, it goes to the dispute adjudication stage. First, the accounts and tokens held by both parties will be locked. Then the system will randomly select 11 users that $Rst_i! = B$ to form the jury. The two users in the dispute, users A and B, will be required to present various pieces of evidence to the jury, such as records of chats, screenshots of games, etc. The jury will need to vote to decide after viewing the evidence, and the vote will be given a weight λ based on the voters' reputation rating. The better the reputation rating is, the higher the λ of the voting is. Algorithm 3 shows how user i's votes are counted.

    l_i is the final result of user i's vote, and L is the final decision in dispute adjudication, which is calculated by $\sum_{k=1}^{11} l_k = L$. The rule for judging the adjudication process is shown below. If user i abstains or does not vote within the time limit, $l_{i0} = 0$. When $L = 0$, the system will randomly select a user whose $i_{rst} = G$ to join the jury to vote until $L! = 0$. Users who are found guilty must compensate the victim, and all their pledged tokens will be confiscated while their accounts will be banned.

$$\begin{cases} L > 0, & \text{user } B \text{ is guilty} \\ L < 0, & \text{user } A \text{ is guilty} \end{cases} \quad (5)$$

Algorithm 3 Dispute adjudication.

Input: Initial voting result of user i: l_{i0}.
Output: Final result of user i's vote: l_i.
    if user i supports user A **then**
        $l_{i0} = 1$ ▷ *The Original Voting Result of user i*
    else if user i supports user B **then**
        $l_{i0} = -1$ ▷ *The Original Voting Result of user i*
    end if
    if $i_{rst} = N$ **then**   ▷ *Calculate the voting weight of user i based on reputation state*
        $\lambda = 0.7$
    else if $i_{rst} = W$ **then** ▷ *The weight of user i's voting will be higher when user i's reputation state is higher*
        $\lambda = 1$
    else if $i_{rst} = G$ **then**
        $\lambda = 1.41$
    end if
    $l_i = \lambda * l_{i0}$ ▷ *The Final Voting Result of user i*

Table 2. Item Prices in Diablo II Measured in Forum Token.

Name of Item	Price in fg
Unid eth demonlime tyrant club	5
Unid eth blackhand key	5
Unid shadowkiller	5
Firelizards Talon	5
Rising sun	5
Unid vampire gaze	10
Angelic ring	5
Nats mask	5
Aldurs full set	20
Ber	750
Jah	650

5. Simulation and Discussion

We present the simulation of the reputation value mechanism and handling fee mechanism in this section. For experimental performance, simulations were implemented under various conditions and compared with the traditional reputation value mechanism.

5.1. Simulation of the New Reputation Value Mechanism

Our experimental simulation (except data decryption) was simulated on a PC with Windows 11, 11th Gen Intel(R) Core(TM) i7-11800H @2.30 GHz, and 16 GB RAM. Simulation experiments were conducted for the designed forum reputation value system to prove the effectiveness of the design. Usually, the user's reputation value does not change over time. Therefore, after users have acquired enough reputation value, their motivation to participate decreases rapidly; an aging mechanism can be introduced to the system, which will make reputation values decrease over time [33]. In the first part of the simulation, we will simulate the process of users participating in the election voting and receiving reputation value rewards, as Figure 3 shows. There are five nodes in the experiment: Alice, Bob, Charlie, Dave, and Eve. The probability of their participation in voting is 90%, 60%, 60%, 30%, and 90%. Their fixed reputation values are A_{rep0}: 50, B_{rep0}: 60, C_{rep0}: 50, D_{rep0}: 60, and E_{rep0}: 60. At the beginning of the experiment, their dynamic reputation values are 0. It is worth mentioning that Eve is a malicious user who will intentionally not generate a block after being selected as a witness. Figure 4 a shows the change in their reputation value over 30 epochs under our system design. In the graph, the horizontal coordinates represent the time. An epoch represents an election process. The vertical coordinate indicates nodes' actual reputation values A_{rep}, B_{rep}, C_{rep}, D_{rep}, and E_{rep}. The lower limit of the vertical coordinate is 50. When $i_{rep} = 50$, $i_{rst} = N$, user i cannot be nominated as a candidate.

At the beginning of the experiment, we can see that Bob and Dave take the lead by relying on their high starting reputation value. However, A_{rep} is the highest in *epoch* 30 because of Alice's highest participation rate. The change in C_{rep} is noteworthy. In the beginning, Charlie quickly accumulated reputation value by frequently voting, making a sharp rise in C_{rep}. However, after *epoch* 19 C_{rep} started to drop significantly. It was due to Charlie's non-voting over a while, and the reputation value accumulated earlier started to expire. Dave has the lowest voting intention, so D_{rep} remains in the lower range even though D_{rep0} is 60. Eve will intentionally not generate blocks when Eve becomes a witness. Eve will try to keep voting to earn reputation value. However, due to the penalty mechanism, after *epoch* 17, Eve was disqualified from being nominated as a witness. In *epoch* 30, the users with the highest reputation values are Alice and Bob, the former has the highest willingness to vote, and the latter has a huge number of tokens pledged. It represents that our system can select two types of users that we believe are more trustworthy: those with a high willingness to vote and those who have pledged ample tokens.

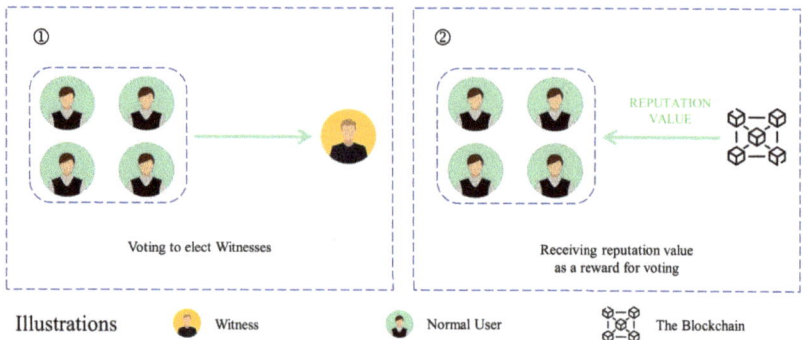

Figure 3. The simulation of the new reputation value mechanism.

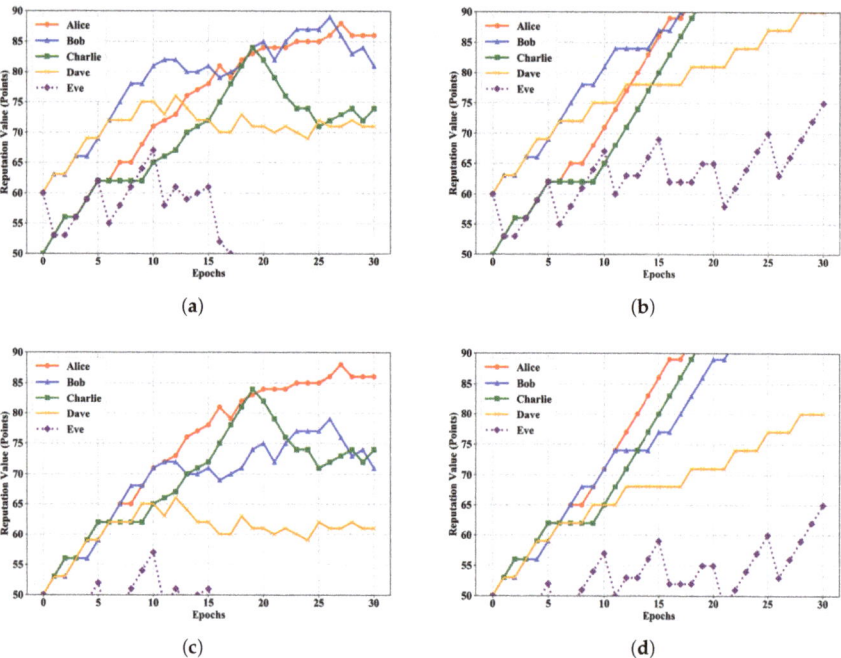

Figure 4. The Simulation of the Reputation Value. (**a**) The reputation value changes in DVIT with the different fixed reputation values. (**b**) The reputation value changes in the traditional DPoS mechanism with the different fixed reputation values. (**c**) The reputation value changes in DVIT with the same fixed reputation values. (**d**) The reputation value changes in the traditional DPoS mechanism with the same fixed reputation values.

Figure 4b shows the result of the same behavior of the same group of users in the traditional reputation value system. Not including a dynamic reputation mechanism poses two main problems. The first one is the reputation value will unlimitedly increase, which will make it hard for new users to catch up with old users. We can see A_{rep}, B_{rep}, and C_{rep} reached 90 before *epoch* 20. Even if an upper limit is designed for the reputation value, users may not participate in voting at all after accumulating enough reputation values. The vitality of the forum will be weakened. The second one is evil users can keep their nomination by constant voting. In *epoch* 21, E_{rep} was deducted for not generating blocks. However, in *epoch* 25, E_{rep} is 70, which is higher than in *epoch* 21. Eve can keep replenishing the reputation value deducted for doing evil. It greatly increases the destructiveness of the forum system by evil users. What is more, we compare the changes in reputation values for Alice and Eve under both the old and new mechanisms in Figure 5a.

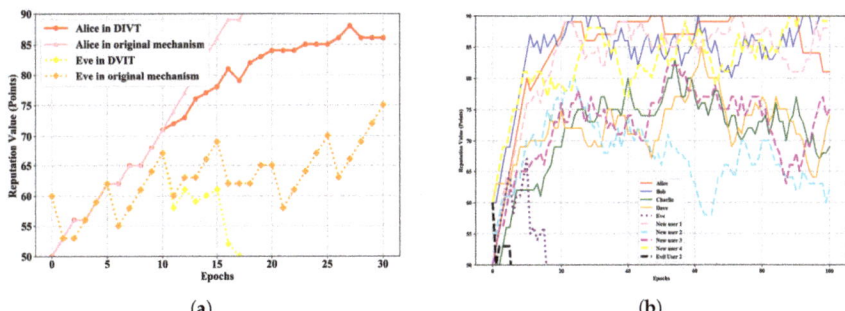

Figure 5. The comparisons of simulation. (**a**) The changes in reputation values for Alice and Eve under both the old and new mechanisms. (**b**) The changes in reputation values with 10 nodes in 100 epochs.

When users have the same fixed reputation value, more active participation can bring more rewards. Figure 4c shows the result of the simulation when users have the same reputation value in the beginning. With the highest voting intention, A_{rep} is the highest after 30 epochs compared to other users. Because of the similar willingness to vote, B_{rep} and C_{rep} are close in the last epochs. As a lazy voter, Dave's reputation value is the lowest after 30 epochs compared to the first three. D_{rep} is lower than 61 in *epoch* 30. Since the reputation value was deducted at the beginning due to rule violations, Eve could not meet the conditions to participate in the witness election for some time afterward.

Figure 4d shows the result of the simulation when users have the same reputation value in the beginning but without a dynamic reputation mechanism. D_{rep} is significantly lower than other users in terms of reputation value due to low voting frequency. After 30 epochs, Alice, Bob, and Charlie have all accumulated a significant reputation value. These cases are similar to Figure 4b. It shows the necessity of a dynamic reputation mechanism.

In Figure 5b, we extended the test period to 100 epochs and added 5 new nodes to show the performance of the DVIT reputation system under longer periods and more users. The fixed reputation value of New user 1 is 55, and the probability of New user 1 participating in voting is 80%; The fixed reputation value of New user 2 is 55, and the probability of New user 2 participating in voting is 30%; The fixed reputation value of New user 3 is 50, and the probability of New user 3 participating in voting is 50%; The fixed reputation value of New user 4 is 60, and the probability of New user 4 participating in voting is 50%; What is more, we add Evil User 2 whose fixed reputation value is 60 and is 30% likely to participate in voting. As the result shows, the new simulation result shows similar outcomes to the original one. Users with a high willingness to vote or have pledged ample tokens gain more reputation value, and we believe those users are more trustworthy. Malicious users are also all quickly removed by the system without administrator intervention. This suggests that our system can also serve to encourage nodes to behave well and select better-quality witnesses over a longer period.

5.2. Simulation of the New Handling Fee Mechanism

In the second part of the experiment, we tested the impact of different reward allocation mechanisms on users with high reputation value. As shown in Figure 6, in the original mechanism, the witness will be randomly assigned to record some transactions and receive a corresponding fee. However, with the new mechanism, the witness with the highest reputation value will obtain the highest value transactions. In the experiment, we simulated the handling fee revenue of two nodes within 30 epochs. Alice has an average reputation value, while Bob has the highest reputation value in the forum. In the simulation environment, it is assumed that the items traded in the forum consist of 90% low-priced items and 90% high-priced items.

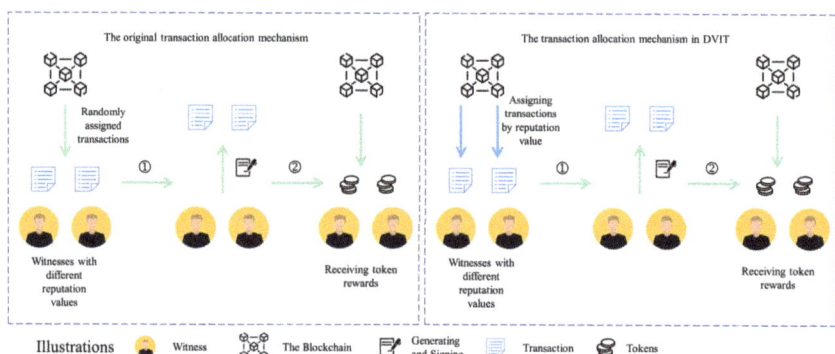

Figure 6. The simulation of the new handling fee mechanism.

The simulation under the traditional DPoS mechanism is shown in Figure 7a; all nodes will be assigned a lot of low-value transactions and a few high-value transactions. In the graph, we use bar charts to compare the handling fees received by Alice and Bob. We set every five epochs as an E_{Period}. We define Alice's handling income in $E_{period}\ k$ as A_{hk} and Bob's handling income in $E_{period}\ k$ as B_{hk}. The percentage of income in $E_{period}\ k\ \Theta_k$ is calculated as:

$$\Theta_k = \frac{A_{hk}}{A_{hk} + B_{hk}} \quad (6)$$

As shown in Figure 7a, Bob earns more in $E_{period}\ 1$, $E_{period}\ 3$ and $E_{period}\ 5$, while Alice earns more in $E_{period}\ 2$, $E_{period}\ 4$ and $E_{period}\ 6$. Θ_1, Θ_3 and Θ_5 are lower than 0.4 while Θ_2, Θ_4 and Θ_6 are higher than 0.6. It shows how random the traditional allocation mechanism is. A higher reputation value does not provide more benefit to the user at this point, which makes users have less incentive to maintain it.

With the new transaction mechanism, since the value of the assigned transaction is proportional to the reputation value of the node, the node with the highest reputation value can record transactions with the highest value all the time. In Figure 7b, Bob's handling fee income is significantly higher than Alice's in every E_{period}. Θ_1 to Θ_6 all stay lower than 0.2. In the simulation of 6 E_{period}, we increased the revenue of users with the highest reputation value, which shows nodes with high reputation value are rewarded. Nodes in the system will work harder to improve their reputation value to compete with other nodes. The problem of low willingness to participate in DPoS can be solved. The forum will also become more dynamic.

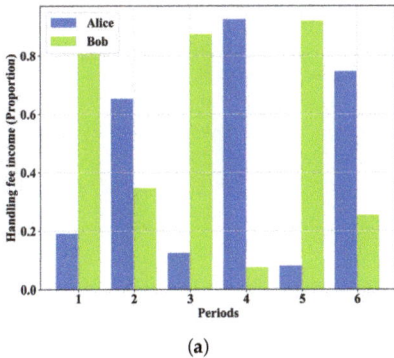 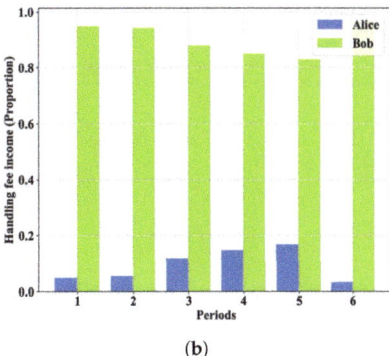

Figure 7. The simulation of handling fees. (**a**) The handling fee incomes in the traditional DPoS mechanism. (**b**) The handling fee incomes in DVIT.

6. Performance Analysis

We present the security, efficiency, and scalability analysis regarding the theoretical analysis in this section.

6.1. Security

The proposed system in this paper has good resistance against data tampering. Using the blockchain, the recorded transactions will not be tampered with. Impersonation attacks are where someone poses as another entity, which has various forms [33]. The identity of the block generator can be verified through the digital signature *sig* in the recorded message *M*. Because of the introduction of *timestamp*, Replay Attacks launched by attackers can also be resisted [34]. Transactions via tokens on the blockchain can reduce the risk of transfers.

6.2. Effectiveness

Our DPoS blockchain-based forum trading system for in-game items has several advantages over the currently available forum systems. It enables decentralized and more transparent trading without making huge changes to the original forum trading system. Compared to the original DPoS algorithm, the DPoS algorithm we use increases the willingness of users to participate in voting by adding a reputation system.

6.3. Scalability

Our system does not need to limit the number of participants. The number of witnesses and the size of the production blocks can be changed by the administrator in **TF**, which brings greater flexibility to our system. Our in-game item-trading NFT has no small prospect as well. With the consent of the administrator, players can use items from other games, or even virtual items from the metaverse, to mint an **iNFT**. Our system can be used to trade virtual items between metaverse in the future.

7. Related Work

In this section, we introduce some relative work about this article, including the state of blockchain technology and a vision of the future of the metaverse.

7.1. Blockchain Technology

7.1.1. Applications of Blockchain Technology

There are many applications of blockchains now. For example, blockchains can contribute to the circular economy (CE). It helps record the consumption of resources so that the general public can audit the environmental friendliness of the production process. People can better manage the destination of various recyclable resources on a waste recycling platform built on blockchain and smart contract technology [35]. Blockchain technology is considered a significant driver for smart initiation along with the Internet of Things (IoT) and fog computing technologies under the background of smart cities. A more trusted and decentralized database can be built using blockchain technology [36]. Metaverse, as the latest buzzword, has attracted great attention from both industry and academia. The flow of data will be beyond the previous scale in the metaverse. The security protection of this data is a very urgent need. The security and decentralized nature of the blockchain makes it a perfect fit for people. It has led to the belief that it is the key to the next round of industrial transformation [37].

7.1.2. Blockchain for Online Trading

In this section, we will introduce some uses of blockchain for online trading. Atomic swaps, which means the quick and automatic exchange of cryptocurrencies between parties or groups, can be performed on-chain or off-chain. It can realize peer-to-peer transfer, which safeguards the privacy of users' transactions and reduces transaction costs by bypassing the exchanges. It is an area with a lot of research potential [38]. Data have become an extremely important asset worth trading. However, traders may encounter problems of a single point of failure (SPOF), opaque transactions, uncontrollability, untraceability, and issues of data privacy. Blockchain and smart contracts can be used in automated transactions of data. Data matching, price negotiation, and reward assigning in data trading will be completed by smart contracts [39]. In addition to the research findings mentioned above, there have also been some attempts at using the blockchain to trade offline physical objects. Peer-to-Peer (P2P) energy trading, which means energy consumers/producers directly trade with each other. In the past, energy trading was rarely performed on a P2P basis because it was hard to have a system that could support such large and complex settlements. Nevertheless, with the help of blockchain, a highly automated, secure, and real-time settlement trading platform can be implemented [40].

Attempts to reduce centralization through blockchain are being made all the time. It has brought innovations in various business domains and spawned a new form of organization—the decentralized autonomous organization (DAO). Steemit is recognized as one of the earliest blockchain-based online communities and a typical example of a DAO. It has more than 1 million registered users. The forum model proposed in this paper can also be considered a DAO after further development [41]. DMarket is a cross-game trading platform based on blockchain and smart contracts. DMT is the only token that users need to use while trading via smart contracts. However, the platform is a bit centralized and only supports games that can offer a trading interface.

7.1.3. Security and Efficiency in Blockchain

Blockchain is widely used in security due to its public and tamper-evident nature. Nevertheless, it also faces multiple security threats. One of the most classic ones is 51% Vulnerability. The 51% attack may occur in PoW-based blockchains if a single miner's hashing power accounts for more than 50% of the total hashing power of the entire blockchain. Double Spending attacks, which means an attacker uses the same cryptocurrency multiple times for transactions, and Criminal Smart Contracts, also pose threats to the blockchain [42]. In the practical application of blockchains, there are still many issues to be solved as how to integrate the new blockchain-based application with the existing legacy system and the data loss and breach risk when a blockchain-based application [43].

Correspondingly, several studies have shown that the proper use of blockchain can maintain user privacy and security. For example, to remap the virtual address to the individual's identity while hiding the user's reality information, blockchain-based meta-native communications need to be introduced to meet the need [44]. Entities can find each other on the blockchain by generating encrypted addresses, which means users from the whole metaverse can acquire the connection information in a decentralized manner. A hierarchical blockchain architecture with the main chain and multiple subchains can be introduced to perform decentralized, secure, and privacy-preserving data training on both physical and virtual spaces. It can help users to build a user-defined privacy-preserving framework with decentralized, federated learning for industrial metaverses [45]. The efficiency of blockchain has also been a topic that has captured the attention of researchers. The issue of efficiency is also a challenge that we cannot avoid if we want to put a blockchain system into practical use. Bitcoin, for example, was split into two separate blockchains—original Bitcoin (BTC) and Bitcoin Cash (BCH) in 2017 due to the overcrowding caused by the overexpansion of users [46]. While the introduction of blockchain can bring a variety of benefits, such as availability, no single point of failure, confidentiality, and privacy, it also increases the chances of escalating overall network costs with high energy and resource consumption [47]. Blockchains with different consensus protocols have performance differences in terms of resource consumption. According to research, Hyperledger Fabric generally surpasses Ethereum against the four performance metrics, including success rate, average latency, throughput, and resource consumption, while executing 100 transactions [48].

7.1.4. Improvements on DPoS

There are many more possibilities for improvements to the DPoS system. Some scholars have improved the election mechanism of DPoS by adding weights to the votes based on reputation value [49]. Some scholars have improved the consensus algorithm by adding a dynamic trust mechanism [50]. Some scholars combine DPoS with other fields and develop a three-stage Stackelberg game to jointly minimize the users' cost and maximize the utilities of the master node and the validation nodes [51]. The improved DPoS has good practicality. For example, it can be against chargeback fraud in e-commerce [52]. These ideas may be helpful to us in future work.

7.2. Metaverse and The Future

Personal computers, the Internet, and mobile devices have been three major technological innovation waves that changed modern society, and the metaverse may be the fourth. The metaverse is a post-reality universe, a perpetual and persistent multiuser environment merging physical reality with digital virtuality [1]. In the past, such technology would have been unthinkable. No matter how high the degree of simulation of the virtual world is, it will always leave people with a sense of alienation due to the limitations of technical means. However, with technologies that enable multisensory interactions with virtual environments, such as virtual reality (VR) and augmented reality (AR), the expressive and infectious power of the meta-universe is unparalleled by the techniques of the past. Some scholars have used immersive virtual reality (iVR) and head-mounted display (HMD) systems to help rehabilitate injured patients [53]. The concept of digital twins, which is related to the metaverse, has also had a profound impact on areas outside the Internet, such as industry [54].

The metaverse has shown strong potential in several areas now. The metaverse can be combined with artificial intelligence to enhance the effectiveness of online education. Some scholars have envisioned a metaverse in which intelligent NPCs (non-player characters) are simulated by artificial intelligence techniques to help students learn. NPCs can become peers and friends that study with the students. When students have problems with lessons, they can turn to NPC students or teachers for help [55]. The metaverse is also promising in the medical field. Due to the impact of COVID-19, the existing offline healthcare system has been affected, and the need for online healthcare has become urgent. The metaverse has brought a lot of innovation to the current healthcare system. Combined with blockchain and Non-Fungible Tokens (NFTs), the metaverse can be applied to telehealth, supply chain, payments, secure data sharing, and remote monitoring. Metaverse has a wide range of applications in clinical care. It allows online immersion in a live simulation of the operating room environment, assisting surgeons complete procedures remotely. Combined with artificial intelligence, it can provide more personalized health assistance to patients. In medical education and training, metaverse technology can give medical students a better practice environment [56]. COVID-19 has also taken a considerable toll on the hospitality and tourism industry, and metaverse technology also can be used to save tourism. Improvements in technology and sophistication in the quality of virtual reality (VR) headsets have made travel in the metaverse as good as offline travel. For example, Japan-based First Airlines has begun offering virtual flights from Tokyo [57].

Among all these applications, the combination of the metaverse and video games is the most striking. Metaverse is learning from the experience of the gaming industry. At present, many metaverses are developed with game engines such as Unreal and Unity [58]. The combination of the metaverse and video games is showing unprecedented appeal. ROBLOX, a sandbox game platform, was the first metaverse concept game stock to be listed on the New York Stock Exchange. Its USD 40 billion valuation proved that the value of the metaverse is recognized [59]. The virtual rewards in the metaverse can even exert an influence on people's real lives. Some researchers suggest that tokenized incentivization in the metaverse can be used to architect people's choices and lead people to live healthy lifestyles. The prospect of the game market is immense in the metaverse [60].

Players' willingness to pay for in-game items has been cultivated over the years. In MMORPGs (Massively Multiplayer Online Role-playing Games), such as World of Warcraft (WoW), a mature inter-player economic system has been established [61]. There are even studios that earn their living by producing in-game items. Players can pay real money to those studios for in-game items they want. A similar situation will occur in the metaverse. Since the interaction between players and the game is more realistic in the metaverse, players are more willing to acknowledge the value of various in-game items. Now in-game items in some metaverse games are much more useful than before. For example, in ZEPETO, a metaverse game launched in 2018 by Snow and owned by the company Naver, users can use in-game currencies, such as coins and gems, to decorate their avatars and maps for space [62]. Concepts such as metaverse and Gamefi, which is a combination of the words Game and Finance, meaning a blockchain game that provides financial incentives for players to earn while they play, are now very prevalent. Many people have already managed to make a profit from them. CryptoKitties is the first game in which game assets and collectible items exist as Non-Fungible Tokens (NFTs) on the blockchain and can be traded for cryptocurrency. It is a relatively successful experiment in the gamification of blockchain [63]. Due to the nature of the metaverse, the scale of buying and selling virtual items in the metaverse is already large and subversive enough. For example, virtual land in the metaverse can be bought and sold just like in reality. There are 90,601 lands in the Decentraland metaverse and 166,464 virtual lands in the Sandbox metaverse [64]. The in-game items trading system designed in this paper can be used in a metaverse context. The growing demand for buying and selling virtual goods in the metaverse must be a bright future for our system.

As Table 3 shows, we introduce a chart containing a comparative study of some representative papers we cited and our work. It can be seen that our work combines the two domains of metaverse and DPoS while incorporating the virtual economy. In our future work, we will continue to draw inspiration from related fields to achieve further results in the exploration of metaverse trading.

Table 3. A comparative study of related papers.

Citation Number	DPoS	Reputation System	Metaverse	Virtual Economy	Incentive Mechanism
[13]	●	●	✗	✗	●
[16]	●	✗	✗	✗	✗
[21]	●	✗	✗	✗	●
[33]	✗	●	✗	✗	●
[44]	✗	✗	●	✗	✗
[45]	✗	✗	●	✗	●
[50]	●	●	✗	✗	✗
[51]	●	●	✗	✗	●
DVIT	●	●	●	●	●

8. Conclusions and Future Work

In this work, we studied the problem of virtual item exchange in the metaverse. We proposed a blockchain-based in-game items trading forum system, combined a DPoS blockchain with an in-game items trading system, and increased the decentralization and security of the system. We added many new features to the system, such as in-game item trading Non-Fungible Token (NFT) and in-game item renting. We designed a user incentive system based on reputation value to guide users to trade correctly in the system. We believe that our solution can substantially improve the existing in-game items trading forum system and can be used in the metaverse for virtual item exchange. In future work, the fairness and rationality of reputation calculation will be reserved for further consideration, and more variables, such as coinday and the number of historical transactions, will be taken into account. Moreover, the economic game theory will also be modularized to facilitate the completeness of the DVIT. To achieve more decentralization, after completing experiments with forum-based virtual item trading, we will try to propose a framework where users can trade directly between consortium-blockchain-based metaverses. We will try to extend our work from in-game item trading to simulations in an environment that is closer to the metaverse.

Author Contributions: Conceptualization, Z.Y. and W.L.; methodology, W.L.; formal analysis, C.D.; investigation, L.L.; data curation, W.L.; writing—original draft preparation, W.L.; writing—review and editing, Z.Y. and W.L.; project administration, X.L. All authors have read and agreed to the published version of the manuscript.

Funding: This research is partially supported by FDCT under its General R&D Subsidy Program Fund (Grant No. 0038/2022/A), Macau, and partially supported by MOST-FDCT Projects (0058/2019/AMJ,2019YFE0110300) (Research and Application of Cooperative Multi-Agent Platform for Zhuhai-Macao Manufacturing Service).

Data Availability Statement: The simulations of this paper can be accessed at https://github.com/LanWusong/DVIT-simulations (accessed on 8 January 2023).

Conflicts of Interest: The authors declare no conflict of interest.

Nomenclature

MK	master key
PK	public key
SP	security parameter
AM	attributes of the **ADM**
k_i	secret key of user i
k_{pi}	public key of user i
i	identification of the User
i_{rep}	actual reputation value of user i
i_{rep0}	fixed reputation value of user i
i_{repa}	reputation value user i got in the last 0–10 epochs
i_{repb}	reputation value user i got in the last 10–20 epochs
w	expired weight
l_{i0}	initial voting result of user i in dispute adjudication
l_i	final result of user i's vote in dispute adjudication
λ	user's vote weight in dispute adjudication
L	the final decision in dispute adjudication
E_{period}	each 5 epochs is a *Period*
Θ_k	the percentage of income in *Period k*
M_{sell}	record of item selling on the blockchain
M_{srent}	record of item renting on the blockchain
sig_k	signature of user k
$Candidate[\ ]$	list of candidates in election process
$Witness[\ ]$	list of witnesses
X	number of witnesses
n	users' node id on the blockchain
in	the information about the in-game items
U_{se}	seller
U_{bu}	buyer
U_{le}	lessee
U_{lo}	lessor
Dep	deposit
Ren	rent
$timestamp$	timestamp of the blocks
U_{is}	issuer of iNFT
I_{pri}	in-game item price
I_{it}	in-game item

References

1. Mystakidis, S. Metaverse. *Encyclopedia* **2022**, *2*, 486–497. [CrossRef]
2. Matthews, J. Ready Player One (Movie Review). 2018. Available online: https://digitalcollections.dordt.edu/faculty_work/886/ (accessed on 1 October 2022).
3. Salvador, R. Facebook Changes Company Name to Meta. Available online: https://www.cnbc.com/2021/10/28/facebook-changes-company-name-to-meta.html/ (accessed on 10 August 2022).
4. Clement, J. When Do You Think the Metaverse Will Start Booming? Available online: https://www.statista.com/statistics/1302240/metaverse-business-boom/ (accessed on 10 August 2022).
5. Ronit, G.; Nisha, S.; Sophia, B.; Kaiwan, M.; Ronak., S.S.; Puneet, S. Metaverse and Money. Available online: https://www.citivelocity.com/citigps/metaverse-and-money/ (accessed on 1 October 2022).
6. Jansen, S. How Cross-Chain Games Are Giving Users the First Look at a Metaverse. Available online: https://cointelegraph.com/news/how-cross-chain-games-are-giving-users-the-first-look-at-a-metaverse (accessed on 25 December 2022).
7. Radahn, C. All About the Open Metaverse Alliance (OMA3). Available online: https://www.altcoinbuzz.io/metaverse/all-about-the-open-metaverse-alliance-oma3/ (accessed on 25 December 2022).
8. Ravenscraft, E. What, Exactly, Is the Metaverse Standards Forum Creating? Available online: https://www.wired.com/story/metaverse-standards-forum-explained/ (accessed on 25 December 2022).
9. Balicer, R.D. Modeling infectious diseases dissemination through online role-playing games. *Epidemiology* **2007**, *18*, 260–261. [CrossRef]

10. Salter, A.W.; Stein, S. Endogenous currency formation in an online environment: The case of Diablo II. *Rev. Austrian Econ.* **2016**, *29*, 53–66. [CrossRef]
11. De Filippi, P.; Mannan, M.; Reijers, W. Blockchain as a confidence machine: The problem of trust & challenges of governance. *Technol. Soc.* **2020**, *62*, 101284.
12. Monrat, A.A.; Schelén, O.; Andersson, K. A Survey of Blockchain From the Perspectives of Applications, Challenges, and Opportunities. *IEEE Access* **2019**, *7*, 117134–117151. [CrossRef]
13. Wei, Y.; Liang, L.; Zhou, B.; Feng, X. A Modified Blockchain DPoS Consensus Algorithm Based on Anomaly Detection and Reward-Punishment. In Proceedings of the 2021 13th International Conference on Communication Software and Networks (ICCSN), Chongqing, China, 4–7 June 2021; pp. 283–288.
14. Saad, S.M.S.; Radzi, R.Z.R.M.; Othman, S.H. Analysis of the Blockchain Consensus Algorithm Between Proof of Stake and DelegatComparativeed Proof of Stake. In Proceedings of the 2021 International Conference on Data Science and Its Applications (ICoDSA), Virtual, 6–7 October 2021; pp. 175–180.
15. Staff, C. What Are Proof of Stake and Delegated Proof of Stake? Available online: https://www.gemini.com/cryptopedia/proof-of-stake-delegated-pos-dpos (accessed on 13 August 2022).
16. Chen, S.; Xie, M.; Liu, J.; Zhang, Y. Improvement of the DPoS Consensus Mechanism in Blockchain Based on PLTS. In Proceedings of the 7th IEEE International Conference on Big Data Security on Cloud, IEEE International Conference on High Performance and Smart Computing, and IEEE International Conference on Intelligent Data and Security, BigDataSecurity/HPSC/IDS 2021, New York, NY, USA, 15–17 May 2021; pp. 32–37.
17. Nguyen, B.M.; Nguyen, T.; Nguyen, T.; Do, B. MPoC—A Metaheuristic Proof of Criteria Consensus Protocol for Blockchain Network. In Proceedings of the IEEE International Conference on Blockchain and Cryptocurrency, ICBC 2021, Sydney, Australia, 3–6 May 2021; pp. 1–8.
18. Dhillon, V.; Metcalf, D.; Hooper, M. Recent developments in blockchain. In *Blockchain Enabled Applications*; Apress: Berkeley, CA, USA, 2017; pp. 151–181.
19. Shin, D.D. Blockchain: The emerging technology of digital trust. *Telemat. Inform.* **2019**, *45*, 101278. [CrossRef]
20. Sun, Y.; Xue, R.; Zhang, R.; Su, Q.; Gao, S. RTChain: A Reputation System with Transaction and Consensus Incentives for E-commerce Blockchain. *ACM Trans. Internet Technol.* **2021**, *21*, 15:1–15:24. [CrossRef]
21. Wang, L.; Xu, P.; Su, W.; Li, Y.; Chen, X. Research on Improvement of Blockchain DPOS Consensus Mechanism Based on HK Clustering. In Proceedings of the 2021 China Automation Congress (CAC), Beijing, China, 22–24 October 2021; pp. 1167–1172.
22. Hu, Q.; Yan, B.; Han, Y.; Yu, J. An improved delegated proof of stake consensus algorithm. *Procedia Comput. Sci.* **2021**, *187*, 341–346. [CrossRef]
23. Johari, R.; Kumar, V.; Gupta, K.; Vidyarthi, D.P. BLOSOM: BLOckchain technology for Security of Medical records. *ICT Express* **2022**, *8*, 56–60. [CrossRef]
24. Merrad, Y.; Habaebi, M.H.; Elsheikh, E.A.A.; Suliman, F.E.M.; Islam, M.R.; Gunawan, T.S.; Mesri, M. Blockchain: Consensus Algorithm Key Performance Indicators, Trade-Offs, Current Trends, Common Drawbacks, and Novel Solution Proposals. *Mathematics* **2022**, *10*, 2754. [CrossRef]
25. Zhu, H.; Guo, Y.; Zhang, L. An improved convolution Merkle tree-based blockchain electronic medical record secure storage scheme. *J. Inf. Secur. Appl.* **2021**, *61*, 102952. [CrossRef]
26. Cho, S.; Park, S.Y.; Lee, S.R. Blockchain consensus rule based dynamic blind voting for non-dependency transaction. *Int. J. Grid Distrib. Comput.* **2017**, *10*, 93–106. [CrossRef]
27. Mitra, D.; Tauz, L.; Dolecek, L. Concentrated stopping set design for coded Merkle tree: Improving security against data availability attacks in blockchain systems. In Proceedings of the 2020 IEEE Information Theory Workshop (ITW), Riva del Garda, Italy, 11–15 April 2021; pp. 1–5.
28. Hellenbrand, A. Asynchronous and Decentral Group Management in Messengers with Delegated Proof of Stake. In *SKILL 2020-Studierendenkonferenz Informatik*; Gesellschaft für Informatik e.V.: Bonn, Germany, 2020.
29. Wang, T.; Guo, J.; Ai, S.; Cao, J. RBT: A distributed reputation system for blockchain-based peer-to-peer energy trading with fairness consideration. *Appl. Energy* **2021**, *295*, 117056. [CrossRef]
30. Chen, Y.; Liu, F. Research on improvement of DPoS consensus mechanism in collaborative governance of network public opinion. *Peer-to-Peer Netw. Appl.* **2022**, *15*, 1849–1861. [CrossRef] [PubMed]
31. Wang, Z.; Xiong, R.; Jin, J.; Liang, C. AirBC: A Lightweight Reputation-based Blockchain Scheme for Resource-constrained UANET. In Proceedings of the 25th IEEE International Conference on Computer Supported Cooperative Work in Design, CSCWD 2022, Hangzhou, China, 4–6 May 2022; pp. 1378–1383.
32. Putra, G.D.; Kang, C.; Kanhere, S.S.; Hong, J.W. DeTRM: Decentralised Trust and Reputation Management for Blockchain-based Supply Chains. In Proceedings of the IEEE International Conference on Blockchain and Cryptocurrency, ICBC 2022, Shanghai, China, 2–5 May 2022; pp. 1–5.
33. Battah, A.; Iraqi, Y.; Damiani, E. A Trust and Reputation System for IoT Service Interactions. *IEEE Trans. Netw. Serv. Manag.* **2022**, *19*, 2987–3005. [CrossRef]
34. Wang, P.; Pan, B.; Tao, Q.; Yang, C.; Luo, S. Distributed Storage and Traceability System for Aviation Equipment Biographies Based on Consortium Blockchain. In Proceedings of the 2022 4th International Conference on Advances in Computer Technology, Information Science and Communications (CTISC), Suzhou, China, 22–24 April 2022; pp. 1–5.

35. Böhmecke-Schwafert, M.; Wehinger, M.; Teigland, R. Blockchain for the circular economy: Theorizing blockchain's role in the transition to a circular economy through an empirical investigation. *Bus. Strategy Environ.* **2022**, *31*, 3786–3801. [CrossRef]
36. Kamruzzaman, M.; Yan, B.; Sarker, M.N.I.; Alruwaili, O.; Wu, M.; Alrashdi, I. Blockchain and Fog Computing in IoT-Driven Healthcare Services for Smart Cities. *J. Healthc. Eng.* **2022**, *2022*, 9957888. [CrossRef] [PubMed]
37. Yang, Q.; Zhao, Y.; Huang, H.; Xiong, Z.; Kang, J.; Zheng, Z. Fusing Blockchain and AI with Metaverse: A Survey. *IEEE Open J. Comput. Soc.* **2022**, *3*, 122–136. [CrossRef]
38. Mohanty, D.; Anand, D.; Aljahdali, H.M.; Villar, S.G. Blockchain Interoperability: Towards a Sustainable Payment System. *Sustainability* **2022**, *14*, 913. [CrossRef]
39. Hu, D.; Li, Y.; Pan, L.; Li, M.; Zheng, S. A blockchain-based trading system for big data. *Comput. Netw.* **2021**, *191*, 107994. [CrossRef]
40. Esmat, A.; de Vos, M.; Ghiassi-Farrokhfal, Y.; Palensky, P.; Epema, D. A novel decentralized platform for peer-to-peer energy trading market with blockchain technology. *Appl. Energy* **2021**, *282*, 116123. [CrossRef]
41. Liu, Z.; Li, Y.; Min, Q.; Chang, M. User incentive mechanism in blockchain-based online community: An empirical study of steemit. *Inf. Manag.* **2022**, *59*, 103596. [CrossRef]
42. Li, X.; Jiang, P.; Chen, T.; Luo, X.; Wen, Q. A survey on the security of blockchain systems. *Future Gener. Comput. Syst.* **2020**, *107*, 841–853. [CrossRef]
43. Islam, M.R.; Rahman, M.M.; Mahmud, M.; Rahman, M.A.; Mohamad, M.H.S. A Review on Blockchain Security Issues and Challenges. In Proceedings of the 2021 IEEE 12th Control and System Graduate Research Colloquium (ICSGRC), Shah Alam, Malaysia, 7 August 2021; pp. 227–232.
44. Xu, H.; Li, Z.; Li, Z.; Zhang, X.; Sun, Y.; Zhang, L. Metaverse Native Communication: A Blockchain and Spectrum Prospective. In Proceedings of the 2022 IEEE International Conference on Communications Workshops, ICC Workshops 2022, Seoul, Republic of Korea, 16–20 May 2022; pp. 7–12.
45. Kang, J.; Ye, D.; Nie, J.; Xiao, J.; Deng, X.; Wang, S.; Xiong, Z.; Yu, R.; Niyato, D. Blockchain-based Federated Learning for Industrial Metaverses: Incentive Scheme with Optimal AoI. In Proceedings of the IEEE International Conference on Blockchain, Blockchain 2022, Espoo, Finland, 22–25 August 2022; pp. 71–78.
46. Jiang, S.; Li, Y.; Wang, S.; Zhao, L. Blockchain competition: The tradeoff between platform stability and efficiency. *Eur. J. Oper. Res.* **2022**, *296*, 1084–1097. [CrossRef]
47. Shahzad, I.; Maqbool, A.; Rana, T.; Mirza, A.; Khan, W.Z.; Kim, S.W.; Zikria, Y.B.; Din, S. Blockchain-based green big data visualization: BGbV. *Complex Intell. Syst.* **2022**, *8*, 3707–3718. [CrossRef]
48. Dabbagh, M.; Kakavand, M.; Tahir, M.; Amphawan, A. Performance Analysis of Blockchain Platforms: Empirical Evaluation of Hyperledger Fabric and Ethereum. In Proceedings of the 2020 IEEE 2nd International Conference on Artificial Intelligence in Engineering and Technology (IICAIET), Kota Kinabalu, Malaysia, 26–27 September 2020; pp. 1–6. [CrossRef]
49. You, L.; Wang, Z.; Hu, G.; Cao, C. An Improved Model on the Vague Sets-Based DPoS's Voting Phase in Blockchain. *IACR Cryptol. ePrint Arch.* **2022**, 391.
50. Sun, Y.; Yan, B.; Yao, Y.; Yu, J. DT-DPoS: A delegated proof of stake consensus algorithm with dynamic trust. *Procedia Comput. Sci.* **2021**, *187*, 371–376. [CrossRef]
51. Wang, D.; Jia, Y.; Liang, L.; Dong, M.; Ota, K. A Game for Task Offloading in Reputation-Based Consortium Blockchain Networks. *IEEE Wirel. Commun. Lett.* **2022**, *11*, 1508–1512. [CrossRef]
52. Liu, D.; Lee, J.H. CFLedger: Preventing chargeback fraud with blockchain. *ICT Express* **2021**, *8*, 352–356. [CrossRef]
53. Elor, A.; Powell, M.; Mahmoodi, E.; Teodorescu, M.; Kurniawan, S. Gaming Beyond the Novelty Effect of Immersive Virtual Reality for Physical Rehabilitation. *IEEE Trans. Games* **2022**, *14*, 107–115. [CrossRef]
54. Jiang, Y.; Yin, S.; Li, K.; Luo, H.; Kaynak, O. Industrial applications of digital twins. *Philos. Trans. R. Soc. A* **2021**, *379*, 20200360. [CrossRef] [PubMed]
55. Hwang, G.J.; Chien, S.Y. Definition, roles, and potential research issues of the metaverse in education: An artificial intelligence perspective. *Comput. Educ. Artif. Intell.* **2022**, *3*, 100082. [CrossRef]
56. Thomason, J. MetaHealth-How will the Metaverse Change Health Care? *J. Metaverse* **2021**, *1*, 13–16.
57. Gursoy, D.; Malodia, S.; Dhir, A. The metaverse in the hospitality and tourism industry: An overview of current trends and future research directions. *J. Hosp. Mark. Manag.* **2022**, *31*, 527–534. [CrossRef]
58. Chia, A. The metaverse, but not the way you think: Game engines and automation beyond game development. *Crit. Stud. Media Commun.* **2022**, *39*, 191–200. [CrossRef]
59. Huang, J.; Sun, P.; Zhang, W. Analysis of the Future Prospects for the Metaverse. In Proceedings of the 2022 7th International Conference on Financial Innovation and Economic Development (ICFIED 2022), Zhuhai, China, 21–23 January 2022; pp. 1899–1904.
60. Thomason, J. Metaverse, Token Economies, and Chronic Diseases. *Glob. Health J.* **2022**, *1*, 13–16.
61. Linnainmaa, H. Virtual economy design in MMORPGs. Bachelor's Thesis, Aalto University, Espoo, Finland, 2021.
62. Han, J.; Heo, J.; You, E. Analysis of metaverse platform as a new play culture: Focusing on roblox and zepeto. In Proceedings of the 2nd International Conference on Human-Centered Artificial Intelligence (Computing4Human 2021), CEUR Workshop Proceedings, Da Nang, Vietnam, 28–29 October 2021.

3. Serada, A. Vintage CryptoKitties and the Quest for Authenticity. In Proceedings of the 2021 IEEE Conference on Games (CoG), Copenhagen, Denmark, 17–20 August 2021; pp. 1–10.
4. Sonmezer, S.; Çelik, G.G. How returns of metaverse tokens are interrelated? *Int. J. Soc. Sci.* **2022**, *8*, 213–223. [CrossRef]

Disclaimer/Publisher's Note: The statements, opinions and data contained in all publications are solely those of the individual author(s) and contributor(s) and not of MDPI and/or the editor(s). MDPI and/or the editor(s) disclaim responsibility for any injury to people or property resulting from any ideas, methods, instructions or products referred to in the content.

Article

DDSG-GAN: Generative Adversarial Network with Dual Discriminators and Single Generator for Black-Box Attacks

Fangwei Wang, Zerou Ma, Xiaohan Zhang, Qingru Li * and Changguang Wang *

Key Laboratory of Network and Information Security of Hebei Province, College of Computer & Cyber Security, Hebei Normal University, Shijiazhuang 050024, China
* Correspondence: qingruli@hebtu.edu.cn (Q.L.); wangcg@hebtu.edu.cn (C.W.)

Abstract: As one of the top ten security threats faced by artificial intelligence, the adversarial attack has caused scholars to think deeply from theory to practice. However, in the black-box attack scenario, how to raise the visual quality of an adversarial example (AE) and perform a more efficient query should be further explored. This study aims to use the architecture of GAN combined with the model-stealing attack to train surrogate models and generate high-quality AE. This study proposes an image AE generation method based on the generative adversarial networks with dual discriminators and a single generator (DDSG-GAN) and designs the corresponding loss function for each model. The generator can generate adversarial perturbation, and two discriminators constrain the perturbation, respectively, to ensure the visual quality and attack effect of the generated AE. We extensively experiment on MNIST, CIFAR10, and Tiny-ImageNet datasets. The experimental results illustrate that our method can effectively use query feedback to generate an AE, which significantly reduces the number of queries on the target model and can implement effective attacks.

Keywords: artificial intelligence; security threat; adversarial attacks; adversarial examples; generative adversarial networks

MSC: 68T07

1. Introduction

With the emergence of deep neural networks, the security issues of artificial intelligence (AI) have become increasingly prominent. Because of the wide application of deep learning technology, the security of deep neural networks has also been increasingly questioned. The existence of an AE makes deep neural networks (DNN) cause disastrous consequences in many fields, such as the occurrence of traffic accidents in the field of automatic driving [1], malicious code successfully escaping detection [2], etc. AE is a major obstacle that various machine learning systems and even artificial intelligence (AI) must overcome. Its existence not only makes the output results of the model deviate greatly but can even make this deviation inevitable. This indicates that machine learning models rely on unreliable features to maximize performance. If the features are disturbed, it will lead to the misclassification of the model. For example, FGSM [3] enables a machine-learning model that classifies the original image as a panda with a probability of 57.7% but classifies its AE as a gibbon with a very high probability of 99.3%.

The vulnerability of DNN to AE has led to adversarial learning. On the one hand, studying an AE is to understand the mechanism of adversarial attacks to better develop corresponding defense technologies and construct more robust deep learning models. In addition, the existence of an AE reveals the serious security threat of DNN. Research on AE can provide a more comprehensive index for evaluating the robustness of DNN.

In adversarial attacks, because different models own different information access rights, the attackers need to consider different attack scenarios to design AE. Adversarial attacks contain two categories: white-box and black-box attacks.

In white-box attacks, adversaries can acquire the structure and parameter information of the target model. Therefore, they can use the target model's gradient information to construct the AE. However, black-box attacks are more challenging to implement. In a black-box attack, the attackers can only interact with the target model through the input, which increases the difficulty of constructing AE. Still, it is more consistent with real-world attack scenarios.

Black-box attacks contain query-based and transfer-based attacks. Although the former can achieve a good attack effect, the query complexity is high, the query results are not fully utilized in the current attack methods, and masses of queries are easily resisted by defense mechanisms. The latter attack avoids the query to the target model. However, its attack effect is not ideal.

Combining transfer-based and query-based attacks, we design a generative adversary network (GAN) with dual discriminators and a single generator (DDSG-GAN) to generate an AE with better attack performance. We use the generator G of the DDSG-GAN to generate the adversarial perturbation, and the trained discriminator D_1 can act as a surrogate model of the target model T. The discriminator D_2 is used to distinguish whether the input image is original. We experimentally evaluate our method on the MNIST [4], CIFAR10 [5], and Tiny-ImageNet [6] datasets and compare it with the state-of-the-art (SOTA) experimental results. The experiment results demonstrate that the proposed method has a high attack success rate and greatly reduces the number of queries to the target model. The generated AE with our proposed method has a higher visual quality. The main contributions are the following:

(1) This study presents a novel image AE generation method based on the GANs of dual discriminators. The generator G generates adversarial perturbation, and two discriminators constrain the generator in different aspects. The constraint of discriminator D_1 guarantees the success of the attack, and the constraint of discriminator D_2 ensures the visual quality of the generated AE.

(2) This study designs a new method to train the surrogate model; we use original images and AEs to train our substitute model together. The training process contains two stages: pre-training and fine-tuning. To make the most of the query results of the AE, we put the query results of the AEs into the circular queue for the subsequent training, which greatly reduces the query requirement of the target model and makes efficient use of the query results.

(3) This study introduces a clipping mechanism so that the generated AEs are within the ϵ neighborhood of the original image.

The remainder of our paper is organized as follows. Section 2 introduces the related work of adversarial attacks. The proposed method of generating AE is described in Section 3. Section 4 demonstrates the effectiveness of the attack method through extensive experiments. Section 5 summarizes this paper.

2. Related Work

AEs can exist in many areas of artificial intelligence (AI), such as images, voice, text, and malware, and bring many potential risks to people's lives. This study mainly focuses on adversarial attacks in image classification tasks. Adversarial attacks mainly contain white-box and black-box attacks. This section will summarize and review the relevant studies of adversarial attacks.

2.1. White-Box attack

In a white-box attack, the adversaries can acquire the structure and parameter information of the attacked target model, while in a black-box attack, the adversaries can only gain the prediction results of the target model about the input. The white-box attack has been developed earlier and is simpler to implement. At present, it can achieve a good attack effect.

White-box attacks mainly include three categories, which are summarized as follows:

(1) Optimize the objective function directly: Szegedy et al. [7] proposed directly optimizing the objective function with the box-constrained L-BFGS algorithm to generate adversarial perturbation. C&W [8] put forward three optimization-based attack methods after the defense distillation, successfully broke the defense distillation, and made the white-box attack reach a new height. Although the optimization-based methods can achieve a good attack effect, the optimization process takes a long time.

(2) Gradient-based attack method: FGSM [3] maintains that the existence of AEs is mainly due to the linear nature of the neural network and can add perturbations in the direction of the maximum gradient change of DNN to increase the classification loss of images. Due to FGSM being a one-step attack algorithm, the attack effect has yet to be improved. The success of FGSM has based on the hypothesis that the loss function is locally linear. If it is nonlinear, the attack's success cannot be guaranteed. Based on this, Kurakin Alexey et al. [9] put forward I-FGSM, which obtains AEs through continuous iteration of the FGSM algorithm. Compared to FGSM, the I-FGSM can construct a more accurate perturbation, but from the performance of AEs in transfer attacks, I-FGSM is less effective than FGSM. Similar to the I-FGSM attack, the PGD [10] attack has more iterations and a better attack effect, whose disadvantage is its poor transfer attack ability.

(3) The attack method based on the generated neural network can train the neural network to generate AEs. Once the network training is completed, it can generate AEs in batches. For example, ATN [11] can convert an input image into AEs against the target model. It also has a strong attack capability, but the effect of a transfer attack is poor. AdvGAN [12] introduced the GANs into the method of generating AEs based on the generative neural network for the first time, and the trained AdvGAN network can convert random noise into AEs.

Other white-box attack algorithms, such as DeepFool [13], are based on the consideration of how to add the minimum perturbation to the original image. It is by reducing the distance between the image and the decision boundary of the target model to iteratively generate the minimum perturbation that can make the target model misclassified, which is relatively simple to implement and can achieve a good attack effect. One-pixel attack [14] is based on differential evolution. Each attack attempt to modify one pixel of data of an example achieves the result of model misclassification. This method has a good attack performance on less pixel information datasets, but for the datasets with a larger pixel space, the performance of the algorithm declined. The current white-box attack methods have been relatively mature and have achieved a good attack effect in MNIST, CIFAR10, ImageNet [6], and other datasets.

2.2. Black-Box attack

Compared with a white-box attack, a black-box attack is more difficult to implement. In the black-box attack setting, the adversary can only interact with the target model through input, which increases the difficulty of constructing the AEs. Black-box attacks are divided into query-based attacks and transfer-based attacks. Querying different target models will get different types of feedback results. According to the query results of the target model, query-based attacks can be divided into score-based attacks and decision-based attacks.

In the query-based attacks, by interacting with the target model, the Zero Order Optimization (ZOO) attack [15] uses the confidence score of the model's feedback to estimate the target model's gradient. Then, it uses the estimated gradient information to generate AEs. AutoZOOM [16] is the improved version of the ZOO attack, which introduces an autoencoder structure and greatly reduces the cost of useless pixel search. At the same time, AutoZOOM adopts a dynamic attack mechanism to further reduce the number of queries. After that, Bandits attack [17] uses the gradient prior information to improve the black-box attacks and introduces data-dependent and time-dependent priors to improve the query efficiency. However, the above methods are used for high-precision gradient estimation, so these inevitably require a lot of time and computing storage. Guo et al. put forward SimBA [18], which does not need to estimate the gradient of the target model and generates query samples by continuously greedily adding randomly sampled perturbation to the original image. According to the query results, it is decided to add or remove the perturbation on the target image. LeBA [19] combined transfer-based and query-based attacks to optimize SimBA further and achieve more efficient attacks.

With the outstanding performance of meta-learning in various classification tasks, Meta attacks [20] first combine adversarial attacks, and meta-learning First uses meta-learning to train a general Meta attack model. Then, it uses real attack information to fine-tune the Meta attack model, which greatly improves the query efficiency. The Simulator attack [21] further improves the attack model based on the Meta attack, which realizes the accurate simulation of any unknown target model. It improves the overall query efficiency of the model. However, because the model is relatively complex, there are comparatively high requirements for computer hardware configuration, and the training time is pretty long. Query-based black-box attacks can achieve a higher success rate. Still, this type of attack requires many query requirements and computing storage, and a large number of queries are easily resisted by the defense mechanism. Therefore, how to improve the efficiency of the query is the key to the current research.

Biggio et al. [22] found that the AEs generated against a certain machine learning model can be used to attack other models, which led researchers to think about transfer attacks. The goal of the transfer-based attack is that the AEs generated for one model can still attack other models. The core idea of the transfer-based black-box attack method [23,24] is to generate AEs on the source model and then transfer them to the target model. This method does not need to know the network structure and the parameters of the target model, nor does it need to query the target model. However, because there is a large distance between the source model and the target model, the attack effect is not satisfactory. The precondition for the realization of transfer-based attacks is the transfer ability of AE. Therefore, training a surrogate model that can highly simulate the target model will improve the AEs' transferability. Therefore, the model-stealing attacks [25–27] are gradually applied to adversarial attacks. The model-stealing attacks obtain the labels of input data by querying the target model and then using the input and query results to train the black-box model's surrogate model. The surrogate model trained by model stealing attacks can more accurately fit the target model and greatly improve the success rate of transfer attacks.

In recent research, many scholars have applied GANs [28] to the adversarial attack. Zhao et al. [29] built the semantic space of images on the architecture of GANs to obtain more natural AE. Xiao et al. [12] first introduced the idea of GANs in the attack algorithm based on neural networks to generate AE. They proposed a network architecture including a generator, discriminator, and target model. The trained generator can efficiently generate AEs for any input image, but it can only generate AEs for a single target class. Later, Zhou et al. [30] proposed a data-free surrogate model training based on GAN's architecture to attack the target model. This method does not need a training data set but needs to combine a white-box attack algorithm, such as FGSM or PGD, to generate AE, and the training time is very long. Because it needs a lot of queries, this attack is easy to be avoided by the defense mechanism. In this paper, we focus on the black-box attack, based on the architecture of GANs, and combine it with the model-stealing attack to generate adversarial samples with a higher attack success rate and better visual quality.

3. Methodology

3.1. Preliminaries

3.1.1. Adversarial Examples and Adversarial Attack

Modifying the original images in a human-imperceptible way so that the modified images can be misclassified by the machine learning model, and the modified images are called AE. For a victim image classification model T, we use (x, y) as the original image-label pair. The goal of the adversarial attack is to generate an AE $\hat{x}$ so that target model T can misclassify it. For the untargeted attack setting, it can be formulated as follows:

$$argmax\ T(x) = y,\ and\ argmax\ T(\hat{x}) \neq y, s.t. \|\hat{x} - x\| \leq \epsilon. \quad (1)$$

For the targeted attack setting, it can be formulated as follows:

$$argmax\ T(x) = y,\ and\ argmax\ T(\hat{x}) \neq y, s.t. \|\hat{x} - x\|_p \leq \epsilon. \quad (2)$$

where $\|\cdot\|_p$ denotes the l_p norm, t is the target class in the targeted attack, and ϵ is the upper bound of the perturbation.

3.1.2. Attack Scenarios

In this paper, we consider the adversarial attack in the black-box scenario. Query-based black-box attacks can be divided into decision-based attacks and score-based attacks. In this paper, we focus on a decision-based attack scenario.

(1) Score-based attacks. In this scenario, the attacker is unknown to any structure and parameter information of the target model, but for any input, the adversary can acquire the classification confidence.
(2) Decision-based attacks. Similar to the attack scenario of score-based attacks, the adversary doesn't know any structure and parameter information of the target model, but for any input, the attacker can acquire the classification label.

3.2. Model Architecture

In this section, we will introduce the method of generating AEs based on the dual discriminators and single generator of GAN (DDSG-GAN). This paper introduces the model architecture of GAN and designs a GAN with dual discriminators and a single generator to generate AEs. DDSG-GAN uses generator G to generate adversarial perturbations and uses discriminators D_1 and D_2 to constrain the generated perturbations. Then, the trained discriminator D_1 can be used as a surrogate model of the target model T, and the overall structure of DDSG-GAN is shown in Figure 1. The input of Generator G is the original image x, and the output is perturbation vector $\delta = G(x; \theta_g)$. Adding the perturbation vector to the original image and clipping it to obtain the query sample $\hat{x}$. Input x and $\hat{x}$ into the target model T to acquire the output $T(x)$ and $T(\hat{x})$. Discriminator D_1 uses image-output pairs $(x, T(x))$ and $(\hat{x}, T(\hat{x}))$ for training, and Discriminator D_2 uses image-output pairs $(x, 1)$ and $(\hat{x}, 0)$ for training.

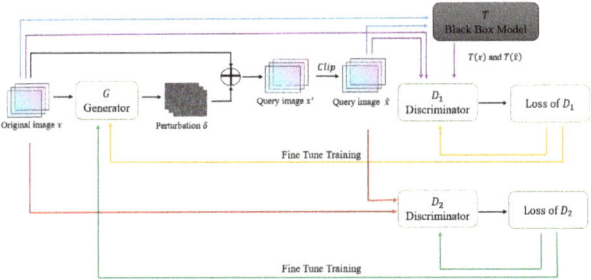

Figure 1. The proposed DDSG-GAN model.

In DDSG-GAN, T is the victim image classification black-box model. The generator G will generate the perturbation vector δ of the input image x and add δ to x. Then, through clip operation, we can get query sample $\hat{x}$. The T's query result is used to train discriminator D_1, and discriminator D_2 is used to identify whether the input is the original image. Both discriminators, D_1 and D_2, will constrain the generated perturbations.

In this training process, the generator and discriminator play a game relationship with each other. In each iteration, target model T and discriminators D_1 and D_2 will calculate corresponding prediction results for each input. The discriminator D_1 fits the target model according to the output of the target model T. With the increasing of iterations, the fitting ability of the discriminator D_1 to T is constantly enhanced so that the attack ability of generator G to target model T continues to increase. At the same time, the discriminator D_2 is increasingly capable of classifying true and fake samples so that generator G will generate AEs closer to the original data distribution. This training process forms discriminators D_1 and D_2 with generator G to keep playing games and making progress.

3.2.1. The Training of Discriminator D_1

The input of generator G is the original image x, and the output is the perturbation vector $\delta = G(x; \theta_g)$ about the original image x. Add the generated perturbation vector to x to get the query sample x'. To ensure that the generated sample is within the ϵ neighborhood of the original image, we clip x' or δ to get the final query sample $\hat{x}$. In the l_2 norm attack,

$$\hat{x} = Clip(x', x) = \begin{cases} x + \frac{\epsilon}{\|x'-x\|_p} \cdot (x' - x), & \|x' - x\|_p \geq \epsilon, \\ x', & \|x' - x\|_p < \epsilon, \end{cases} \quad (3)$$

where $\|x' - x\|_p$ denotes the l_p norm between x and x', and ϵ is the upper bound of the perturbation.

In the l_∞ norm attack,

$$\delta' = clip(\delta, \alpha_1, \alpha_2) = \begin{cases} \alpha_1, & \delta < \alpha_1; \\ \delta, & \alpha_1 \leq \delta \leq \alpha_2, \\ \alpha_2, & \delta > \alpha_2; \end{cases} \quad (4)$$

where α_1 and α_2 are the upper bound and lower bound of clipping respectively. The final query sample $\hat{x} = x + \delta'$.

The adversarial attack's goal is to make the target model misclassify the AE. It can be formulated as follows:

$$T(\hat{x}) \neq y, \quad (5)$$

For the convenience of training, we convert (5) to maximize the following objective function:

$$\max_{\hat{x}} L(T(\hat{x}), y), \quad (6)$$

where $L(\cdot, \cdot)$ measures the difference between the output of target model T and y.

In the process of solving the optimization problem (6), it is necessary to continuously query the target model T to obtain $T(\hat{x})$. However, this will make the query calculation very large, which is easily avoided by the defense mechanism. In the cause of reducing the number of queries to the target model, we train the discriminator D_1 as a surrogate model for T so that the query of T can be transferred to D_1, which will greatly reduce the number of queries to the target model.

The training goal of the discriminator D_1 is to make it to be used as a surrogate model to simulate the function of model T. For the purpose of improving the fitting ability of D_1, we use the original image x and the generated query sample $\hat{x}$ to train D_1 together. The loss function for training the discriminator D_1 is as follows:

$$L_{D1} = \beta_1 \times d(D_1(x; \theta_{d1}), T(x)) + \beta_2 \times d(D_1(\hat{x}; \theta_{d1}), T(\hat{x})), \quad (7)$$

where $T(x)$ and $T(\hat{x})$ are the query results obtained by inputting x and $\hat{x}$ into the target model T, respectively, θ_{d1} is the parameters of model D_1, $D_1(\hat{x}; \theta_{d1})$ is the predicting result of the discriminator D_1 about the query sample $\hat{x}$, and $D_1(x; \theta_{d1})$ is the predicting result of the discriminator D_1 about the original image x. β_1 and β_2 are the weight factors used to control the relative importance. In this paper, we set $\beta_1 = 2$, $\beta_2 = 1$.

For the decision-based black-box attack, the loss function of D_1 can be formulated as follows:

$$L_{D1} = \beta_1 \times CEL(D_1(x;\theta_{d1}), T(x)) + \beta_2 \times CEL(D_1(\hat{x};\theta_{d1}), T(\hat{x})), \tag{8}$$

where $CEL(a, b)$ denotes the cross-entropy function between a and b.

For the score-based black-box attack, the adversary is obtained through query T to get the classification probability for each class. So, we can convert the $T(x)$ obtained by the query into the corresponding label value and bring it into (8) to calculate the loss function of D_1 in this attack setting. Algorithm 1 presents the training procedure of D_1.

Algorithm 1	Training procedure of the Discriminator D_1
Input:	Training dataset $(x, T(x))$ and $(x', T(x'))$, where x is the original image and x' is the sample after adding perturbation, target model T, the discriminator D_1 and its parameters θ_{d1}, the generator G and its parameters θ_g; loss function $L(\cdot, \cdot)$ is defined in Equation (7).
Parameters:	Batch number B, learning rate λ_1, iterations N, weight factor β_1 and β_2, clipping upper bound α_1 and lower bound α_2.
Output:	The trained Discriminator D_1.
1:	**for** $epoch \leftarrow 1$ to N **do**
2:	**for** $b \leftarrow 1$ to B **do**
3:	$\delta = G(x;\theta_g)$
4:	**if** $norm = 2$ **do**
5:	$x' = x + \delta$
6:	$\hat{x} = Clip(x', x)$
7:	**elif** $norm = \infty$ **do**
8:	$\delta' = clip(\delta, \alpha_1, \alpha_2)$
9:	$\hat{x} = x + \delta'$
10:	**end if**
11:	$\hat{x} \leftarrow clip(\hat{x}, 0, 1)$
12:	$loss_{d1} = \beta_1 \times d(D_1(x;\theta_{d1}), T(x)) + \beta_2 \times d(D_1(\hat{x};\theta_{d1}), T(\hat{x}))$
13:	$\theta_{d1} \leftarrow \theta_{d1} - \lambda_1 \times \nabla_{\theta_{d1}} loss_{d1}$
14:	**end for**
15:	**end for**
16:	**return** D_1

3.2.2. The Training of Discriminator D_2

We train the discriminator D_1 as a surrogate model for T, so most of the queries on T can be transferred to discriminator D_1. When the attack is successful, the AEs must be close to x, so discriminator D_2 can be set to distinguish whether the sample is sampled from the original images. If it is the original image, the label is 1. If it is the AE, the label is 0. The objective function for training the discriminator D_2 is:

$$L_{D2} = E_{x \sim P_{data}(x)}[\log(D_2(x;\theta_{d2})) + \log(1 - D_2(\hat{x};\theta_{d2}))], \tag{9}$$

where $P_{data}(x)$ is the data distribution of the original image x, E denotes the calculation of the mean of the expression, θ_{d2} is the parameters of model D_2, $D_2(x;\theta_{d2})$ is the predicting result of the discriminator D_2 about the original image x, and $D_2(\hat{x};\theta_{d2})$ is the predicting result of the discriminator D_2 about the query sample $\hat{x}$.

The discriminator D_2 is used to judge whether the sample is true or fake and uses D_2 to train a good generator to fool D_2 so that the distribution of the generated AE can be closer to the original image. Algorithm 2 presents the training procedure of D_2.

Algorithm 2	Training procedure of the Discriminator D_2
Input:	Training dataset $(x, 1)$ and $(\hat{x}, 0)$, where x is the original image and $\hat{x}$ are the query samples, the discriminator D_2 and its parameters θ_{d2}, loss function $L(\cdot, \cdot)$ is defined in Equation (9).
Parameters:	Batch number B, Learning rate λ_2, iterations N.
Output:	The trained Discriminator D_2.
1:	**for** $epoch \leftarrow 1$ to N **do**
2:	**for** $b \leftarrow 1$ to B **do**
3:	$loss_{d2} = E_{x \sim P_{data}(x)}[\log(D_2(x; \theta_{d2})) + \log(1 - D_2(\hat{x}; \theta_{d2}))]$
4:	$\theta_{d2} \leftarrow \theta_{d2} + \lambda_2 \times \nabla_{\theta_{d2}} loss_{d2}$
5:	**end for**
6:	**end for**
7:	**return** D_2

3.2.3. The Training of Generator G

The input of generator G is the original image x, and the output is the perturbation vector δ about x. On behalf of making the generated AE to fool the target model T, which needs to maximize the objective function (6). In this way, each update of generator G needs to query T, and the parameter information of target model T needs to be used in the backpropagation process, which does not conform to the scenario settings of black-box attacks. Therefore, we replace the target model T with the discriminator D_1 and approximate (6) as follows (10):

$$\max_{\hat{x}} L(D_1(\hat{x}; \theta_{d1}), y), \quad (10)$$

where $L(\cdot, \cdot)$ is the cross-entropy function. Since the output of D_1 has passed softmax, the denominator of (11) will not be 0, and (10) is equivalent to the following (11):

$$\min_{\hat{x}} \frac{1}{L(D_1(\hat{x}; \theta_{d1}), y)}, \quad (11)$$

generator G's loss function regarding discriminator D_1 can be defined as follows (12):

$$L_{G\_D1} = \frac{1}{L(D_1(\hat{x}; \theta_{d1}), y)}. \quad (12)$$

While the attack is successful in ensuring that the generated AEs are closer to the distribution of the original image, the loss function of the generator G, with respect to the discriminator D_2, is defined as (13):

$$L_{G\_D2} = \log[1 - D_2(\hat{x}; \theta_{d2})]. \quad (13)$$

To obtain a high attack success rate, it is necessary to continuously input $\hat{x}$ into the target model T and use the loss of output $T(\hat{x})$ with the ground truth (untargeted attack) or the target class (targeted attack) to optimize generator G. The objectivate loss function of the attack can be formulated as follows:

$$L_{att\_score} = \begin{cases} \hat{y}_T - \hat{y}_t, & if\ untargeted\ attack, \\ \hat{y}_t - \hat{y}_T, & if\ targeted\ attack, \end{cases} \quad (14)$$

where $\hat{y}_t$ denotes the prediction probability of T for the target class in the targeted attack or the prediction probability of T for the real class in the untargeted attack, and $\hat{y}_T$ denotes the maximum value among the predicted probabilities of other classes by T.

To reduce the number of queries and be more consistent with the black-box setting, we use discriminator D_1 instead of T to optimize the training process. The objectivate loss function can be formulated as follows:

$$L_{att} = \begin{cases} \hat{y}_{D_1} - \hat{y}_t, & \text{if untargeted attack,} \\ \hat{y}_t - \hat{y}_{D_1}, & \text{if targeted attack,} \end{cases} \quad (15)$$

where $\hat{y}_t$ denotes the prediction probability of D_1 for the target class in the targeted attack or the prediction probability of D_1 for the real class in the untargeted attack, and $\hat{y}_{D_1}$ denotes the maximum value among the predicted probabilities of other classes by D_1.

We train the generator G by minimizing the following objectivate function:

$$L_G = \gamma_1 \times L_{G\_D1} + \gamma_2 \times L_{G\_D2} + \gamma_3 \times L_{att}, \quad (16)$$

where γ_i ($i = 1, 2, 3$) is the weight factor of the three losses, which controls the relative importance of the three losses. L_{G_D1} makes the generated AE deceive discriminator D_1 step by step. L_{G_D2} makes generated AEs to be closer to the actual data distribution. L_{att} is the attack loss, and its optimization produces a better attack effect. In this paper, the generator G and discriminators D_1 and D_2 are obtained by solving the minimax function $\min_G \min_{D_1} \max_{D_2} L_G$.

3.2.4. Improved Model

We can find from the training of discriminator D_1 that every training update of D_1 needs to query T. To reduce the number of queries to T while ensuring the fitting ability of D_1, we design a circular queue to limit the training of D_1. We divide the training process of D_1 into two stages: model pre-training and fine-tuning.

First, when the number of iterations $iter \leq n$, setting $\beta_1 = 3$, and $\beta_2 = 0$. We use $(x, T(x))$ to train D_1 according to the Equation (7). When the number of iterations $iter > n$ and $iter \bmod m = 0$, we add the query result $(\hat{x}, T(\hat{x}))$ of this iteration to circular queue H. So, when $iter > n$, setting $\beta_1 = 2$ and $\beta_2 = 1$ and when using $(x, T(x))$, the query result $(\hat{x}, T(\hat{x}))$ is saved in the circular queue to fine-tuned D_1 according to the Equation (7).

In each iteration training, since we constantly use the query results of T to train D_1, D_1 and T are highly approximate. Therefore, the ultimate goal of generator G can be converted to realize the discriminator D_1's misclassification of AE. If the AE can successfully lead to D_1 misclassifying them, we can think that the AE can also successfully fool the target model T with a high probability. Therefore, in the whole training process, we also trained a surrogate model that can highly simulate the target model while generating the adversarial perturbation, combining GANs and model-stealing attacks to improve the transferability of the AEs. Algorithm 3 presents the training procedure of the whole model.

Algorithm 3	Training procedure of the DDSG-GAN.
input:	Target model T, generator G and it's parameters θ_g, discriminator D_1 and its parameters θ_{d1}, discriminator D_2 and it's parameters θ_{d2}, original image–label pair (x, y) the learning rate η_g, η_{d1} and η_{d2}.
output:	The trained generator G.
1:	Initialize the model of G, D_1 and D_2.
2:	**for** $i \leftarrow 1$ to N **do**
3:	**for** $j \leftarrow 1$ to n_1 **do**
4:	$\delta \leftarrow G(x; \theta_g)$
5:	**if** $norm = 2$ **do**
6:	$x' = x + \delta$
7:	$\hat{x} \leftarrow Clip(x', x)$
8:	**elif** $norm = \infty$ **do**
9:	$\delta' = clip(\delta, \alpha_1, \alpha_2)$
10:	$\hat{x} \leftarrow x + \delta'$
11:	**end if**

Algorithm 3	Cont.

```
12:       x̂ ← clip(x̂, 0, 1)              ▷ query example
13:       if i > n and i mod m = 0 do
14:           Input x̂ into the targeted model T to get the query result
              Add (x̂; T(x̂)) to the circular queue H
16:       end if
17:       if i ≤ n do                      ▷ pre-training of D₁
18:           L_{D1} = d(D₁(x; θ_{d1}), T(x))
19:       elif i > n do                    ▷ fine tuning of D₁
20:           L_{D1} = β₁ × d(D₁(x; θ_{d1}), T(x)) + β₂ × d(D₁(x̂; θ_{d1}), T(x̂))
              ▷(x̂; T(x̂)) is taken from the circular queue H
21:       end if
22:       θ_{d1} ← θ_{d1} − η_{d1} ∇_{d1} L_{D1}(θ_{d1})
23:   end for
24:   for j ← 1 to n₂ do
25:       L_{D2} = E_{x∼P_{data(x)}} [log(D₂(x; θ_{d2})) + log(1 − D₂(x̂; θ_{d2}))]
26:       θ_{d2} ← θ_{d2} + η_{d2} × ∇_{L_{D2}}(θ_{d2})
27:   end for
28:   for j ← 1 to n₃ do
29:       L_G = γ₁ × L_{G_D1} + γ₂ × L_{G_D2} + γ₃ × L_{att}
30:       θ_g ← θ_g − η_g × ∇_{L_G}(θ_g)
31:   end for
32: end for
33: return G
```

3.2.5. Generate Adversarial Examples

Firstly, according to algorithm 3, the adversary trains the generator G for the target model T under a specific attack setting. Secondly, we input the original image x into the trained generator G to obtain the corresponding perturbation vector δ, and then add δ to the original sample to get the initial AE $x' = x + \delta$. In order to ensure that the perturbation of the AE is within a small range, we perform the corresponding clipping operation on x' to obtain the AE $\hat{x}$. If it is a l_2 norm attack, the clipping operation is performed according to the formula (3). If it is a l_2 norm attack, the clipping operation is performed according to the formula (4). Input the AE $\hat{x}$ to the corresponding target T model to attack.

Figure 2 shows the specific attack process of the MNIST dataset. As shown in Figure 2, after the training of DDSG-GAN, we input the original image x into the trained generator to make AE $\hat{x}$. Then, input $\hat{x}$ into the corresponding target model to attack. The generator designed in this paper consists of an encoder and a decoder. The encoder is a 5-layer convolution network, and the decoder is a 3-layer convolution network. For different target models, DDSG-GAN will train different generators and get different attack results.

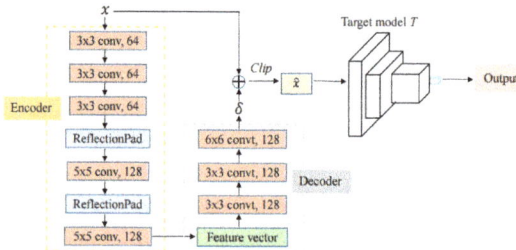

Figure 2. The attack procedure on MNIST dataset.

4. Experiment

4.1. Experiment Setting

In this section, we will introduce the specific details of the experiment, including datasets, target model architecture, method settings, and evaluation indicators.

Dataset: We evaluate the effectiveness of the proposed method through experimental results on MNIST, CIFAR10, and Tiny-ImageNet. For these datasets, we select images with the correct classification of the target model in their testing sets as their respective testing sets for evaluation. The number of selected images is 1000, 1000, and 1600, respectively.

Attack scenario: We use a decision-based attack in the black-box attack setting to evaluate the proposed method. The attackers can acquire the output results of the target model but cannot obtain any structure and parameter information about the target model.

Target model architecture: In the l_∞ norm attack, for the MNIST dataset, we follow the advGAN [12] trained three image classification models for attack testing. Models A and B are from the paper [31], and model C is from the paper [8]. In the l_∞ norm attack, we trained model D as the target model. The structure of these models is shown in Table 1.

Table 1. MNIST classification model.

A	B	C	D
		Conv(32,3,3) + Relu	
Conv(64,5,5) + Relu	Dropout (0.2)	Conv(32,3,) + Relu	
Conv(64,5,5) + Relu	Conv(64,8,8) + Relu	Conv(64,3,3) + Relu	Conv(128,3,3) + tanh
Dropout(0.25)	Conv(128,6,6) + Relu	Conv(64,3,3) + Relu	Conv(64,3,3) + tanh
FC(128) + Relu	Conv(128,5,5) + Relu	FC(200) + Relu	FC(128) + Relu
Dropout(0.5)	Dropout(0.5)	Dropout (0.5)	FC + Softmax
FC + Softmax	FC + Softmax	FC(200) + Relu	
		FC + Softmax	

For the CIFAR10 dataset, we perform an l_∞ norm attack. We also follow advGAN to train ResNet32 as the target model. In a Tiny-ImageNet dataset, we train the ResNet34 classification model as the target model, and perform l_2 norm attack.

DDSG-GAN model details: The DDSG-GAN model contains dual discriminators and a single generator. The generator consists of an encoder and a decoder. For MNIST and CIFAR10 data sets, we design the same generator structure. The encoder is a 5-layer convolutional network, and the decoder is a 3-layer convolutional network. Refer to Figure 2 for the specific generator structure. For the Tiny-ImageNet, we add a convolution layer in the encoder and generator, respectively. For the MNIST data set, the discriminator D_1 is a 4-layer convolutional neural network. The discriminator D_1 for the CIFAR10 data set is ResNet18 without pre-training. For the Tiny-ImageNet data set, there are two types of discriminators D_1, ResNet18 and ResNet50, which are pre-trained. We design the same discriminator D_2 for all data sets. The discriminator D_2 is a 2-classification network model composed of a 4-layer convolutional network, which is used to distinguish whether the sample is sampled from the original images.

Method setting: Multiple classification models are trained for MNIST, CIFAR10, and Tiny-ImageNet datasets. First, algorithm 3 is used to train the generator G. Then, the trained G is used to generate the adversarial perturbation. Then, it is added to the original sample, and the AE is obtained by clipping operation. Finally, we use these AEs to attack classification models. In the targeted attack, the target class is set to $t = (y + 1) \bmod C$, where y is the ground truth, and C is the total number of categories.

Evaluation indicators: (1) Attack success rate. In the untargeted attack, it is the proportion of the AE successfully divided into any other classes. In the targeted attack, it is the probability of classifying the image into a specific target class. (2) The magnitude of the perturbation. We conduct attack experiments under the l_2 and l_∞ norm and set the corresponding perturbation threshold.

4.2. Experiments on MNIST

In this section, we use the l_2 and l_∞ norms to perform targeted and untargeted attacks on MNIST, respectively. Table 2 shows the specific parameter settings. The untargeted attack aims to generate AEs that make the classification result of the target model different from the ground truth. The targeted attack aims to generate AEs that make the classification result of the target model in the specified category. The experimental results are shown in Tables 3–5.

Table 2. Experimental parameter setting of MNIST.

Name	l_∞ Norm	l_2 Norm	Description
η_{d1}	0.0001	0.0001	the learning rate for updating θ_{d1}
η_{d2}	0.0001	0.0001	the learning rate for updating θ_{d2}
η_g	0.001	0.001	the learning rate for updating θ_g
H	20	10	query target model's interval
$H's$ length	60,001	60,001	the maximum length of H
n	20	5	updating queue H's interval
γ_1	1	1	weight factor of γ_1 (15)
γ_2	1	1	weight factor of γ_2 (15)
γ_3	10 (epoch $\leq$ 20) 20 (epoch $>$ 20)	1	weight factor of γ_3 (15)

Table 3. Training results of the surrogate model.

		Target Model A	Target Model B	Target Model C
Untargeted attack	Accuracy	99.33%	99.01%	99.16%
	Similarity	99.19%	99.04%	99.13%
Targeted attack	Accuracy	99.29%	99.12%	99.27%
	Similarity	99.19%	99.16%	99.22%

Table 4. Experimental results of untargeted attack under l_∞ norm (ASR: the attack success rate).

Target Model	Accuracy	Method	ASR	ϵ
A	98.97%	Black-box (Surrogate Model [32] + FGSM)	69.4%	0.4
		Black-box (Surrogate Model [32] + PGD)	68.0%	0.4
		Black-box (D_1 as Surrogate Model + FGSM)	74.1%	0.3
		Black-box (D_1 as Surrogate Model + PGD)	90.2%	0.3
		DaST [30]	76.4%	0.3
		DDSG-GAN (Proposed)	100%	0.3
B	99.6%	Black-box (Surrogate Model [32]+ FGSM)	74.7%	0.4
		Black-box (Surrogate Model [32]+ PGD)	70.6%	0.4
		Black-box (D_1 as Surrogate Model + FGSM)	77.1%	0.3
		Black-box (D_1 as Surrogate Model + PGD)	82.8%	0.3
		DaST [30]	82.3%	0.3
		DDSG-GAN (Proposed)	99.9%	0.3
C	99.17%	Black-box (Surrogate Model [32]+ FGSM)	69.2%	0.4
		Black-box (Surrogate Model [32]+ PGD)	67.4%	0.4
		Black-box (D_1 as Surrogate Model + FGSM)	73.5%	0.3
		Black-box (D_1 as Surrogate Model + PGD)	91.3%	0.3
		DaST [30]	68.4%	0.3
		DDSG-GAN (Proposed)	100%	0.3

Table 5. Experimental results of targeted attack under l_∞ norm.

Target Model	Accuracy	Method	ASR	ϵ
A	98.97%	Black-box (Surrogate Model [32]+ FGSM)	11.3%	0.4
		Black-box (Surrogate Model [32]+ PGD)	24.9%	0.4
		AdvGAN [12]	93.4%	0.3
		Black-box (D_1 as Surrogate Model + FGSM)	18.3%	0.3
		Black-box (D_1 as Surrogate Model + FGSM)	50.3%	0.3
		DaST [30]	28.7%	0.3
		DDGS-GAN (proposed)	98.0%	0.3
B	99.6%	Black-box (Surrogate Model [32]+ FGSM)	17.6%	0.4
		Black-box (Surrogate Model [32]+ PGD)	22.3%	0.4
		AdvGAN [12]	90.1%	0.3
		Black-box (D_1 as Surrogate Model + FGSM)	25.1%	0.3
		Black-box (D_1 as Surrogate Model + PGD)	53.9%	0.3
		DaST [30]	40.3%	0.3
		DDGS-GAN (proposed)	97.6%	0.3
C	99.17%	Black-box (Surrogate Model [32]+ FGSM)	11.0%	0.4
		Black-box (Surrogate Model [32]+ PGD)	29.3%	0.4
		AdvGAN [12]	94.02%	0.3
		Black-box (D_1 as Surrogate Model + FGSM)	18.0%	0.3
		Black-box (D_1 as Surrogate Model + PGD)	65.8%	0.3
		DaST [30]	25.6%	0.3
		DDGS-GAN (proposed)	94.6%	0.3

First, we attack the target models under l_∞ norm. We train discriminator D_1 as a T's surrogate model. We calculate the classification accuracy and similarity with the model T (the proportion of the same number of output results of the surrogate model and that of the target model) against the MNSIT test set. The experimental results are shown in Table 3. The classification accuracy of several surrogate models and the similarity between them and the target model is close to above 99%, indicating that the surrogate model we trained can replace the target model's function.

In the l_∞ norm attack, we set the maximum perturbation threshold $\epsilon = 0.30$ to evaluate the proposed approach. We compare DDSG-GAN with surrogate model-based black-attack, DaST, and advGAN. The surrogate model is trained by two methods, respectively. The first is to train the surrogate model according to [32]. This method uses 150 images in the test set as the original training set S_0, which sets the Jacobian augmentation parameter $\lambda = 1$, and runs 30 Jacobian augmentation iterations. The second is to use the trained discriminator D_1 as the surrogate model and combine FGSM and PGD for the black-box attacks. We set an upper bound on the number of queries to the target model in the DaST method. For MNIST data sets, the query of each image is set to 1000. Under this premise, the total query upper bound of the DaST method is 6×10^7.

For a surrogate model-based attack, we use the same DNN model as the surrogate model and attack the target model by combining FGSM and PGD attack algorithms. To make the surrogate model trained by the first method have a better attack effect, set $\epsilon = 0.40$, and the perturbation thresholds of other methods are set to $\epsilon = 0.30$. Table 4 shows that our proposed method (DDSG-GAN) achieves an attack success rate of nearly 100%, which is much higher than black-box attacks based on surrogate models and DaST. At the same time, we also calculated the average query numbers of the target model. For the target models A, B, and C, the query numbers of each image in the train set were 15, 20, and 28, respectively, which ensured a low query quantity. Because the target model is unknown, black-box attacks based on the surrogate model have a low success rate. If D_1 is the surrogate model, compared with the surrogate model trained by [32], if combined with the FGSM algorithm to attack, the attack success rate is increased by 3.8% (4.7%, 2.4%, 4.3%) on average. If combined with the PGD algorithm to attack, the attack success rate is increased by 19.4% (22.2%, 12.2%, 23.9%) on average, and the attack effect is significantly improved. It demonstrates that the surrogate model we trained can replace the target model to a large extent, and this method can also achieve a good attack effect.

Table 5 shows the result of the targeted attack under the l_∞ norm, and we also compare it with the advGAN method. Compared with advGAN, the attack success rate of DDSG-GAN is 4.23% (6.5%, 7.5%, 0.58%) higher than advGAN on average, and three–four times higher than DaST. It also is much higher than the surrogate-model-based black-box attack. For target models A, B, and C, each image query numbers in the train set are 70, 75, and 109 times, respectively, also maintained at a low level. If D_1 is the surrogate model, compared with the surrogate model trained by [32], if combined with the FGSM algorithm to attack, the ASR is increased by 7.17% (7%, 7.5%, 7%) on average. If combined with the PGD algorithm to attack, the ASR is increased by 31.17% (25.4%, 31.6%, 36.5%) on average. The attack effect has also been significantly improved. In this attack setting, we visualize the generated AEs by DDSG-GAN on MNIST, which is shown in Figure 3. The top row shows the original samples of each class randomly selected from the training set. Other rows show the AEs generated by DDSG-GAN for the corresponding target model. The probability that each AE is classified into the target class is shown below the image.

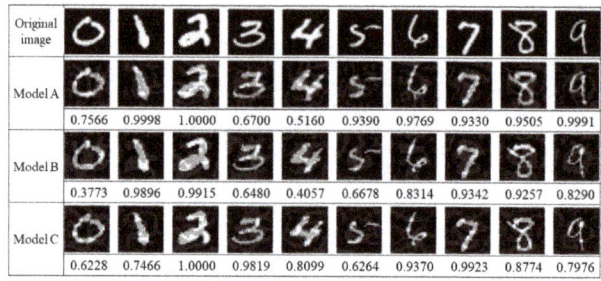

Figure 3. Visualization of the AE in targeted l_2 attack.

We also carried out an untargeted attack under the l_2 norm, and the results are shown in Table 6. In the l_2 norm attack, DDSG-GAN achieved comparable ASR and perturbation size to other attack methods but reduced the number of queries.

Table 6. Experimental results of untargeted attack under l_2 norm.

Attack Type	Method	ASR	ϵ	Agv. Queries
	Bandits [17]	73%	1.99	2771
Untargeted attack	Decision Boundary [33]	100%	1.85	13,630
	Opt-attack [34]	100%	1.85	12,925
	DDSG-GAN	90.6%	1.85	1431

4.3. Experiments on CIFAR10 and Tiny-ImageNet

We perform the untargeted and targeted attacks on CIFAR10 under l_∞ norm. Different from the setting of experimental parameters of MNIST, we set $m = n = 1$, $\eta_g = 0.00001$, $\eta_{d1} = 0.001$, and the maximum length of H is set to 50,001. The target model of the attack is ResNet32, and its classification accuracy is 92.4%. In the targeted attack, the classification accuracy of the trained D_1 for the test set reaches 54.82%, and the similarity with the target model is 73.26%. The classification accuracy of the surrogate model trained by DaST is only 20.35%, and the accuracy of D_1 is 2.69 times higher. To verify the effectiveness of DDSG-GAN, we also compare it with DaST, advGAN, and the black-box attack based on the surrogate model on CIFAR10. The results are shown in Table 7.

Table 7. Attack results under l_∞ norm on CIFAR10.

Target Model/ Accuracy	Attack Type	Method	ASR	ϵ
ResNet-32/ 92.4%	Untargeted attack	Black-box (Surrogate Model [32]+ FGSM)	79.5%	0.4
		Black-box (Surrogate Model [32] + PGD)	20.7%	0.031
		Black-box (D_1 as Surrogate Model + FGSM)	84.4%	0.031
		Black-box (D_1 as Surrogate Model + PGD)	86.9%	0.031
		DaST [30]	68.0%	0.031
		DDSG-GAN (Proposed)	89.5%	0.031
	Targeted attack	Black-box (Surrogate Model [32]+ FGSM)	7.6%	0.4
		Black-box (Surrogate Model [32]+ PGD)	4.7%	0.031
		Black-box (D_1 as Surrogate Model + FGSM)	19.5%	0.031
		Black-box (D_1 as Surrogate Model + PGD)	16.9%	0.031
		AdvGAN [12]	78.47%	0.032
		DaST [30]	18.4%	0.031
		DDSG-GAN (Proposed)	79.4%	0.031

Under the setting of a targeted attack and untargeted attack, we have realized FGSM and PGD attacks based on the surrogate model. For FGSM, we set $\epsilon = 0.4$, as it is shown to be effective in [32]. For the other attack methods, we uniformly set the perturbation threshold to $\epsilon = 0.031$. We also set an upper bound on the number of queries to the target model in the DaST method on CIFAR10. We set the query of each image to 1000. Under this premise, the total query upper bound of the DaST method is 5×10^7. As can be seen from Table 7, DDSG-GAN has an obvious advantage over the other attack methods. Compared with advGAN, DDSG-GAN's ARS in targeted attack is improved by 0.93%, and it is much higher than the black box attack based on the surrogate model and DaST. At the same time, the surrogate model we trained also achieved a good fitting effect. In the untargeted attack (targeted attack), if D_1 as the surrogate model combined with the FGSM algorithm to attack the target model, the ASR is 4.9% (10.9%) higher than the surrogate trained by [32], and the ASR combined with the PGD algorithm is increased by 10% (8.1%). The attack effect has obviously been improved. In the untargeted attack setting, visualization of AE generated by DDSG-GAN is shown in Figure 4. Figure 4a denotes original samples randomly selected from the training set. Figure 4b denotes AE generated by DDSG-GAN for the corresponding target model.

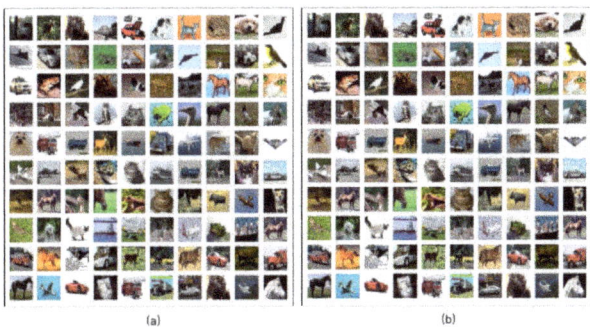

Figure 4. Visualization of AE generated by DDSG-GAN for attacking the ResNet32 on CIFAR10. (**a**) original samples randomly selected from the training set; (**b**) AE generated by DDSG-GAN for the corresponding target model.

We perform an untargeted attack on Tiny-ImageNet under l_2 norm. Because the Tiny-ImageNet data set is large, only about 1/3 of the training set, that is, 32,000 pictures, are randomly selected for training in each iterative training. We set $m = n = 1$, $\eta_g = 0.001$, $\eta_{d1} = \eta_{d2} = 0.0001$, and $\epsilon = 4.6$. The maximum length of H is set to 32,001. The pre-trained

ResNet18 and ResNet50 are used as discriminators D_1. The classification accuracy of the trained D_1 for the test set is 52.3% and 45.8%, respectively. The results are shown in Table 8. As can be seen from Table 8, the more complex the surrogate model, the better the attack effect. Therefore, in order to improve the attack effect, the complexity of the surrogate model can be appropriately increased.

Table 8. Attack results under l_2 norm on Tiny-ImageNet.

Attack Type	ϵ	D_1	ASR
Untargeted attack	4.6	ResNet18	72.15%
		ResNet50	83.76%

4.4. Model Analysis

As can be seen from the above experimental results, compared with the black-box attack based on the surrogate model (under l_∞ norm), DDSG-GAN has great advantages and a significantly higher attack success rate. In a black-box attack experiment based on the surrogate model, the surrogate model trained in this paper has a higher success rate of attack. In the l_2 norm attack, we can find that the query requirement of the target model is greatly reduced, and the success rate is kept at a high level. In addition, the attack effect of the model depends largely on the network architecture of the generator and the discriminator. When we use a fully connected neural network as the generator to perform algorithm 3, the ASR of the untargeted attack is only 80%. Therefore, designing a better network architecture helps improve the attack ability of the model.

5. Conclusions

Based on the structure of GAN, we design the architecture of generating AE with dual discriminators and a single generator and use the generator to generate the adversarial perturbation. Two discriminators constrain the generated perturbation, respectively. While ensuring the attack success rate and low image distortion, it also ensures a low query level. While training the generator, the discriminator D_1 gradually fits the target model, and, finally, it is trained as a surrogate model that can highly simulate the target model. In this way, D_1 combined with the white-box attack algorithm can carry out a black-box attack based on a surrogate model, and this attack method reaches a higher attack level, which shows that the surrogate model we trained has a good effect. When training the discriminator D_1, we added the structure of a circular queue to save the query results, which made efficient use of the query results and greatly reduced the query requirements. In future work, we will consider adding perturbation in key areas to ensure the attack effect and reduce unnecessary image distortion. At the same time, it is considered to select a broader data set, such as ImageNet, to improve the universality of the method.

Author Contributions: Methodology, F.W., Z.M. and X.Z.; validation, Z.M. and Q.L.; formal analysis, F.W., Z.M. and C.W.; investigation, F.W. and Z.M.; data curation, Z.M. and Q.L.; writing—original draft preparation, F.W., Z.M. and X.Z.; writing—review and editing, F.W., C.W. and Q.L.; visualization, Z.M.; supervision, F.W. and C.W.; funding acquisition, F.W. and C.W. All authors have read and agreed to the published version of the manuscript.

Funding: This research was funded by NSFC under Grant 61572170, Natural Science Foundation of Hebei Province under Grant F2021205004, Science and Technology Foundation Project of Hebei Normal University under Grant L2021K06, Science Foundation of Returned Overseas of Hebei Province Under Grant C2020342, and Key Science Foundation of Hebei Education Department under Grant ZD2021062.

Institutional Review Board Statement: Not applicable.

Informed Consent Statement: Not applicable.

Data Availability Statement: The MNIST dataset is available at http://yann.lecun.com/exdb/mnist/ (accessed on 10 January 2023). The CIFAR10 dataset is available at http://www.cs.toronto.edu/~kriz/cifar-10-python.tar.gz (accessed on 10 January 2023). The Tiny-ImageNet dataset is available at http://cs231n.stanford.edu/tiny-imagenet-200.zip (accessed on 8 February 2023).

Acknowledgments: We would like to thank Yong Yang, Dongmei Zhao, and others for helping us check the details and providing us with valuable suggestions for this paper.

Conflicts of Interest: The authors declare no conflict of interest.

References

1. McAllister, R.; Gal, Y.; Kendall, A.; Van Der Wilk, M.; Shah, A. Concrete problems for autonomous vehicle safety: Advantages of bayesian deep learning. In Proceedings of the Twenty-Sixth International Joint Conferences on Artificial Intelligence, Melbourne, Australia, 19–25 August 2017; pp. 4745–4753.
2. Grosse, K.; Papernot, N.; Manoharan, P.; Backes, M.; McDaniel, P. Adversarial perturbations against deep neural networks for malware classification. *arXiv* **2016**, arXiv:1606.04435.
3. Goodfellow, I.J.; Shlens, J.; Szegedy, C. Explaining and harnessing adversarial examples. *arXiv* **2014**, arXiv:1412.6572.2014.
4. LeCun, Y. The Mnist Database of Handwritten Digits. Available online: http://yann.lecun.com/exdb/mnist/ (accessed on 10 January 2023).
5. Krizhevsky, A.; Hinton, G. *Learning Multiple Layers of Features from Tiny Images*; Technical Report; University of Toronto: Toronto, CA, USA, 2009.
6. Deng, J.; Dong, W.; Socher, R.; Li, L.-J.; Li, K. Imagenet: A large-scale hierarchical image database. In Proceedings of the 2009 IEEE Conference on Computer Vision and Pattern Recognition, Miami, FL, USA, 20–25 June 2009; pp. 248–255.
7. Szegedy, C.; Zaremba, W.; Sutskever, I.; Bruna, J.; Erhan, D.; Goodfellow, I.; Fergus, R. Intriguing properties of neural networks. *arXiv* **2013**, arXiv:1312.6199.
8. Carlini, N.; Wagner, D. Towards evaluating the robustness of neural networks. In Proceedings of the 2017 IEEE Symposium on Security and Privacy (SP), San Jose, CA, USA, 22–24 May 2017; pp. 39–57.
9. Kurakin, A.; Goodfellow, I.J.; Bengio, S. Adversarial examples in the physical world. In *Artificial Intelligence Safety and Security*; Roman, V.Y., Ed.; Chapman and Hall/CRC: Boca Raton, FL, USA, 2018; pp. 99–112.
10. Madry, A.; Makelov, A.; Schmidt, L.; Tsipras, D.; Vladu, A. Towards Deep Learning Models Resistant to Adversarial Attacks. *arXiv* **2017**, arXiv:1706.06083.
11. Baluja, S.; Fischer, I. Adversarial Transformation Networks: Learning to Generate Adversarial Examples. *arXiv* **2017**, arXiv:1703.09387.
12. Xiao, C.; Li, B.; Zhu, J.Y.; He, W.; Liu, M.; Song, D. Generating Adversarial Examples with Adversarial Networks. *arXiv* **2018**, arXiv:1801.02610.
13. Moosavi-Dezfooli, S.M.; Fawzi, A.; Frossard, P. Deepfool: A Simple and Accurate Method to Fool Deep Neural Networks. In Proceedings of the 2016 IEEE Conference on Computer Vision and Pattern Recognition, Las Vegas, NV, USA, 27–30 June 2016; pp. 2574–2582.
14. Su, J.; Vargas, D.V.; Sakurai, K. One pixel attack for fooling deep neural networks. *IEEE Trans. Evol. Comput.* **2019**, 23, 828–841. [CrossRef]
15. Chen, P.Y.; Zhang, H.; Sharma, Y.; Yi, J.; Hsieh, C.J. Zoo: Zeroth order optimization based black-box attacks to deep neural networks without training substitute models. In Proceedings of the 10th ACM Workshop on Artificial Intelligence and Security, Dallas, TX, USA, 3 November 2017; pp. 15–26.
16. Tu, C.C.; Ting, P.; Chen, P.Y.; Liu, S.; Zhang, H.; Yi, J.; Cheng, S.M. Autozoom: Autoencoder-based zeroth order optimization method for attacking black-box neural networks. In Proceedings of the Thirty-Third AAAI Conference on Artificial Intelligence, Honolulu, HI, USA, 27 February 2019; pp. 742–749.
17. Ilyas, A.; Engstrom, L.; Madry, A. Prior convictions: Black-box adversarial attacks with bandits and priors. *arXiv* **2018**, arXiv:1807.07978.
18. Guo, C.; Gardner, J.; You, Y.; Wilson, A.G.; Weinberger, K. Simple black-box adversarial attacks. In Proceedings of the International Conference on Machine Learning, Boca Raton, FL, USA, 16–19 December 2019; pp. 2484–2493.
19. Yang, J.; Jiang, Y.; Huang, X.; Ni, B.; Zhao, C. Learning black-box attackers with transferable priors and query feedback. In Proceedings of the NeurIPS 2020, Advances in Neural Information Processing Systems 33, Beijing, China, 6 December 2020; pp. 12288–12299.
20. Du, J.; Zhang, H.; Zhou, J.T.; Yang, Y.; Feng, J. Query efficient meta attack to deep neural networks. *arXiv* **2019**, arXiv:1906.02398.
21. Ma, C.; Chen, L.; Yong, J.H. Simulating unknown target models for query-efficient black-box attacks. In Proceedings of the 2021 IEEE/CVF Conference on Computer Vision and Pattern Recognition, Nashville, TN, USA, 20–25 June 2021; pp. 11835–11844.
22. Biggio, B.; Corona, I.; Maiorca, D.; Nelson, B.; Šrndić, N.; Laskov, P. Evasion attacks against machine learning at test time. In Proceedings of the Joint European Conference on Machine Learning and Knowledge Discovery in Databases, Prague, Czech Republic, 22–26 September 2013; pp. 387–402.

23. Xie, C.; Zhang, Z.; Zhou, Y.; Bai, S.; Wang, J.; Ren, Z.; Yuille, A.L. Improving transferability of adversarial examples with input diversity. In Proceedings of the 2019 IEEE/CVF Conference on Computer Vision and Pattern Recognition, Long Beach, CA, USA, 15–20 June 2019; pp. 2730–2739.
24. Demontis, A.; Melis, M.; Pintor, M.; Matthew, J.; Biggio, B.; Alina, O.; Roli, F. Why do adversarial attacks transfer? explaining transferability of evasion and poisoning attacks. In Proceedings of the 28th USENIX Security Symposium, Santa Clara, CA, USA, 14–16 August 2019; pp. 321–338.
25. Kariyappa, S.; Prakash, A.; Qureshi, M.K. Maze: Data-free model stealing attack using zeroth-order gradient estimation. In Proceedings of the 2022 IEEE/CVF Conference on Computer Vision and Pattern Recognition, Nashville, TN, USA, 18–24 June 2022; pp. 13814–13823.
26. Wang, Y.; Li, J.; Liu, H.; Wang, Y.; Wu, Y.; Huang, F.; Ji, R. Black-box dissector: Towards erasing-based hard-label model stealing attack. In Proceedings of the 2021 European Conference on Computer Vision, Montreal, Canada, 11 October 2021; pp. 192–208.
27. Yuan, X.; Ding, L.; Zhang, L.; Li, X.; Wu, D.O. ES attack: Model stealing against deep neural networks without data hurdles. *IEEE Trans. Emerg. Top. Comput. Intell.* **2022**, *6*, 1258–1270. [CrossRef]
28. Goodfellow, I.; Pouget-Abadie, J.; Mirza, M.; Xu, B.; Warde-Farley, D.; Ozair, S.; Bengio, Y. Generative adversarial nets. *Commun. ACM* **2020**, *63*, 139–144. [CrossRef]
29. Zhao, Z.; Dua, D.; Singh, S. Generating Natural Adversarial Examples. *arXiv* **2017**, arXiv:1710.11342.
30. Zhou, M.; Wu, J.; Liu, Y.; Liu, S.; Zhu, C. Dast: Data-Free Substitute Training for Adversarial Attacks. In Proceedings of the IEEE/CVF Conference on Computer Vision and Pattern Recognition, Seattle, WA, USA, 13–19 June 2020; pp. 234–243.
31. Tramèr, F.; Kurakin, A.; Papernot, N.; Goodfellow, I.; Boneh, D.; McDaniel, P. Ensemble adversarial training: Attacks and defenses. *arXiv* **2017**, arXiv:1705.07204.
32. Papernot, N.; McDaniel, P.; Goodfellow, I.; Jha, S.; Celik, Z.B.; Swami, A. Practical black-box attacks against machine learning. In Proceedings of the 2017 ACM on Asia Conference on Computer and Communications Security, Abu Dhabi, United Arab Emirates, 2–6 April 2017; pp. 506–519.
33. Brendel, W.; Rauber, J.; Bethge, M. Decision-based adversarial attacks: Reliable attacks against black-box machine learning models. *arXiv* **2017**, arXiv:1712.04248.
34. Cheng, M.; Le, T.; Chen, P.Y.; Yi, J.; Zhang, H.; Hsieh, C.J. Query efficient hard-label black-box attack: An optimization based approach. *arXiv* **2018**, arXiv:1807.04457.

Disclaimer/Publisher's Note: The statements, opinions and data contained in all publications are solely those of the individual author(s) and contributor(s) and not of MDPI and/or the editor(s). MDPI and/or the editor(s) disclaim responsibility for any injury to people or property resulting from any ideas, methods, instructions or products referred to in the content.

Article

Privacy-Preserving Public Route Planning Based on Passenger Capacity

Xin Zhang [†], Hua Zhang [*,†], Kaixuan Li and Qiaoyan Wen

State Key Laboratory of Networking and Switching Technology, Beijing University of Posts and Telecommunications, Beijing 100876, China; zxby233@bupt.edu.cn (X.Z.); lkx1118@bupt.edu.cn (K.L.); wqy@bupt.edu.cn (Q.W.)
* Correspondence: zhanghua_288@bupt.edu.cn
† These authors contributed equally to this work.

Abstract: Precise route planning needs huge amounts of trajectory data recorded in multimedia devices. The data, including each user's location privacy, are stored as cipher text. The ability to plan routes on an encrypted trajectory database is an urgent necessity. In this paper, in order to plan a public route while protecting privacy, we design a hybrid encrypted random bloom filter (RBF) tree on encrypted databases, named the encrypted random bloom filter (eRBF) tree, which supports pruning and a secure, fast k nearest neighbor search. Based on the encrypted random bloom filter tree and secure computation of distance, we first propose a reverse k nearest neighbor trajectory search on encrypted databases (RkNNToE). It returns all transitions, in which each takes the query trajectory as one of its k nearest neighbor trajectories on the encrypted database. The results can be the indicator of a new route's capacity in route planning. The security of the trajectory and query is proven via the simulation proof technique. When the number of points in the trajectory database and transition database are 1174 and 18,670, respectively, the time cost of an R2NNToE is about 1200 s.

Keywords: public route planning; reverse trajectory query; encrypted trajectory database

MSC: 68P27

Citation: Zhang, X.; Zhang, H.; Li, K.; Wen, Q. Privacy-Preserving Public Route Planning Based on Passenger Capacity. *Mathematics* **2023**, *11*, 1546. https://doi.org/10.3390/math11061546

Academic Editors: Ximeng Liu, Xinbin Miao and Zuobin Ying

Received: 8 March 2023
Revised: 18 March 2023
Accepted: 20 March 2023
Published: 22 March 2023

Copyright: © 2023 by the authors. Licensee MDPI, Basel, Switzerland. This article is an open access article distributed under the terms and conditions of the Creative Commons Attribution (CC BY) license (https://creativecommons.org/licenses/by/4.0/).

1. Introduction

Public route planning is used to find a new route that can cover a large area and carry a greater amount of passengers. The operation of a new public route can ease traffic congestion as well as reduce fuel consumption and pollution. Public route planning requires a lot of trajectory data recorded in various GPS-equipped multimedia devices and online location-based services (Bikely, Didi, Twitter, and Facebook) [1]. Since trajectory data include locations, data owners encrypt the trajectory data to preserve their locations' privacy. Public route planning on an encrypted database is necessary.

In a typical scenario of planning a bus route, a passenger's transition includes two points: the source and the destination. The passenger prefers to take the bus, which has stations close to the two points. If a bus company wants to develop a new route (trajectory) that provides services to more passengers, it is necessary to predict the passenger flow of the new route. Note that passengers do not want to leak their location privacy. The new route should not be published until it is applied. Basically, it is a reverse k nearest neighbor trajectory (RkNNT) search on an encrypted trajectory database. The transition data and trajectory data are collected by online location-based service providers; they outsource their encrypted data to the cloud server to release their storage space. In a secure RkNNT search on an encrypted trajectory database, the operations of computing and comparing the distances between different trajectories are frequent, which leads to repeated access to the online location-based service providers. A proxy cloud can represent all the online location-based service providers to cooperate with the server cloud, which can reduce the online computational burden of the online location-based service providers. The details of the two-cloud model are introduced in Section 3.3.

Various kinds of queries on encrypted points are proposed, such as k nearest neighbor (NN) points queries, reverse kNN points queries, range queries, skyline queries and liner range queries. However, all these schemes cannot be applied to an encrypted trajectory query, because the similarity measure of trajectories is based on a more complex aggregation of distances and order between trajectory points, such as dynamic time warping [2], longest common subsequence [3], and edit distance on a real sequence [4]. There are also some schemes study the reverse kNN trajectories query [5,6]. However, they only return the single point, which takes the query trajectory as one of the kNN trajectories. In addition, the locations are not protected, which leaks the locations of users and the points in trajectories. These problems motivate us to investigate the RkNNT search on the encrypted databases.

There are two challenges to search the RkNNT on the encrypted databases. One is to reduce the search space, since computation on large encrypted data is time-consuming. The other is to search on a certain space without leaking the location's privacy. To overcome these two challenges, our main contributions are as follows:

- In this paper, we first design a hybrid tree, eRBFtree. It divides the search space into subspaces according to the distribution of trajectory points. The division of the subspace is according to the distribution of transition points. The eRBFtree supports spatial pruning and fast kNN search on ciphertext.
- We propose a reverse kNN trajectory search on the encrypted database, RkNNToE. We use eRBFtree to prune the space of encrypted transitions. Then, we give a distance list (DList), which helps to refine the transitions and reduce the times of the kNN search. To ensure the correctness of results, we apply the fast kNN search for every transition as a result.
- Theoretical analysis proves that clouds and users cannot know the locations of data and the distance between two locations at the same time. The experiment results confirm that our scheme is practicable in the GeoLife project in Beijing and the bus lines dataset in Beijing.

2. Related Work

In this section, we present an overview of the existing protocols in terms of trajectory search on plain text [7] and secure RkNN search [8], which are related to our work in this paper. The comparison between related schemes and RkNNToE is listed in Table 1. Note that a trajectory can degrade into a point, so the search method in RkNNT can deal with the RkNNP search, and a two-type database can degrade into a one-type database.

Table 1. Comparison with related works.

Schemes	Plaintext				Ciphertext	
	[5,6]	[9]	[10]	[11]	[8]	RkNNToE
Search Type	RkNNT	RkNNT	RkNNT	RkNNP	RkNNS	RkNNT
Query Type	T	T	P	P	S	T
Result Type	P	T	T	P	S	T
Database Type	P and T	T and T	P and T	P	S	T and T

P: point; T: trajectory; S: set.

RkNNT Search. In [12,13], an RkNN points search was studied, which is the foundation of RkNNT search. Refs. [5,6] investigated the problem to find the single points—that is, the kNN points—for the query trajectory. In 2018, Wang et al. [9] proposed an RkNN trajectory search, which studies transitions with multiple points. It does not include any semantic information [10]. In [14,15], the reverse spatial–keyword nearest neighbor queries were studied. Pan et al. [10] introduced the geo-textual object sequences to achieve an

RkNN semantic trajectories search. None of the above schemes focus on the privacy of both the query and data.

Privacy-Preserving RkNN Search. In [16], the private information retrieval was used to protect the query to achieve the privacy-preserving RkNN search. It does not protect the database stored in the cloud [17]. Li et al. [17] designed a reference-locked order-preserving based RNN query, which protects the database, but it is only used for two-dimensional data. In [11], RkNN over-encrypted multi-dimensional data were proposed, which only support point data and cannot support trajectory data. In 2023, Zheng et al. [8] proposed a privacy-preserving set reverse kNN query, which is not suitable for the two-type trajectory database.

3. Problem Formulation

The notations are shown in Table 2.

Table 2. Notations.

Notation	Definition
dist(a,b)	The distance between a and b
DB_p	The database of all points
DB_τ	The database of points in all trajectories
DB_o	The database of points in all transitions
S_τ, S_{can}	The set of trajectories and the set of candidate transitions
S_{ref}, S_{res}	The set of refined transitions and the set of results
$node(\cdot)$	The node with identity $(\cdot)$
loc	The vector of location
N_τ	The max number of trajectory points in a leaf node of the father tree
N_o	The max number of transition points in a leaf node of the child tree
$i \in (a, b)$	$i \in (a, \ldots, b)$

3.1. RkNNT Problem and Definitions

The RkNNT on the plain-text database is introduced in [9]. In this paper, we follow their definitions.

Definition 1. *(Transition) A transition of an object $O = (s, d)$ is a pair of points, describing the motive object's source and destination. $\mathcal{D}_o$ is the set of transitions.*

Definition 2. *(Trajectory) A trajectory (route) τ of length l is a sequence of points $< p_1, p_2, \ldots, p_{N_p} >$, where N_p is the number of points in the trajectory, and $\mathcal{D}_\tau$ is the set of trajectories.*

Definition 3. *(Point-to-trajectory distance) The distance between a point p_i and a trajectory τ_j is defined as:*

$$Dist(p_i, \tau_j) = \max_{p_j \in \tau_j} dist(p_i, p_j) \qquad (1)$$

Definition 4. *(RkNNT) Given a transition set $\mathcal{D}_o$, a trajectory set $\mathcal{D}_\tau$ and a query trajectory Q, RkNNT(Q) returns all the transitions in a set $\mathcal{D}_1 \in \mathcal{D}_o$. For each $O = (s, d) \in \mathcal{D}_1$, all trajectories $\tau \in \mathcal{D}_\tau$ that meet $Dist(s, \tau) \leq Dist(s, Q)$ and $Dist(d, \tau) \leq Dist(d, Q)$ are stored in a set $\mathcal{D}_2$, whose size less is than k.*

3.2. Basic Security Primitives

3.2.1. CKKS Encryption

CKKS encryption [18] is a fully homomorphic encryption. It can directly encrypt a vector and support calculating the inner product on cipher text. In this paper, $CKKS_{enc}(\cdot)$, $CKKS_{dec}(\cdot), CKKS_{sub}(\cdot, \cdot)$ and $CKKS_{dot}(\cdot, \cdot)$ represent the operation of encryption, decryption, subtraction and inner product, respectively. If $CKKS_{enc}(v_1) = c_1$, $CKKS_{enc}(v_2) = c_2$, $v_1 = (x_1, y_1)$ and $v_2 = (x_2, y_2)$, then $CKKS_{dec}(CKKS_{dot}(c_1, c_2)) = v_1 \cdot v_2$, $CKKS_{dec}(CKKS_{sub}(c_1, c_2)) = (x_1 - x_2, y_1 - y_2)$ and $CKKS_{dec}(CKKS_{dot}(CKKS_{sub}(c_1, c_2), CKKS_{sub}(c_1, c_2))) = (x_1 - x_2)^2 + (y_1 - y_2)^2$. In this paper, we use the above operations to obtain the distance of two points and denote a new operation as $CKKS_{dis^2}(c_1, c_2) = CKKS_{dot}(CKKS_{sub}(c_1, c_2), CKKS_{sub}(c_1, c_2))$.

3.2.2. Security kNN

In our algorithm, a secure kNN point search is based on the Fast and Secure kNN query (FSknn [19]). In this paper, we will briefly give the main changes compared to the FSknn.

Index-building. In this phase, a data owner (DO) firstly random generates two vectors $v_1 \perp v_2$. The method of computing every point's prefix families is the same as it in FSknn. However, in this paper, the DO treats all prefixes of all points in subspace of a node as keywords kw to embed in one RBF rather than all prefixes of a point. As shown in Figure 1, an empty RBF is initialized as a two-row and m-column random binary array. The two elements in the same column are different. $RB[i][j]$ is the element in the i-th row and j-th column of RBF. For every keyword, the DO sets $RBF[H(h(h_k(kw)) \oplus r_k)][h_k(kw)] = 1$ and $RBF[1 - H(h(h_k(kw)) \oplus r_k)][h_k(kw)] = 0$, where $h(\cdot) = HMAC(\cdot) mod 2$, $h_k(\cdot) = HMAC(\cdot)$, $H(\cdot) = SHA256(\cdot) mod 2$ and k is the number of hash functions for RBF. Every RBF point is a node rather than a point. An example of inserting a keyword is shown in Figure 1. An RBF tree is generated based on $RBF_p[H(h(h_l(kw)) \oplus r_p)][i] = RBF_l[H(h(h_l(kw)) \oplus r_l)][i] \vee RBF_r[H(h(h_r(kw)) \oplus r_r)][i]$, where RBF_p is the parent RBF of child $RBF_i, i \in (1, 4)$. An example of constructing an RBF tree is shown in Figure 2.

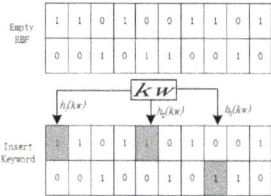

Figure 1. Inserting a keyword on an empty RBF.

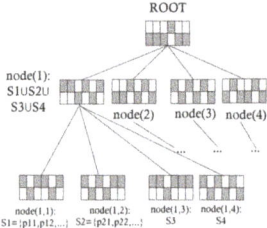

Figure 2. Index structure: RBF tree.

Token generation. When a data user (DU) wants to find the kNN in the database, the DU needs to generate k pairs of hashes and locations that serve as the search token following the same method in FSknn. However, when the token is generated by the DO, it only needs to generate the token based on one radius dis_{ref} rather than L radiuses.

Query processing. The method of the cloud is the same as it in FSknn. However, the stop condition is to find kNN trajectories in all query points' kNN points set rather than to find more than kNN points for every query point.

Post-processing. If there are not kNN trajectories in all query points' kNN points set, the DU needs to expand the search radius and repeat search kNN points following the same method in FSknn. However, if the token is generated by the DO, it does not need to expand the search radius or repeat search for kNN points.

3.3. The System and Threat Models

As shown in Figure 3, there are four entities: a data owner (DO), two clouds ($cloud_1$ and $cloud_2$) and a data user (DU). The details are described as follows.

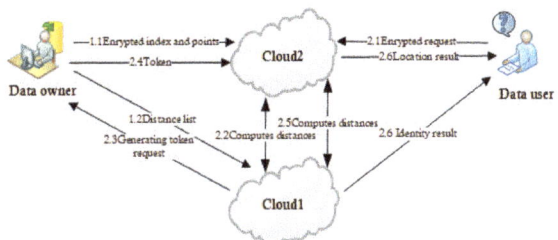

Figure 3. The model of RkNNToE search.

The DO is a data owner. The data include the transition data and the trajectory data. The DO wants to update the encrypted trajectory data and transition data to $cloud_2$ to release the storage space.

The DU is a user who wants to process the RkNNT search on the database stored in $cloud_2$. The DU sends a query to trigger the service; the query includes the encrypted information of the data user's trajectory.

$cloud_1$ (proxy cloud) is the proxy of the DU and DO, which is responsible for directing $cloud_2$ to filter and refine the transitions, and calling the DU to construct the token for every point in the refined transitions.

$cloud_2$ (server cloud) provides storage space for data owners. $cloud_2$ is responsible for searching nearest neighbor points for every point in a query trajectory and refined transitions, computing the distance between points or points and nodes with the $cloud_1$'s help, and sending the encrypted transition points to the DU.

Overview: As shown in Figure 3, the DO sends the index and encrypted points to $cloud_2$ and a distance list (DList) to $cloud_1$ to complete data outsourcing. If the DU wants to conduct an RkNN trajectory search, he sends the encrypted request to $cloud_2$. $cloud_2$ cooperates with $cloud_1$ to prune and refine transitions that cannot be the RkNN transition of the query trajectory. $cloud_1$ obtains the refined transitions and sends a request for NN points token for every point in refined transitions to the DO. The DO generates and sends the tokens to $cloud_2$. $cloud_2$ cooperates with $cloud_1$ to find the NN trajectories of all refined transitions based on the NN points. $cloud_1$ obtains the transitions that take the query trajectory as one of the kNN trajectories and returns the results to the DU.

3.4. Secure Requirements for MTS

Our scheme is under the assumptions that two clouds follow the processing of search and cannot actively attack the system or collude with each other (honest-but-curious). The DO and DU cannot collude with any cloud, but they can be a malicious attacker. Note that we mainly focus on the location privacy of points. The identity is on plain text.

Data Security. The location of every point in the transition and trajectory should not be learned by both clouds. An attacker cannot know the points' locations in the encrypted database.

Index Security. The index is secure, which means that $cloud_2$ cannot know the specific point pointed by every leaf node of the index, and every node cannot reveal the location of both trajectories and transitions.

Query Security. Both the encrypted requests cannot reveal the location of every point in the query trajectory. Both clouds cannot know the specific location.

4. The Proposed Scheme

In this section, first, we generalize the main idea of the search. However, all information of the index is not protected, and the trajectories and transitions are not encrypted. Then, we proposed a secure scheme with encrypted index and encrypted data, which should be processed in a two-cloud model. It can satisfy the secure requirements and counter-threat model.

4.1. Main Idea of RkNNT Search

The reverse trajectories searching are divided into four steps: building a hybrid quad tree, generating a filter set and pruning transition, refining transitions and returning results. The whole processing is shown in Algorithm 1.

Algorithm 1: Reverse Trajectory Search (Q, DB_p)

Input: Q: query, DB_p: all points in the database $DB_p = DB_\tau \cup DB_o$
Output: $RkNN(Q)$: The reverse kNN trajectories for Q
1   $DB_p \rightarrow$ hybrid Quadtree
2   **for** all $q_i \in Q$ **do**
3     $kNN(q_i, DB_\tau) \rightarrow$ Table
4   FilterSet(Table) $\rightarrow S_\tau$
5   PruneTransition(S_τ, DB_o) $\rightarrow S_{can}$
6   RefineTransition($S_{can}, DList$) $\rightarrow S_{ref}$
7   **for** all $O = \{s, d\} \in S_{ref}$ **do**
8     $kNN(s, DB_\tau) \rightarrow S_s$, $kNN(d, DB_\tau) \rightarrow S_d$ kNNTrajectorySet(S_s, S_d) $\rightarrow S_{\tau'}$
     CompareDistance($dis(\tau_{k-th}, O), dis(Q, O)$) $\rightarrow S_{res}$
9   **return** S_{res}

4.1.1. Building Hybrid Quad Tree

On the plain-text trajectory database, we build a hybrid quad tree base on quad tree [20] in DB_p. DB_p includes all the points in DB_τ and DB_o. The space in a node is partitioned into four equal subspaces. The subspace is stored in the child node. The partitioning will not be stopped until there are less than n points in the subspace. First, the partitioning is based on DB_τ, it will not be stopped until there are less than N_τ points in the subspace. The quad tree in this phase is called the father tree. The trajectory points are stored in every leaf node of the father tree. Then, every subspace in the leaf node of the father tree is partitioned. The partitioning is based on all points in this subspace; it will not be stopped until there is less than N_o points in one leaf node. The quad tree takes the leaf node of the father tree, as its root node is called the child tree. Figure 4 shows the structure of a hybrid quad tree. The bold tree is the father tree. The others are child trees. Every non-leaf node of the hybrid quad tree stores the location vectors of four vertexes. Every leaf node stores the identities and location vectors of points in this leaf node. This is shown in line 1 of Algorithm 1.

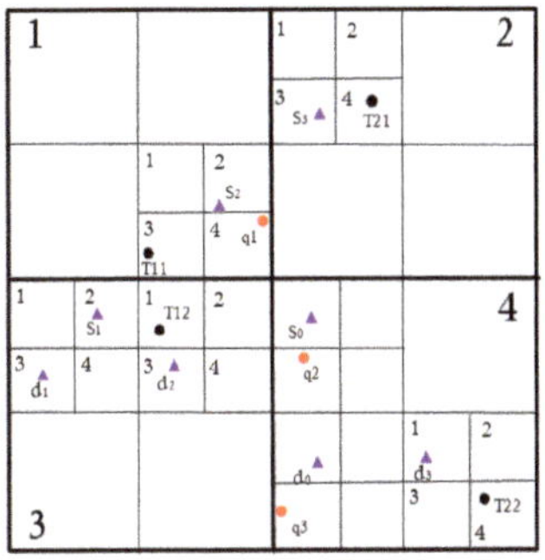

Figure 4. The partition for all points.

4.1.2. Generating Filter Points and Pruning Transitions

If a reverse trajectory search is needed, we find the NN trajectory points for every query trajectory point and construct a table. In Figure 5, the NN points of query points (q_1, q_2, q_3) are in $node(1)$, $node(2)$, $node(3)$ and $node(4)$. Then, we find the trajectory, which has more than two points in the table, such as $T1$. All points in these trajectories are called filter points. In Figure 6, the filter points are $T11$ and $T12$. We form a polyline based on perpendicular bisectors between the points from one trajectory and the query points. The polyline divides the space into two subspaces. If one node is intersected by the polyline, then we check whether the child node meets the above condition. Then, $node(1)$ and the $node(3)$ are intersected by the polyline in Figure 5. Its child node needs to be checked. If the node is the leaf node of the child tree, we list all the transitions' identity and compute the distance between the transition points and the filter points. If there are more than k trajectories closer to the transition than the query trajectory, the transition is pruned. In Figure 6, leaf $node(3, 2, 3)$ is intersected by the polyline, and we compare the distance $dist(O_2, Q)$ with the distance $dist(O_2, T1)$. Since $dist(O_2, Q) > dist(O_2, T1)$, transition O_2 can be pruned. If one node is in the subspaces of two filter points with one trajectory identity, the node is closer to the trajectory than the query trajectory. If there are more than k polylines that make one node meet the above condition, there are more than k trajectories closer to the node than to the query trajectory. All transitions in these nodes are closer to the k trajectories than to the query trajectory. All transitions in these nodes can be pruned. In Figure 5, the $node(3, 1)$ is in the subspace of $T11$ and $T12$, all points in $node(3, 1)$ are closer to trajectory $T1$ than to query trajectory Q. Since transition $O_1 = (s_1, d_1)$ is in $node(3, 1)$, it can be pruned. All the rest of the transitions are called candidate transitions. The candidate transitions in Figure 5 are O_0 and O_3.

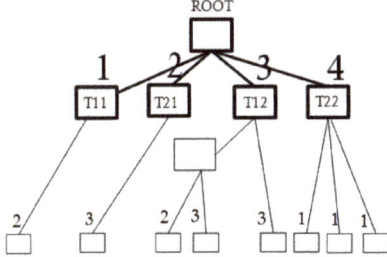

Figure 5. The quad tree structure for all points.

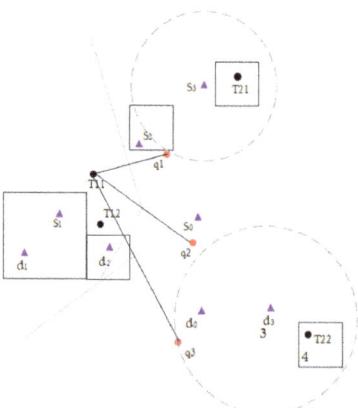

Figure 6. The example of RkNN search.

4.1.3. Refining Transitions and Returning Results

For every candidate transition, we compute the distance between every point in transition and the query trajectory. We check the nodes in the quad tree by using a circle, of which the radius is the distance and the center point is the transition point. For the nodes in the circles of one transition, we record the identities of trajectories in these nodes. For the nodes that intersect with the circle, the child node needs to be checked further. If the node is a leaf node, we compute the distance between every transition point and trajectory in the leaf node. We record the identities of trajectories which are closer to the transition than the query trajectory. If the total number of recorded identities is more than k, then the candidate transition is deleted. In Figure 6, the circles of point s_3 and d_3 are drawn. The nodes $(2,1,4)$ and $(4,4,1)$ are in the circle, respectively. The trajectory $T2$ is closer to the transition O_3. It can be deleted in the candidate transitions. The rest of the candidate transitions are called refined transitions. For every point of the refined transitions, we find the NN points in the quad tree and check whether there are two points of query trajectory in it. If two points of the query trajectory are in the NN points of one transition, it is inserted in the set $RkNN(Q)$. The $RkNN(Q)$ is the search results. In Figure 5, the NN point for the point s_0 is q_2 and the NN point for the point d_0 is q_3. The $RkNNT(Q)$ in Figure 5 is O_1.

4.2. Reverse Search on Encrypted Trajectory Database

In this section, the points of transitions and trajectories are encrypted, and the hybrid quad tree is replaced by an encrypted RBF tree (eRBFtree) and the distance list (DList). This section is consists of four phases: setup, eRBFtree building, query encryption and search.

4.2.1. Setup

The data owner generates the parameters of CKKS and RBF tree as shown in Section 3.2. It encrypted all the location vectors of points in database DB_p. For a point with identity ID and location loc, its item is $\{ID, CKKS_{enc}(loc)\}$. The $cloud_2$ generates its private key sk_2 and public key pk_2; it publishes the public key pk_2 to the DO and DU.

4.2.2. eRBFtree and DList Building

As shown in Figure 7, building an eRBFtree includes two steps. The first step is building the RBF tree in the database DB_τ and the partitioning of space is the same to the partitioning of the father tree in Section 4.1.1. Every leaf node of the RBF tree stores the encrypted items of trajectory points. Every non-leaf node stores an RBF and four encrypted points $\{CKKS_{enc}(V_1), \ldots, CKKS_{enc}(V_4)\}$, where $V_i, i \in (1,4)$ is the four vertices of the node. The second step is building the child trees in the database DB_o. Every leaf node of the child tree stores encrypted items of transition points. Every non-leaf node stores four encrypted points $\{CKKS_{enc}(V_1), \ldots, CKKS_{enc}(V_4)\}$. The DList is a table, in which every row records $(ID_o, p) : \{dis_1, SID_\tau^1\}, \{dis_2, SID_\tau^2\}, \ldots$. The keywords (ID_o, p) are the identity of transition and one point in the transition. The value dis_i is the maximum distance from the point p to its nearby nodes. The value SID_τ^i is the set of trajectories' identities in these nodes. The values are listed in increasing order by the dis_i. The eRBFtree and the DList are constructed by the data owner. The DO encrypts the eRBFtree with all the items by the public key pk_2 and sends the cipher text to $cloud_2$. The DO sends the DList and the secret key of CKKS to $cloud_1$.

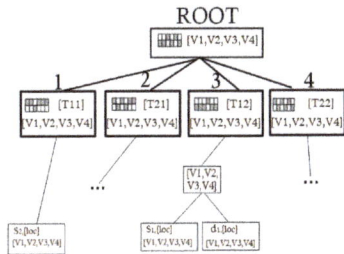

Figure 7. The structure of eRBFtree. $[\cdot]$ is the encryption of $\cdot$.

4.2.3. Query Encryption

The query includes tokens and items for points $q_j, j \in (1, N_p)$ in the query trajectory. N_p is the number of points in the query trajectory. The token $Token(q_j)$ is for a secure kNN search in eRBFtree, which is constructed as shown in Section 3.2.2. The center point is the point of the query trajectory, and the search radius is set by the DO. The item $\{CKKS_{enc}(q_j)\}$ is the encrypted location vector of the point q_j. The query $Q = \{(Token(q_1), CKKS_{enc}(q_1)), \ldots, (Token(q_{N_p}), CKKS_{enc}(q_{N_p}))\}$ is encrypted by the public key of $cloud_2$; then, it is sent to $cloud_2$ to start a reverse search.

4.2.4. Search

In this phase, $cloud_2$ decrypts the query with the private key sk_2. Then, $cloud_2$ uses the tokens $Token(q_j), j \in (1, N_p)$ to search the eRBF tree, obtains the NN trajectory points for every point in the query trajectory, checks the identities of points and constructs the filter set. The item in the filter set is $\{ID_\tau, CKKS_{enc}(loc_1), CKKS_{enc}(loc_2), \ldots, CKKS_{enc}(loc_{N_p})\}$, where $CKKS_{enc}(loc_1), CKKS_{enc}(loc_2), \ldots, CKKS_{enc}(loc_{N_p})$ are NN points of N_p query points. They have the same trajectory identity ID_τ. $Cloud_2$ computes distances between every vertex in the node and the filter points by $DIS_1 = CKKS_{dis^2}(CKKS_{enc}(loc_i), CKKS_{enc}(V_j)), i \in (1,2), j \in (1,4)$. Then, $cloud_2$ computes the distance between every vertex in the node and the query trajectory by $DIS_2 = CKKS_{dis^2}(CKKS_{enc}(q_i), CKKS_{enc}(V_j)), i \in (1, N_p), j \in (1,4)$. Afterwards, $cloud_2$ sends DIS_1, DIS_2 to the $cloud_1$. $Cloud_1$ decrypts them and obtains the distance between every vertex and the filter points $dist(loc_i, V_j), i \in (1,2), j \in (1,4)$ and the distance between every vertex in node and the query trajectory $dist(q_i, V_j), i \in (1, N_p), j \in (1,4)$. The process is from the root node to the leaf node, using the pruning transition in Section 4.1.2. If one node is filtered, $cloud_1$ notifies $cloud_2$. Then, $cloud_2$ stops computing the distance of its child node. If the node is a leaf node, $cloud_2$ and $cloud_1$ compute the distance between every transition point in the node and the query trajectory $dist(loc_i, q_j), i \in (1,2), j \in (1, N_p)$. After filtering the transitions, $cloud_2$ cooperates with $cloud_1$ to compute the distance between the candidate transitions and the query trajectory. The identities of transitions and the cipher text of distance are sent to $cloud_1$. Then, $cloud_1$ decrypts the cipher text and obtains the distance $d = dist(loc_i^{can}, q_j), i \in (1,2), j \in (1, N_p)$. For every candidate point $loc_i^{can}, i \in (1,2)$ in one transition, $cloud_1$ refers to the DList, locates the row of keyword loc_i^{can} and finds the maximum values for dis_{h_i} meet $dis_{h_i} \leq min\{dist(loc_i^{can}, q_j), j \in (1, N_p)\}$. Then, $cloud_1$ counts the number of trajectories, of which two points come from two sets $SID_\tau^{h_1}$ and $SID_\tau^{h_2}$. If the number of the trajectories is more than k, the transition $(loc_1^{can}, loc_2^{can})$ can be pruned. Then, $cloud_1$ sends the identities of refined transitions S_{ref} to $cloud_2$. For every refined transition (s,d) with identity in S_{ref}, $cloud_2$ sends the identity and a distance $dis_{ref} = dist(s,Q) + dist(d,Q)$ to the DO. Then, $cloud_2$ sends the encrypted transition $(CKKS_{enc}(loc_s), CKKS_{enc}(loc_d))$ points to the DO. The tokens $Token_{ref}$ for every point in the refined transition are constructed after the DO obtains the request $\{ID_O, dis_{ref}\}, ID_O \in S_{ref}$ from $cloud_1$ and decrypts $(CKKS_{enc}(loc_s), CKKS_{enc}(loc_d))$. The DO constructs two tokens for every transition, as shown in Section 3.2.2. The center points are the points of location loc_s and loc_d, respectively. The radius is dis_{ref}. The DO sends the set of tokens $Token_{ref}$ to $cloud_2$. $Cloud_2$ searches the NN points and checks if there is less than k trajectories in the NN points. If there are, the transition is one of the reverse k transitions for the query trajectory. Otherwise, $cloud_2$ computes the distance between trajectories and transitions with the help of $cloud_1$. $Cloud_1$ compares the distance between the trajectory and transitions as wel as between the query trajectory and transitions. If more than k trajectories are closer to one transition, the transition is deleted. The rest of the refined transitions are the results. Then, $cloud_1$ returns the identities to the DU and $cloud_2$ returns the encrypted locations to the DU.

5. Theoretical Analysis

5.1. Correctness Analysis

In this section, we will discuss the returned results, which are all reverse transitions for the query trajectory. The discussion is divided into three steps.

(1) In the first step, we find the filter set S_τ and prune the $O = (s,d) \in DB_o$ so that $\exists \mathcal{D}_\tau = \{\tau_1, \ldots, \tau_k\}$ such that $dist(s, \tau_i) < dist(s, Q)$ and $dist(d, \tau_i) < dist(d, Q)$, $i \in (1, \ldots, k)$. According to Definition 4, the transition cannot be in RkNNT(Q). We call the transition that is not in RkNNT(Q) a negative transition and the transition that is in RkNNT(Q) a positive transition. In this step, we only prune a part of the negative transitions. There are also many negative transitions in set S_{can}.

(2) In the second step, we use the candidate set S_{can} and DList to delete the $O = (s,d), s \in S_{can}$ or $d \in S_{can}$ so that there exists $\{dis_s < dist(s,Q), SID_\tau^s\}$ in the row of point s, $\{dis_d < dist(d,Q), SID_\tau^d\}$ in the row of point d and $SID_\tau^s \cap SID_\tau^d$ has more than k trajectory identities. It also means that $\exists \mathcal{D}_{\tau'} = \{\tau'_1, \ldots, \tau'_k\} \subset (SID_\tau^s \cap SID_\tau^d)$ such that $dist(s, \tau_i) < dist(s,Q)$ and $dist(d, \tau_i) < dist(d,Q)$, $i \in (1', \ldots, k')$. In this step, we also delete a part of negative transitions. It is unclear whether there are any negative transitions in set S_{ref}.

(3) In the third step, we know that if a transition takes the query trajectory as one of its kNN trajectories, the transition must be the RkNNT of the query trajectory. For every transition $O = (s,d) \in S_{ref}$, we find all trajectory points with distance to s or d less than $dis_{ref} = dist(s,Q) + dist(d,Q)$. If a trajectory τ has only a point with distance to s or d less than dis_{ref}, then $dist(s, \tau) + dist(d, \tau) > dis_{ref}$. If a trajectory τ has no point with distance to s or d less than dis_{ref}, then $dist(s, \tau') + dist(d, \tau') > 2dis_{ref}$. So if only a trajectory has one point with distance to s less than dis_{ref} and the other one point has distance to d less than dis_{ref}, it is possibly closer to the transition $O = (s,d)$ than the query trajectory Q. For every transition $O = (s,d) \in S_{ref}$, we list all NN trajectories τ_i meets $dist(s, \tau_i) + dist(d, \tau_i) \leq 2dis_{ref}$ and check the size of $\mathcal{D}_\tau = \{\tau_1, \ldots, \tau_j\}$ such that $dist(s, \tau_i) + dist(d, \tau_i) < dist(s,Q) + dist(d,Q)$, $i \in (1, \ldots, j)$. If the size of $\mathcal{D}_\tau$ is not more than k, the transition must be the positive transitions; otherwise, the transition must be the negative transition.

5.2. Security Definitions and Analysis

The two-clouds model is honest-but-curious, and the RkNNToE is processed in two phases. The definition of leakage functions [21] of two phases and the formal proof are proposed. It shows that RkNNToE is secure in an honest-but-curious clouds model.

Definition 5. *In an honest-but-curious clouds model, there are two participants $C_i, i \in (1,2)$ in a protocol $\mathcal{P}$. For C_i, f_i and O_i are the execution function and its output, while $view_i$ is the view* during an execution of $\mathcal{P}$. The protocol $\mathcal{P}$ is secure against a probabilistic polynomial time (PPT) honest-but-curious adversary if there exist simulators $\mathcal{S}_1$ and $\mathcal{S}_2$ such that:

$$(\mathcal{S}_1(f_1, \mathcal{L}_1), f_2) \equiv (view_1, O_2) \quad (2)$$

$$(f_1, \mathcal{S}_2(f_2, \mathcal{L}_2)) \equiv (O_1, view_2) \quad (3)$$

where $\equiv$ means computational indistinguishability.

$\mathcal{L}_i^j$ is the leakage function of cloud $i \in (1,2)$ in phase $j \in \{setup, search\}$. Given a collection of points DB_p from the DO and a query trajectory Q from the DU,

$$\mathcal{L}_1^{setup}(DB_p) = \{DL, [\mathbb{EI}, [id, p]]\}$$

$$\mathcal{L}_2^{setup}(DB_p) = \{\mathbb{EI}, (OID, [loc])_i, (TID, [loc])_j, |DB_p|, |DB_\tau|, |DB_O|\}$$

$$\mathcal{L}_1^{search}(DB_p, Q) = \{\mathbb{D}(Q), DL, S_{can}, S_{ref}\}$$

$$\mathcal{L}_2^{search}(DB_p, Q) = \{Token_i, Token_j, |Q|, |S_{ref}|, |S_{can}|, \mathbb{S}(Q), \mathbb{A}(Q), (OID, [loc])_i, (TID, [loc])_j\},$$

where DL is the distance list, EI is the eRBF tree, id is the identity of point p, $[\cdot]$ is the cipher text of $\cdot$, $|\cdot|$ is the size of $\cdot$, OID_i is the identity of transition i and TID_j is the identity of trajectory j.

Definition 6. *(Search Pattern $\mathbb{S}$) The search pattern leakage reveals whether the keywords in the token of every query point have appeared before.*

Definition 7. *(Access Pattern $\mathbb{A}$) Given a search query Q, the access pattern is defined as the identifier of trajectory points in the nearest neighbor of query points.*

Definition 8. *(Distance Pattern $\mathbb{D}$) Given a search query Q, $\mathbb{D}(Q) = dist(p_i, q_j), q_j \in Q, p_i \in S_{can}$. Informally, this part of leakage can be derived from the query, $\mathbb{D}$ leaks the distances between the points in candidate transitions and query points.*

Theorem 1. *Under the permitted leakage functions $\mathcal{L}_1^{Setup}$, $\mathcal{L}_2^{Setup}$, $\mathcal{L}_1^{Search}$ and $\mathcal{L}_2^{Search}$, if CKKS and the FSknn [19] are secure in the two honest-but-curious clouds model, then RkNNToE is secure in the two honest-but-curious clouds model.*

Proof. We introduce the leakage function to Definition 5 and prove that for any PPT adversary, there exist simulators S_1 and S_2 such that:

$$(\mathcal{S}_1(f_1, \mathcal{L}_1^{setup}), f_2) \equiv (view_1, O_2) \quad (4)$$

$$(\mathcal{S}_1(f_1, \mathcal{L}_1^{search}), f_2) \equiv (view_1, O_2) \quad (5)$$

[Simulating Setup] Given $\mathcal{L}_1^{setup}(DB_p) = \{DL, [\mathbb{EI}, [id, p]]\}$, $\mathcal{S}_1$ randomly generates a message as the plain text m and encrypts it by using a CPA-secure encryption to obtain $[m]$. $\mathcal{S}_1$ randomly generates the identity of trajectories and transitions. The number of these trajectories is the same as the one listed in DL. $\mathcal{S}_1$ randomly generates many increasing arrays to represent the distance between the transition points and vertices of each node. Since the PPT adversary does not know the real distribution of points, and the encryption in the above simulation is secure, a PPT adversary cannot distinguish between the simulated view and the real view.

[Simulating Search] Given $\mathcal{L}_1^{search}(DB_p, Q) = \{\mathbb{D}(Q), DL, S_{can}, S_{ref}\}$, $\mathcal{S}_1$ knows the identities of transitions that are deleted in the phase of refining transitions $S_{del} = S_{can} - S_{ref}$. From $\mathbb{D}(Q)$, $\mathcal{S}_1$ knows the distance between the point in S_{can} and query points. In the simulated DL', if a transition is in S_{del}, it must have kNN trajectories closer than the query.

A PPT does not know the locations of every point; it only knows the distance and the identities of deleted transitions. It cannot distinguish between the simulated DL' and the real DL.

$$(f_1, \mathcal{S}_2(f_2, \mathcal{L}_2^{setup})) \equiv (O_1, view_2), \qquad (6)$$

$$(f_1, \mathcal{S}_2(f_2, \mathcal{L}_2^{search})) \equiv (O_1, view_2) \qquad (7)$$

[Simulating Setup] Given $\mathcal{L}_2^{setup}(DB_p) = \{\mathbb{EI}, (OID, [loc])_i, (TID, [loc])_j, |DB_p|, |DB_\tau|, |DB_O|\}$, $\mathcal{S}_2$ randomly chooses $|DB_p|$ points, encrypts points by CKKS to obtain $[loc]'$ and assigns the identity to these points. Then, $\mathcal{S}_2$ constructs an eRBF tree $\mathbb{EI}'$, which has the same structure with $\mathbb{EI}$. For each node, $\mathcal{S}_2$ randomly generates four vectors $V_1', \ldots, V_4'$ and encrypts them by CKKS. $\mathcal{S}_2$ associates encrypts $[loc]'$ with its corresponding OID or TID in $\mathbb{EI}$. According to secure analysis in [19], a PPT adversary cannot distinguish between the simulated view and the real view.

[Simulating Search] Given $\mathcal{L}_2^{search}(DB_p, Q) = \{Token_i, Token_j, |Q|, S_{can}, S_{ref}, \mathbb{S}(Q), \mathbb{A}(Q), (OID, [loc])_i, (TID, [loc])_j\}$, $\mathcal{S}_2$ randomly generates plain text loc' and encrypts it by using CKKS to get $[loc]'$. From $\mathbb{S}(Q)$, $\mathcal{S}_2$ knows whether a point in query has been searched before or not. From $\mathbb{A}(Q)$, $\mathcal{S}_2$ knows the identifiers of points which are NN points for a query point. If a $q_i \in Q$ is searched before by comparing the token of q_i and in previous tokens, $\mathcal{S}_2$ reuses the previous simulated token and returns the previous NN points as search results. Otherwise, $\mathcal{S}_2$ simulates a new search token $Token'$, which is the token of one point including k hashes $h(kw)$ and a location. Since $\mathcal{S}_2$ knows which leaf node of the eRBF tree matches the search token $Token_j$, $\mathcal{S}_2$ randomly generates a k-bit string as the search token $Token$. The string has the same size as $h(kw)$ and matches with the same leaf node of eRBF. A PPT cannot distinguish between the simulated $Token'$ and the real $Token$. □

5.3. Computational Complexity Analysis

In this section, we analyze the time complexity of RkNNToE, in which the most complexity is caused by computing the distance between two points securely. The complexity of kNN is shown in [19]. To generate the set S_{can}, every query point is checked against nodes and cost $\mathcal{O}(|Q| \cdot (N_{vis}(eRBFtree) + N_{vis}(O_{leaf})))$ at most, where $N_{vis}(eRBFtree)$ is the number of vertexes in the visited nodes and $N_{vis}(O_{leaf})$ is the number of transition points in the leaf nodes that are intersected by the polyline. All filter points are checked against nodes and the cost of computing the distance is $\mathcal{O}(k \cdot |Q| \cdot (N_{vis}(eRBFtree) + N_{vis}(O_{leaf})))$ at most. After obtaining S_{can}, the cost of computing the distances between all transitions in set S_{can} and the query trajectory is $\mathcal{O}(|Q| \cdot |S_{can}|)$. After obtaining S_{ref}, the cost of computing the distances between all transitions in set S_{ref} and their kNN trajectories is $\mathcal{O}(2|S_{T'}| \cdot |S_{ref}|)$, where $S_{T'}$ is a set of all kNN trajectories of a transition. The total complexity is $\mathcal{O}(RkNNToE) = \mathcal{O}((k+1) \cdot |Q| \cdot (N_{vis}(eRBFtree) + N_{vis}(O_{leaf}))) + \mathcal{O}(|Q| \cdot |S_{can}|) + \mathcal{O}(2|S_{T'}| \cdot |S_{ref}|)$. According to [9], the visited nodes are proportional to the number of points in DB_p, f is the fanout of the eRBFtree, and $DB_\tau \ll DB_o$. The complexity is $\mathcal{O}(RkNNToE) = \mathcal{O}((k+1) \cdot |Q| \cdot (N_{vis}(eRBFtree) + N_{vis}(O_{leaf}))) + \mathcal{O}(|Q| \cdot |S_{can}|) + \mathcal{O}(2|S_{T'}| \cdot |S_{ref}|) = \mathcal{O}((k+2) \cdot |Q| \cdot (|DB_o|/f))$.

6. Performance Evaluation

In this section, we conduct experiments on the two databases: the aGPS trajectory dataset (Transition dateset) collected in Geolife project in Beijing [22–24] and the bus lines dataset (Trajectory dataset) in Beijing [25]. There are 18,670 transitions in the transition database. The bus lines dataset has 1891 trajectories and 1174 bus stations. All algorithms are implemented in Python language in Windows 10 and examined on a computer with an Intel(R) Core (TM)i5-10505 and 16.00 GB RAM. We randomly generate a query trajectory by selecting an ordered sequence from the trajectory database, since the randomly generated points cannot keep the spatial continuity as a trajectory. In the experiment, the NN k trajectories do not share any one point with the query trajectory. The trajectory that is shared by multiple bus lines is just recorded as one trajectory.

6.1. Constructing eRBF Tree and DList

Before outsourcing the data, the DO needs to build the eRBF tree. The time cost of constructing the eRBF index includes two parts: the time of constructing the RBF tree in database D_τ and the time of constructing the encrypted quad tree in database D_p. The first part is related with the maximum number (N_τ) of trajectory points in a leaf node of the father tree. Table 3 shows the time cost of constructing the RBFs in the father tree with different N_τ. The second part is related to the maximum number (N_o) of transition points in a leaf node of the child tree. The total time of constructing the eRBF tree is shown in Figure 8; the main cost is for encrypting the four vertexes in every node of eRBF tree. With N_τ or N_o increasing, the cost of constructing eRBF decreases, since the DList is constructed based on plain text, and the DO only needs to compute the distance between every transition point with vertexes in its nearby nodes. Here, we set the nodes in the range of 25 to 200 steps, and the mean time of constructing the DList is shown in Table 3.

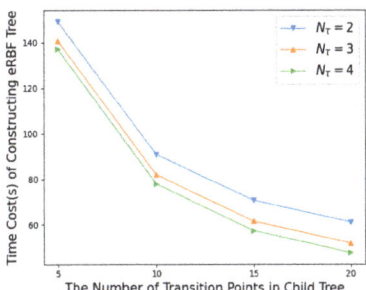

Figure 8. The time cost of constructing the eRBF tree.

Table 3. The cost of constructing father tree and DList.

DB	N_τ	Step Length in Latitude and Longitude	Time Cost of RBF Tree(s)	Time Cost of DList(s)
DB_τ	2	[0.000230, 0.001237]	5.600787	3.559773
	3	[0.000460, 0.002474]	3.796525	3.468612
	4	[0.001840, 0.009896]	2.861059	3.470150
	5	[0.001840, 0.009896]	2.698736	3.444898

6.2. Generating Query

A query of one point includes the encrypted location and an NN search token. The time cost of encrypting a location vector is about 0.004516 seconds by CKKS encryption. The cost of generating a token is related with the search radius. Here, we denote the minimum range of the leaf node in the father tree as a step length and use the number of steps to determine the search radius. The step length does not decrease as N_τ increases, which is shown in Table 3. As shown in Figure 9, the line of "Enc." is the time of encryption of a location. As the number of steps increases, the time of generating a token increases. So, the total time to generate a trajectory query is related to the number of points included in this trajectory and the search radius for every point in the query.

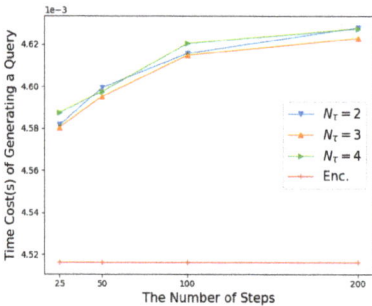

Figure 9. The time cost of generating a query.

6.3. Search

In this section, we firstly demonstrate the time cost of the kNN search for a point. Then we show the total time of two clouds after receiving a RkNNToE request.

6.3.1. NN Trajectories Search

Since the DO needs to search NN trajectories for the refined transitions, it is necessary to illustrate the efficiency of the kNN search for every transition point. As shown in Figure 10, as the number of trajectory points in a leaf node of the father tree increases, the time of searching the NN points increases. As the number of steps in the search radius increases, the time cost of searching NN points increases. The total cost of searching NN trajectories for a transition requires twice as much time as that for NN points in Figure 10.

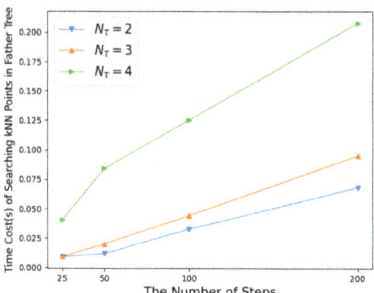

Figure 10. The time cost of searching NN trajectory points.

6.3.2. RkNNToE Search

In this section, we simulate the whole search process in two clouds, which includes finding NN points for every query point, constructing a filter set and pruning transitions, refining transitions and finding NN trajectories for every refined transition. In the simulated search, the eRBF tree is built with $N_\tau = 2$ and $N_o = 2$. The experiment settings are as follows:

The number of points in a query(N_p): 2 to 5, default 3. The k in RkNNToE: 1 to 4, default 2. The number of steps in NN points search: 20 to 200.

The random behavior of a time cost is caused by the random generation query trajectory. The effect of pruning differs widely when the queries are different. According to Section 5.3, the complexity is mainly affected by S_{can} and (DB_O/f) rather than operations of search k NN trajectories. S_{can} and (DB_O/f) are the outputs of pruning, and the size of the filter set does not linearly increase as k increases. In most cases, when $k = 2$, the points in the filter set are a, b, c. $\{a, c\}$ and $\{a, b\}$ can form two trajectories. It also causes the random behavior of time cost. So, we use the median of time cost to analyze the distribution trend of the results. As shown in Figure 11, when the number of points in a query is 3, the median time cost decreases as k increases. As k increases, the number of trajectories in the filter set increases, and the filtered transition increases. In the refining phase, the number of candidate transitions decreases, which leads to the reduction of time. As shown in Figure 12, when $k = 2$, the median of the time cost is increased as the number of points in a query increases. As the number of points in a query increases, the number of points in the trajectories in the filter set increases, which leads to the increased times of computing distance. It also results in the decrease of pruning space, which means the number of refined transitions increases. Both conditions cause the cost time to increase.

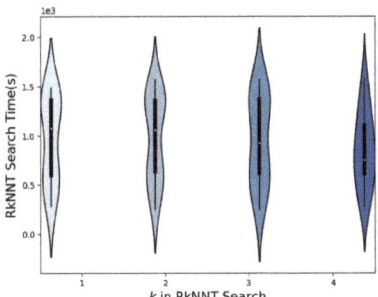

Figure 11. The effect of k in RkNNToE search ($N_P = 3$).

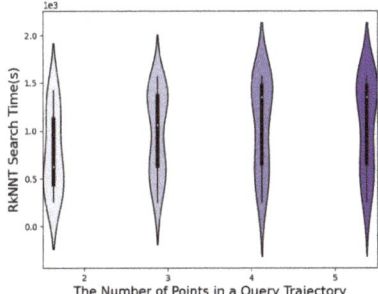

Figure 12. The effect of the number of points in query ($k = 2$).

7. Conclusions

In this paper, we studied a method of route planning on an encrypted trajectory database, RkNNToE, that securely returns all transitions, which are the reverse k nearest neighbor trajectories of the query trajectory. We designed a hybrid encrypted bloom filter tree (eRBFtree) for search in the encrypted trajectory database, which supports space pruning and fast kNN search. Combined with eRBFtree, we gave the pruning strategies to prune the transition as much as possible and to improve the search efficiency. The security analysis showed that the query, data and index are secure in the process of RkNNToE. The experiments showed that RkNNToE can find the results in the RkNNT search efficiently and correctly.

Author Contributions: Conceptualization, X.Z., H.Z. and Q.W.; methodology, X.Z.; software, X.Z.; validation, H.Z., X.Z. and K.L.; formal analysis, X.Z. and H.Z.; investigation, H.Z.; resources, X.Z.; writing—original draft preparation, X.Z.; writing—review and editing, H.Z.; visualization, X.Z. and K.L.; supervision, Q.W. and K.L.; project administration, H.Z.; funding acquisition, H.Z. All authors have read and agreed to the published version of the manuscript.

Funding: This work was supported by the National Natural Science Foundation of China (Grant Nos. 62072051, 61976024, 61972048, 62272056).

Data Availability Statement: GPS trajectory dataset (Transition dateset) collected in Geolife project in Beijing [22–24] and the bus lines dataset (Trajectory dataset) in Beijing [25].

Conflicts of Interest: The authors declare no conflict of interest.

References

1. Chen, Z.; Shen, H.T.; Zhou, X.; Zheng, Y.; Xie, X. Searching trajectories by locations: An efficiency study. In Proceedings of the ACM SIGMOD International Conference on Management of Data, Indianapolis, IN, USA, 6–10 June 2010; pp. 255–266. [CrossRef]
2. Keogh, E.J. Exact indexing of dynamic time warping. In Proceedings of the VLDB, Hong Kong, China, 20–23 August 2002; pp. 406–417.
3. Vlachos, M.; Gunopulos, D.; Kollios, G. Discovering similar mul- tidimensional trajectories. In Proceedings of the ICDE, San Jose, CA, USA, 26 February–1 March 2002; pp. 673–684.
4. Chen, L.; Özsu, M.T.; Oria, V. Robust and fast similarity search for moving object trajectories. In Proceedings of the SIGMOD, Baltimore, MD, USA, 14–16 June 2005; pp. 491–502.
5. Cheema, M.A.; Zhang, W.; Lin, X.; Zhang, Y.; Li, X. Continuous reverse k nearest neighbors queries in Euclidean space and in spatial networks. *VLDB J.* **2012**, *21*, 69–95. [CrossRef]
6. Emrich, T.; Kriegel, H.P.; Mamoulis, N.; Niedermayer, J.; Renz, M.; Zufle, A. Reverse-nearest neighbor queries on uncertain moving object trajectories. In *Database Systems for Advanced Applications*; Springer: Berlin/Heidelberg, Germany, 2014; pp. 92–107.
7. Feng, Z.; Zhu, Y. A Survey on Trajectory Data Mining: Techniques and Applications. *IEEE Access* **2017**, *4*, 2056–2067. [CrossRef]
8. Zheng, Y.; Lu, R.; Zhu, H.; Zhang, S.; Guan, Y.; Shao, J.; Wang, F.; Li, H. SetRkNN: Efficient and Privacy-Preserving Set Reverse kNN Query in Cloud. *IEEE Trans. Inf. Forensics Secur.* **2023**, *18*, 888–903. [CrossRef]
9. Wang, S.; Bao, Z.; Culpepper, J.S.; Sellis, T.; Cong, G. Reverse k nearest neighbor serach over trajectories. *IEEE Trans. Knowl. Data Eng.* **2018**, *30*, 757–771. [CrossRef]
10. Pan, X.; Nie, S.; Hu, H.; Yu, P.S.; Guo, J. Reverse Nearest Neighbor Search in Semantic Trajectories for Location-Based Services. *IEEE Trans. Serv. Comput.* **2022**, *15*, 986–999. [CrossRef]
11. Tzouramanis, T.; Manolopoulos, Y. Secure reverse k-nearest neighbors search over encrypted multi-dimensional databases. In Proceedings of the 22nd International Database Engineering & Applications Symposium (IDEAS), Villa San Giovanni, Italy, 18–20 June 2018; pp. 84–94.
12. Tao, Y.; Papadias, D.; Lian, X. Reverse kNN search in arbitrary dimensionality. In Proceedings of the 30th International Conference Very Large Data Bases, Toronto, ON, Canada, 31 August–3 September 2004; pp. 744–755.
13. Wu, W.; Yang, F.; Chan, C.-Y.; Tan, K.-L. FINCH: Evaluating reverse k-nearest-neighbor queries on location data. *Proc. Vldb Endow.* **2008**, *1*, 1056–1067. [CrossRef]
14. Lu, J.; Lu, Y.; Cong, G. Reverse spatial and textual k nearest neighbor search. In Proceedings of the ACM SIGMOD International Conference on Management Data, Athens, Greece, 12–16 June 2011; pp. 349–360.
15. Lu, Y.; Cong, G.; Lu, J.; Shahabi, C. Efficient algorithms for answering reverse spatialkeword nearest neighbor queries. In Proceedings of the 23rd SIGSPATIAL International Conference on Advances in Geographic Information Systems, Bellevue, WA, USA, 3–6 November 2015; pp. 1–4.
16. Pournajaf, L.; Tahmasebian, F.; Xiong, L.; Sunderam, V.; Shahabi, C. Privacy preserving reverse k-nearest neighbor queries. In Proceedings of the 19th IEEE International Conference Mobile Data Manage, (MDM), Aalborg, Denmark, 25–28 June 2018; pp. 177–186.
17. Li, X.; Xiang, T.; Guo, S.; Li, H.; Mu, Y. Privacy-preserving reverse nearest neighbor query over encrypted spatial data. *IEEE Trans. Serv. Comput.* **2022**, *15*, 2954–2968. [CrossRef]
18. Wang, Q.; He, M.; Du, M.; Chow, S.S.; Lai, R.W.; Zou, Q. Searchable encryption over feature-rich data. *IEEE Trans. Dependable Secur. Comput.* **2016**, *15*, 496–510. [CrossRef]
19. Lei, X.; Tu, G.H.; Xie, A.X.L.T. Fast and Secure kNN Query Processing in Cloud Computing. In Proceedings of the 2020 IEEE Conference on Communications and Network Security (CNS), Avignon, France, 29 June–1 July 2020.
20. Finkel, R.A.; Bentley, J.L. Quad trees a data structure for retrieval on composite keys. *Acta Inform.* **1974**, *4*, 1–9. [CrossRef]
21. Lindell, Y. How to simulate it—A tutorial on the simulation proof technique. In *Tutorials on the Foundations of Cryptography*; Springer: Berlin/Heidelberg, Germany, 2017; pp. 277–346.
22. Zheng, Y.; Zhang, L.; Xie, X.; Ma, W. Mining interesting locations and travel sequences from GPS trajectories. In Proceedings of the International conference on World Wild Web (WWW 2009), Madrid, Spain, 20–24 April 2009; ACM Press: New York, NY, USA, 2009; pp. 791–800.
23. Zheng, Y.; Li, Q.; Chen, Y.; Xie, X.; Ma, W. Understanding Mobility Based on GPS Data. In Proceedings of the ACM conference on Ubiquitous Computing (UbiComp 2008), Seoul, Republic of Korea, 21–24 September 2008; ACM Press: New York, NY, USA, 2008; pp. 312–321.

24. Zheng, Y.; Xie, X.; Ma, W. GeoLife: A Collaborative Social Networking Service among User, location and trajectory. *IEEE Data Eng. Bull.* **2010**, *33*, 32–40.
25. BeiJIngBusStation. Available online: https://github.com/FFGF/BeiJIngBusStation (accessed on 7 March 2023).

Disclaimer/Publisher's Note: The statements, opinions and data contained in all publications are solely those of the individual author(s) and contributor(s) and not of MDPI and/or the editor(s). MDPI and/or the editor(s) disclaim responsibility for any injury to people or property resulting from any ideas, methods, instructions or products referred to in the content.

Article

Cloud-Assisted Private Set Intersection via Multi-Key Fully Homomorphic Encryption

Cunqun Fan [1,2], Peiheng Jia [3], Manyun Lin [1,2], Lan Wei [1,2,*], Peng Guo [1,2], Xiangang Zhao [1,2] and Ximeng Liu [4]

[1] Key Laboratory of Radiometric Calibration and Validation for Environmental Satellites, National Satellite Meteorological Center (National Center for Space Weather), China Meteorological Administration, Beijing 100081, China
[2] Innovation Center for FengYun Meteorological Satellite (FYSIC), Beijing 100081, China
[3] School of Mathematics and Computer Science, Shanxi Normal University, Taiyuan 030031, China
[4] College of Computer and Data Science, Fuzhou University, Fuzhou 350108, China
* Correspondence: weilan@cma.cn

Abstract: With the development of cloud computing and big data, secure multi-party computation, which can collaborate with multiple parties to deal with a large number of transactions, plays an important role in protecting privacy. Private set intersection (PSI), a form of multi-party secure computation, is a formidable cryptographic technique that allows the sender and the receiver to calculate their intersection and not reveal any more information. As the data volume increases and more application scenarios emerge, PSI with multiple participants is increasingly needed. Homomorphic encryption is an encryption algorithm designed to perform a mathematical-style operation on encrypted data, where the decryption result of the operation is the same as the result calculated using unencrypted data. In this paper, we present a cloud-assisted multi-key PSI (CMPSI) system that uses fully homomorphic encryption over the torus (TFHE) encryption scheme to encrypt the data of the participants and that uses a cloud server to assist the computation. Specifically, we design some TFHE-based secure computation protocols and build a single cloud server-based private set intersection system that can support multiple users. Moreover, security analysis and performance evaluation show that our system is feasible. The scheme has a smaller communication overhead compared to existing schemes.

Keywords: private set intersection; homomorphic encryption; multi-key TFHE; cloud computing; privacy protection

MSC: 68U99; 68U99; 68T09; 68Q06

1. Introduction

With the rapid growth of data in the Internet era, the demand for data storage and computing capacity in various fields far exceeds the capacity of their own devices. To solve this problem, cloud computing has been proposed. Cloud computing is generally defined as an internet-based computing method. In this way, the shared software and hardware information and resources can be provided to various terminals and other devices of the computer as required. Cloud computing technology can transmit various information to the Internet and store and calculate data, and users can view the calculation results and data information. However, current security issues in the context of cloud computing are more prominent [1]. Data security issues in cloud computing mainly include storage data security, computing data security, and transmission data security. When users store data on the cloud server, the cloud server will obtain the users' data first, but the abnormal use of malicious users can also cause a risk of data leakage. In the process of cloud server computing, the cloud server will know the calculation results and additional data. This information that should only be known by users also has a risk of leakage. In addition,

Citation: Fan, C.; Jia, P.; Lin, M.; Wei, L.; Guo, P.; Zhao, X.; Liu, X. Cloud-Assisted Private Set Intersection via Multi-Key Fully Homomorphic Encryption. *Mathematics* 2023, 11, 1784. https://doi.org/10.3390/math11081784

Academic Editor: Antanas Cenys

Received: 21 March 2023
Revised: 4 April 2023
Accepted: 4 April 2023
Published: 8 April 2023

Copyright: © 2023 by the authors. Licensee MDPI, Basel, Switzerland. This article is an open access article distributed under the terms and conditions of the Creative Commons Attribution (CC BY) license (https://creativecommons.org/licenses/by/4.0/).

data theft can easily occur during data transmission, and user data can show problems of theft and tampering [2].

Private set intersection (PSI), as an interactive encryption protocol, calculates the intersection of two data owners' data and returns it to one of them. We generally refer to the party receiving the data as the receiver and the party receiving nothing as the sender. It is important and necessary to protect the privacy of the set in computing, especially when the information in the set is important private information such as the customer transaction information of a bank or the address book of a user. With the concerted efforts of many researchers, PSI technology has developed rapidly, and more and more efficient solutions have been proposed [3–15]. After several years of development, PSI technology has been applied to the fields of internet of vehicles [16], profile matching [17], and private contact search [18]. In the current situation where the data volume is large and scattered in the hands of different participants, PSI technology can well balance the relationship between privacy and information sharing. Leveraging the storage and computing power of cloud servers allows PSI protocols to compute larger datasets, but current cloud-assisted PSI schemes suffer from information leakage [19] or large communication overhead [20].

Fully homomorphic encryption (FHE) refers to the computation of data that has been homomorphically encrypted, and the computed decryption result is the same as that obtained by the same computation for unencrypted data. The concept of FHE has been proposed as early as the late 1970s, but it has only started to develop rapidly in the last two decades. The development of fully homomorphic encryption is generally divided into three stages. In 2009, the first generation of fully homomorphic encryption started to develop, and Gentry constructed the first fully homomorphic encryption scheme [21]. The scheme first constructs a somewhat homomorphic encryption (SHE) scheme that can homomorphically compute circuits of a certain depth, then compresses and decrypts the circuits and performs bootstrapping operations in an orderly manner, and finally obtains a scheme that can homomorphically compute arbitrary circuits. The second generation of fully homomorphic encryption schemes arose in 2011 when Brakerski and Vaikuntanathan implemented FHE for the first time under the LWE assumption using linearization and modulo conversion [22] and implemented FHE under the RLWE assumption [23]. These schemes do not require compression and decryption circuits, and the security and efficiency are greatly improved. In 2013, the third generation of fully homomorphic encryption schemes was born, and Gentry et al. for the first time designed a fully homomorphic encryption scheme, Gentry–Sahai–Waters (GSW), that does not require the computation of a key using the approximate eigenvector technique [24].

There are two broad categories of fully homomorphic algorithms, the BGV [25] scheme proposed by Professor Brakerski of Stanford University, Research Fellow Gentry of IBM, and Professor Vaikuntanathan of the University of Toronto, and the GSW [24] scheme proposed by Gentry of IBM, Sahai of the University of California and Waters of the University of Austin. Fully homomorphic encryption over toru (TFHE) [26] is an improvement of the GSW scheme with higher efficiency. TFHE can accomplish fast comparisons, supports arbitrary boolean circuits, and allows fast bootstrapping to reduce the noise due to ciphertext computation. In previous studies, the BGV scheme has been used to focus on the unbalanced privacy aggregation scenario [27–29]. Unlike previous works, this paper uses the TFHE encryption scheme for the first time to implement privacy-seeking protocol based on cloud computing. At a high level, our contributions can be summarized as follows:

- We have designed a series of security sub-protocols for the MKTFHE cryptosystem, including some basic circuit gate operations and security comparison protocols.
- We have built a cloud-assisted multi-key private set intersection (CMPSI) system based on a single cloud server. Our system can prevent collusion attacks between servers and participants.
- We strictly prove the security of the proposed CMPSI system under the semi-honest model.

- We have conducted extensive experimental evaluation on the performance of the scheme, which proves that our scheme has greatly reduced the communication cost of the participants.

The rest of the paper is organized as follows. In Section 2, we describe the related work of private set intersection. In Section 3, we provide the preliminaries. Section 4 details the system model, threat model, and design goals. Section 5 elaborates on the cryptographic protocol for the private set intersection. Section 6 analyzes the security of our proposed protocols. Section 7 conducts a series of experimental comparisons. Finally, Section 8 concludes this paper.

2. Related Work

PSI was first proposed by Freedman et al. [30], who transformed the element comparison problem into the polynomial root problem and realized PSI through multiplicative homomorphic encryption. However, when the polynomial order is large, it will lead to a costly exponential computation of the homomorphic encryption. In recent years, many researchers have intensively studied the PSI problem, and many PSI protocols with high efficiency and low communication overhead have emerged. PSI computing protocols are mainly divided into two categories according to whether there is a third party, namely, the traditional PSI computing protocol based on public key encryption, obfuscation circuit [31–33] and inadvertent transmission [34] technology and the cloud-assisted PSI computing protocol that uses cloud servers to complete computing.

Traditional PSI computing protocols rely on a series of basic cryptography technologies for computing. These basic cryptography technologies are mainly divided into PSI based on public key encryption mechanism, PSI based on obfuscation circuit, and PSI based on inadvertent transmission. The PSI calculation protocol proposed by Freedman et al. [34] is based on the public key encryption mechanism. This scheme represents the elements in the set as the roots of polynomials and uses polynomials to calculate the intersection. However, the cost of calculation will become large with the increase in the order of polynomials. Hazay et al. also improved the article [30] and adopted the bit commitment protocol to prevent the scenario of inconsistent input data on the server [35], so that the PSI protocol can be applied to the protocol of malicious adversaries. In 2012, Huang et al. first proposed PSI computing protocols based on obfuscated circuits [36], which are Bitwise-AND (BWA), Pairwise-Comparisons (PWC), and Sort-Compare-Suffle (SCS) protocols. In 2013, the PSI protocol proposed by Dong et al. [37] used OT technology for the first time. The author used OT technology to ensure the security of the protocol. Pinkas et al. [38] proposed a new PSI protocol based on Hash and random OT protocols and optimized the SCS protocol in [36]. The computational efficiency of the protocol was greatly improved, and the complexity of the algorithm was also reduced. Based on the article [34], Freedman et al. further optimized and improved their scheme in 2014 [39]. Specifically, the scheme uses different hash functions for the client and server when mapping the set elements. In 2018, Pinkas et al. realized PSI based on unintentional pseudorandom function [40] through the circuit. In 2020, Pinkas et al. [12] constructed a PSI protocol with malicious security based on the protocols [41] in the literature. The traditional PSI does not need the assistance of a third party, but in the application, the participants are generally resource-constrained users, who are insufficient in providing sufficient data storage and computing power.

With the development of cloud computing, the PSI protocol based on cloud servers began to develop. The cloud-assisted PSI scheme provides a new optimization method for the existing PSI scheme by the excellent storage and computing capabilities of the cloud server. The cloud-assisted PSI uses the third-party cloud computing framework to complete the calculation and uses the storage and computing resources of the cloud server to enable the protocol to calculate large-scale datasets. Kerschbaum [42] implemented the anti-collusion outsourcing PSI protocol through two single functions, but the method has the risk of brute force cracking. Then, Kerschbaum [43] proposed another kind of cloud-assisted PSI using bloom filter and homomorphic encryption. Liu et al. [19] proposed a relatively simple PSI protocol, but it can disclose the cardinality of set intersection. Abadi et al. [44] implemented the PSI protocol using homomorphic encryption and polynomial interpolation in 2015. This protocol outsources the collection of clients to a third-party server to perform infinite PSI operations. Based on this work, a verifiable cloud outsourcing PSI protocol [45] is proposed to ensure the privacy and integrity of data. Ali et al. [46] proposed an attribute-based private set intersection scheme. The cloud server can calculate the corresponding access rights of the participants. The PSI protocol based on the cloud server can use the computing and storage capabilities of the cloud server, but it has produced the privacy disclosure problem of data outsourcing, and the excessive cost of users in the operation of the protocol is another problem that needs to be solved. Table 1 shows the comparison between our scheme and the existing scheme.

Table 1. Comparison with existing schemes.

	CMPSI	[46]	[47]	[48]	[19]	[42]	[43]
The year	2023	2020	2019	2014	2014	2012	2012
Private against the CSP	52	52	52	52	56	52	52
PSI computation authorization	52	52	52	52	56	52	52
Supports multiple user queries	52	52	52	52	56	56	56
Participants can go offline after uploading data	52	52	56	56	56	56	56
CSP can collude with participants	52	56	56	56	56	56	56

3. Preliminaries

In this section, we first introduce the concept of private set intersection and have an example to better understand the concept. Then, we introduce the cryptosystem MKTFHE used in our system and present the algorithm as an example of a NAND gate. Table 2 lists some of the symbols used in this paper.

Table 2. Notation used.

Notations	Definition
λ	Security parameter
$\mathbb{Z}$	Integer set
$\mathbb{T}$	(R)LWE over the real torus
s_i	Private key of participant i
$(\mathbf{PK}_i, \mathbf{BK}_i, \mathbf{KS}_i)$	Public key set of participant i
$[\![x]\!]_{s_i}$	Encrypted data x under s_i
$\mathbf{MKHE}_{\mathbf{NAND}}$	NAND gate in multi-key TFHE
CMPSI	Cloud-assisted multi-party private set intersection

3.1. Private Set Intersection

PSI allows two parties holding sets to compare encrypted versions of these sets to compute the intersection. Let the two parties holding the sets be sender X and receiver Y. The sender and receiver hold datasets of size N_x and N_y respectively, each with a number of bits σ. In a basic PSI protocol, receiver Y encrypts its own dataset and sends it to sender X. For each of Y's data, sender X calculates the homomorphic product of the difference with all of its own terms and sends the result to receiver Y. Y decrypts the result of X's calculation and obtains the final intersection information. The result of the calculation is sent to the receiver Y. Y decrypts the result of X's computation and obtains the final intersection information. The basic PSI protocol is shown in Figure 1.

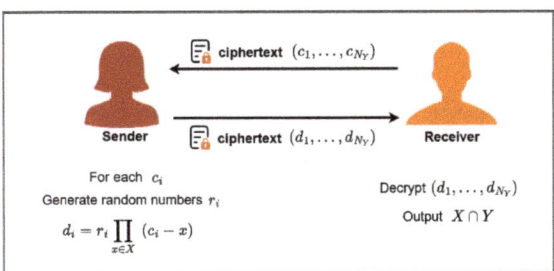

Figure 1. Basic PSI protocol.

In the scheme of this paper, the storage of data and the computation are performed on the cloud server. We construct a new PSI scheme using fully homomorphic encryption. Both the sender and the receiver encrypt the data locally and then send it to the cloud server. Suppose that the sender has encrypted data $a_1, \ldots, a_{N_X}$ and the receiver has encrypted data $b_1, \ldots, b_{N_Y}$. Both parties send their encrypted data to the cloud server. On the cloud server, for each data b_i of the receiver, $c_i = \prod_{0<j\leq N_X}(b_i - a_j)$ is computed. c_i is a Boolean value that represents whether the data b_i of the receiver are in the sender X or not. Figure 2 shows the handshake model of this scheme.

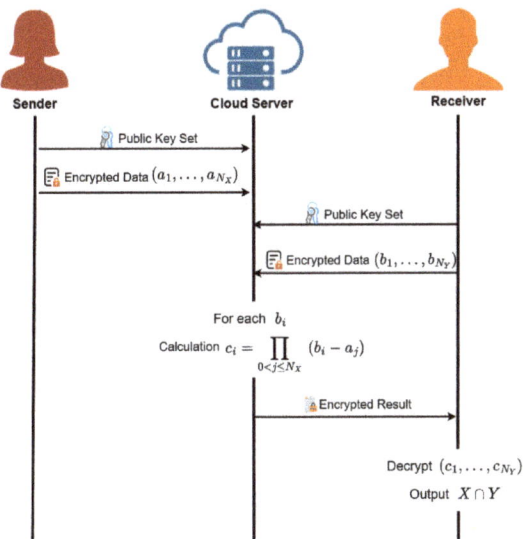

Figure 2. Handshake model.

3.2. MKTFHE Cryptosystem

Homomorphic encryption is the computation of the encrypted data to obtain the encrypted computational result, and the result of the decryption of the obtained encryption result is the same as the result obtained by performing the same operations on the unencrypted plaintext. Fully homomorphic encryption [24,25] is a homomorphic encryption that can satisfy both additive and multiplicative operations. Fully homomorphic encryption over the toru (TFHE) [26] is a type of fully homomorphic encryption that can accomplish fast comparisons and support operations on arbitrary Boolean circuits. TFHE differs from other FHE schemes in that it can be fast bootstrapping to reduce noise during ciphertext operations. In this paper, we use multi-key TFHE [49] to meet the needs of our system. MKTFHE is a multi-key version of TFHE that can compute Boolean circuits on ciphertexts encrypted under different keys, and then performs bootstrapped to refresh the noise as each binary gate is computed. However, the MKTFHE library only implements multi-key homomorphic NAND gates, which cannot meet the needs of our system. The following describes the five components of MKTFHE and gives an example of the homomorphic computation process with a multi-key homomorphic NAND gate.

1. **Setup**(1^λ): Takes as input the security parameter λ and returns the public parameter pp^{MKTFHE}.

    (a) Run **LWE.Setup**(1^λ) to generate the LWE parameter $pp^{LWE} = (n, \chi, \alpha, B', d')$. In the LWE parameters, n is the dimension of the LWE secret, χ is the key distribution of the LWE secret, α is the error rate, B' is the decomposition basis, and d' is the dimension of the key transformation gadget vector. We use the key-switching gadget vector $g' = \left(B'^{-1}, \ldots, B'^{-d'}\right)$.

    (b) Run **RLWE.Setup**(1^λ) to generate the RLWE parameter $pp^{RLWE} = (N, \psi, B, d, \mathbf{a})$. We define N as the dimension of RLWE secret (a power of 2), ψ as the distribution of RLWE secret over R and with error rate α, $B \geq 2$ as an integer base, decomposition dimension d, and gadget vector $g = \left(B^{-1}, \ldots, B^{-d}\right)$. $\mathbf{a}$ is a uniformly distributed sample over distribution T^d.

    (c) Returns the generated public parameter $pp^{MKTFHE} = \left(pp^{LWE}, pp^{RLWE}\right)$.

2. **KeyGen**(pp^{MKTFHE}): Each participant generates its keys independently. Take the public parameter pp^{MKTFHE} as input and return the key s_i and the public key set (PK_i, BK_i, KS_i).

    (a) Generate the LWE secret $s_i \leftarrow$ **LWE.KeyGen**(). This step is only for sampling the key from distribution χ.

    (b) Run $(z_i, b_i) \leftarrow$ **RLWE.KeyGen**(), and set the public key to $PK_i = b_i$. Sample z from distribution ψ, and then, set $\mathbf{z} = (1, z)$. Take an error vector $\mathbf{e}$ from D_α^d and calculate the public key $\mathbf{b} = -z \cdot \mathbf{a} + \mathbf{e} \pmod 1$. For $z_i = z_{i,0} + z_{i,1}X + \ldots + z_{i,N-1}X^{N-1}$, note $\mathbf{z}_i^* = (z_{i,0}, -z_{i,N-1}, \ldots, z_{i,1}) \in \mathbb{Z}^N$.

    (c) For $j \in [n]$, generate $(\mathbf{d}_{i,j}, \mathbf{F}_{i,j}) \leftarrow$ **RLWE.UniEnc**($s_{i,j}, z_i$), this step is to encrypt the LWE secret using the RLWE secret. In addition, set the bootstrap key to $BK_i = \{(\mathbf{d}_{i,j}, \mathbf{F}_{i,j})\}_{j \in [n]}$. Taking a random value r from ψ, one can think of $\mathbf{d}$ as the LWE key s under the encryption of the random value r and $\mathbf{F}$ as the random value r under the encryption of the RLWE key z.

    (d) Generate a key conversion key $KS \leftarrow$ **LWE.KSGen**(z_i^*, s_i), capable of converting an LWE ciphertext corresponding to $\mathbf{t} \in \mathbb{Z}^N$ into another LWE ciphertext for the same message under $\mathbf{s} \in \mathbb{Z}^N$ encryption.

    (e) Returns key s_i, a triple (PK_i, BK_i, KS_i) of public keys, public key, bootstrap key and key transformation key, respectively.

3. **Enc**(m): The data m to be encrypted are taken as input, and return TLWE ciphertext $[\![m]\!] = (b, \mathbf{a}) \in \mathbb{T}^{n+1}$ satisfies $b + \langle \mathbf{a}, \mathbf{s} \rangle \approx \frac{1}{4}m \pmod 1$.

    (a) Using standard LWE encryption, uniformly sample from $\mathbb{T}^n$ to obtain $\mathbf{a}$ as the mask and sample from D_α to obtain e as the error.

    (b) Output ciphertext $[\![m]\!] = (b, \mathbf{a}) \in \mathbb{T}^{n+1}$, where $b + \langle \mathbf{a}, \mathbf{s} \rangle \approx \frac{1}{4}m \pmod 1$.

4. **Dec**($[\![m]\!], \{s_i\}_{i \in [k]}$): Takes as input the TLWE ciphertext $[\![m]\!] = (b, \mathbf{a}_1, \ldots, \mathbf{a}_k) \in \mathbb{T}^{kn+1}$ with a set of keys ($s_1, \ldots, s_k$) and returns the decrypted message m which minimizes $|b + \sum_{i=1}^k \langle \mathbf{a}_i, \mathbf{s}_i \rangle - \frac{1}{4}m|$.

    (a) Input $[\![m]\!] = (b, \mathbf{a}_1, \ldots, \mathbf{a}_k) \in \mathbb{T}^{kn+1}$ with a set of keys ($s_1, \ldots, s_k$).

    (b) Returns the bit $m \in \{0, 1\}$ that minimizes $|b + \sum_{i=1}^k \langle \mathbf{a}_i, \mathbf{s}_i \rangle - \frac{1}{4}m|$.

5. **NAND**($[\![m_1]\!], [\![m_2]\!], \{(PK_i, BK_i, KS_i)\}_{i \in [k]}$): Takes two TLWE ciphertexts and the public key as input. Expand $[\![m_1]\!] \in \mathbb{T}^{k_1 n + 1}$ and $[\![m_2]\!] \in \mathbb{T}^{k_1 n + 1}$ to $[\![m_1']\!], [\![m_2']\!] \in \mathbb{T}^{kn+1}$ and evaluate the gate homomorphically on encrypted bits. Then the algorithm evalu-

ates the decryption circuit of the TLWE ciphertext and execute the multi-key switching algorithm. Finally, returning the TLWE ciphertext of the same message under joint key encryption.

(a) Given two ciphertexts $[\![m_1]\!] \in \mathbb{T}^{k_1 n+1}$ and $[\![m_2]\!] \in \mathbb{T}^{k_1 n+1}$, let k be the number of participants, associated with either $[\![m_1]\!]$ or $[\![m_2]\!]$. For a public key set, $\mathbf{PK}_i = \mathbf{b}_i$ represents the public key, $\mathbf{BK}_i = \{(\mathbf{d}_{i,j}, \mathbf{F}_{i,j})\}_{j \in [n]}$ represents the bootstrap key, and $\mathbf{KS}_i$ represents the key transformation key of the j-th participant. Expand ciphertext $[\![m_1]\!]$ and $[\![m_2]\!]$ to $[\![m_1]\!]'$, $[\![m_2]\!]' \in \mathbb{T}^{kn+1}$, i.e., the same message under joint key $\bar{\mathbf{s}} = (\mathbf{s}_1, \ldots, \mathbf{s}_k) \in \mathbb{Z}^{kn}$ encryption. The process of expansion is the process of rearrangement, and 0 is put into the empty slot. Using the expanded ciphertext to perform the calculations. Only the calculation of NAND gate is supported in the document.

(b) Use the Mux gate to implement the main calculation, for $i \in [k]$, let $\tilde{\mathbf{a}}_i = (\tilde{a}_{i,j})_{j \in [n]}$. For $i \in [k]$ and $j \in [n]$, recursively compute
$$[\![c]\!] \leftarrow [\![c]\!] + \mathbf{RLWE.Prod}\Big([\![c]\!] \cdot X^{\tilde{a}_{ij}} - [\![c]\!], (\mathbf{d}_{i,j}, \mathbf{F}_{i,j}), \{\mathbf{b}_l\}_{l \in [k]}\Big),$$
where $\mathbf{RLWE.Prod}\Big([\![c]\!], (\mathbf{d}_i, \mathbf{F}_i), \{\mathbf{b}_j\}_{j \in [k]}\Big)$ is a hybrid product algorithm that multiplies a single encrypted ciphertext $(\mathbf{d}_i, \mathbf{F}_i)$ by a multi-key RLWE ciphertext $[\![c]\!]$.

(c) For $[\![c]\!] = (c_0, c_1, \ldots, c_k) \in \mathbb{T}^{k+1}$, let b^* be a constant term of c_0 and for $i \in [k]$, let $\mathbf{a}_i^*$ be a vector of coefficients of c_i. Compute the LWE ciphertext $[\![m]\!]^* = (b^*, \mathbf{a}_1^*, \ldots, \mathbf{a}_k^*) \in \mathbb{T}^{kn+1}$. Finally a multi-key key conversion algorithm is executed and returns the ciphertext $[\![m]\!]'' \leftarrow \mathbf{LWE.MKSwitch}\Big([\![m]\!]^*, \{\mathbf{KS}_i\}_{i \in [k]}\Big)$, where $\mathbf{LWE.MKSwitch}\Big([\![m]\!]^*, \{\mathbf{KS}_i\}_{i \in [k]}\Big)$ inputs the expanded ciphertext and a series of key conversion keys, returning the ciphertext of the same message under joint key encryption.

4. System Model and Design Goal

4.1. Problem Formulation

Suppose the receiver Y has a dataset T_Y, and Y wants to know their intersection with other data owners but does not want to expose more information. The data owners encrypt their datasets separately and send them to the cloud server. The cloud server can store this encrypted information but cannot decrypt it. Data receiver Y encrypts its data and uploads it to the cloud server, which executes privacy intersection and obtains the intersection information of dataset T_Y with other datasets. The cloud server computes and returns the cryptographic result to receiver Y. Y decrypts the intersection result and obtains the intersection information. Note that each data owner including the data receiver has their separate key to encrypt the data.

4.2. System Model

In Section 3.1, we mention the flow of the basic PSI protocol, in which the sender interacts directly with the receiver for information. Unlike the basic PSI protocol, our system consists of four entities, which are Parameter Generation Center (PGC), Cloud Server (CS), Data Receiver (DR), and Data Owners (DOs). DO owns its own dataset and is able to let other participants obtain information about the intersection of the dataset but does not want to expose more information. DR wants to query the intersection of its own dataset with the dataset of other participants and does not want to expose more information. Specifically, PGC is responsible for generating public parameters in the system and sending them to other entities. CS can store a large amount of data and has excellent computing resources. DR needs to query the intersection. DOs provide their encrypted data to CS. Note that in our system, the data owners can be multiple participants. The general model of our private set intersection system is shown in Figure 3.

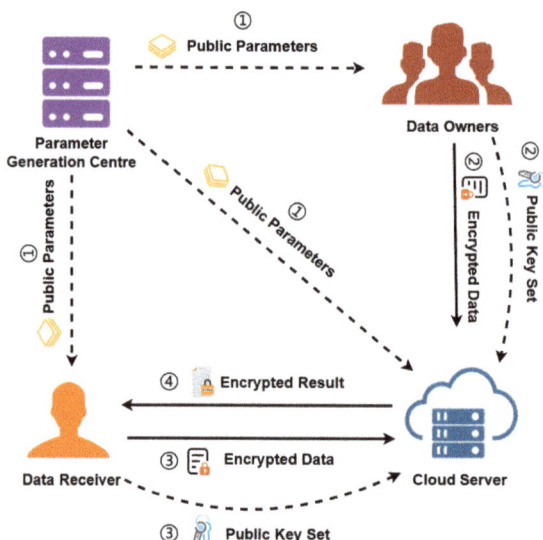

Figure 3. System model.

1. PGC: PGC generates public parameters for our system and sends them to each entity involved in the computation (See ①).
2. CS: CS has huge storage resources to store the encrypted data of the participating parties. At the same time, CS has large enough computing power to satisfy the intersection of the datasets of the participating parties.
3. DR: DR generates its own private key and public key set using public parameters, encrypts its own data using the private key and sends it to CS (See ③), and receives the computation results sent by CS (See ④).
4. DOs: Each DO generates its own private key and public key set using public parameters, encrypts its own dataset using the private key, and sends it to CS (See ②).

Please note that in our system, the participants do not need to be online all the time. Since CS can store the encrypted data, the DOs can go offline after they send their encrypted data to CS. Similarly, DR can be offline after sending data until CS returns the calculation results. In our scheme, DO can be used as DR for frequent item set queries, and the DR can query the intersection information with multiple DOs to achieve multi-user query.

4.3. Threat Model

In our system model, the participating entities are curious but honest individuals. Curious means that the server and the participants try to use existing resources and data to obtain the data of other participants and are curious about the data of other entities; honest means that the server and the participants do not falsify the experimental data and follow the developed protocols to complete the computation. $\mathcal{A}$ is the active adversary we introduce to obtain the real data from other entities. Specifically, $\mathcal{A}$ desires to obtain the real data of DOs and DR. We assume that adversary $\mathcal{A}$ has the following capabilities.

1. $\mathcal{A}$ can obtain all the data that passes through the public channel.
2. $\mathcal{A}$ may collude with CS. Try to obtain the original values of the encrypted data uploaded by DOs and DR.
3. $\mathcal{A}$ may be a DR used to obtain its dataset information, the cryptographic query results returned by the CS, and the encryption and decryption capabilities of the DR.
4. $\mathcal{A}$ may be a DO used to obtain its dataset information and encryption and decryption capabilities.

Note that in our threat model, the attacking adversary $\mathcal{A}$ can be a DR. Since the joint key of multiple participants must be used in decryption to decrypt the computed result of CS, the final decryption result is also not available when $\mathcal{A}$ has only the key of DR. Unlike existing schemes when the attacking adversary $\mathcal{A}$ is a CSP, $\mathcal{A}$ can collude with DR or DO. In our scheme, decryption requires the keys of all participants to perform; thus, CSP colluding with some DR or DO still cannot decrypt the computation results.

4.4. Design Goal

According to the system model and threat model proposed above, the design objectives of this paper are as follows.

1. Data privacy: the original data of DR and the query intersection result as well as the original dataset of DOs cannot be revealed to adversary $\mathcal{A}$.
2. Calculation accuracy: The accuracy of the calculation results of the system cannot be reduced compared with other methods.
3. Low overhead: The time and upload overhead of the calculation cannot be too large compared with other methods.
4. Offline participant: The participant should be able to go offline after encrypting the data and uploading it to ensure the scalability of the system.

5. Cloud-Assisted Multi-Party Private Set Intersection

In this section, we first introduce the initialization of the system. Then, we design the secure computing sub-protocol based on MKTFHE. Finally, we describe our private set intersection scheme.

5.1. System Initialization

Our system can satisfy the DR to query the information of its intersection with multiple participants, and we assume that there is a DR and n DOs. First, PGC generates public parameters for each participant and the cloud server and sends the public parameters to CS, DR, and n DOs. Then, each entity that receives the public parameters generates its own public key set (**PK**, **BK**, **KS**) and private key s based on the public parameters.

5.2. Security Protocol Design

In this paper, four secure computation protocols are proposed to help complete the privacy-seeking intersection, which is a secure AND gate computation protocol (**SC$_{AND}$**), secure OR gate computation protocol (**SC$_{OR}$**), secure XNOR computation protocol (**SC$_{XNOR}$**), and secure comparison protocol (**SCP**).

5.2.1. Secure AND Gate Computation Protocol

We implement the AND operation between two MKLwe samples. We implement the addition between multi-key Lwe samples (**MKlweAddTo**) to implement this secure computation protocol. Suppose CS has two MKLwe samples ca and cb: initialize an intermediate sample $temp$, add ca and cb using **MKlweAddTo** twice, and finally return the result to res (Algorithm 1).

Algorithm 1 Secure AND gate computation protocol (**SC$_{AND}$**).

Input: MKLwe Sample ca, cb.
Output: MKLwe Sample res.
1: CS initializes $temp$ using the public parameter **pp** to hold the intermediate variable LWE sample.
2: $AndConst = modSwitchToTorus32(-1,8)$
3: $temp \leftarrow$ **MKlweNoiselessTrivial**($AndConst$, **pp**)
4: $temp \leftarrow$ **MKlweAddTo**($temp + ca$)
5: $res \leftarrow$ **MKlweAddTo**($temp + cb$)

5.2.2. Secure OR Gate Computation Protocol

We implement the OR operation between two MKLwe samples. As with **SC$_{AND}$** above, we use the addition **MKlweAddTo** between multi-key Lwe samples to implement this secure computation protocol. Suppose CS has two MKLwe samples ca and cb, initialize an intermediate sample $temp$, add ca and cb using **MKlweAddTo** twice respectively, and finally, return the result to res to obtain the result of the OR gate operation between ca and cb (Algorithm 2).

Algorithm 2 Secure OR gate computation protocol (**SC$_{OR}$**).

Input: MKLwe Sample ca, cb.
Output: MKLwe Sample res.
1: CS initializes $temp$ using the public parameter **pp** to hold the intermediate variable LWE sample.
2: $ORConst = modSwitchToTorus32(1, 8)$
3: $temp \leftarrow$ **MKlweNoiselessTrivial**$(ORConst, \mathbf{pp})$
4: $temp \leftarrow$ **MKlweAddTo**$(temp + ca)$
5: $res \leftarrow$ **MKlweAddTo**$(temp + cb)$

5.2.3. Secure XNOR Gate Computation Protocol

We implement the XNOR operation between two MKLwe samples. We implement this secure computation protocol using the addition and multiplication of multi-key Lwe samples **MKlweAddMulTo**. Suppose CS has two MKLwe samples ca and cb: initialize an intermediate sample $temp$, add $2 * ca$ and $2 * cb$ using **MKlweAddMulTo** twice, return the result to $temp$ to obtain the XOR gate operation result of ca and cb, and use the multi-key homomorphic NOT gate **SC$_{NOT}$** once to obtain the XNOR gate operation result. Note that in the cryptographic scheme we use, MKTFHE, the computation of the NOT gate does not require bootstrapping operations; thus, the computation overhead is very small (Algorithm 3).

Algorithm 3 Secure XNOR gate computation protocol (**SC$_{XNOR}$**).

Input: MKLwe Sample ca, cb.
Output: MKLwe Sample res.
1: CS initializes $temp$ using the public parameter **pp** to hold the intermediate variable LWE sample.
2: $XNORConst = modSwitchToTorus32(1, 8)$
3: $temp \leftarrow$ **MKlweNoiselessTrivial**$(XNORConst, \mathbf{pp})$
4: $temp \leftarrow$ **MKlweAddMulTo**$(temp + 2 * ca)$
5: $temp \leftarrow$ **MKlweAddMulTo**$(temp + 2 * cb)$
6: $res \leftarrow$ **SC$_{NOT}$**$(temp)$

5.2.4. Secure Comparison Protocol

SCP is important in our protocol and is used to determine whether the two input ciphertext vectors are equal or not. Suppose DR has its own encrypted data $[\![\mathbf{x}]\!]_{s_{DR}} = ([\![x_1]\!]_{s_{DR}}, \ldots, [\![x_n]\!]_{s_{DR}})$ sent to CS and DO has its own encrypted data $[\![\mathbf{y}]\!]_{s_{DO}} = ([\![y_1]\!]_{s_{DO}}, \ldots, [\![y_n]\!]_{s_{DO}})$ also sent to CS, where s_{DR} and s_{DO} are the private keys of DR and DO, respectively. For each of $[\![\mathbf{x}]\!]_{s_{DR}} = ([\![x_1]\!]_{s_{DR}}, \ldots, [\![x_n]\!]_{s_{DR}})$ and $[\![\mathbf{y}]\!]_{s_{DO}} = ([\![y_1]\!]_{s_{DO}}, \ldots, [\![y_n]\!]_{s_{DO}})$, the protocol performs **SC$_{XNOR}$** and **SC$_{AND}$** protocols to finally obtain a ciphertext with a Boolean value (Algorithm 4).

Algorithm 4 Secure Comparison Protocol (SCP).

Input: Encrypted data vectors $[\![\mathbf{x}]\!]_{s_{DR}} = ([\![x_1]\!]_{s_{DR}}, \ldots, [\![x_n]\!]_{s_{DR}}), [\![\mathbf{y}]\!]_{s_{DO}} = ([\![y_1]\!]_{s_{DO}}, \ldots, [\![y_n]\!]_{s_{DO}})$.
Output: Encrypted Boolean values $[\![z]\!]_{s_i}$.
1: CS initializes the intermediate data vector $[\![\mathbf{v}]\!] = ([\![v_1]\!], \ldots, [\![v_n]\!])$ using the public parameter **pp**.
2: **for** $k = 0$ to $n - 1$ **do**
3: $\quad [\![v_k]\!]_{s_i} \leftarrow [\![x_k]\!]_{s_{DR}} \text{XNOR} [\![y_k]\!]_{s_{DO}}$
4: $\quad [\![z]\!]_{s_i} \leftarrow [\![v_k]\!]_{s_i} \text{AND} [\![z]\!]_{s_i}$
5: **end for**

5.3. Private Set Intersection

CMPSI is performed by CS, DR, and DOs working together. Now DR wants to obtain the intersection information of their dataset and DOs dataset. First DOs encrypt their dataset with their own private key s_{DO}, send the encrypted dataset $A_{DO} = \{[\![\mathbf{a_1}]\!]_{s_{DO}}, [\![\mathbf{a_2}]\!]_{s_{DO}}, \ldots, [\![\mathbf{a_m}]\!]_{s_{DO}}\}$ with the public key set ($\mathbf{PK}_{s_{DO}}, \mathbf{BK}_{s_{DO}}, \mathbf{KS}_{s_{DO}}$) to CS, and then they can go offline. DR encrypts the dataset with its own private key s_{DR} and then sends the encrypted dataset $B_{DR} = \{[\![\mathbf{b_1}]\!]_{s_{DR}}, [\![\mathbf{b_2}]\!]_{s_{DR}}, \ldots, [\![\mathbf{a_n}]\!]_{s_{DR}}\}$ with its public key set ($\mathbf{PK}_{s_{DR}}, \mathbf{BK}_{s_{DR}}, \mathbf{KS}_{s_{DR}}$) to CS, and then, it can be offline until CS completes the calculation. CS receives the encrypted dataset sent by DOs and DR, saves the data, and performs the secure computation in a secure environment. Finally, DR receives the encryption result calculated by CS and decrypts it using the joint key to obtain the intersection. Let there be m items in the encrypted dataset $A_{DO} = \{[\![\mathbf{a_1}]\!]_{s_{DO}}, [\![\mathbf{a_2}]\!]_{s_{DO}}, \ldots, [\![\mathbf{a_m}]\!]_{s_{DO}}\}$ of DOs with k Boolean values in each item, and n items in the encrypted dataset $B_{DR} = \{[\![\mathbf{b_1}]\!]_{s_{DR}}, [\![\mathbf{b_2}]\!]_{s_{DR}}, \ldots, [\![\mathbf{b_n}]\!]_{s_{DR}}\}$ of DR with k Boolean values in each item.

S1(DOs): Each DO encrypts its dataset using its own key s_{DO} generated by the public parameter **pp** issued by PGC and sends it to CS. CS stores the encrypted dataset of all DOs, and for item i of dataset $A_{DO} = \{[\![\mathbf{a_1}]\!]_{s_{DO}}, [\![\mathbf{a_2}]\!]_{s_{DO}}, \ldots, [\![\mathbf{a_m}]\!]_{s_{DO}}\}$, we have $[\![\mathbf{a_i}]\!]_{s_{DO}} = ([\![a_1]\!]_{s_{DO}}, \ldots, [\![a_k]\!]_{s_{DO}})$.

S2(DR): DR uses the public parameter **pp** to generate its own key s_{DR} to encrypt its dataset and sends it to CS. CS uses DR's encrypted database for secure computation and has $[\![\mathbf{b_j}]\!]_{s_{DR}} = ([\![b_1]\!]_{s_{DR}}, \ldots, [\![b_k]\!]_{s_{DR}})$ for item j of dataset $B_{DR} = \{[\![\mathbf{b_1}]\!]_{s_{DR}}, [\![\mathbf{b_2}]\!]_{s_{DR}}, \ldots, [\![\mathbf{b_n}]\!]_{s_{DR}}\}$.

S3(CS): CS receives the encrypted data message $B_{DR} = \{[\![\mathbf{b_1}]\!]_{s_{DR}}, [\![\mathbf{b_2}]\!]_{s_{DR}}, \ldots, [\![\mathbf{b_n}]\!]_{s_{DR}}\}$ from DR and the encrypted data message $A_{DO} = \{[\![\mathbf{a_1}]\!]_{s_{DO}}, [\![\mathbf{a_2}]\!]_{s_{DO}}, \ldots, [\![\mathbf{a_m}]\!]_{s_{DO}}\}$ from DO. For $j \in \{1, 2, \ldots, n\}$ and $i \in \{1, 2, \ldots, m\}$, each item $[\![\mathbf{b_j}]\!]_{s_{DR}} = ([\![b_1]\!]_{s_{DR}}, \ldots, [\![b_k]\!]_{s_{DR}})$ in $B_{DR} = \{[\![\mathbf{b_1}]\!]_{s_{DR}}, [\![\mathbf{b_2}]\!]_{s_{DR}}, \ldots, [\![\mathbf{b_n}]\!]_{s_{DR}}\}$ performs SCP with each item $[\![\mathbf{a_i}]\!]_{s_{DO}} = ([\![a_1]\!]_{s_{DO}}, \ldots, [\![a_k]\!]_{s_{DO}})$ in $A_{DO} = \{[\![\mathbf{a_1}]\!]_{s_{DO}}, [\![\mathbf{a_2}]\!]_{s_{DO}}, \ldots, [\![\mathbf{a_m}]\!]_{s_{DO}}\}$, i.e., $\mathbf{SCP}([\![\mathbf{a_i}]\!]_{s_{DO}}, [\![\mathbf{b_j}]\!]_{s_{DR}})$. The result $[\![\mathbf{g_i}]\!]_s = ([\![g_1]\!]_s, \ldots, [\![g_k]\!]_s)$ is obtained as the result of whether the current $[\![\mathbf{b_j}]\!]_{s_{DR}} = ([\![b_1]\!]_{s_{DR}}, \ldots, [\![b_k]\!]_{s_{DR}})$ is the same as each item in $A_{DO} = \{[\![\mathbf{a_1}]\!]_{s_{DO}}, [\![\mathbf{a_2}]\!]_{s_{DO}}, \ldots, [\![\mathbf{a_m}]\!]_{s_{DO}}\}$.

S4(CS): For each computed $[\![\mathbf{g_i}]\!]_s = ([\![g_1]\!]_s, \ldots, [\![g_k]\!]_s)$, CS runs $\mathbf{SC_{OR}}$ to obtain $[\![c_j]\!]_s = ([\![c_1]\!]_s, \ldots, [\![c_k]\!]_s)$. $[\![\mathbf{c_j}]\!]_s = ([\![c_1]\!]_s, \ldots, [\![c_k]\!]_s)$ is a cryptographic Boolean value indicating whether each item in $B_{DR} = \{[\![\mathbf{b_1}]\!]_{s_{DR}}, [\![\mathbf{b_2}]\!]_{s_{DR}}, \ldots, [\![\mathbf{b_n}]\!]_{s_{DR}}\}$ exists in $A_{DO} = \{[\![\mathbf{a_1}]\!]_{s_{DO}}, [\![\mathbf{a_2}]\!]_{s_{DO}}, \ldots, [\![\mathbf{a_m}]\!]_{s_{DO}}\}$. A value of 1 means it exists and 0 means it does not.

S5 (CS): For $j \in \{1, 2, \ldots, n\}$, execute S4, and send the calculated result $C = \{[\![c_1]\!]_s, [\![c_2]\!]_s, \ldots, [\![c_n]\!]_s\}$ to DR.

S6 (DR): Receive the calculation result from $C = \{[\![c_1]\!]_s, [\![c_2]\!]_s, \ldots, [\![c_n]\!]_s\}$ sent by CS and decrypt it using the joint key to obtain the result.

Please note that in our PSI scheme, the dense state computation is performed by FHE cryptography. All the calculations are performed on the cloud server, and the data on the cloud server are all cryptographic data, so that the privacy of the participants is protected. During the calculation process, the DR does not obtain any information other than its own information and the query result. The DOs do not obtain any information other than their own information and do not expose their information to other participants. The result of the CS calculation is in cryptographic form and cannot be decrypted by the participants except by the DR, which protects the privacy of the calculation result.

6. Security Analysis

In this section, we prove that our scheme is secure under a semi-honest model. We will prove the security of the MKTFHE cryptosystem, SC_{AND}, SC_{OR}, SC_{XOR}, SCP and PSI schemes separately. We first present the security of the semi-honest model below.

Definition 1 (Security of the semi-honest model). *According to protocol π, let a_i be the input of participant P_i and b_i be the output of P_i. $REAL_i^\Pi(\pi)$ is the viewpoint of P_i when protocol π is actually executed. $IDEAL_i^\Pi(\pi)$ is the viewpoint of P_i, simulated by a_i and b_i, executed in the ideal world of protocol π. If $REAL_i^\Pi(\pi)$ is computationally indistinguishable from $IDEAL_i^\Pi(\pi)$, then protocol π is secure in the semi-fair model [50].*

Note that in our protocols, the execution image usually consists of the exchanged data and the information that can be computed from these data. It follows from Definition (1) that when proving the security of these protocols, the image we simulate should be indistinguishable from the actual execution image when we compute it.

6.1. Security of MKTFHE Cryptosystem

Privacy of LWE Assumption: The j-th component K_j of a key-switching key $KS = \{K_j\}_{j \in [N]}$ from $t \in \mathbb{Z}^N$ to $s \in \mathbb{Z}^N$ is generated by adding $t_j \cdot g'$ to the first column of the $\mathbb{T}^{d' \times (n+1)}$ matrix, the rows of which are instances of LWE under the secret s. Therefore, $KS \leftarrow LWE.KSGen(t, s)$ is computationally indistinguishable from a uniform distribution over $(\mathbb{T}^{d' \times (n+1)})^N$ where LWE assumes a parameter of (n, χ, β) and s is sampled according to χ.

Privacy of RLWE Assumption: Under the assumption that the parameter is (N, ψ, α), a uniform distribution over $T^{d \times 5}$ is computationally indistinguishable from the distribution $\mathcal{D}_0 = \{(a, b, d, F) : pp^{RLWE} \leftarrow RLWE \cdot Setup(1^\lambda), (z, b) \leftarrow RLWE.KeyGen(), (d, F) \leftarrow RLWE \cdot UniEnc(\mu, z)\}$ for any $\mu \in R$. We consider the following distribution: First, we transform $F = [f_0 \mid f_1]$ and (b, a) into independent uniform distributions of $T^{d \times 2}$ using the RLWE assumption of a secret z. Therefore, $\mathcal{D}_0$ is indistinguishable from $\mathcal{D}_1$ in terms of calculation. $\mathcal{D}_1 = \{(a, b, d, F) : a, b \leftarrow U(T^d),$ $F \leftarrow U(T^{d \times 2}), r \leftarrow \psi, e_1 \leftarrow D_\alpha^d, d = r \cdot a + \mu \cdot g + e_1 \pmod{1}\}$. Then, d is made uniformly distributed using the RLWE assumption with a secret of r. Therefore, $\mathcal{D}_1$ is indistinguishable from the distribution $\mathcal{D}_2$. $\mathcal{D}_2 = \{(a, b, d, F) : a, b, d \leftarrow U(T^d), F \leftarrow U(T^{d \times 2})\}$. Since $\mathcal{D}_2$ is independent from μ, our RLWE scheme is semantically private.

In summary, under the (R)LWE assumption, our cryptosystem is semantically private; thus, we can appropriately choose parameters pp^{LWE} and pp^{RLWE} to achieve a security level of at least λ-bit.

6.2. Security of Secure Computing Protocols

In this section, we demonstrate the security of our secure computing subprotocols, including SC_{AND}, SC_{OR}, SC_{XOR} and SCP.

Theorem 1. *The SC_{AND} proposed is secure under the semi-honest model.*

Proof of Theorem 1. We use $REAL^{\Pi}_{CS}(SC_{AND})$ to denote the execution view in the real world of the of CS, where it is specified as $REAL^{\Pi}_{CS}(SC_{AND}) = \{[\![ca]\!], [\![cb]\!], [\![AndConst]\!], [\![temp]\!], [\![res]\!]\}$. $[\![AndConst]\!]$ is obtained from $[\![-1]\!]$ and $[\![8]\!]$ by $modSwitchToTorus32$. $[\![temp]\!]$ is obtained from $[\![AndConst]\!]$ and $[\![ca]\!]$ by **MKlweAddTo** and **MKlweNoiselessTrival**. We assume that $IDEAL^{\Pi}_{CS}(SC_{AND}) = \{[\![ca']\!], [\![cb']\!], [\![temp']\!], [\![res']\!], [\![AndConst']\!]\}$ is the execution view of the simulation in the ideal world, where $[\![ca']\!], [\![cb']\!], [\![temp']\!], [\![res']\!]$ and $[\![AndConst']\!]$ are chosen randomly from $\mathbb{T}^{n+1}$. The semantic privacy of our encryption scheme makes $[\![ca]\!], [\![cb]\!], [\![temp]\!]$ and $[\![AndConst]\!]$ computationally indistinguishable from $[\![ca']\!], [\![cb']\!], [\![temp']\!]$ and $[\![AndConst']\!]$ respectively. In addition, $[\![res]\!]$ is computationally indistinguishable from $[\![temp']\!]$ and $[\![AndConst']\!]$ respectively. Thus, it can be concluded that $REAL^{\Pi}_{CS}(SC_{AND})$ and $IDEAL^{\Pi}_{CS}(SC_{AND})$ are computationally indistinguishable. We can obtain that SC_{AND} is secure under the semi-honest model. □

Theorem 2. *The SC_{OR} proposed is secure under the semi-honest model.*

Proof of Theorem 2. We use $REAL^{\Pi}_{CS}(SC_{OR})$ to denote the execution view in the real world of CS, where it is specified as $REAL^{\Pi}_{CS}(SC_{OR}) = \{[\![ca]\!], [\![cb]\!], [\![temp]\!], [\![ORConst]\!], [\![res]\!]\}$. $[\![ORConst]\!]$ is obtained from $[\![1]\!]$ and $[\![8]\!]$ by $modSwitchToTorus32$. $[\![temp]\!]$ is obtained from $[\![ca]\!]$ and $[\![ORConst]\!]$ by **MKlweNoiselessTrivial** and **MKlweAddTo**. $[\![res]\!]$ is obtained from $[\![temp]\!]$ and $[\![cb]\!]$ by **MKlweAddTo**. We assume that $IDEAL^{\Pi}_{CS}(SC_{OR}) = \{[\![ca']\!], [\![cb']\!], [\![temp']\!], [\![ORConst']\!], [\![res']\!]\}$ is the execution view of the simulation in the ideal world, where $[\![ca']\!], [\![cb']\!], [\![temp']\!], [\![ORConst']\!]$ and $[\![res']\!]$ are chosen randomly from $\mathbb{T}^{n+1}$. The semantic privacy of our encryption scheme makes $[\![ca]\!]$ and $[\![cb]\!]$ computationally indistinguishable from $[\![ca']\!], [\![cb']\!], [\![temp']\!]$ and $[\![ORConst']\!]$, respectively. In addition, $[\![res]\!]$ is computationally indistinguishable from $[\![ca']\!], [\![cb']\!], [\![temp']\!]$ and $[\![ORConst']\!]$ respectively. Thus, it can be concluded that $REAL^{\Pi}_{CS}(SC_{OR})$ and $IDEAL^{\Pi}_{CS}(SC_{OR})$ are computationally indistinguishable. We can obtain that SC_{OR} is secure under the semi-honest model. □

Theorem 3. *The SC_{XOR} proposed is secure under the semi-honest model.*

Proof of Theorem 3. Since the design ideas of SC_{AND} and SC_{OR} are similar, we can prove the theorem based on Theorem (1). □

Theorem 4. *The SCP proposed is secure under the semi-honest model.*

Proof of Theorem 4. We use $REAL^{\Pi}_{CS}(SCP)$ to denote the execution view in the real world of the CS, where it is specified as $REAL^{\Pi}_{CS}(SCP) = \{([\![\mathbf{x}]\!], [\![\mathbf{y}]\!]), [\![z]\!]\}$. $[\![\mathbf{x}]\!]$ and $[\![\mathbf{y}]\!]$ are the encrypted data vectors. $[\![z]\!]$ is the result of determining whether the encrypted data vectors $[\![\mathbf{x}]\!]$ and $[\![\mathbf{y}]\!]$ are equal. $[\![z]\!]$ is a random number between 0 and 1 in the ciphertext. We assume that $IDEAL^{\Pi}_{CS}(SCP) = \{([\![\mathbf{x}']\!], [\![\mathbf{y}']\!]), [\![z']\!]\}$ is the execution view of the simulation in the ideal world, where the encrypted data in both $[\![\mathbf{x}']\!]$ and $[\![\mathbf{y}']\!]$ are chosen randomly from $\mathbb{T}^{n+1}$. $[\![z']\!]$ are chosen randomly from $\mathbb{T}^{n+1}$. The semantic privacy of our encryption scheme makes $[\![\mathbf{x}]\!]$ and $[\![\mathbf{y}]\!]$ computationally indistinguishable from $[\![\mathbf{x}']\!]$ and $[\![\mathbf{y}']\!]$, respectively. In addition, $[\![z']\!]$ takes 0 or 1 with equal probability. $[\![z]\!]$ are computationally indistinguishable from $[\![z']\!]$, respectively. Thus, it can be concluded that $REAL^{\Pi}_{CS}(SCP)$ and $IDEAL^{\Pi}_{CS}(SCP)$ are computationally indistinguishable. We can obtain that SCP is secure under the semi-honest model. □

6.3. Security of CMPSI

Theorem 5. *The $CMPSI$ proposed is secure under the semi-honest model, and the security of encrypted data, mining results, and query data can be guaranteed.*

Proof of Theorem 5. We can use the above method to prove that our proposed **CMPSI** is secure under the semi-honest model. In S1, CS obtains the encrypted dataset from DOs. In S2, CS obtains the encrypted dataset from DR. From Section 6.1, our cryptosystem is semantically secure, and the semi-honest CS cannot distinguish these messages from the random values of $\mathbb{T}^{n+1}$. In S3, **SCP** is executed to obtain the intersection information of the encryption of individual items in the dataset. Since **SCP** is secure in our system, it can be confirmed that the protocol in S3 is secure. In S4, **SC_OR** is used to obtain the final encryption result. Since **SC_OR** is secure in our system, the protocol in S4 is secure. In S5 and S6, the execution of S4 is repeated, the DR receives the message and decrypts it using the joint key, and the protocol is secure from the security of **MKTFHE**. □

Theorem 6. *The* **CMPSI** *proposed is able to resist man-in-the-middle attacks.*

Proof of Theorem 6. As shown in Figure 4, the participants represent the DR and DOs in our scenario. Under normal conditions, the participants can communicate with the CS, and Figure 4a shows the communication under normal conditions. The man-in-the-middle attack changes the original communication channel and can access the communication data between the participant and the cloud server, and Figure 4b shows the impact of the man-in-the-middle attack on the communication. We will prove that our model is resistant to man-in-the-middle attacks in three ways. First, DO encrypts its own dataset T_{DO} into $[\![T_{DO}]\!]_{s_{DO}}$ using its own key s_{DO} and then sends $[\![T_{DO}]\!]_{s_{DO}}$ to CS. Intermediary $\mathcal{A}$ obtains $[\![T_{DO}]\!]_{s_{DO}}$ through the new channel, but $\mathcal{A}$ does not have DO's key, and it is known from the security of **MKTFHE** that $\mathcal{A}$ cannot decrypt $[\![T_{DO}]\!]_{s_{DO}}$. Thus, our model can resist the man-in-the-middle attack during the data transmission from DO to CS. Second, DR wants to obtain the intersection information and sends the encrypted data $[\![T_{DR}]\!]_{s_{DR}}$ to CS. Intermediary $\mathcal{A}$ obtains $[\![T_{DR}]\!]_{s_{DR}}$ through the illegal channel. By the security of **MKTFHE**, $\mathcal{A}$ does not have s_{DR} and cannot obtain T_{DR} from $[\![T_{DR}]\!]_{s_{DR}}$. Thus, our model can resist the man-in-the-middle attack from DR to CS man-in-the-middle attack during the data transfer. Finally, CS needs to return the computed intersection information $[\![T_{DR \cap DO}]\!]_s$ to DR. The middleman $\mathcal{A}$ obtains the information $[\![T_{DR \cap DO}]\!]_s$, and it is known from the security of **MKTFHE** that $\mathcal{A}$ does not have the key to obtain $T_{DR \cap DO}$. Thus, our model can resist the man-in-the-middle attack during the data transmission from CS to DR. □

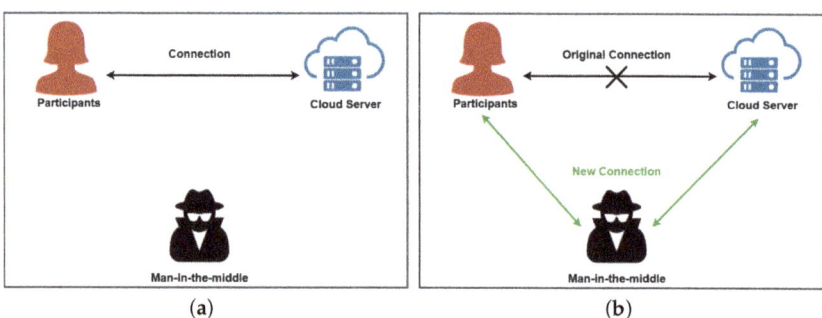

Figure 4. Man-in-the-middle attack; (**a**) normal communication; (**b**) post-attack communication.

6.4. Security Services

According to the above proof of CMPSI security, Table 3 shows the security services provided by the scheme and a demonstration from our model of how the method provides each of these functions.

Table 3. Security services provided.

Security Services	Definition	Proof
Confidentiality	Network information is not disclosed to non-authorized users, entities, or processes.	In our system, DO uses its own key s_{DO} to encrypt its own dataset T_{DO} into $[\![T_{DO}]\!]_{s_{DO}}$ and then sends $[\![T_{DO}]\!]_{s_{DO}}$ to CS. An unauthorized user $\mathcal{A}$ illegally obtains $[\![T_{DO}]\!]_{s_{DO}}$, and according to the security of the MKTFHE cryptosystem in Section 6.1, it is known that without the key, s_{DO} cannot perform decryption. Therefore, unauthorized illegal users $\mathcal{A}$ cannot obtain the information of DO's dataset T_{DO}.
Integrity	Information is transmitted, exchanged, stored, and processed in such a way that it remains uncorrupted or unmodified, that it is not lost, and that it cannot be changed without authorization.	In our system, DR encrypts the dataset T_{DR} as $[\![T_{DR}]\!]_{s_{DR}}$ using the key s_{DR} and sends $[\![T_{DR}]\!]_{s_{DR}}$ to CS. Attacker $\mathcal{A}$ obtains the dataset $[\![T_{DR}]\!]_{s_{DR}}$ through the intermediate channel, and according to the definition of the semi-honest model in Section 4.3, $\mathcal{A}$ does not modify or corrupt the data, and CS can obtain the dataset $[\![T_{DR}]\!]_{s_{DR}}$ intact.
Availability	Assurance that information is available to authorized users, i.e., assurance that legitimate users can use the required information when needed.	In our system, DR is the legal user. When DR wants to obtain the intersection information of its dataset T_{DR}, DR sends $[\![T_{DR}]\!]_{s_{DR}}$ to CS, and CS sends the computed intersection result $[\![T_{DR \cap DO}]\!]_s$ to DR. The legitimate user DR can obtain the required data when needed, which proves the usability of our system.
Non-repudiation	The two parties of information exchange cannot deny that they send or receive information in the exchange process.	In our system, DO sends its encrypted dataset $[\![T_{DO}]\!]_{s_{DO}}$ to CS. According to the definition of the semi-honest model in Section 4.3, DO will not deny that the dataset $[\![T_{DO}]\!]_{s_{DO}}$ is its data, proving the non-repudiation of our system.

7. Performance Analysis

In this section, we evaluate the time overhead and communication overhead of our proposed scheme. The experimental parameters we used [51] are shown in Table 4 below. According to one study [52], the parameters we use reach a privacy level of at least 110 bits, which is a common reference in this field.

Table 4. Parameter sets.

LWE-n	LWE-α	LWE-B′	LWE- d′	RLWE-N	RLWE-β	RLWE-B	RLWE-d
560	3.05×10^{-5}	2^2	8	1024	3.72×10^{-9}	2^9	3

The test environment used for our experiments was as follows: a 2.30 GHz Intel (R) Core(TM) i5-8300H Dell laptop. The programming language we used was C++, and our system was based on the MKTFHE library. First, we tested the efficiency of the security subprotocols separately. Then, we tested the communication overhead of our scheme and compared it with existing schemes. Finally, we tested our scheme.

7.1. Experiments on Security Computing Protocols

Our secure subprotocol experiments were performed using the MKTFHE library (https://github.com/ilachill/MK-TFHE) (1 February 2023). MKTFHE is a proof-of-concept implementation of a multi-key version of TFHE. The code is written on top of the TFHE library (https://tfhe.github.io/tfhe/) (1 February 2023). The computation of secure NAND gates is given in the MKTFHE library. In the MKTFHE-based implementation, our goal is to implement the MKLwe sample addition and multiplication operations as a way to implement the other circuit gates needed in our scheme in addition to the NADN gate. We first performed experiments on single circuit gates, including experiments on secure AND gate computation protocol, secure OR gate computation protocol, and secure XNOR computation protocol, and the experimental results are shown in Table 5. We compared these with NAND gates and found that the efficiency of individual gate computation is close.

Table 5. Experimental results for single circuit gates.

Gate Circuit	Key Generation Time (s)	FFT Conversion Time (s)	Bootstrapping Time (s)
AND	1.973	0.039	0.226
NAND	1.982	0.038	0.227
OR	1.956	0.040	0.227
XNOR	1.975	0.039	0.220

Then, as shown in Table 6, we tested the experimental time overhead of **SCP** for $k = 8$, 16, and 32, where k is the bits of data. The results show that the time overhead of the **SCP** protocol is linearly related to the number of bits of input.

Table 6. Running time of **SCP**.

k	8	16	32
Running time (s)	3.52	7.17	14.20

7.2. Overhead Evaluation

In our scenario, DOs and DRs are resource-constrained users; thus, it is important to have a smaller communication overhead. In our scheme, each participant uses their key to encrypt the data and uploads it to the cloud server; thus, the total communication overhead is related to the total data size. We tested the communication overhead of our scheme on datasets with aggregate sizes of 2^8, 2^{12}, 2^{16}, and 2^{20}. We compared our scheme with the scheme based on RSA [53] and the scheme based on pseudorandom permutation (PRP) [48]. As shown in Figure 5, our scheme is significantly superior to the privacy intersection scheme based on RSA. For the server-assisted scheme with limited security [48], the communication cost of our scheme is also lower. Our experimental results are the average of ten experiments.

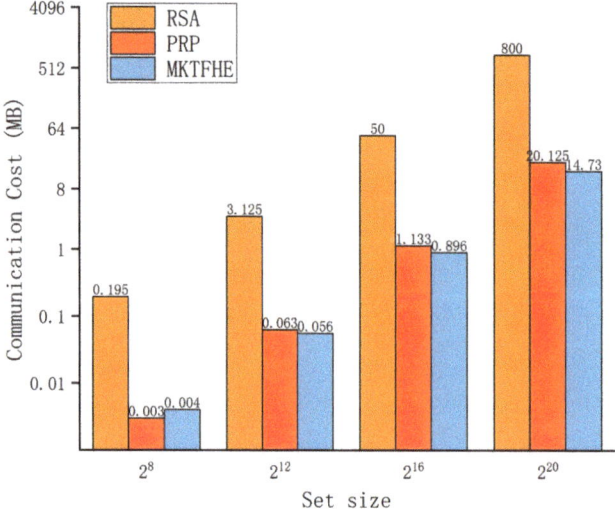

Figure 5. Communication overhead.

Our scheme is based on the underlying PSI protocol, and the computation of the ciphertext is performed directly on the cloud server. To the best of our knowledge, our proposed scheme is the first scheme that uses MKTFHE to achieve the ideal PSI, and the time overhead of the scheme is a very important metric. For users with limited resources, low overhead in the process of data encryption and decryption is necessary. We tested the time cost of using encryption and decryption and the size of ciphertext on datasets with sizes of 2^8, 2^{12}, 2^{16} and 2^{20}. Table 7 shows that for DOs and DR with limited resources, the cost of our scheme in data encryption and decryption is very small. Finally, we tested the computing cost of the cloud server. In the experiment, we used data from 16, 32, and 64 bit systems to test the performance of our proposed scheme. Table 8 shows our experimental results. The results show that the time cost of the scheme is linearly related to the size of the dataset and the number of bits of data. Please note that the cloud has excellent computing power, so that the efficiency of the solution can be faster in actual use.

Table 7. Cost during encryption.

	2^8	2^{12}	2^{16}	2^{20}
Encryption time (ms)	13.5	208.2	3162.2	47,987.1
Cipher size (kb)	3.5	57.3	917.5	15,083.6

Table 8. Cloud computing time (min).

Data Set Size	16bit	32bit	64bit
2^2	0.51	0.99	1.98
2^4	8.47	16.02	31.70
2^6	137.68	273.83	547.66

8. Conclusions

In this paper, we proposed CMPSI, a cloud-assisted private set intersection via multi-key fully homomorphic encryption, which allows the participants to outsource the encrypted data to cloud servers for storage and computation. We also designed some MKTFHE-based secure computing protocols to complete the design of our system. We analytically demonstrated the security of our scheme under a semi-honest model. Through experiments, we tested the performance of our proposed scheme and proved that our scheme has less communication overhead by comparing it with existing schemes. We also proved the feasibility of the scheme.

As future research work, we plan to apply our proposed MKTFHE to a wider range of areas, such as association rule mining systems in large shopping malls. In addition, we will improve our framework to handle more complex computations and further improve the performance of our system.

Author Contributions: Conceptualization, C.F.; Methodology, X.L.; Software, C.F. and P.J.; Validation, P.J.; Formal analysis, M.L.; Investigation, M.L. and P.G.; Data curation, X.Z.; Writing—original draft, X.Z.; Writing—review & editing, L.W. and X.L.; Visualization, P.G.; Supervision, L.W. All authors have read and agreed to the published version of the manuscript.

Funding: This work was funded by the National Key Technology Research and Development Program of China (grant nos. 2021YFB3901000 and 2021YFB3901005); the Civil Aerospace Technology Advance Research Project of China (D040405); the Application Pilot Plan of Fengyun Satellite (FY-APP-2021.0501).

Data Availability Statement: Not applicable.

Conflicts of Interest: The authors declare no conflict of interest.

Abbreviations

The following abbreviations are used in this manuscript:

PSI   Private set intersection
CMPSI   Cloud-assisted multi-key private set intersection
TFHE   Fully homomorphic encryption over toru
MKTFHE   Multi-key fully homomorphic encryption over toru

References

1. Abdulsalam, Y.S.; Hedabou, M. Security and privacy in cloud computing: technical review. *Future Internet* **2022**, *14*, 11. [CrossRef]
2. Aburukba, R.; Kaddoura, Y.; Hiba, M. Cloud Computing Infrastructure Security: Challenges and Solutions. In Proceedings of the 2022 International Symposium on Networks, Computers and Communications (ISNCC), Shenzhen, China, 19–22 July 2022; pp. 1–7.
3. Shao, Z.; Bo, Y. Private set intersection via public key encryption with keywords search. *Secur. Commun. Netw.* **2015**, *8*, 396–402. [CrossRef]
4. Shi, R.H.; Mu, Y.; Zhong, H.; Cui, J.; Zhang, S. An efficient quantum scheme for Private Set Intersection. *Quantum Inf. Process.* **2016**, *15*, 363–371. [CrossRef]
5. Yang, X.; Luo, X.; Xu, A.W.; Zhang, S. Improved outsourced private set intersection protocol based on polynomial interpolation. *Concurr. Comput. Pract. Exp.* **2018**, *30*, e4329. [CrossRef]
6. Tajima, A.; Sato, H.; Yamana, H. Outsourced Private Set Intersection Cardinality with Fully Homomorphic Encryption. In Proceedings of the 2018 6th International Conference on Multimedia Computing and Systems (ICMCS), Rabat, Morocco, 10–12 May 2018.
7. Ruan, O.; Huang, X.; Mao, H. An efficient private set intersection protocol for the cloud computing environments. In Proceedings of the 2020 IEEE 6th International Conference on Big Data Security on Cloud (BigDataSecurity), Baltimore, MD, USA, 25–27 May 2020; pp. 254–259.
8. Jiang, Y.; Wei, J.; Pan, J. Publicly Verifiable Private Set Intersection from Homomorphic Encryption. In Proceedings of the Security and Privacy in Social Networks and Big Data: 8th International Symposium, SocialSec 2022, Xi'an, China, 16–18 October 2022; pp. 117–137.
9. Debnath, S.K.; Kundu, N.; Choudhury, T. Efficient post-quantum private set-intersection protocol. *Int. J. Inf. Comput. Secur.* **2022**, *17*, 405–423. [CrossRef]
10. Wang, Q.; Zhou, F.; Xu, J.; Peng, S. Tag-based verifiable delegated set intersection over outsourced private datasets. *IEEE Trans. Cloud Comput.* **2020**, *10*, 1201–1214. [CrossRef]
11. Pinkas, B.; Rosulek, M.; Trieu, N.; Yanai, A. SpOT-light: lightweight private set intersection from sparse OT extension. In Proceedings of the Advances in Cryptology—CRYPTO 2019: 39th Annual International Cryptology Conference, Santa Barbara, CA, USA, 18–22 August 2019; pp. 401–431.
12. Pinkas, B.; Rosulek, M.; Trieu, N.; Yanai, A. PSI from PaXoS: fast, malicious private set intersection. In Proceedings of the Advances in Cryptology—EUROCRYPT 2020: 39th Annual International Conference on the Theory and Applications of Cryptographic Techniques, Zagreb, Croatia, 10–14 May 2020; pp. 739–767.
13. Chase, M.; Miao, P. Private set intersection in the internet setting from lightweight oblivious PRF. In Proceedings of the Advances in Cryptology—CRYPTO 2020: 40th Annual International Cryptology Conference, CRYPTO 2020, Santa Barbara, CA, USA, 17–21 August 2020; pp. 34–63.
14. Rindal, P.; Schoppmann, P. VOLE-PSI: fast OPRF and circuit-psi from vector-ole. In Proceedings of the Advances in Cryptology—EUROCRYPT 2021: 40th Annual International Conference on the Theory and Applications of Cryptographic Techniques, Zagreb, Croatia, 17–21 October 2021; pp. 901–930.
15. Shi, R.H.; Li, Y.F. Quantum private set intersection cardinality protocol with application to privacy-preserving condition query. *IEEE Trans. Circuits Syst. Regul. Pap.* **2022**, *69*, 2399–2411. [CrossRef]
16. Zhou, Q.; Zeng, Z.; Wang, K.; Chen, M. Privacy Protection Scheme for the Internet of Vehicles Based on Private Set Intersection. *Cryptography* **2022**, *6*, 64. [CrossRef]
17. Qian, Y.; Xia, X.; Shen, J. A profile matching scheme based on private set intersection for cyber-physical-social systems. In Proceedings of the 2021 IEEE Conference on Dependable and Secure Computing (DSC), Aizuwakamatsu, Japan, 30 January–2 February 2021; pp. 1–5.
18. Demmler, D.; Rindal, P.; Rosulek, M.; Trieu, N. *PIR-PSI: Scaling Private Contact Discovery*; Cryptology ePrint: Archive, CA, USA, 2018.
19. Liu, F.; Ng, W.K.; Zhang, W.; Han, S.; et al. Encrypted set intersection protocol for outsourced datasets. In Proceedings of the 2014 IEEE International Conference on Cloud Engineering, Boston, MA, USA, 11–14 March 2014; pp. 135–140.
20. De Cristofaro, E.; Tsudik, G. Practical private set intersection protocols with linear complexity. In Proceedings of the Financial Cryptography and Data Security: 14th International Conference, FC 2010, Tenerife, Canary Islands, 25–28 January 2010; pp. 143–159.
21. Gentry, C. Fully homomorphic encryption using ideal lattices. In Proceedings of the 41st Annual ACM Symposium on Theory of Computing, Bethesda, MA, USA, 31 May–2 June 2009; pp. 169–178.

22. Brakerski, Z.; Perlman, R. Lattice-based fully dynamic multi-key FHE with short ciphertexts. In Proceedings of the Advances in Cryptology—CRYPTO 2016: 36th Annual International Cryptology Conference, Santa Barbara, CA, USA, 14–18 August 2016; pp. 190–213.
23. López-Alt, A.; Tromer, E.; Vaikuntanathan, V. On-the-fly multiparty computation on the cloud via multikey fully homomorphic encryption. In Proceedings of the 44th Annual ACM Symposium on Theory of Computing, New York, NY, USA, 20–22 May 2012; pp. 1219–1234.
24. Gentry, C.; Sahai, A.; Waters, B. Homomorphic encryption from learning with errors: Conceptually-simpler, asymptotically-faster, attribute-based. In Proceedings of the Annual Cryptology Conference, Barbara, CA, USA, 18–22 August 2013; pp. 75–92.
25. Brakerski, Z.; Gentry, C.; Vaikuntanathan, V. (Leveled) fully homomorphic encryption without bootstrapping. *ACM Trans. Comput. Theory (TOCT)* **2014**, *6*, 1–36. [CrossRef]
26. Chillotti, I.; Gama, N.; Georgieva, M.; Izabachene, M. Faster fully homomorphic encryption: Bootstrapping in less than 0.1 seconds. In Proceedings of the International Conference on the Theory And Application of Cryptology and Information Security, Taipei, Taiwan, 5–9 December 2016; pp. 3–33.
27. Chen, H.; Laine, K.; Rindal, P. Fast private set intersection from homomorphic encryption. In Proceedings of the 2017 ACM SIGSAC Conference on Computer and Communications Security, Dallas, TX, USA, 30 October–3 November 2017; pp. 1243–1255.
28. Chen, H.; Huang, Z.; Laine, K.; Rindal, P. Labeled PSI from fully homomorphic encryption with malicious security. In Proceedings of the 2018 ACM SIGSAC Conference on Computer and Communications Security, Toronto, ON, Canada, 15–19 October 2018; pp. 1223–1237.
29. Cong, K.; Moreno, R.C.; da Gama, M.B.; Dai, W.; Iliashenko, I.; Laine, K.; Rosenberg, M. Labeled PSI from homomorphic encryption with reduced computation and communication. In Proceedings of the 2021 ACM SIGSAC Conference on Computer and Communications Security, Copenhagen, Denmark, 15–19 November 2021; pp. 1135–1150.
30. Freedman, M.J.; Nissim, K.; Pinkas, B. Efficient private matching and set intersection. In Proceedings of the Advances in Cryptology-EUROCRYPT 2004: International Conference on the Theory and Applications of Cryptographic Techniques, Interlaken, Switzerland, 2–6 May 2004; pp. 1–19.
31. Yao, A.C. Protocols for secure computations. In Proceedings of the 23rd Annual Symposium on Foundations of Computer Science (SFCS 1982), Chicago, IL, USA, 3–5 November 1982; pp. 160–164.
32. Micali, S.; Goldreich, O.; Wigderson, A. How to play any mental game. In Proceedings of the 19th ACM Symposium on Theory of Computing, New York, NY, USA, 1 January 1987; pp. 218–229.
33. Kolesnikov, V. Gate evaluation secret sharing and secure one-round two-party computation. In Proceedings of the Advances in Cryptology-ASIACRYPT 2005: 11th International Conference on the Theory and Application of Cryptology and Information Security, Chennai, India, 4–8 December 2005; pp. 136–155.
34. Even, S.; Goldreich, O.; Lempel, A. A randomized protocol for signing contracts. *Commun. ACM* **1985**, *28*, 637–647. [CrossRef]
35. Hazay, C.; Nissim, K. Efficient Set Operations in the Presence of Malicious Adversaries. In Proceedings of the Public Key Cryptography, Paris, France, 26–28 May 2010; Volume 6056; pp. 312–331.
36. Huang, Y.; Evans, D.; Katz, J. Private set intersection: Are garbled circuits better than custom protocols? In Proceedings of the NDSS, San Diego, CA, USA, 5–8 February 2012.
37. Dong, C.; Chen, L.; Wen, Z. When private set intersection meets big data: An efficient and scalable protocol. In Proceedings of the 2013 ACM SIGSAC Conference on Computer & Communications Security, Berlin, Germany, 4–8 November 2013; pp. 789–800.
38. Pinkas, B.; Schneider, T.; Zohner, M. Faster Private Set Intersection based on OT Extension (Full Version). In Proceedings of the USENIX Security Symposium, San Diego, CA, USA, 20–22 August 2014.
39. Freedman, M.J.; Hazay, C.; Nissim, K.; Pinkas, B. Efficient set intersection with simulation-based security. *J. Cryptol.* **2016**, *29*, 115–155. [CrossRef]
40. Pinkas, B.; Schneider, T.; Zohner, M. Scalable private set intersection based on OT extension. *ACM Trans. Priv. Secur. (TOPS)* **2018**, *21*, 1–35. [CrossRef]
41. Orrù, M.; Orsini, E.; Scholl, P. Actively secure 1-out-of-N OT extension with application to private set intersection. In Proceedings of the Topics in Cryptology–CT-RSA 2017: The Cryptographers' Track at the RSA Conference 2017, San Francisco, CA, USA, 14–17 February 2017; pp. 381–396.
42. Kerschbaum, F. Collusion-resistant outsourcing of private set intersection. In Proceedings of the 27th Annual ACM Symposium on Applied Computing, Trento, Italy, 25–29 March 2012; pp. 1451–1456.
43. Kerschbaum, F. Outsourced private set intersection using homomorphic encryption. In Proceedings of the Proceedings of the 7th ACM Symposium on Information, Computer and Communications Security, Hong Kong, 7–11 June 2012; pp. 85–86.
44. Abadi, A.; Terzis, S.; Dong, C. O-PSI: delegated private set intersection on outsourced datasets. In Proceedings of the ICT Systems Security and Privacy Protection: 30th IFIP TC 11 International Conference, SEC 2015, Hamburg, Germany, 26–28 May 2015; Proceedings 30; pp. 3–17.
45. Abadi, A.; Terzis, S.; Dong, C. VD-PSI: verifiable delegated private set intersection on outsourced private datasets. In Proceedings of the Financial Cryptography and Data Security: 20th International Conference, FC 2016, Christ Church, Barbados, 22–26 February 2016; Revised Selected Papers 20; pp. 149–168.
46. Ali, M.; Mohajeri, J.; Sadeghi, M.R.; Liu, X. Attribute-based fine-grained access control for outscored private set intersection computation. *Inf. Sci.* **2020**, *536*, 222–243. [CrossRef]

47. Abadi, A.; Terzis, S.; Metere, R.; Dong, C. Efficient Delegated Private Set Intersection on Outsourced Private Datasets. *IEEE Trans. Dependable Secur. Comput.* **2019**, *16*, 608–624. [CrossRef]
48. Kamara, S.; Mohassel, P.; Raykova, M.; Sadeghian, S. Scaling private set intersection to billion-element sets. In Proceedings of the Financial Cryptography and Data Security: 18th International Conference, FC 2014, Christ Church, Barbados, 3–7 March 2014; Revised Selected Papers 18; pp. 195–215.
49. Chen, H.; Chillotti, I.; Song, Y. Multi-key homomorphic encryption from TFHE. In Proceedings of the International Conference on the Theory and Application of Cryptology and Information Security, Kobe, Japan, 8–12 December 2019; pp. 446–472.
50. Oded, G. *Foundations of Cryptography: Volume 2, Basic Applications*; Cambridge University Press: Cambridge, MA, USA, 2009.
51. Pradel, G.; Mitchell, C. Privacy-Preserving Biometric Matching Using Homomorphic Encryption. In Proceedings of the 2021 IEEE 20th International Conference on Trust, Security and Privacy in Computing and Communications (TrustCom), Shenyang, China, 18–20 August 2021; pp. 494–505.
52. Albrecht, M.R.; Player, R.; Scott, S. On the concrete hardness of learning with errors. *J. Math. Cryptol.* **2015**, *9*, 169–203. [CrossRef]
53. Ciampi, M.; Orlandi, C. Combining private set-intersection with secure two-party computation. In Proceedings of the Security and Cryptography for Networks: 11th International Conference, SCN 2018, Amalfi, Italy, 5–7 September 2018; pp. 464–482.

Disclaimer/Publisher's Note: The statements, opinions and data contained in all publications are solely those of the individual author(s) and contributor(s) and not of MDPI and/or the editor(s). MDPI and/or the editor(s) disclaim responsibility for any injury to people or property resulting from any ideas, methods, instructions or products referred to in the content.

Article

XTS: A Hybrid Framework to Detect DNS-Over-HTTPS Tunnels Based on XGBoost and Cooperative Game Theory

Mungwarakarama Irénée [1,2,*], Yichuan Wang [1,*], Xinhong Hei [1,*], Xin Song [1], Jean Claude Turiho [2] and Enan Muhire Nyesheja [2]

1. School of Computer Science and Engineering, Xi'an University, Xi'an 710071, China; songxin@xaut.edu.cn
2. Computing and Information Science, University of Lay Adventists of Kigali, Kigali 6392, Rwanda; tulije@gmail.com (J.C.T.); nyenani@unilak.ac.rw (E.M.N.)
* Correspondence: fezanava@stu.xaut.edu.cn (M.I.); chuan@xaut.edu.cn (Y.W.); heixinhong@xaut.edu.cn (X.H.)

Abstract: This paper proposes a hybrid approach called XTS that uses a combination of techniques to analyze highly imbalanced data with minimum features. XTS combines cost-sensitive XGBoost, a game theory-based model explainer called TreeSHAP, and a newly developed algorithm known as Sequential Forward Evaluation algorithm (SFE). The general aim of XTS is to reduce the number of features required to learn a particular dataset. It assumes that low-dimensional representation of data can improve computational efficiency and model interpretability whilst retaining a strong prediction performance. The efficiency of XTS was tested on a public dataset, and the results showed that by reducing the number of features from 33 to less than five, the proposed model achieved over 99.9% prediction efficiency. XTS was also found to outperform other benchmarked models and existing proof-of-concept solutions in the literature. The dataset contained data related to DNS-over-HTTPS (DoH) tunnels. The top predictors for DoH classification and characterization were identified using interactive SHAP plots, which included destination IP, packet length mode, and source IP. XTS offered a promising approach to improve the efficiency of the detection and analysis of DoH tunnels while maintaining accuracy, which can have important implications for behavioral network intrusion detection systems.

Keywords: DNS tunneling; DoH-based C2 covert channels; XGBoost; cooperative game theory; SHAP values; feature importance analysis; dimensionality reduction; imbalanced data; XAI

MSC: 91A12; 41A58

1. Introduction

As the deployment of fifth-generation (5G) technology continues to increase, potential shortfalls [1–3] and use cases [4] have started to drive researchers all over the world to move their focus towards sixth-generation technology (6G). Its proposed frameworks and methods envision the use of AI/ML as the eminent enabler of these new network technologies [5–8].

The problems of high-dimensional feature spaces, commonly known as the "curse of dimensionality" [9], have been major challenges in the machine learning research community and among practitioners for decades. Several research articles have since studied its effects and how the various classes of traditional feature selection (FS) algorithms attempt to solve these challenges [10–14]. While these techniques can help us to improve the accuracy of the ML models, a significant number of them fail to provide sensible explanations as to why a particular decision or prediction is made; additionally, they mostly have the potential to suffer from issues such as instability, scalability and inconsistency [13,15–18].

In this study, we focus on the application of behavior-based intelligent network intrusion detection systems, which are known to be affected by high-dimensional data [19]. This is due to the fact that open source and proprietary IP traffic flow feature collectors have the capability to generate numerous flow features, sometimes numbering in the hundreds [9]. As per the definition provided by the Internet Engineering Task Force (IETF), a flow refers to a sequence of packets that are monitored by a meter as they transit across a network between two endpoints or from a single endpoint [20]. These packets, as will be shown latter in Section 3.3, are then summarized by the traffic meter for the purposes of facilitating analysis.

Flow-based features are used in encrypted traffic analysis because traditional decryption methods, such as deep packet inspection (DPI), have become less effective in the face of recent advances in complex encryption algorithms. This encryption is in response to the increased demand for user privacy, which has led to the widespread use of encrypted traditional protocols such as DNS-over-HTTPS(DoH). Figure 1 shows how adding another layer of security to the classical domain name system has changed the way communication takes place. Although it can be beneficial to the end user, it is a major challenge to security operational control systems. Recently, records of attacks leveraging DoH protocols to cover command and control (C2) communications have emerged. The use of flow-based features in combination with machine learning algorithms has yielded promising results in terms of detecting network behavior and identifying applications, users, and malware [16,18–22]. However, one of the potential challenges associated with these techniques is the high dimensionality of the generated data [9]. The analysis of flow properties and statistical features often results in a large number of dimensions, a fact which can pose difficulties in terms of computational resources, feature selection, and interpretability. Finding effective methods to handle high-dimensional data with remains an important area of research in the field of behavioral network intrusion detection.

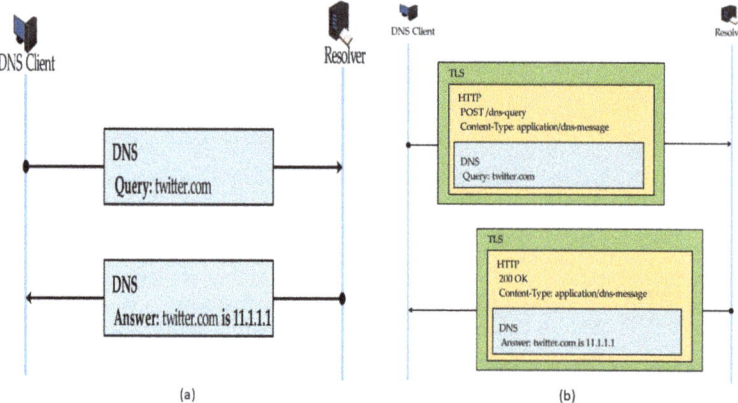

Figure 1. Advancement in privacy protection: (**a**) illustrates a traditional unencrypted DNS system, where DNS queries and responses are transmitted in plain text. While it is possible to monitor browsing activities through DNS logs, the effectiveness of security controls and DPI systems in preventing malware attacks is limited. (**b**) represents the modern encrypted DNS system, DNS-over-HTTPS (DoH). With DoH, DNS queries and responses are encrypted, ensuring that browsing activities remain private and protected from unauthorized monitoring.

With respect to the detection of DNS-over-HTPPS tunnels or any other vulnerability, the need for a security analyst or practitioner to intuitively understand and explain the model's decision in a particular instance, such as flow, session or other network artifacts; or to calibrate network intrusion detection systems is paramount. The belief in the need for explainability, combined with the inherent high dimensionality of network traffic data, provides a strong rationale for our proposed low-dimensional representation framework. We propose a framework that combines cutting-edge ML models with the significance of explainable artificial intelligence (XAI) in enhancing the adoption and trustworthiness of machine learning models in order to study the current research trends in the field of network intrusion detection systems, specifically DNS/DoH tunneling detection.

This framework will provide human-friendly explanations for model decisions by creating a clear link between the input features and the output predictions, making it easier for security analysts to understand the reasoning behind a model's detection or classification decisions. Furthermore, reducing the number of features used in the models will increase computational efficiency, which is particularly relevant in the context of real-time network traffic analysis. In summary, our proposed low-dimensional representation framework tackles the challenges posed by high-dimensional network traffic data and aims to improve the explainability of machine learning models. By doing so, it is assumed that we will be able to enhance the efficiency and effectiveness of network intrusion detection systems. To this end, our contributions are summarized as follows: We propose a hybrid framework combining three components: Cost-sensitive and GPU-Aware, eXtreme Gradient Boosting (XGBoost), Tree Shapley Additive eXplanations (TreeSHAP), combined with the Sequential Forward and Evaluation (SFE) algorithm, collectively dubbed as XTS. To break down our contributions into manageable objectives:

(1) We hypothesize that command and control traffic can assumably be detected based on unique connections at the IP level (the source, destination IPs), and that this probably is also the case for packet size factors such as packet length mode, median or mean. Possessing prior efficiency assumptions in terms of XGBoost, we compare its performance to other well-known machine learning models, ultimately selecting the best performer for our specific use case.

(2) We construct a GPU-aware $f(x)$ from unfamous but powerful hyperparameters, particularly gpu_hist, an optimized version of the histogram-based tree building algorithm used in XGBoost that leverages the parallel computing power of GPUs to perform computations faster than they are on a CPU. With gpu_hist, XGBoost can build decision trees on large datasets more efficiently, making it the preferred choice for tasks with high-dimensional and large-scale data. It also optimizes memory usage, enabling users to train models on larger datasets that may not fit into CPU memory.

(3) We turn the base model of XGBoost into a cost-sensitive algorithm that has a bias towards the majority class. By increasing the weights of the minority class instances, the algorithm is penalized more for misclassifying those instances, leading to a better balance between the minority and majority classes. This technique, unlike its counterpart sampling methods, is simple but efficient.

(4) We use a tree-specific SHAP model to explain $g'(f(x))$ in order to learn SHAP values $\varnothing$ that explain the unique and consistent features making contributions towards $f(x)$ predictions. We interpret the results via rich visualization, using SHAP plots at both local and global levels to verify our subjective hypothesis.

(5) Based on the most influential flow features, we create a subset $S_M \subseteq M$ ranging from the most significant feature (MSF) to the least significant feature (LSF) and design a new algorithm E to sequentially fit and evaluate f on subsets $S_1, S_2, S_3, \ldots S_n$, $S_i \subseteq S_M$ until the loss function $L \simeq 0$. This helps us to achieve the highest prediction accuracy with a low-dimensional representation. This presumably decreases computational cost.

The remainder of this paper is organized as follows. We first review the recent abuse of DNS and the current ML methods to detect the attacks in Section 2. We then describe the design of the proposed model in Section 3. In Section 4, we carry out the experiment and we discuss the results in Section 5. We conclude with Section 6.

2. Related Work

The use of machine learning (ML) algorithms to detect network intrusions, especially in high-dimensional and imbalanced data sets, has gained significant attention in recent years [21–28]. Several studies have proposed different ML-based solutions to detect DNS and DoH tunnels in network traffic [21–28]. In this section, we focus specifically on the assumption that despite the TLS encryption concealing certain information, a limited set of relevant features, such as IP addresses and packet size-related characteristics, could still provide valuable insights for detecting the frequency of command and control (C2) communication in HTTPS traffic. By leveraging these key features, our research revolves around the idea that anomaly detection/classification can still be conducted in encrypted traffic analysis, even without full access to DNS logs.

We investigate the application and effectiveness of state-of-the-art machine learning models to classify high-dimensional and imbalanced data in the field of anomaly detection, focusing specifically on encrypted traffic where the traditional NIDS lacks the capacity to see into DNS logs due to the use of advanced TLS versions that even hide SNI extensions. We propose the rationale that a subset of relevant features, such as IP and packet size-related features, can potentially be sufficient for detecting the frequency of C2 in HTTPS traffic.

The objective of this section is to explore studies focusing on the use of these models to extract meaningful insights from extensive feature sets and leverage the selected features to improve training and detection speed, as well as to enhance security decision-making processes. By combining advanced machine learning techniques with the identification of informative features, we conjecture that this approach would optimize computational efficiency, resource utilization, and the overall effectiveness of security analysis in the context of encrypted network intrusion detection.

2.1. Recent Abuse of DNS

The Internet was designed more than 50 years ago. Its foundation architecture and protocols remain the backbones of even the emerging technologies, such as DNS. DNS is considered as the phonebook and the backbone of the Internet. DNS system translates IP addresses—a unique number used to communicate between devices on the Internet, such as 107.20.1.23—into a memorable name like www.rdb.co.rw.

A recent global DNS threat report [29] shows that 88% of the surveyed organizations experienced an attack and that there were 7 attacks per year on average for each organization. The survey results indicate an increasing number of DNS-based attacks compared to the previous year. DNS-based attacks are among the most growing and worrying attacks because their traffic is mostly not filtered by security controls. Despite the privacy intentions for which this protocol was designed, it is commonly exploited by attackers. For instance, two recent reviews compiled different abuse and trends in DNS-C2 covert channel to show how this means of malware disguising itself in the legitimate traffic is increasing in use and is being adopted by malware developers. The usage of this protocol in terms of attack involves command and control (C&C or C2) covert channels. These channels may serve two purposes to the attacker: (a) as a beacon signal—used to call back to the controller (sever); or (b) in data exfiltration.

Although the methods applying deep packet inspection (DPI) with middle boxes are the most effective ways to detect vulnerabilities, they are also privacy-evasive [30]. These solutions may suffer from the complexity of advanced modern encryption schemes and privacy violation issues. As the Internet is moving towards the encryption of all web traffic [31,32], cybercriminals have also switched to tunneling their malicious code inside legitimate protected protocols. For example, the use of TLS to spread covert malware traffic increased in recent years [33]. In a case of DNS-based malware use, metadata collected during the traffic analysis, such as the length of the packet, request/response time, packet time, flow bytes, and flow bytes sent/received duration, were also studied [34]. Ref. [35] gathered studies about port-based and flow-based approaches used to detect encrypted malware traffics without decrypting the packet. The strength of these approaches is that they do not evade privacy.

2.2. High-Dimension Features Problems in Machine Learning

With the pervasive adoption of DNS-over-HTTPS (DoH) methods along with the design advancement of TLS protocol TLS 1.3, collecting traffic flow metadata remains the only viable option to achieve cybersecurity privacy and regulatory compliance. Both open source and proprietary IP traffic flow feature collectors are able to produce hundreds of flow features for the use of the intrusion detection systems in analyzing traffic. For example, Moore et al. [9] extracted 249 flow features. This production of features comes with the following challenges: (1) many features are redundant, which adds noise to the model and may lead to an overfitting problem [23,36,37]; (2) the use of more features increases computational cost (training, detection time and memory space) [38]; and the use of (3) a greater quantity of features, as well as some redundant features, may lead to the failure of model interpretability.

Feature importance analysis and selection would be the desired methods to alleviate the data dimensionality problem. Feature importance is the process of finding the feature set $S \subseteq M$ in the feature vector space M, whose values have more influence on the model's output than others. The main challenges for the classical feature analysis methods are scalability, stability and lack of better alignment with human intuition. Chandrashekar et al. [18] and Tang et al. [39] classified traditional feature importance selection methods and reported the challenges of their use. [12] defined scalability as the tendency of the feature selection algorithm to require the sufficient sample size to provide statistically significant results. The stability of a feature selection algorithm was defined by [13] as the capacity of an algorithm to consistently provide a consistent feature subset when additional training samples are added or when some training samples are removed. To overcome the above challenges, a rigorous mathematically founded game theory method was proposed, namely, the Tree Shapley Additive eXplanations (TreeSHAP) method.

2.3. DNS Tunneling Detection with ML Methods

There have been more efforts made by different researchers to utilize the properties and statistical features of the traffic flow to classify DNS-over-HTTPS (DoH) and DoH-based C2 tunnels using machine learning and deep learning models. Notwithstanding previous research on HTTPS traffic analysis, the malware use of HTTPS, or TLS with machine learning using flow-based features [40–45], this section focused on studies conducted on DoH traffic and DoH-based tunneling detection using machine learning methods.

Commonly used ML algorithms include the random forest, support vector machine (SVM), and deep learning algorithms. In addition to these algorithms, XGBoost has been reported to achieve strong performances in various classification tasks. For instance, S. Cerna et al. [46] used it in the fire services to predict public service breakdowns; it was used in weather forecasts for wind power prediction by H. Arcolez et al. [47]; S. Robert et al. [48] used it in emergency medical services (EMS) to predict both victim mortality and need for transportation to health facilities; additionally, it has found uses in fraud detection, and vehicular ad hoc networks (VANETs) [49,50].

The results of these and other more unreferenced previous studies are the reasons behind selecting this robust model. Furthermore, the SHAP (SHapley Additive eXplanations) method developed by Scott M Lundberg, et al. [51] has been wildly adopted by many researchers in various disciplines and studies to explain feature importance and draw some close-to-human intuitive explanation of the underlying ML model. The SHAP values provide a global view of the feature importance and enable the detection of any biases in the model. Apart from the studies by Scott M Lundberg, et al. [52,53], the pioneers of this field, other studies have also shown the success of these complex but efficient methods. For example, in malware and stress detection [54–56], SHAP values have shown excellent results.

In 2019, ref. [23] showed the emergence of the first malware that could bypass network traffic monitoring systems using DNS-over-HTTPS, catching the attention of researchers in the field of malware traffic analysis. In response, Drew Hjelm [42] proposed some solutions for the issues of detecting DoH traffic and highlighted the limitations of existing intrusion detection systems, such as Zeek and Security Information and Event Management (SIEM) such as Real Intelligence Threat Analytics (RITA). One solution involved using packet capture and TLS inspection to decrypt and log DNS queries, while the other relied on the use of network events logs to detect DoH-based command and control communication without decrypting traffic. While Hjelm's research was successful, the focus of this technical report is on showcasing the control solutions that are already in use.

The adoption of DNS-over-HTTPS (DoH) has garnered much attention in recent years, leading to increased research into its potential security vulnerabilities and mitigation strategies. In [25], the distributed generation of NTP server pools, designed using multiple DoH resolvers, was proposed as a more secure alternative to plaintext DNS queries. However, practical studies such as [26] have shown the susceptibility of DoH to downgrade attacks, where attackers can force the communication to use insecure DNS protocols. To address these concerns, ref. [27] proposed a multilabel support vector machine (SVM) to detect and classify various DNS tunnelling techniques, including DoH. Similarly, ref. [28] evaluated five different machine learning algorithms and demonstrated their effectiveness in accurately detecting DoH traffic and identifying the applications that use it. Despite these advances, challenges still remain in monitoring and filtering DoH traffic at end gateways, as highlighted in [29]. In [30], a new technique called live memory forensics was proposed to detect URLs from the RAM of end client machines in to monitor and control user content, even when DoH was used. Finally, ref. [31] demonstrated how data exfiltration can be achieved through DoH queries using different tools, while [32] revealed privacy weaknesses in DoH traffic by analyzing packet-level information with machine learning classifiers. Mohammadreza et al. developed a two-layered architecture to classify HTTPS traffic into DoH and normal web HTTPS traffic (NonDoH). Their study contributed significantly to the field of DoH detection, and their dataset was cited extensively in subsequent research. The authors created a deep learning model (LSTM) and used packet clumps created from the timeseries feature of the full flow as the input feature set. Although the packet clumping approach is interesting and has yielded attractive results, the number of packets required to make a clump is not clear, and the window size claimed by the authors may not be suitable for real-time traffic with longer inter-packet arrival times [19]. This research has served as a foundation for many other researchers to build upon and has been an essential reference in the field of DoH detection.

For example, in the realm of DoH traffic analysis, the research of Banaki [57], whose methods follow the same approach of a two-layered architecture incorporating both flow properties and statistical features, has been the subject of several studies. While his focus was on prediction performance metrics and feature importance, he did not thoroughly investigate the time factor. The lack k of clarity in his method and results, along with a small sample size, caught the attention of other researchers.

To address these concerns, Jafar et al. [58], Behnke et al. [36] and Zebin et al. [59] took a different approach by reproducing [57]'s studies while removing its flow property features. Using chi-square and Pearson correlation coefficients to select the best features via the Sequential Forward Selection method (SFS), feature importance was examined. Of the 10 machine learning models studied including XGBoost, the LGBM model was recommended as the best-performing model in both prediction performance and computational cost.

In the study by Ahakonye et al. [37], the authors aimed to address the issue of overlooking the time factor in previous solutions using machine learning models to counter DNS vulnerability attacks. They applied several machine learning models such as XGB, GB, AD, RF, and DT to CI-RA-CIC-DoHBrw-2020 dataset to evaluate the trade-off between prediction performance and computational time. While their study provided valuable insights, it is important to note that their results were presented in an ambiguous manner in terms of time units. The same results were interpreted four times with different units, including seconds and milliseconds, which could have potentially misled the comparison and interpretation of the findings. To conclude our review on previous DoH tunnel detection studies, the final study in question was carried out by [59]. The author proposed a balanced and stacked random forest solution to classify DNS-over-HTTPS traffics. Additionally, he used explainable AI methods to highlight some insights into the model decisions. This approach achieved great results; however, he did not consider the time factor.

After a thorough review of into the previous literature, the authors in this paper appreciated the previous studies carried out on this subject but found some gaps therein. For instance, studies such as [36,59] underestimated IP addresses as potential contributors to DoH and C2 DoH tunnels. The latter also used unsuitable, and unstable techniques to rank and select features. Others, like [58], lack clarity and consistency in their results and data pre-processing. The study only used the accuracy metric, which is not suitable for application to highly imbalanced dataset. Additionally, the study's time metrics had no time units, which raised some doubts in the results and limited direct comparison. The same problems regarding the lack of time units and inconsistency are also found in [37]. To the authors' best knowledge, no study of this kind has demonstrated a method combining prediction results, computational cost and model interpretability. Hence, this paper comes as a solution. In order to build a more effective and accurate solution to the problem of DoH tunnel detection and to address feature dimensionality challenges while having the model explain predictors with close similarity to the expert's knowledge, it is important to address the limitations of previous studies. As noted in the literature review, some previous studies have overlooked important factors such as the time factor, the role of IP addresses, and the stability of feature selection techniques. Additionally, some studies have used unsuitable evaluation metrics, leading to inaccurate results, as stated above.

To overcome these limitations, the proposed framework combines a cost-sensitive XGBoost algorithm, trained with GPU_hist tree_method using an explainable AI technique, to achieve a strong prediction performance while maintaining computational efficiency. Feature selection is also incorporated in order to evaluate the models on subsets created sequentially from the list of important features. By incorporating these approaches, the proposed framework is expected to outperform previous studies in terms of accuracy and computational efficiency. The cost-sensitive nature of the XGBoost algorithm will address the issue of class imbalance in the dataset, while the GPU_hist tree_method will significantly reduce computational time compared to traditional tree-based methods. Furthermore, the use of explainable AI will provide insights into the decision-making process of the model, allowing for greater interpretability and transparency. The inclusion of feature selection will also aid in identifying the most important features for DoH tunnel detection, improving the overall performance of the model. This approach will eliminate irrelevant features and reduce the likelihood of overfitting, resulting in the development of a more robust and accurate model.

In summary, the proposed framework addresses the limitations of previous studies and offers a more effective and efficient solution to DoH tunnel detection. The combination of cost-sensitive XGBoost, GPU_hist tree_method, explainable AI, and feature selection techniques will result in a model with high accuracy, computational efficiency, and interpretability.

3. Proposed Framework

This section describes the graphical and analytical modeling of DNS-over-HTTPS tunnels in HTTPS traffic using the proposed framework—XTS. The section ends with a proposed application of our framework in the network environment. For the sake of space, we describe the modeling process using graphical representation accompanied by a short description. We believe that "a picture is worth 1000 words".

3.1. Preliminaries

In this section, we present notations and background information to help the reader to follow along in subsequent sections. The proposed method is hereafter dubbed XTS to denote the hybrid structure of the framework which comprises of three parts:

1. Cost-Sensitive eXtreme Gradient Boosting—optimized black-box ML model used for classification of HTTPS traffic in this study.

2. Tree Explainer—A SHAP (SHapley Additive exPlanations)-based model designed specifically to provide explanations for tree-based models.
3. Sequential Forward Evaluation—algorithm designed to evaluate the newly optimized model of the subsets of features selected as a result of the Tree Explainer list of the most significant features.

This section does not include the preliminary task of selecting XGBoost as the best performer among other state-of-the-art machine learning models. Although it is one part of our framework, it is described in Section 4.2.

XTS is designed firstly to contribute to the challenges faced in different research directions shown in Figure 2. It is designed to classify HTTPS traffic in binary-class imbalanced dataset using the state-of-the-arts machine learning model—cost-sensitive eXtreme Gradient Boosting. Second, it leverages the most recent advances in the field of eXplainable Artificial Intelligent (XAI) to explain the output decision made by the underlying XGBoost model through feature importance explanations with more elegant and human-friendly presentation. Finally, XTS uses a newly designed simple algorithm to create a low-dimensional representation to address the challenges of the high-dimensional problems discussed in Sections 1 and 2. Figure 3 graphically describes how the components of XTS interact with one another. More details will be seen in subsequent sections.

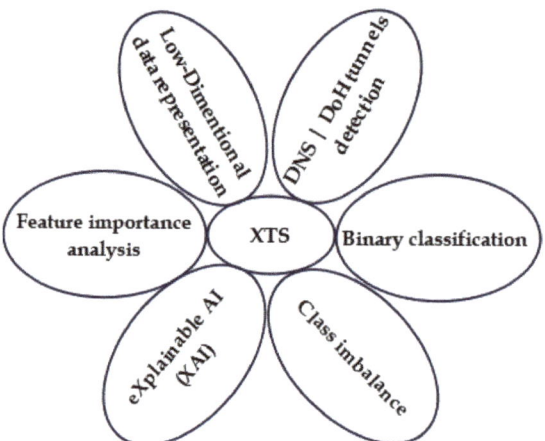

Figure 2. Research directions or problems that XTS framework revolves around.

Let the number of positive instances in the dataset be denoted as P, and the number of negative instances as N. If P << N, meaning that the number of positive instances is significantly smaller than the number of negative instances, then the dataset is said to be imbalanced. In the context of machine learning models, this imbalance can cause the model to have a bias towards the majority class as it will have more data to learn from the majority class than the minority class. This can result in poor model performance when used on the minority class, which is often the class of interest in real-world applications.

The issue with class imbalance is that machine learning algorithms are designed to optimize for overall accuracy, which can lead to a bias towards the majority class, resulting in poor performance in predicting the minority class. This can be especially problematic when the minority class is the one of interest, such as in fraud detection or malware detection and medical diagnosis.

To address the problem of class imbalance, various sampling techniques such as the synthetic minority over-sampling technique (SMOTE) [60] have become common approaches in the field of imbalance data. This technique, however, come with the cost of increased training time and label noise [26]. To address this problem, the cost-sensitive parameter c of cost-sensitive designed models can be the best alternate simplified solution.

This method assigns heavy weight to the loss function of the activated model to penalize the misclassification of the minority or positive class.

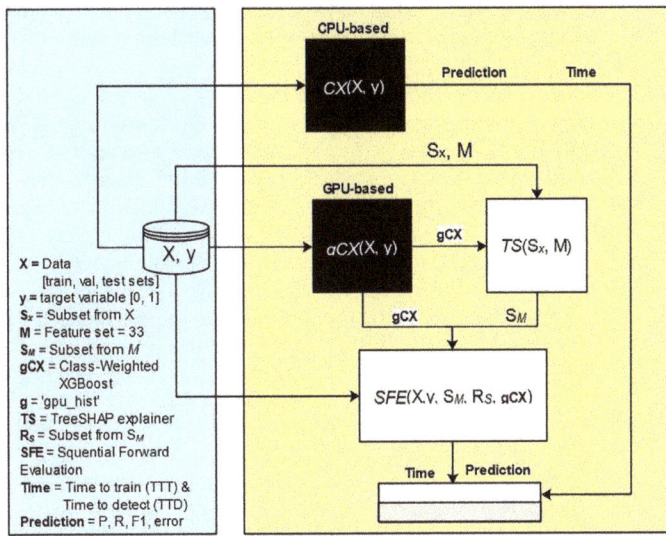

Figure 3. Abstract view of the proposed framework. The figure shows interaction between three components of XTS and how they access the data. X represents the set of traffic flow samples in a dataset while, while y represents a binary vector consisting of labels [0, 1]. CPU-based CX means cost-sensitive XGB trained on a CPU, while gCX shows an optimized CX to use gpu_hist —a tree split method parameter designed for in-speed optimization. TS is a TreeSHAP explainer for gCX. SFE is a newly developed algorithm to evaluate gCX model on data subsets.

Additionally, we investigated the use of the GPU-based histogram optimization method for tree-based models to speed up training times on CUDA-enabled computers [61].

In subsequent sections, particularly the framework design and other parts of the paper, we will write the following notations as:

- XTS: The dubbed term of our framework. X represents collectively the cost-sensitive and GPU-aware eXtreme Gradient Boosting; T is for Tree Explainer; and S is for Sequential Forward Evaluation algorithm, designed in this study.
- CX: The non-cost-sensitive version of XGBoost, trained with CPU-only capability, where C stands for cost-sensitive or, more technically, the parameter "scale_pos_weight" in XGB algorithm.
- gCX: The GPU-aware version of XGB. Where g stands for GPU capability activation or, more technically, the string "gpu_hist" for tree method parameter.
- Dataset (X, y) represents any dataset used to train, evaluate, test or explain the models specified above.
- TTT: The time to train a machine learning model.
- TTD: The time to detect—the time taken by the model to predict test examples.
- Layer 1: The task of classifying HTTPS traffic into DNS-over-HTTPS (DoH) and normal web browsing activities (NonDoH). Dataset for this task is denoted as D.
- Layer 2: The task of characterizing DNS-over-HTTPS (DoH). Classifying DoH traffic into malicious or benign DoH. The dataset for this task is denoted as B. It is important to mention that we keep lower traffic samples of benign class in D as is and consider it to be the positive class for detection. Contrary to the commonly practiced methods of making malicious a minority, positive class, we deviate a little in order to prove otherwise.

3.2. Analytical Modeling of DoH Tunnels Using XTS

This section presents mathematical analysis of the proposed framework and its application to the detection of DNS-over-HTTPS tunnels in HTTPS traffic. We also explain the performance metrics used for highly imbalanced data.

3.2.1. XGB Mathematical Abstract

Analytical modeling of HTTPS traffic flows using XTS framework involves using the XGBoost algorithm to learn a function that can predict the type of traffic flows in a network based on a set of input features. XGBoost uses classification decision trees called estimators as the base or weak learners. The final model output of a sample is a summation results of all the learners' trained iteratively, as shown in Figure 4. Let $P = \{1, 2, 3, \ldots M\}$ denote the set of weak learners, where M is the total number of trees in the model. If y_i is used to represent the true label DoH (1) or NonDoH (0), or Malicious (0), Benign (1) of a traffic flow x_i in the dataset D or B respectively—in our case, then the predicted value $f_M(x_i)$ of the XGBoost model can be expressed in Equation (1) as:

$$f_M(x_i) = \sum_{m=1}^{M} f_m(x_i), \; f \in F \qquad (1)$$

where F represents a set of all classification trees and $f_m(x_i)$ the individual base classifier's prediction. The raw output or scores from each tree in XGBoost is referred to as the "raw prediction" and is denoted by z [62]. The predicted probability is then obtained by passing the raw prediction through the sigmoid function in Equation (2)

$$P(z) = \frac{1}{1+e^{-z}} \qquad (2)$$

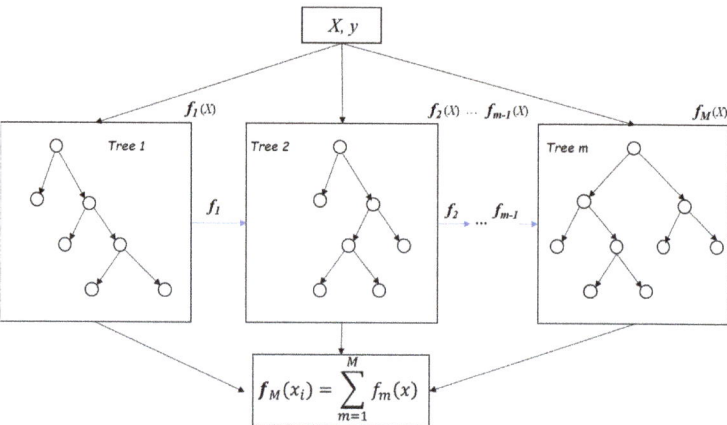

Figure 4. A general architecture of XGB showing abstract graphical representation of internal forest. Each tree in the model represents a decision tree classifier. x_i refers to a single traffic flow instance. $f_M(x_i)$ refers to the final XGB output.

To minimize the objective function $obj(\theta)$, Equation (3) is computed as:

$$obj(\theta) = L(\theta) + \Omega(\theta) \qquad (3)$$

where $L(\theta) = \sum_{i=1}^{n} l(y_i, \hat{y}_i)$ is the loss function and $\Omega(\theta) = \sum_{m=1}^{M} \Omega(f_m)$ the regularization parameter that penalizes the complexity of the model. Since training happens in iteration process, the prediction value $\hat{y}_i^{(t)}$ of an instance ith in iteration t, is expressed in Equation (4).

$$\hat{y}_i^{(t)} = \hat{y}_i^{(t-1)} + f_t(x_i) \tag{4}$$

Since the problem is a binary classification, we let the model use the predetermined loss function which is the cross entropy.in Equation (5).

$$L(y_i, \hat{y}_i) = -[y_i log(\hat{y}_i) + (1 - \hat{y}_i) log(1 - \hat{y}_i)] \tag{5}$$

where y is the true label (either 0 or 1) and $\hat{y}$ is the predicted probability of the positive class (i.e., the output of the sigmoid function) $P(z)$ as shown in Equation (2). The loss is minimized when the predicted probabilities $\hat{y}$ are as close as possible to the true labels y.

3.2.2. Dealing with Imbalance Data Using CX

Cost-Sensitive XGB assigns weights to training samples according to class proportions. This allows the algorithm to associate the cost of misclassification. Let i be a predicted class and j the actual class of an instance x. Let also $C(i, j)$ a function that computes the cost of predicting actual class j as i, for instance, a model predict class DoH as nonDoH or Benign as Malicious, we assign heavy cost according to the class ratio. If we let n be the total number of majority class, negative (0) and p the minority, positive class (1), the cost of misclassifying minority will be n/p shows a matrix of how the algorithm assigns the cost for a binary classification. In Layer 1, we assign

The expected cost of classifying x into class i can be expressed in Equation (6).

$$C(i|x) = \sum_j P(j|x) \, C(j, i) \tag{6}$$

In order to incorporate weighting and cost sensitivity into our XGBoost model for the classification of DoH and non-DoH traffic in Layer 1, as well as the classification of Benign and Malicious traffic in Layer 2, we adjusted the parameter C to assign different weights to each class as shown in Equation (6) and Table 1. This allows us to consider the costs associated with misclassifying samples and tailor the model's behavior accordingly.

Table 1. Cost matrix for binary classification.

	Predicted Positive	Predicted Negative
Actual Positive	C (1, 1) = 1	C (0, 1) = n/p
Actual Negative	C (1, 0) = 1	C (0, 0) = 1

3.2.3. Compared Models' Computation Time Complexity

Let $D^{n \times m}$ be a dataset with n samples and m feature variables. Assume v is the number of support vectors, K the number of trees, d the depth of the tree and $\|X\|_0$ the number of non-missing entries in the training data. Table 2 shows the computational time complexity for each model that was used in this paper. To choose the best model, the time parameter was equally considered, with the assumption that, based on Table 3, if M is a vector space of dataset features, reducing M to a very significant number $S \subseteq M$ will result in low-dimensional representation data, thus presumably reducing computational cost (time and space). In our experiment, we performed empirical tests while observing the model's prediction performance. Overfitting was observed diligently.

Table 2. Computational time complexity of baseline models.

Model	TTT	TTD
LR	$O(n \times m)$	$O(m)$
SVM	$O(n^2)$	$O(v \times m)$
RF	$O(K \times n \times \log n \times m)$	$O(K \times m)$
XGB	$O(K \times d \times \|X\|_0 + \|X\|_0 \times \log n)$	$O(K \times d)$

Table 3. Traffic flows features.

Category	Feature Name
Flow Direction	F1: Source IP, F2: Destination IP, F3: Source Port, F4: Destination Port.
Packet Bytes	F5: Duration, F6: Number of flow bytes sent, F7: Rate of flow bytes sent, F8: Number of flow bytes received, F9: Rates of flow bytes received.
Packet Length	F10: Mean, F11: Median, F12: Mode, F13: Variance, F14: Standard deviation, F15: Coefficient of variation, F16: Skew from median, F17: Skew from mode.
Packet Time	F18: Mean, F19: Median, F20: Mode, F21: Variance, F22: Standard Deviation, F23: Coefficient of variation, F24: Skew from median, F25: Skew from mode
Request/response time difference	F26: Mean, F27: Median, F28: Mode, F29: Variance, F30: Standard Deviation, F31: Coefficient of variation, F32: Skew from median, F33: Skew from mode.

3.2.4. Speed Optimization Using gCX

The XGB model provides many parameters and methods commonly used to minimize computational cost, such as reducing the number of trees, column sampling, pruning a tree, among others. Finding the optimum parameters require trial and error process, which takes more time. However, with the pervasive use of GPU-based processors in today's laptops, many researchers have not realized the great speed benefits of running a GPU-based XGB model. This paper demonstrates the difference between running a GPU and CPU-based XGB models as a simple but effective means of minimizing computational cost.

According to Tianqi et al. [62,63], there are 4 tree methods, namely exact, approx, hist and gpu_hist used as split finding methods; they have a great impact on XGB computational time. exact tree method is slower in performance by $O(K \times d \|X\|_0 + \|X\|_0 \times \log n)$ and not scalable. approx tree method makes the algorithm faster than the previous by $O(K \times d \times \|X\|_0 + \|X\|_0 \times \log B)$, where B is the maximum number of rows in each block. Unlike approx., which generates a new set of bins for each iteration, the hist method reuses the bins over multiple iterations. It is a faster tree construction method on CPU computers. Although the hist method was faster than all its predecessors, Mitchell et al. [64] developed a CUDA-capable GPU method to construct a tree algorithm, namely the gpu_hist method. We only set the following parameters in our experiment, namely, generic XGB speedup to (11 times, 1.08 times) in layer 1, and (5 times, 1.14 times) in layer 2 for TTT and TTD, respectively. This model is represented as gCX in the framework.

3.2.5. Feature Importance Modeling and Analysis

In this section, we employ the Tree Explainer method to interpret the prediction output of our gCX model and learn the importance of features in predicting the samples in our datasets, or in a specific sample x_i. The Tree Explainer is a variation of SHAP (SHapley Additive exPlanations) kernels, which are based on the concept of SHAP values.

SHAP values were introduced by Lundberg and Lee in 2017 [65], drawing inspiration from the coalitional game theory developed by Lloyd Shapley [66]. These values provide a principled approach to fairly distribute the contributions of features towards the model's output, ensuring interpretability and an understanding of feature importance.

We choose to utilize the Tree Explainer method instead of the kernel explainer due to its computational efficiency. The Tree Explainer leverages the tree-based structure of the

XGB model to approximate the SHAP values, resulting in faster computation times while still providing reliable interpretations of feature importance [67].

To model the feature importance using SHAP values, let M denote a set of all input features of a dataset D or B and gCX indicate the previously optimized XGB classifier (that maps input feature vector $x \in \mathbb{R}^{|N|}$ to an output $f(x) \in [0, 1]$ for DoH tunnels classification. SHAP values present the only single solution to "fairly" spread the features contributions towards $f(x)$ and satisfies three desirable properties: local accuracy, missingness, and consistency [60,61].

Let $f_x(s)$ denote the model's output constrained to the feature subset $S \cup M$. Based on the classical Shapley values [original], SHAP values are generally computed as follows:

$$\varnothing i = \sum_{S \subseteq M \setminus \{i\}} \frac{|S|!(M-|S|-1)!}{M!} [f_x(S \cup \{i\}) - f_x(S)] \tag{7}$$

where $f_x(S \cup \{i\})$ is the model's output of the instance x constrained to the feature set $S \cup M$, excluding the ith feature. SHAP was designed as an model-agnostic explainer g to mimic the process that the original model f used to predict a specific prediction so that $f(x_i) \approx g(x_i)$. To compute the contribution of a feature j, referred to as I_j, where $j \in M$ feature set, its mean absolute SHAP values across the dataset is calculated as follows:

$$I_j = \frac{1}{n} \sum_{i=1}^{n} \left| \varnothing_j^{(i)} \right| \tag{8}$$

TreeSHAP: It is a variant of SHAP Kernel method. Kernel method is model-agnostic, whereas TreeSHAP was designed specifically for tree-based models such as decision tree, random forest and gradient boosting models. Unlike Kernel SHAP, Tree SHAP computes SHAP values in polynomial, rather than exponential, time to reduce the computational time by $O(TLD^2)$ from of $O(TL2^M)$, which makes it faster than its counterpart; T is the number of trees; L is the maximum number of leaves in any tree; and D is the maximum depth of any tree. Due to the additive nature of SHAP, the output SHAP value on an ensemble model is a weighted average of the SHAP values of the individual tree.

SHAP values plots: a feature SHAP value can be calculated for all or some samples in the dataset. The SHAP library provides plots to summarize features at the local and global view. In this paper, three plots (force plot, feature importance plot and the summary plot) were chosen to present the results.

The force plot [53,65,65] shows how each feature value pushes to increase the baseline towards the model's output value.

A baseline or base value on the plot is the value that would be predicted if the features contributions were unknown to the current model output $f(x)$. In other words, it is the mean prediction of the model's explainer on the passed dataset. Equation (9) shows the formula used to compute the baseline value.

$$\bar{y} = \frac{1}{n} \sum_{i=1}^{n} \hat{y} \tag{9}$$

In the force plot as shown in Figure 5, features are stacked in colored (red/blue) arrows or bars according to their SHAP values ($\varnothing$). Red bars, pushing towards right, means that, the corresponding feature's original value pushes the model to the higher output $f(x)$ from the base value calculated in Equation (10). By higher output, it means positive class, in a binary problem. On another hand, the blue bars, pushing towards left, means that, the corresponding feature's original value pushes the model to the lower output $f(x)$ negative class (0) from the base value.

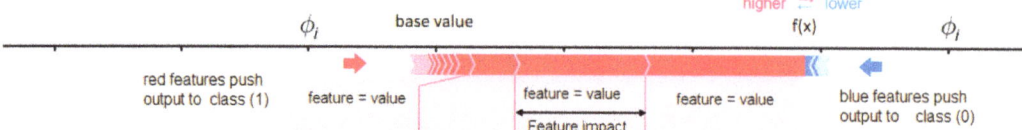

Figure 5. Generic view of the SHAP force plot.

The magnitude of the bar indicates the degree of influence, measured in SHAP values, which a feature has on the model's output. For a binary problem, the positive model output, which could be the probabilities or log odds, indicates a positive (1) prediction. Conversely, a negative output means a negative class (0) prediction. It is to be noted that Tree Explainer library in the Scikit-learn library as of the writing of this paper, allows the model output to be 'raw', indicating the score values of the underlying tree model before the sigmoid function is used to compute probabilities. They are real-valued numbers in the form of log-odds. The positive numbers represent the high confidence of the model to predict a sample x_i as a positive class (1). To achieve this, we set the link function to logit for the model to transform the log-odds back into probabilities, something which can be achieved separately using the sigmoid function shown in Equation (2). This is due to the known property of inversibility between logit/log-odds function and sigmoid.

A feature importance plot displays sorted global SHAP values of the features on (x, y) axis, where x indicates a scale of SHAP values ranging from (low to high) and y the features from MSF (top) to LSF (bottom).

The summary plot shows the relationship between the values of the feature and their impact on the prediction. The SHAP values of individual samples are plotted onto a 2D graph as dots across the x axis against their corresponding features to a form SHAP value distribution (a bee-like swarm), as seen in Figure 6. Each dot (SHAP value) is presented in color (red, blue) to indicate the magnitude of the original feature value. The intensity of the colors on the color bar (right of the plot) indicates the degree of the original feature's values across the entire column in the dataset. A strong red (top of the bar) means a higher value and a strong blue (bottom of the bar) means a lower value. To determine whether a value is high or low, it is compared to its column's average value. If the value of the feature is greater than its average, its corresponding SHAP value is colored with red. In the inverse situation, it is colored blue.

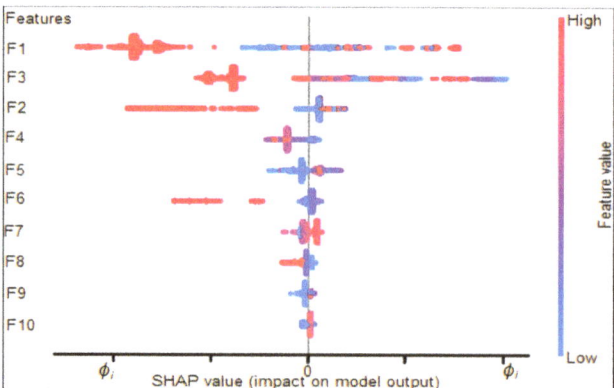

Figure 6. Generic view of SHAP summary plot.

3.2.6. Low-Dimensional Representation Using SFE

A Sequential Forward Evaluation algorithm is developed in this paper to evaluate how the gCX model performs on features subsets. Algorithm 1 shows how gCX is evaluated on each subset. S_M is a set of integer numbers $(u_1, u_2, u_3, \ldots, u_m)$. They are the indices of features in S_M. The process starts by initializing a variable R_s to hold a set of feature indices. The algorithm employed in this approach does not rely on complex mathematical constructs, such as permutation or shuffling. Instead, it adopts a simple feed-forward design principle. Despite its simplicity, this algorithm enables us to sequentially evaluate the model's performance and gain valuable insights into the importance of different features in determining a model's output.

By creating subsets of features and evaluating the model using these subsets, we are able to achieve high prediction scores while keeping the dimensionality relatively low. This approach allows us to effectively analyze and understand the contribution of individual features to the model's output. It also addresses the challenges posed by high dimensionality in the dataset, which is an important consideration in many real-world applications. For each iteration, the model operates on the next newly formed S_i. This allows the model to access all samples of the dataset by using the selected features to study the contribution of the feature subsets without changing their contribution order.

For each iteration, error rate or loss and aucpr curves are displayed to monitor the model's learning process. TTT and TTD are each recorded in a variable set to keep track of computational time by subset. Additionally, other evaluation metrics are recorded for comparison.

Algorithm 1: Sequential Forward Evaluation.

Input: A list of m top 10 selected features from the main feature set M
Output: Computational time (TTT, TTD), evaluation metrics (P, R, $F1$, $AUCPR$, $loss$) for all subsets

1 **Require:** $S_M \leftarrow [u_1, u_2, u_3, \ldots, u_m]; u \in \mathbb{Z}^+; S \subseteq M$
    Create a subset S_M of selected top features m from original feature set M
2 **Initialize:** $R_s \leftarrow \emptyset; t_{train} \leftarrow \emptyset; t_{pred} \leftarrow \emptyset; R_s \subseteq S_M$ // initialize features index and time sets to null
3 **Procedure** ($X_{train}; X_{val}; X_{test}; y_{train}; y_{val}; y_{test}$)
4   **for all** $u \in S_M$ **do** // create a subset for each iteration
5          $R_s \leftarrow R_s \cup \{u_i\}$ // add one feature to create a new subset
6          $t_0 \leftarrow time.time()$ // time before training and validation
7          $cfr \leftarrow f(X_{train}[:, R_s], y_{train}, [(X_{train}[:, R_s], y_{train}), (X_{val}[:, R_s], y_{val})])$ // train the model
8          $t_1 \leftarrow time.time$ // time after training and validation
9          $t_t \leftarrow t_1 - t_0$ // Time-to-Train (TTT) including validation time
10   **append** t_t to t_{train} // add TTT of a subset to training time set
11         $t'_0 \leftarrow time.time()$ //time before testing
12         $y \leftarrow cfr(X_{test}[:, R_s])$ //test the model
13         $t'_1 \leftarrow time.time()$ //time after testing
14         $t_d \leftarrow t'_1 - t'_0$ //Time-to-Detect (TTD)
15   **append** t_d to t_{test} // add TTD of a subset to prediction time set
16   **record** log
17   **call** plot functions (y_{test}, y_{pred})
18   **end for**
20 **end procedure**

3.2.7. Model Performance Metrics

Throughout this paper, the model's performance evaluation is measured in two dimensions: model's prediction performance using (precision, recall, F1-Score, AUCPR, confusion matrix) and computational time (time to train and time to detect). Prediction performance metrics: precision (P), recall (R), F1-Score ($F1$) and AUCPR are the ML metrics suitable for application to problems with highly imbalanced or skewed data.

DoH samples in layer 1 represent the positive class (minority), while NonDoH samples represent the negative class (majority). Benign flows in layer 2 represent the positive class (minority) and malicious flows represent the negative class (majority). For highly imbalanced data, the model tends to be biased towards the majority class, where huge number of actual positive samples are predicted as negative (FN). In rare cases, the actual negative samples may be predicted as positive (FP). Hence, in the most cases as in our case of security incident monitoring, the success of the model is measured on how it correctly predicts the positive class (low FN). Since the benign class is the minority/positive class in our case, we pay attention to how the model detects this class rather than the malicious class, as described in Section 3.1.

To achieve this goal, a confusion matrix for binary classification is created to further help in calculating other metrics.

- Precision: Precision metric shows, from all the instances that the model predicted as belonging to the positive class (TP + FP), the percentage of those which were actually true positive (TP). In this paper, it refers to how many DoH samples were predicted correctly out of all predicted as DoH and/or how many benign samples were predicted correctly out of all predicted as benign, in layer 1 and layer 2, respectively.

$$P = \frac{TP}{TP + FP} \qquad (10)$$

- Recall: Recall metric shows, from all the instances of positive class (TP + FN), the percentage of those which the model predicted correctly. In this paper, it refers to how many DoH or Benign flows were predicted correctly in layer 1 or 2 respectively.

$$R = \frac{TP}{TP + FN} \qquad (11)$$

- F1-Score: F1-Score measures the overall average of both Precision and Recall.

$$F1 = 2\frac{P * R}{P + R} \qquad (12)$$

- AUCPR: Area Under the (Precision-Recall) Curve also known as Average precision (AP), shows a relationship between the Recall and Precision on a scale between 0 and 1. Equation (13), shows how to compute AP, where R_n and P_n mean the recall and precision at the ith threshold. Unlike AUC-ROC curves which considers the balance between positive and negative classes, AUCPR/AP focuses on how correctly the positive (minority) class is predicted [68]

$$AP = \sum_n (R_n - R_{n-1}) P_n \qquad (13)$$

If these metrics are used by the IDS implementing this model, FP may be noisy warnings but less dangerous than FN in layer 1, which is opposite in layer 2. However, security guidelines are defined by the company rules. In this paper both metrics are equally important, though much focus is put on the minority class to avoid the errors which may be caused by the imbalance and skewness of the dataset [24].

3.3. Proposed Application Domain

At the edge AI network, IoT or other devices may be compromised by a remote C2 implementing DoH tunneling attacks, as shown in Figure 7. A rule-based firewall may not be able to detect intrusion due to similarity with normal HTTPS traffic. For a supervised task of this kind, XTS would be recommended, among other solutions. The idea of this framework was inspired by the recent research buzz surrounding the newly envisioned 6G technology and intelligent multimedia [5–8].

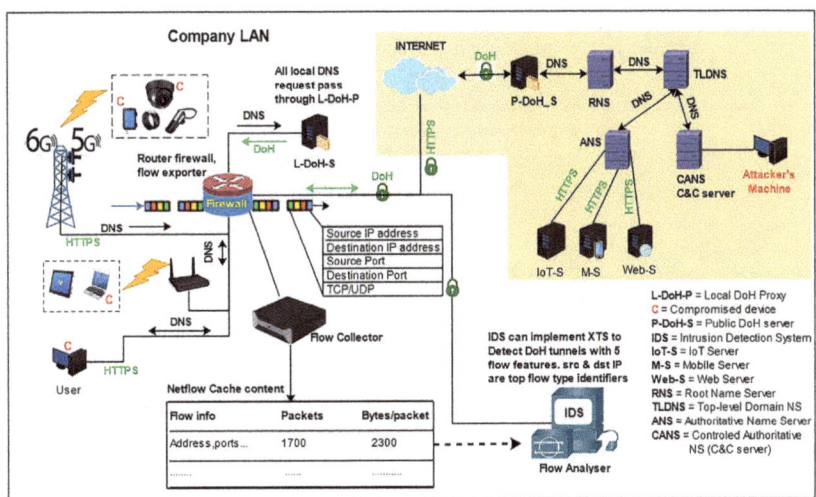

Figure 7. A graphical view of positioning a proposed method as an engine in the intrusion detection system (IDS) at the edge AI network. At the edge AI, IoT or other devices may be compromised by a remote C2 implementing DoH tunneling attacks. Rule-based firewall may not be able to detect intrusion due to similarity with normal https traffic. A flow collector would collect flow metadata and send them to IDS for analysis.

This new technology, as was mentioned in Section 1, anticipate enormous amount of heterogeneous data due to the sparsity of data and their imbalanced nature; TTT and TTD are among the concerned parameters. Information security is also among areas that will undoubtedly be affected. Therefore, an approach is needed that reduces data dimensionality and enables small devices to collect only a small number of variables and improve model interpretability. The solution should not only help us to minimize computation cost but also should assist users to understand consistency and individualized model output decisions. Additionally, it may need to minimize the attack surface due to reduced user features. This framework would serve as an abstract view of how security devices such as IDS or SIEM at the edge network would be optimized to report more accurate and understandable results, while reducing computation costs in a growing ecosystem of faster data.

4. Materials and Methods

This study is a computer experimental-based design. This section explains the experimental procedures used to empirically evaluate the design of the XTS framework redescribed in the previous sections.

4.1. Dataset Description

The dataset namely CIRA-CIC-DoHBrw-2020, used to evaluate the proposed method, was created by the Canadian Institute for Cybersecurity (CIC) project, which was funded by Canadian Internet Registration Authority (CIRA). It was made publicly available by [69]. The authors of this dataset conducted DNS-over-HTTPS tunneling attack using proof-of-concepts tools in a lab-controlled environment. They followed a two-layered architecture: in layer 1, they classified HTTPS traffic into DNS-over-HTPPS (DoH) and normal HTTPS web browsing activities (NonDoH). In layer 2, DoH traffic flows were characterized into malicious DoH and benign DoH.

The data were captured in two phases: In the first phase of data capturing, web browsers (Google Chrome and Mozilla Firefox) were configured to send DNS requests to the public DoH resolvers (AdGuard, Cloudflare, Google DNS, and Quad9) through a local DoH proxy server. The flow samples were captured between the proxy server and the public DoH server to include both (benign DoH) and normal HTTPS browsing activities (NonDoH). In the second phase, three DoH-based C2 tunnelling tools (namely, Iodine [70], DNS2TCP [71], and DNScat2 [72]) were used to communicate with malicious C2 servers on the Internet. To make sure that only malicious DoH traffic (malicious DoH) was captured, other browsing activities were prevented. All traffic were captured as bi-directional traffic (where requests and responses are combined in one flow) and saved in PCAP files. A new custom application namely DOHLyser [73] was developed to extract flow-based statistical and timeseries features and saved as CSV files.

4.2. Experimental Setup

4.2.1. Overview

The experimental setup in this study aimed to rigorously evaluate the performance of the proposed XTS framework in DNS/DoH tunnels detection as described in Figure 8. The selection and preparation of suitable datasets, along with careful parameter tuning and model comparisons, were conducted to ensure the obtention of robust and meaningful results.

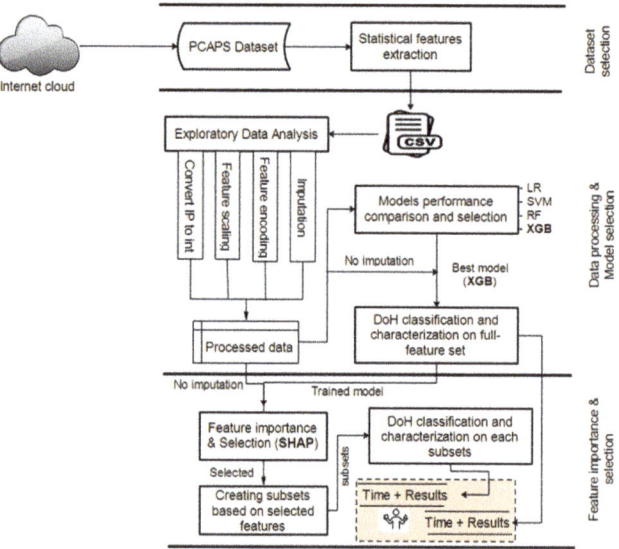

Figure 8. A workflow diagram showing experimental process.

The datasets used in this experiment consisted of a diverse range of network traffic, including normal HTTPS, benign, and malicious traffic. These datasets were obtained from a publicly available repository, ensuring the availability of real-world and representative samples. To ensure that the datasets were appropriately processed, several steps were taken. IP addresses were converted into numerical integer values to facilitate analysis and modeling. Feature scaling, imputation of missing variables, and the label encoding of target classes were performed to ensure compatibility with the chosen machine learning algorithms. A comprehensive comparison was conducted among five well-known machine learning models, excluding deep learning models. In this comparison, default parameter settings were used for all models, except for models that could be transformed into cost-sensitive models. Models not designed with this feature, such as Bayes models, were excluded from initial consideration.

Standard XGB was hyper-parameterized, taking into account cost sensitivity and speed optimization. GPU acceleration was utilized to leverage computational power for use in efficient training and testing. To gain insights into the model's decision-making process, the SHAP Tree Explainer was applied to provide interpretable explanations. Three types of SHAP plots were generated: a global SHAP summary plot, local explanations, and individualized sample explanations. These visualizations helped use to identify the most influential features and understand how they contributed to the model's predictions. Additionally, feature subset evaluation was conducted to assess the impact of different feature combinations on the model's performance. A sequential algorithm was employed to create subsets of increasing size, and training and testing were performed for each subset. This analysis allowed for a deeper understanding of the importance and relevance of specific features in the DNS/DoH tunnels detection task.

The experimental setup was designed to be rigorous, scientifically valid, and comprehensive. By leveraging appropriate datasets, conducting model comparisons, hyperparameter tuning, and utilizing explainability techniques, the XTS framework demonstrated its effectiveness in addressing the DNS/DoH tunnel detection problem. The subsequent sections will present the results and discuss their implications in detail.

We trained the newly hyper-parameterized XGBoost on full features datasets, split divided into three distinct subsets: training, validation, and testing, with sizes of 60%, 20%, and 20%, respectively. The experiments were conducted on a Lenovo laptop, which featured an Intel i7-9750H CPU with 6 cores clocked at 2.6 GHz, a Pascal GTX 1050 GPU with 2 GB of memory, and 8 GB of RAM. Important parameters were set as follows: objective function = 'binary:logistic', booster = 'gbtree', n_estimators = 100, scale_pos_weight = majority_class/minority_class, tree_method = 'gpu_hist', eval_metric = ['logloss', 'aucpr']. To track the results of separate datasets, an instance for each dataset was created. There were, on average, 20 epochs on average and 7-fold CV.

The loss/AUCPR log results were collected to plot loss and AUCPR values. A trained model instance was fitted in the SHAP Tree Explainer for interpretation. Three SHAP plots were created—global shap summary plot, local explanations and individualized sample explanations. We selected the top 10 most significant features and created 10 subsets sequentially using written Algorithm 1. These were recorded for each training and testing time, along with prediction scores, each time a new subset was created. Finally, the different results were compared.

4.2.2. Data Engineering

To begin with, the source and destination features, represented as string objects, were converted into numeric whole numbers. We performed this with the intuition that the model could learn some insights from the numerical representation of the source and destination. Another study considered this before and argued that the model would present its decision in numerical format. For us, these features were crucial in our working hypothesis. Feature scaling using standardization Equation (14) was applied to all integer features to reduce their magnitudes, thus increasing the chance to prevent model's overfitting and speed up its convergence.

$$z = \frac{x - \mu}{\sigma} \tag{14}$$

A new score z or standard is computed from μ (the mean) and σ (the standard deviation from the mean). This technique scales the feature values in the range $[-1, 1]$, so that they will have properties of the standard normal distribution with the mean $\mu = 0$ and the standard deviation $\sigma = 1$. Since this is a binary classification problem, a vector y is encoded and assumed to represent the target variable such that, $y_1 = [0, 1]$ represents the target variable in layer 1, where 0 means NonDoH and 1 is the DoH class. On another hand, $y_2 = [0, 1]$ represents the target variable in layer 2, where 0 means Malicious and 1 is the Benign class.

Both datasets D and B exhibit a high degree of class imbalance, as revealed by the samples per layer presented in Figure 9.

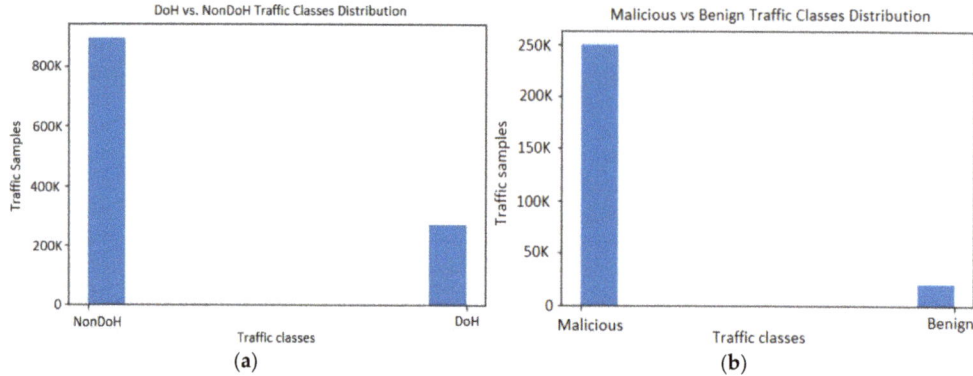

Figure 9. Classes distribution. (**a**) shows that, the distribution of classes in layer 1, DoH class is the minority (Positive class). (**b**) shows that Benign DoH class is the minority (Positive class) in layer 2.

Based on the numbers in Table 4, the graphical distribution of classes depicted in Figure 9, specifically, Figure 9a, displays a class ratio of 8:2, while Figure 9b exhibits a more imbalanced ratio of 9:1. Moreover, both datasets contain 16,056 missing values each, and therefore, imputation was performed on the relevant variables by filling the missing values with the column mean, as per Equation (15).

$$\hat{x} = \frac{1}{n}\sum_{i=1}^{n} x_i \qquad (15)$$

Table 4. Sample sizes per class.

Layer 1: Classification of HTTPS Traffics	
Class	Sample size
NonDoH	897,493
DoH	269,643
Layer 2: DoH Characterization	
Benign DoH	19,807
Malicious DoH	249,836

4.2.3. Model Selection

Based on a comparative analysis with other popular machine learning models, including logistic regression (LR), support vector machine (SVM), and random forest (RF), we found that XGB outperforms other models on the selected datasets. Our selection of XGB was based on its empirical performance in terms of accuracy and computational efficiency. Additionally, our choice was motivated by its popularity and its widespread use in the machine learning research community [74]. All the models were trained with default parameters, with their respective cost-sensitive parameters being set as indicated in Section 3.2.2.

The comparison of both dataset D and B indicates that LR exhibits faster training and detection times compared to other models, albeit with the lowest F1-score, Figure 10. SVM, on the other hand, achieves excellent F1-score but at the expense of being the slowest model. RF and XGB demonstrate outstanding F1-scores, with XGB outperforming RF in terms of training latency and detection speed. Specifically, RF's training latency is nearly 5 times that of XGB, while its detection speed is approximately 20 times slower than XGB. The selection of XGB was based on its higher prediction performance, lower training latency, and faster detection speed. The elimination criteria were primarily based on prediction performance and computational time. Other factors, such as missing value handling and scalability, were also taken into account, especially in cases where models had similar results, as shown by RF and XGB in Section 5.

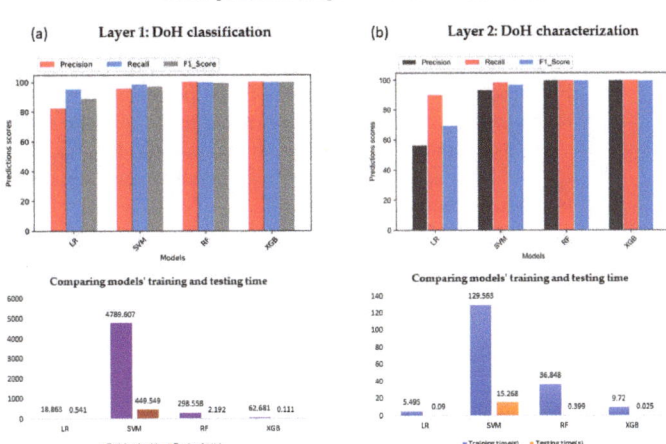

Figure 10. Performance comparisons of the most commonly used ML models across two layers using two separate datasets, D and B. The results presented in Table 1, clearly demonstrate that XGB consistently outperforms all other models on average in both Layer 1 (**a**) and Layer 2 (**b**). These initial results provide a compelling reason to prioritize XGB for further investigation and analysis. Its consistently strong performance suggests that it possesses characteristics and capabilities that make it particularly well-suited to the task at hand.

5. Results and Discussion

The gCX model demonstrated unrivaled performance compared to other models in the experiments. It outperformed the baseline models in terms of predictive accuracy, precision, recall, and F1-score as shown in Figure 10. The utilization of weighted parameters and the incorporation of SHAP values for feature importance analysis played a role in achieving this superior performance. The gCX model's ability to handle class imbalance and its effective utilization of the underlying structure in the data contributed to its exceptional results. These findings highlight the effectiveness of the gCX model in tackling the challenges posed by the DoH tunnels dataset and its potential to make accurate and reliable predictions in the context of highly imbalanced-binary classification tasks.

5.1. Prediction vs. Computational Time

This section of the findings addresses the concern of overfitting that may arise from the results presented in Figures 11 and 12. While the possibility of overfitting is acknowledged, we have not found substantial empirical evidence to support this assumption. Several reasons contribute to this perspective. Firstly, gCX, our chosen model, is optimized using the best parameters specifically tailored for the problem under investigation, as outlined in Section 4. This optimization process enhances the model's performance and reduces the likelihood of overfitting. Secondly, the models employed in this research have been widely recognized as exceptional within the research community. Their effectiveness and reliability have been extensively demonstrated in various studies, providing further confidence in their robustness. Thirdly, the evaluation metrics used, such as the confusion matrix and log-based measures (log loss, AUC–PR), are well-established and trustworthy for use in assessing imbalanced models. These metrics offer reliable insights into the model's performance and its ability to handle imbalanced datasets. Fourthly, the dataset used in this study is relatively large, providing a sufficient number of samples for training and evaluation. Adequate sample size plays a crucial role in mitigating the risk of overfitting, and our dataset meets this requirement. Furthermore, we employed scientifically accepted methodologies to split the data and applied 7-fold cross validation, a widely recognized unbiased estimation method used by researchers in various machine leaning domains. For instance, K. Nkurikiyeyezu [75] provided convincing arguments on the same issue. Additionally, we conducted evaluations on subsets of the most significant features, Figure 11, further strengthening the reliability and generalizability of our findings. Based on these arguments, we are inclined to reject the notion that the model's exceptional performance on our labeled datasets is solely due to overfitting. However, we acknowledge the need for further research and exploration to deepen our understanding of both the data and the model's capabilities. By conducting additional investigations, we aim to gain more insights and validate the model's performance in diverse scenarios and datasets.

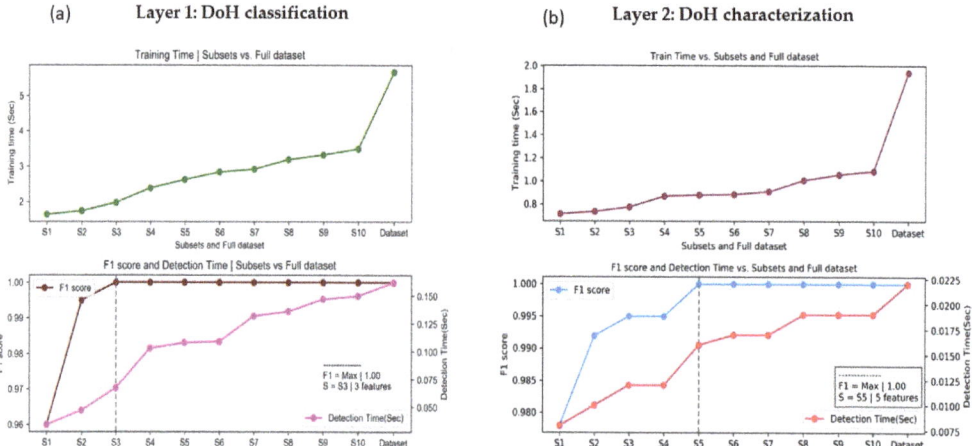

Figure 11. Prediction performance and computational time by different subsets created by Algorithm 1, subsets result vs. Dataset. S_i, $i = 1, 2, 3, \ldots$ 10, is a subset containing the number of features selected sequentially and additively in a forward manner. Taking 10 most important features generated by TS, we created 10 subsets. $S_i = S_{i-1} + 1$, where 1 is the next feature to the S_i in the selection list. Each S_i is fed to the model and the metrics in this figure are computed. The threshold line (vertically dotted line in the second row) indicates at which subset (how many important features) required for the model to achieve the highest (1.00) prediction scores (F1), how much time (TTT), TTD did the model use to train and detect (test) on that subset. As observed, the results are exceptionally good: even with just one of the most significant features, the model can detect desired class.

As stated, starting this section, we can observe in Figure 12a that when the model is trained only with one feature (S1) in the S_M list—Destination IP—according to Figure 13, it successfully recognizes all instances of DoH traffic and avoids false negatives, ensuring that no DoH traffic goes undetected. However, the relatively high number of false positives indicates that the model is also misclassifying a significant amount of non-DoH traffic as DoH. It is also the case in (b), where the model successfully detected many instances of benign DoH traffic, missing (FN) only around 21% (663) but misclassifying more than 14% (7123) of malicious traffic (FP). Expectedly, when the model is trained on the combined destination and source IP (S2) features (a), FP is reduced towards 0 (only 30 out of 179, 549), which is also the case in (b). These results confirm our hypothesis that C2 traffic is likely to be detected based only on unique connections at the IP level (the source and destination IPs) and probably with packet length statistical features such as packet length mode, mean, or median. The packet length effect was shown in (a), where 0 FN and FP are achieved only with 3 features (S3)—the first three most important features according to Figure 13, Layer 2. Consequently, based on the above empirical evidence, we can objectively reject the assumption of overfitting for the gCX model.

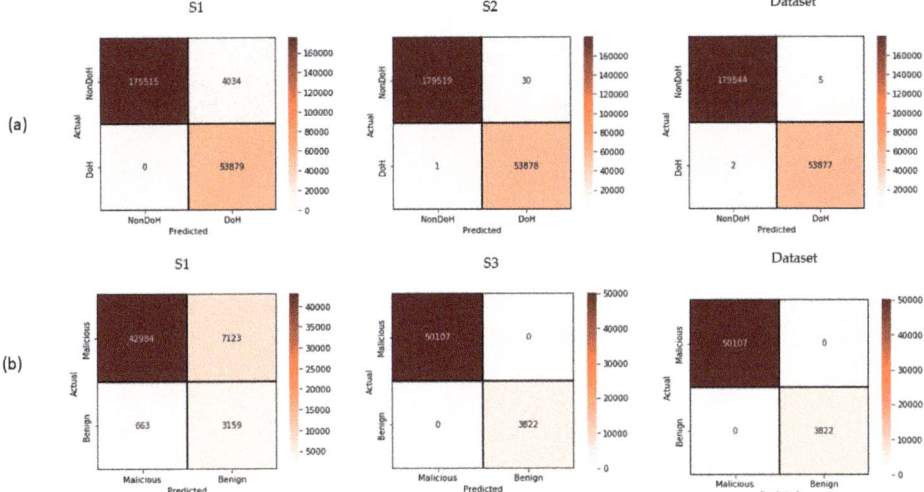

Figure 12. A confusion matrix showing the FP, FN, in both datasets (**a**,**b**). Overall, we observe that gCX can separate classes with minimum of two features. Since it performed poorly on one feature —(S1) in both (**a**,**b**), and improved exponentially after adding another one, and continue to improve even to the maximum, it is strong evidence that it's hard to accept the assumption of overfitting subjectively.

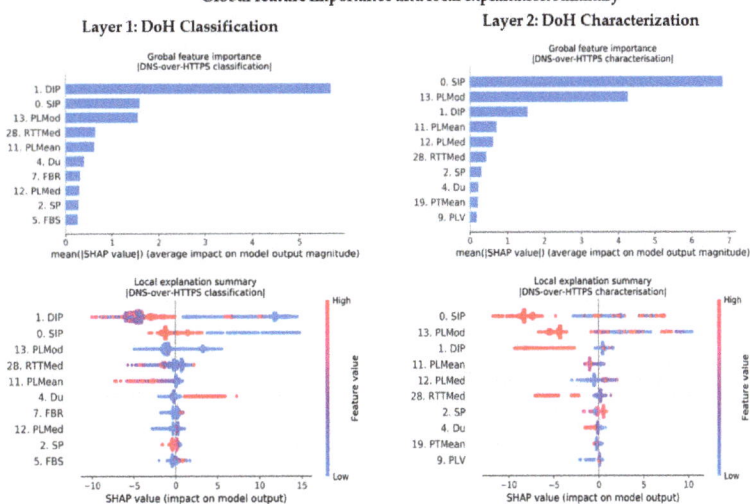

Figure 13. Global view of feature importance analysis. Both figures represent the global view of the features importance. While figures in the first row show a simplified summary of the features average arranged by their contributions, from top (more impact) to bottom (less impact), figures in the second row show a more detailed summary distribution of combined individual SHAP values of a single feature across the entire dataset, showing the relationship between the value of the feature and the impact of the prediction. The numbers before a feature name represent the index numbers in Table 3.

5.2. Feature Importance

In Figure 13, it is observed that at the global view, the model is likely to classify HTTPS traffic based mostly on three features, destination IP (DIP), packet length mode (PLMod) and source IP (SIP). Local explanation provides further insights about these features. For instance, there is a clear cut showing that, as the values of the feature samples become higher (which specifies that their values are higher than their respective column mean) in detecting benign flows (lower right), the model grows certain about the malicious class (negative SHAP values). The same is observed in Figure 14 (lower right) for sample 1996. It shows that, values of DIP, SIP and PLMod push the model to predict positive class (Benign), which is also the case for sample 7 (lower left).

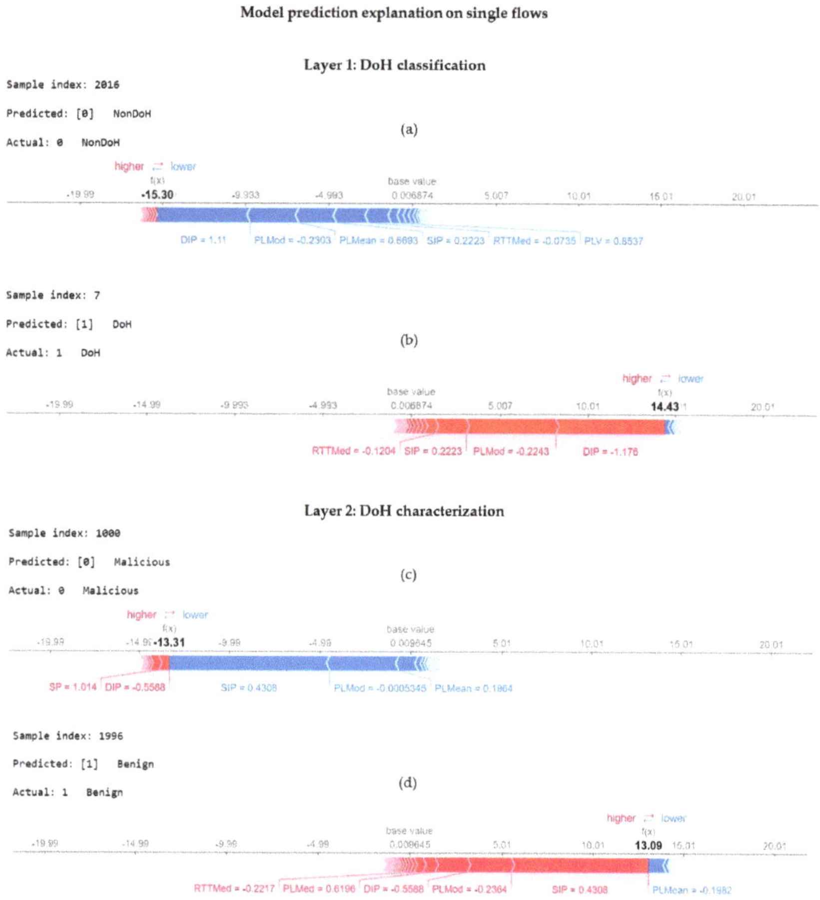

Figure 14. Single random traffic flow samples analysis using force plot (**a–d**). The number shown on the line as $f(x)$, indicates the log-odds value (raw prediction scores of gCX before a sigmoid function is applied) as was discussed in Section 3. This number indicates the confidence of predicting a positive class by gCX. As the number becomes higher (far from 0) the model increases the chances in predicting the positive class. The four samples were selected randomly from both datasets D (**a,b**) and B (**c,d**) to avoid bias interpretation. We can agree with high confidence that gCX was able to detect both classes with the highest accuracy based mostly on the three features that were indicated in Figure 13, being the most influential features.

Although this might not be generalized to the real-world scenario, where IP addresses vary significantly, we observed in our study that IP address numbers assigned to DoH tunnel computers are larger than those of benign traffic. In this case, we may assert that may the model was correct in predicting malicious traffic. There is supporting evidence behind the model basing its prediction on both flow connection and packet length size features in traffic flow analysis using statistical modeling.

The bold numbers on the SHAP values line in Figure 14 show the summation of all feature contributions and the expected value of the model towards the prediction of an individual sample [52] and are represented as log-odds. The color shows the magnitude of the feature values—not the SHAP values, where red indicates that the values of particular features were higher than the mean of their respective columns in the dataset and blue indicates otherwise [51]. We can observe in Figure 14a,c that whenever the values of the features are lower than their respective mean (blue), they push the model, gCX, to predict negative classes (non-DoH or malicious) following the order of feature contributions, contrary to the observation seen in (c) and (d), where values higher (red) than their mean push the model to predict positive classes (DoH or benign) following the order of feature contributions. It is important to note that there is not always an exact match between a single sample (Figure 14) and the overall local explanations (Figure 13, second row).

5.3. Comparison and Discussion

This research includes a comprehensive comparison of the proposed XTS model with other studies in the literature that utilized the same dataset and employed similar computational time measurements. It is unfortunate to note that many researchers did not provide extensive details of their experimental setup. However, even with these limitations, our findings highlight the superior performance of XTS as shown in Table 5.

Table 5. Comparison of the proposed framework (XTS) with related studies in the literature. *—the best performing methods before XTS; TTT—training time; TTD—testing time; (-)— indicates that we could not find these values in the mentioned papers. Where there were two values in the cell, it means the authors did not use two-layered architecture, i.e., Layer 1 and Layer 2, respectively. Because all the models have demonstrated exceptionally high prediction scores, we consider the best performers as overall but focus on TTT(s) and TTT(s). For example, ref. [53] shows missing F1, P and R in their methods; however, they demonstrate TTT and TTD earlier than others. The presence of (-) in the Features column means that authors did not conduct the low-dimensionality representation process.

Methods	AUCPR/ROC	F1	P	R	TTT(s)	TTD(s)	Features
Layer 1: Classification of HTTPS into DoH and NonDoH							
LSTM [76]	-	99.3	99.3	99.3	-	0.574	3
LGBM [36] *	99.9	99.9	99.9	99.9	87	0.08	27
Decision tree, random forest [58] *	[98, 1]	-	-	-	[11.9,31.7]	[0.041,0.216]	-
XTS (proposed framework)	99.99	99.96	99.94	99.99	1.8	0.07	3
Layer 2: DoH characterization into Malicious DoH and Benign DoH							
LSTM [76]	-	99.1	99.1	99.1	-	0.502	5
LGBM [36] *	99.9	99.9	99.9	99.9	40	0.08	27
ABG-VAE [77]	-	99.4	99.2	99.6	12.24	1.1	-
Decision tree, random forest [58] *	[1, 1]	-	-	-	[72.24,118.78]	[0.098,0.586]	-
XTS (proposed framework)	1	1	1	1	0.7	0.016	5

Our research emphasizes the unique strengths of the XTS model, including its exceptional computational efficiency and prediction performance. By significantly outperforming previous models in terms of computational speed and maintaining or surpassing their detection capabilities, XTS establishes itself as the best-performing solution for DNS/DoH tunnels detection within the compared space. We welcome other researchers to make further improvements to our work.

In summary, the comparison of XTS with other research using the same dataset and computational time measurements reveals its significant advantages. XTS outperforms previous models in terms of computational efficiency, being substantially faster in both TTT, TTD and reduced features. Additionally, XTS demonstrates equal or superior prediction performance compared to the best performing models in the literature. Moreover, it was the only model found to have combined bridged or at least touched different research problems shown in Figure 2, all together. These findings reaffirm the relevance and importance of our research, positioning XTS as a leading state-of-the-art framework to address the problems of imbalanced-binary classification, low-dimensional representation, with more advanced eXplainable AI to detect DNS/DoH tunnels using labeled datasets.

6. Conclusions

In conclusion, this research paper presents XTS, a hybrid framework designed to increase the low-dimensional representation of data while maintaining high model performance. The framework was successfully tested on two datasets containing HTTPS traffic flows and achieved a prediction efficiency greater than 99.9%. Compared to benchmarked models and previous studies in the literature, XTS was found to be more competitive in terms of both prediction and computational cost. The framework's ability to handle sparse, highly imbalanced, and scaled data, along with its powerful human intuitive results presentation, makes it suitable for use in outlier and anomaly detection systems. Given its positive attributes such as speed, sparsity awareness, scalability, feature learning stability, and imbalance handling, XTS is recommended for use by other researchers working with similar types of data. The research paper provides a promising new framework to increase the efficiency and accuracy of data analysis in outlier and anomaly detection systems.

7. Challenges and Recommendations

During the course of this research, the authors have learned that, in addition to the challenges posed by high directionality problems, new malware behaviors can emerge that in practice render IDS ineffective or powerless. Therefore, it is recommended that researchers focus on developing solutions that do not require a labeled dataset whilst using minimum features. Researchers can also explore the use of explainable AI (XAI) techniques on unsupervised methods, one of the known techniques to identify patterns and anomalies in the data which does not require prior knowledge of the labels. XAI methods can provide insights into the underlying features and patterns that the model is using to make predictions, a factor which can help to identify potential gaps or limitations in the model. This can enable researchers to refine and improve IDS models over time, and provide transparency and accountability for how the model is being used in practice. Additionally, during our experiment, we observed that, when a background dataset is fed to the Tree Explainer, the speed increases exponentially, relative to the depts of the tree. A faster approach should be carefully investigated, such as GPU-based Tree SHAP [78].

Author Contributions: Conceptualization, M.I. and Y.W.; methodology, M.I.; software, M.I.; validation, Y.W. and X.H.; formal analysis, M.I., Y.W. and X.H.; investigation, resources, Y.W., X.H and X.S.; data curation, X.S., J.C.T. and E.M.N.; writing—original draft preparation, M.I.; writing—review and editing, M.I.; visualization, M.I.; supervision, X.H. and Y.W. All authors have read and agreed to the published version of the manuscript.

Funding: This research was funded by the National Natural Science Founds of China, grant number (62072368, U20B2050) and Natural Science Basic Research Program of Shaanxi Province (2023-JC-QN-0742). The APC was funded by Key Research and Development Program of Shaanxi Province (2021ZDLGY05-09, 2022CGKC-09).

Data Availability Statement: The dataset used to support the findings of this study is publicly available and was cited in this paper.

Acknowledgments: The authors gratefully acknowledge the financial support of National Natural Science Founds of China, Key Research and Development Program of Shaanxi Province and Natural

Science Basic Research Program of Shaanxi Province. We acknowledge Canadian Institute for Cybersecurity (CIC) project funded by Canadian Internet Registration Authority (CIRA) as well, for making data publicly available.

Conflicts of Interest: The authors declare no conflict of interest. The funders had no role in the design of the study; in the collection, analyses, or interpretation of data; in the writing of the manuscript; or in the decision to publish the results.

References

1. Rappaport, T.S.; Xing, Y.; Kanhere, O.; Ju, S.; Madanayake, A.; Mandal, S.; Alkhateeb, A.; Trichopoulos, G.C. Wireless Communications and Applications above 100 GHz: Opportunities and Challenges for 6g and Beyond. *IEEE Access* **2019**, *7*, 78729–78757. [CrossRef]
2. Saad, W.; Bennis, M.; Chen, M.; Dang, S.; Amin, O.; Shihada, B.; Alouini, M.S.; Letaief, K.B.; Chen, W.; Shi, Y.; et al. What Should 6G Be? *IEEE Netw.* **2020**, *3*, 134–142. [CrossRef]
3. Saad, W.; Bennis, M.; Chen, M. A Vision of 6G Wireless Systems: Applications, Trends, Technologies, and Open Research Problems. *IEEE Netw.* **2020**, *34*, 134–142. [CrossRef]
4. Zhao, Q.; Li, Y.; Hei, X.; Yang, M. A Graph-Based Method for IFC Data Merging. *Adv. Civ. Eng.* **2020**, *2020*, 8782740. [CrossRef]
5. Yang, H.; Alphones, A.; Xiong, Z.; Niyato, D.; Zhao, J.; Wu, K. Artificial-Intelligence-Enabled Intelligent 6G Networks. *IEEE Netw.* **2020**, *34*, 272–280. [CrossRef]
6. Xiao, Y.; Shi, G.; Li, Y.; Saad, W.; Poor, H.V. Toward Self-Learning Edge Intelligence in 6G. *IEEE Commun. Mag.* **2020**, *58*, 34–40. [CrossRef]
7. Guo, W. Explainable Artificial Intelligence for 6G: Improving Trust between Human and Machine. *IEEE Commun. Mag.* **2020**, *58*, 39–45. [CrossRef]
8. Bandi, A.; Yalamarthi, S. Towards Artificial Intelligence Empowered Security and Privacy Issues in 6G Communications. In Proceedings of the 2022 International Conference on Sustainable Computing and Data Communication Systems (ICSCDS), Erode, India, 7–9 April 2022; pp. 372–378. [CrossRef]
9. Moore, A.; Zuev, D.; Crogan, M. *Discriminators for Use in Flow-Based Classification*; Queen Mary University of London: London, UK, 2005.
10. Li, J.; Cheng, K.; Wang, S.; Morstatter, F.; Trevino, R.P.; Tang, J.; Liu, H. Feature Selection: A Data Perspective. *ACM Comput. Surv.* **2017**, *50*, 1–45. [CrossRef]
11. Ang, J.C.; Mirzal, A.; Haron, H.; Hamed, H.N.A. Supervised, Unsupervised, and Semi-Supervised Feature Selection: A Review on Gene Selection. *IEEE/ACM Trans. Comput. Biol. Bioinforma.* **2016**, *13*, 971–989. [CrossRef]
12. Di Mauro, M.; Galatro, G.; Fortino, G.; Liotta, A. Supervised Feature Selection Techniques in Network Intrusion Detection: A Critical Review. *Eng. Appl. Artif. Intell.* **2021**, *101*, 104216. [CrossRef]
13. AlNuaimi, N.; Masud, M.M.; Serhani, M.A.; Zaki, N. Streaming Feature Selection Algorithms for Big Data: A Survey. *Appl. Comput. Inform.* **2022**, *18*, 113–135. [CrossRef]
14. Azhar, M.A.; Thomas, P.A. Comparative Review of Feature Selection and Classification Modeling. In Proceedings of the 2019 International Conference on Advances in Computing, Communication and Control (ICAC3), Mumbai, India, 20–21 December 2019. [CrossRef]
15. Bolón-Canedo, V.; Rego-Fernández, D.; Peteiro-Barral, D.; Alonso-Betanzos, A.; Guijarro-Berdiñas, B.; Sánchez-Maroño, N. On the Scalability of Feature Selection Methods on High-Dimensional Data. *Knowl. Inf. Syst.* **2018**, *56*, 395–442. [CrossRef]
16. Khaire, U.M.; Dhanalakshmi, R. Stability of Feature Selection Algorithm: A Review. *J. King Saud Univ. Comput. Inf. Sci.* **2022**, *34*, 1060–1073. [CrossRef]
17. Al Hosni, O.; Starkey, A. Assesing the Stability and Selection Performance of Feature Selection Methods Under Different Data Complexity. *Int. Arab J. Inf. Technol.* **2022**, *19*, 442–455. [CrossRef]
18. Chandrashekar, G.; Sahin, F. A Survey on Feature Selection Methods. *Comput. Electr. Eng.* **2014**, *40*, 16–28. [CrossRef]
19. Schölkopf, B.; Platt, J.C.; Shawe-Taylor, J.; Smola, A.J.; Williamson, R.C. Estimating the Support of a High-Dimensional Distribution. *Neural Comput.* **2001**, *13*, 1443–1471. [CrossRef]
20. Brownlee, N.; Mills, C.; Ruth, G. *RFC2722: Traffic Flow Measurement: Architecture*; ACM Digital Library: New York, NY, USA, 1999.
21. Wang, Z.; Zhou, J.; Hei, X. Network Traffic Anomaly Detection Based on Generative Adversarial Network and Transformer. *Lect. Notes Data Eng. Commun. Technol.* **2023**, *153*, 228–235. [CrossRef]
22. Vu, L.; Bui, C.T.; Nguyen, Q.U. A Deep Learning Based Method for Handling Imbalanced Problem in Network Traffic Classification. In Proceedings of the 8th International Symposium on Information and Communication Technology, Nha Trang, Vietnam, 7–8 December 2017; pp. 333–339. [CrossRef]
23. Santos, M.S.; Soares, J.P.; Abreu, P.H.; Araujo, H.; Santos, J. Cross-Validation for Imbalanced Datasets: Avoiding Overoptimistic and Overfitting Approaches [Research Frontier]. *IEEE Comput. Intell. Mag.* **2018**, *13*, 59–76. [CrossRef]
24. Wang, Z.; Zhou, J.; Wang, Z.; Hei, X. Research on Network Traffic Anomaly Detection for Class Imbalance. In *Intelligent Robotics, Proceedings of the Third China Intelligent Robotics Annual Conference, CCF CIRAC 2022, Xi'an, China, 16–18 December 2022*; Springer: Singapore, 2023; pp. 135–144. [CrossRef]

25. Spelmen, V.S.; Porkodi, R. A Review on Handling Imbalanced Data. In Proceedings of the 2018 International Conference on Current Trends towards Converging Technologies (ICCTCT 2018), Coimbatore, India, 1–3 March 2018; Institute of Electrical and Electronics Engineers: Coimbatore, India, 2018; pp. 1–11. [CrossRef]
26. He, S.; Li, B.; Peng, H.; Xin, J.; Zhang, E. An Effective Cost-Sensitive XGBoost Method for Malicious URLs Detection in Imbalanced Dataset. *IEEE Access* **2021**, *9*, 93089–93096. [CrossRef]
27. Abdulhammed, R.; Faezipour, M.; Abuzneid, A.; Abumallouh, A. Deep and Machine Learning Approaches for Anomaly-Based Intrusion Detection of Imbalanced Network Traffic. *IEEE Sens. Lett.* **2019**, *3*, 2018–2021. [CrossRef]
28. Brownlee, J. Cost-Sensitive. In *Imbalanced Classification with Python: Choose Better Metrics, Balance Skewed Classes, and Apply Cost-Sensitive Learning*; Martin, S., Sanderson, M., Koshy, A., Cheremskoy, J.H., Eds.; Machine Learning Mastery: Vermont, Australia, 2020; pp. 237–240.
29. Fouchereau, R. An IDC Info Brief, Securing Anywhere Networking DNS Security for Business Continuity and Resilience 2022 Global DNS Threat Report. 2022. Available online: https://efficientip.com/wp-content/uploads/2022/10/IDC-EUR149048522-EfficientIP-infobrief_FINAL.pdf (accessed on 10 May 2023).
30. Durumeric, Z.; Ma, Z.; Springall, D.; Barnes, R.; Sullivan, N.; Bursztein, E.; Bailey, M.; Halderman, J.A.; Paxson, V. *The Security Impact of HTTPS Interception*; NDSS: New York, NY, USA, 2017.
31. HTTPS Encryption on the Web. Available online: https://transparencyreport.google.com/https/overview?hl=en (accessed on 27 November 2022).
32. Let's Encrypt Stats. Available online: https://letsencrypt.org/stats/ (accessed on 27 November 2022).
33. Nearly Half of Malware Now Use TLS to Conceal Communications–Sophos News. Available online: https://news.sophos.com/en-us/2021/04/21/nearly-half-of-malware-now-use-tls-to-conceal-communications/ (accessed on 24 November 2022).
34. Nguyen, A.T.; Park, M. Detection of DoH Tunneling Using Semi-Supervised Learning Method. In Proceedings of the 2022 International Conference on Information Networking (ICOIN), Jeju-si, Republic of Korea, 12–15 January 2022; pp. 450–453. [CrossRef]
35. Wang, P.A.N.; Chen, X.; Ye, F.; Sun, Z. A Survey of Techniques for Mobile Service Encrypted Traffic Classification Using Deep Learning. *IEEE Access* **2019**, *7*, 54024–54033. [CrossRef]
36. Behnke, M.; Briner, N.; Cullen, D.; Schwerdtfeger, K.; Warren, J.; Basnet, R.; Doleck, T. Feature Engineering and Machine Learning Model Comparison for Malicious Activity Detection in the DNS-Over-HTTPS Protocol. *IEEE Access* **2021**, *9*, 129902–129916. [CrossRef]
37. Venkatesh, B.; Anuradha, J. A Review of Feature Selection and Its Methods. *Cybern. Inf. Technol.* **2019**, *19*, 3–26. [CrossRef]
38. Atashgahi, Z.; Sokar, G.; van der Lee, T.; Mocanu, E.; Mocanu, D.C.; Veldhuis, R.; Pechenizkiy, M. *Quick and Robust Feature Selection: The Strength of Energy-Efficient Sparse Training for Autoencoders*; Springer: New York, NY, USA, 2022; Volume 111, ISBN 0123456789.
39. Tang, J.; Alelyani, S.; Liu, H. Feature Selection for Classification: A Review. In *Data Classification: Algorithms and Applications*; Aggarwal, C.C., Ed.; Taylor & Francis Group: New York, NY, USA, 2014; pp. 37–64. ISBN 9780429102639.
40. Tong, V.; Tran, H.A.; Souihi, S.; Mellouk, A. A Novel QUIC Traffic Classifier Based on Convolutional Neural Networks. In Proceedings of the 2018 IEEE Global Communications Conference (GLOBECOM), Abu Dhabi, United Arab Emirates, 9–13 December 2018.
41. Yaacoubi, O. The Rise of Encrypted Malware. *Netw. Secur.* **2019**, *2019*, 6–9. [CrossRef]
42. Hjelm, D. *A New Needle and Haystack: Detecting DNS over HTTPS Usage*; SANS Institute: North Bethesda, MD, USA, 2021.
43. Piskozub, M.; De Gaspari, F.; Barr-smith, F.; Martinovic, I. MalPhase: Fine-Grained Malware Detection Using Network Flow Data. In Proceedings of the 2021 ACM Asia Conference on Computer and Communications Security (ASIA CCS '21), Hong Kong, China, 7–11 June 2021; Association for Computing Machinery: New York, NY, USA, 2021; Volume 1, pp. 774–786.
44. Singh, A.P.; Singh, M. A Comparative Review of Malware Analysis and Detection in HTTPs Traffic. *Int. J. Comput. Digit. Syst.* **2021**, *10*, 111–123. [CrossRef]
45. Hynek, K.; Vekshin, D.; Luxemburk, J.A.N.; Wasicek, A.; Member, S. Summary of DNS Over HTTPS Abuse. *IEEE Access* **2022**, *10*, 54668–54680. [CrossRef]
46. Cerna, S.; Guyeux, C.; Royer, G.; Chevallier, C.; Plumerel, G. Predicting Fire Brigades Operational Breakdowns: A Real Case Study. *Mathematics* **2020**, *8*, 1383. [CrossRef]
47. Sobolewski, R.A.; Tchakorom, M.; Couturier, R. Gradient Boosting-Based Approach for Short- and Medium-Term Wind Turbine Output Power Prediction. *Renew. Energy* **2023**, *203*, 142–160. [CrossRef]
48. Arcolezi, H.H.; Cerna, S.; Couchot, J.F.; Guyeux, C.; Makhoul, A. A Privacy-Preserving Prediction of Victim's Mortality and Their Need for Transportation to Health Facilities. *IEEE Trans. Ind. Inform.* **2022**, *18*, 5592–5599. [CrossRef]
49. Hashemi, S.K.; Mirtaheri, S.L.; Greco, S. Fraud Detection in Banking Data by Machine Learning Techniques. *IEEE Access* **2023**, *11*, 3034–3043. [CrossRef]
50. Amiri, P.A.D.; Pierre, S. An Ensemble-Based Machine Learning Model for Forecasting Network Traffic in VANET. *IEEE Access* **2023**, *11*, 22855–22870. [CrossRef]
51. Scott, M.; Lundberg, S.-I.L. A Unified Approach to Interpreting Model Predictions. *Adv. Neural Inf. Process. Syst.* **2017**, *30*, 1208–1217.
52. Lundberg, S.M.; Erion, G.; Chen, H.; DeGrave, A.; Prutkin, J.M.; Nair, B.; Katz, R.; Himmelfarb, J.; Bansal, N.; Lee, S.I. From Local Explanations to Global Understanding with Explainable AI for Trees. *Nat. Mach. Intell.* **2020**, *2*, 56–67. [CrossRef]

53. Lundberg, S.M.; Nair, B.; Vavilala, M.S.; Horibe, M.; Eisses, M.J.; Adams, T.; Liston, D.E.; Low, D.K.W.; Newman, S.F.; Kim, J.; et al. Explainable Machine-Learning Predictions for the Prevention of Hypoxaemia during Surgery. *Nat. Biomed. Eng.* **2018**, *2*, 749–760. [CrossRef]
54. Zhong, S.; Fu, X.; Lu, W.; Tang, F.; Lu, Y. An Expressway Driving Stress Prediction Model Based on Vehicle, Road and Environment Features. *IEEE Access* **2022**, *10*, 57212–57226. [CrossRef]
55. Alani, M.M.; Awad, A.I. PAIRED: An Explainable Lightweight Android Malware Detection System. *IEEE Access* **2022**, *10*, 73214–73228. [CrossRef]
56. Li, Z. Extracting Spatial Effects from Machine Learning Model Using Local Interpretation Method: An Example of SHAP and XGBoost. *Comput. Environ. Urban Syst.* **2022**, *96*, 101845. [CrossRef]
57. Banadaki, Y.M. Detecting Malicious DNS over HTTPS Traffic in Domain Name System Using Machine Learning Classifiers. *J. Comput. Sci. Appl.* **2020**, *8*, 46–55. [CrossRef]
58. Jafar, M.T.; Al-fawa, M.; Al-hrahsheh, Z.; Jafar, S.T. Analysis and Investigation of Malicious DNS Queries Using CIRA-CIC-DoHBrw-2020 Dataset. *Manch. J. Artif. Intell. Appl. Sci.* **2021**, *2*, 65–70.
59. Zebin, T.; Rezvy, S.; Luo, Y. An Explainable AI-Based Intrusion Detection System for DNS Over HTTPS (DoH) Attacks. *IEEE Trans. Inf. Forensics Secur.* **2022**, *17*, 2339–2349. [CrossRef]
60. Chawla, N.V.; Bowyer, K.W.; Hall, L.O.; Kegelmeyer, W.P. SMOTE: Synthetic Minority Over-Sampling Technique. *J. Artif. Intell. Res.* **2002**, *16*, 321–357. [CrossRef]
61. Mitchell, R.; Adinets, A.; Rao, T.; Frank, E. XGBoost: Scalable GPU Accelerated Learning. *arXiv* **2018**, arXiv:1806.11248.
62. Chen, T.; Guestrin, C. XGBoost: A Scalable Tree Boosting System. In Proceedings of the 22nd ACM SIGKDD International Conference on Knowledge Discovery and Data Mining, San Francisco, CA, USA, 13 August 2016; Association for Computing Machinery: New York, NY, USA, 2016; pp. 785–794.
63. Tree Methods. Available online: https://xgboost.readthedocs.io/en/stable/treemethod.html (accessed on 26 November 2022).
64. Mitchell, R.; Frank, E. Accelerating the XGBoost Algorithm Using GPU Computing. *PeerJ Comput. Sci.* **2017**, *3*, e127. [CrossRef]
65. Lundberg, S.M.; Lee, S.-I. A Unified Approach to Interpreting Model Predictions. In Proceedings of the 31st International Conference on Neural Information Processing Systems, Long Beach, CA, USA, 4–9 December 2017; Curran Associates Inc.: Red Hook, NY, USA, 2017; pp. 4768–4777.
66. Shapley, L.S. *Notes on the N-Person Game–I: Characteristic-Point Solutions of the Four-Person Game*; RAND Corporation: Santa Monica, CA, USA, 1951.
67. Yang, J. Fast TreeSHAP: Accelerating SHAP Value Computation for Trees. *arXiv* **2021**, arXiv:2109.09847.
68. Saito, T.; Rehmsmeier, M. The Precision-Recall Plot Is More Informative than the ROC Plot When Evaluating Binary Classifiers on Imbalanced Datasets. *PLoS ONE* **2015**, *10*, e0118432. [CrossRef]
69. DoHBrw 2020 Datasets. Available online: https://www.unb.ca/cic/datasets/dohbrw-2020.html (accessed on 25 November 2022).
70. Kryo.Se: Iodine (IP-over-DNS, IPv4 over DNS Tunnel). Available online: https://code.kryo.se/iodine/ (accessed on 26 November 2022).
71. GitHub-Alex-Sector/Dns2tcp. Available online: https://github.com/alex-sector/dns2tcp (accessed on 26 November 2022).
72. GitHub-Iagox86/Dnscat2. Available online: https://github.com/iagox86/dnscat2 (accessed on 26 November 2022).
73. GitHub-Ahlashkari/DoHLyzer: DoHlyzer Is a DNS over HTTPS (DoH) Traffic Flow Generator and Analyzer for Anomaly Detection and Characterization. Available online: https://github.com/ahlashkari/DoHlyzer (accessed on 26 November 2022).
74. Kaggle. State of Data Science and Machine Learning 2021. Available online: https://www.kaggle.com/kaggle-survey-2021 (accessed on 26 November 2022).
75. Nkurikiyeyezu, K.; Yokokubo, A.; Lopez, G. Effect of Person-Specific Biometrics in Improving Generic Stress Predictive Models. *Sensors Mater.* **2020**, *32*, 703. [CrossRef]
76. Montazerishatoori, M.; Davidson, L.; Kaur, G.; Habibi Lashkari, A. Detection of DoH Tunnels Using Time-Series Classification of Encrypted Traffic. In Proceedings of the 2020 IEEE Intl Conf on Dependable, Autonomic and Secure Computing, Intl Conf on Pervasive Intelligence and Computing, Intl Conf on Cloud and Big Data Computing, Intl Conf on Cyber Science and Technology Congress (DASC/PiCom/CBDCom/CyberSciTech), Calgary, AB, Canada, 17–22 August 2020; pp. 63–70.
77. Ding, S.; Zhang, D.; Ge, J.; Yuan, X.; Du, X. Encrypt DNS Traffic: Automated Feature Learning Method for Detecting DNS Tunnels. In Proceedings of the 2021 IEEE Intl Conf on Parallel & Distributed Processing with Applications, Big Data & Cloud Computing, Sustainable Computing & Communications, Social Computing & Networking (ISPA/BDCloud/SocialCom/SustainCom), New York, NY, USA, 30 September–3 October 2021; pp. 352–359. [CrossRef]
78. Mitchell, R.; Frank, E.; Holmes, G. GPUTreeShap: Massively Parallel Exact Calculation of SHAP Scores for Tree Ensembles. *PeerJ Comput. Sci.* **2022**, *8*, e880. [CrossRef]

Disclaimer/Publisher's Note: The statements, opinions and data contained in all publications are solely those of the individual author(s) and contributor(s) and not of MDPI and/or the editor(s). MDPI and/or the editor(s) disclaim responsibility for any injury to people or property resulting from any ideas, methods, instructions or products referred to in the content.

MDPI
St. Alban-Anlage 66
4052 Basel
Switzerland
Tel. +41 61 683 77 34
Fax +41 61 302 89 18
www.mdpi.com

Mathematics Editorial Office
E-mail: mathematics@mdpi.com
www.mdpi.com/journal/mathematics

www.ingramcontent.com/pod-product-compliance
Lightning Source LLC
LaVergne TN
LVHW070452100526
838202LV00014B/1707